RAND

POW/MIA Issues

Volume 3, Appendixes

Paul M. Cole

Prepared for the
Under Secretary of Defense for Policy

National Defense Research Institute

PREFACE

This report consists of three volumes. Volume 1 addresses American prisoners of war (POW) and missing in action cases (MIA) who were not repatriated following the Korean War, with particular emphasis on whether any American servicemen were transferred to USSR territory during the war.

Volume 2 examines three issues: First, it examines whether American servicemen liberated by Soviet forces from Nazi German POW camps in the European theater of operations in World War II were not repatriated. Second, it examines whether American aircrews in the Far East and European theaters were detained in USSR territory. Third, early Cold War incidents are examined to determine whether archive materials indicate that American servicemen and civilians were held alive in USSR territory.

Volume 3, an appendix volume, contains a number of POW rosters, primary source documents, and other lists. It is intended to complement Volumes 1 and 2.

Throughout Volumes 1 and 2, the evolution of U.S. POW/MIA policy is documented as are U.S. government efforts to obtain a full accounting of missing American citizens. This report is documented extensively, in accordance with the guidance from the Department of Defense, so that other researchers may use it as a reference work or as a guide to sources. This report is not intended, however, to be a comprehensive history of World War II, the Cold War, or the Korean War.

This report was prepared as a part of "The POW/MIA Issue in U.S.-North Korean Relations," a project sponsored between October 1991 and April 1993 by the Office of the Under Secretary of Defense for Policy. Research for this report was conducted within the International Security and Defense Strategy Program of RAND's National Defense Research Institute, a federally funded research and development center supported by the Office of the Secretary of Defense and the Joint Staff.

This report should be of interest to government officials involved in MIA/POW affairs, casualty resolution officers, family members, and others in and out of government interested in the efforts that have been made by the U.S. government to resolve POW/MIA issues.

CONTENTS

Appendix 1

MEMBERS OF THE U.S.-RUSSIAN JOINT COMMISSION ON POW/MIAs

Found In: Chapter One, Volume 1
Source of this information: U.S.-Russian Joint Commission

U.S. DELEGATION

Commissioners

Ambassador Malcolm Toon
Senator John Kerry
Senator Bob Smith
Representative John Miller
Representative Pete Peterson
Mr. Alan C. Ptak, DASD, DoD, MIA-POW Affairs
Mr. Richard Kauzlarich, DAS, DoS, European Affairs
Mr. Kenneth Quinn, DAS, DoS, East Asian and Pacific Affairs
Mr. A. Denis Clift, Chief of Staff, Defense Intelligence Agency
Ms. Trudy Peterson, Assistant United States Archivist

Experts

Brig. General Eldon W. Joersz, USAF, Director ISA/POW-MIA
  Affairs[1]
Major Charles W. Gittins, USMC, ISA/MIA-POW Affairs
Lt. Thomas Vhay, USN, ISA/MIA-POW Affairs
Mr. Steve Mann, OASD/ISP (Russia Desk Officer)
Mr. David Sisson, DIA (PW-MIA)
Mr. Michael Sasek, DIA (PW-MIA)
Lt. Col. Alan Young, USA, DIA (PW-MIA)
Mr. David Hess, DoS, Russia/CIS Director
Mr. Dan Sainz, DoS, Russia Desk Officer
Mr. Frank Light, DoS, Vietnam Desk Officer
Lt. Yuri Tabach, USN, Interpreter/Assistant to Mr. Ptak

Congressional

Mr. Mark Bitterman, OASD/LA, Congressional Liaison
Ms. Francis Zwenig, Staff Director, Senate Select Committee
Mr. Robert Taylor, Senate Select Committee Staff
Ms. Pat Ravalgi, Staff, House Foreign Relations Committee
Ms. Heike Nussbaum, Staff, Congressman Miller
Ms. Susan Farmer, Staff, Congressman Peterson

RUSSIAN DELEGATION

Chairman

Dimitri Petrovich Volkogonov, Presidential Advisor on Military
  Issues

---

[1]By July 1992, General Joersz had been replaced by Edward W. Ross
as Office Director.

Deputy Chairman

Vladimir Petrovich Kozlev, Deputy Chairman, Russian Archives Committee

Members

Yevgeniy Arshakovich Ambartsumov, Acting Chairman, Parliamentary Committee on International Affairs

Nikolay Mikhailovich Arzhannikov, Deputy Chairman, Parliamentary Committee on Human Rights

Igor Nokolayevich Venkov, Director, Historical and Memorial Center of the Armed Forces General Staff

Yuriy Ivanovich Kalinin, Director, General Enforcement Directorate, Ministry of Internal Affairs

Sergey Adamovich Kovalev, Chairman, Parliamentary Human Rights Committee

Anatoliy Afanasevich Krayushkin, Section Chief, Ministry of Security

Gennadiy Lukyanovich Lezhikov, Director, Ministry of Internal Affairs Information Center

Vyacheslav Petrovich Mazyrov, Senior Assistant to Section Chief of the External Intelligence Service

Vladimir Fedorovich Mironov, Consultant, Ministry of Justice

Iosip Nikolaevich Podrazhanetz, Acting Director, USA and Canada Administration, Ministry of Foreign Affairs

Experts

Viktor Mikhailovich Arkhipov, MFA, Human Rights Administration

Viktor Nikolaevich Bondarev, Director, Central State Special Archives

Nikolai Petrovich Brileb, Director, Central Ministry of Defense Archives

Vladimir Konstantinovich Vinogradov, Deputy Section Director, Ministry of Security

Vladimir Ivanovich Korotayev, Deputy Director, Central State Special Archives

Tatiana Fedorovna Pavlova, Acting Director, State Archives of the October Revolution, Higher State Organs and State Administration

Valentin Konstantinovich Parkhomenko, MFA, USA and Canada Administration

Vladimir Vasiliyevich Sokolov, MFA, Deputy Director of Documents Division

Aleksandr Maksimovich Shubin, Ministry of Internal Affairs, Section Director in Information Center

Appendix 2

ACCESS TO INFORMATION IN THE UNITED STATES

Found in: Chapter One, Volume 1
Source of this information: National Archives and Records
Administration, and Army Central Identification Laboratory, Hawaii
(CILHI)

Access to official primary source material is a political act in
any country. American citizens enjoy unequaled access to government
records. In the United States the Freedom of Information Act (5 U.S.C.
552) provides that various records should be made available to the
public unless they are exempted from public disclosure. The government
is obligated to state the grounds on which documents are denied. Of the
approximately one dozen categories and statutes that permit the U.S.
government to deny access to archive materials, perhaps the most common
reason when access is denied is the following:

> (b) This section (of 5 U.S.C. 552) does not apply to matters
> that are:

> (1)(A) specifically authorized under criteria established by
> an Executive order to be kept secret in the interest of
> national defense or foreign policy and (B) are in fact
> properly classified pursuant to such Executive order.

> Section (7) of 5 U.S.C. 552 permits the government to withhold
> records that "could reasonably be expected to disclose the
> identity of a confidential source, including a State, local,
> or foreign agency or authority or any private institution
> which furnished information on a confidential basis...." The
> grounds for withholding or redacting material must be stated.
> U.S. law allows for denials to be appealed under the Freedom
> of Information Act.

U.S. federal laws on access to primary source material apply
equally to a wide range of historic documentation. These laws have kept
pace, for the most part, with the changes in the way the historical
record is accumulated. No legislation or executive order similar to the
one affecting Vietnam War era documents has been needed or issued to
make available the source material for this study. The vast majority of

documents containing information related to the subjects touched on in this study have been available for research in the various repositories of the U.S. National Archives and Records Administration (NARA) for years. The factor limiting research into World War II, Korean War, and early Cold War incidents is not excessive government secrecy.

There is no single repository of information in any country that can resolve all of the issues raised in this study. The U.S. government does not possess in one place all of the information required to piece together a complete picture of the POW/MIA story. The absence of information in one archive should not always be interpreted as a sign that it does not exist in another file stored elsewhere. Several archivists in the National Archives have been extraordinarily helpful during the course of this study. Two of them compiled the following guide to information about American prisoners of war from World War II:

WORLD WAR II U.S. POWs: RECORDS IN THE U.S. NATIONAL ARCHIVES

Record Group (RG) 334, Records of Interservice Agencies, Military Mission to Moscow, Subject File POWs, boxes 22-25, 17w4

RG165, Records of War Department General and Special Staffs, Operations Division, OPD Decimal File TS 383.6 case 13 1945, OPD 383.6 1945

RG165, Chief of Staff, Decimal File 383.6 TS 1945, 15w3

RG165, Personnel, Subject File 1943-1947, Sec. 58, Box 2, 13w4/2/3/d

RAMP's: The Recovery and Repatriation of Liberated Prisoners of War, Reference Collection 2058

RG389, Records of the Provost Marshall General, American POW Information Bureau, entry 460A, "List of Repatriates--Germany." "List, Returned to Military Control from European Theater of Operations," Box 2221

RG389, American POW Information Bureau, IBM Index 1943-6, Deceased American POWs (Germany), American Escapees, American POWs Returned to Military Control by the Germans

RG389, Lists of American POWs Germany, 12w3/11/14

RG389, Enemy POW Information Bureau, Subject File 1942-6, Repatriation, Boxes 2691-2695

RG389, POW Operations Division, Information Bureau, Subject File 1942-5, Repatriation--Summary of numbers by Robert Murphy, Box 1592

RG389, American POW Information Bureau, General Subject File 1942-6, RMC Lists--Return of Liberated Personnel from Europe, Boxes 2247-2254, 12w3/7/17-18/e-a

RG389, Historical File 1941-8, "The Exchange with Soviet Forces of Liberated Personnel--World War II," Box 7, 12w3/20/22a

RG319, Records of the Army Staff, Plans and Operations Division (1946-8), Decimal File 320, case 20/2, study 103, "Report of the General Board USFET, Military Police Activities in Connection with the Evacuation and Detention of Prisoners of War, Civilian Internees and Military Personnel Recovered from the Enemy," Box 227, 17w4

RG331, Records of Allied Operational and Occupation Headquarters, World War II, Supreme Headquarters Allied Expeditionary Force, Secretary to the General Staff, 383.6/11; G-1, 383.6-15

RG407, Records of the Adjutant General's Office, formerly classified Decimal File 1943-5, 383.6, 17w4

RG407, Records of the Adjutant General's Office, Legislative and Policy Precedent Files 1943-1975, 150 (299), Official Number of American Prisoners of War Captured During World War II, Box 22, 14w3/12/31c

RG242 being transferred to RG 389--Cards on American POWs created by Germans and captured by American Army (3rd Army, 26th Infantry). Microfilm T-84, rolls 384-374, 15w/16/8/drawer 3, Boxes 1-74, 16w3/25/29-30

RG319, Records of the Army Staff, Army Intelligence, Project Decimal File 1941-5, 383.6 USSR (NNRR)

RG319, Army Intelligence, Decimal File 1941-8, 383.6 (NNRR)

RG342, Records of U.S. Air Force Commands, Activities, and Organizations, 5th Air Force interrogations of Japanese POWs returning from the Far East (NNRR)

RG332, Records of U.S. Theaters of War, World War II, European Theater of Operations/United States Forces European Theater, SGS 383.6 (NNRR)

RG332, Records of U.S. Theaters of War, World War II, ETOUSA/Provost Marshal General (NNRR)

RG407, Strength and Accounting Branch, List of POWs (NNRR)

RG492, Mediterranean Theater of Operations, Provost Marshal, Register of POWs (NNRR)

RG331, AF HQ, Adjutant General and Provost Marshal, 383.6 (NNRR)

RG342, Air Force Commands. Air Force Intelligence, Wringer Reports, debriefing reports, microfilm, no index (NNRR)

RG242, Downed American Flyers (NNRR)

RG92, Missing Aircrew Reports (NNRR)

The Casualty Data Section of the U.S. Army's Central Identification Laboratory, Hawaii (CILHI) has an important collection of original documents and two automated data bases that contain historical, geographical, unit, cemetery, POW camp, and individual information that can be used to resolve cases involving unrecovered or unaccounted for UN Command casualties from the Korean conflict. These records and systems are described in the following section.

RECORDS AND DATA BASES ON THE KOREAN CONFLICT MAINTAINED BY THE ARMY CENTRAL IDENTIFICATION LABORATORY, HAWAII (CILHI)

"293 Files," also known as casualty jackets. Approximately 3,000 293 files are on hand including those for UN KIA(BNR). The resolved Korean War 293 files are stored at the Washington National Records Center, Suitland, MD.

"5 x 8 card files," also known as "8200 Case Status Cards." These cards provide name, status, dates, Field Search Case number, map grid coordinates and unit information. The "7700 Casualty Data Cards" provide information on POW camp, ante mortem physical data, and dental charts.

Microfiche. Ref. No. 601-07, Rosters of U.S. dead, Korea (all services), Korean War, May 23, 1956, Fiche 0001-0027. Ref. No. 601-07, POW, MIA, Non-Battle Casualties, Korean Operation (all services) Korean War March 31, 1954, Fiche 0001-0008. Ref. No. 601-07, Rosters Non-Recoverable and Buried At Sea, Korean Operations. Casualty files (293 File) of the UNCMAC "389" list.

Casualty Lists and Indexes: American Battle Monuments Commission Register, Volume III, Korea Missing or Lost or Buried at Sea; Marine Casualties who appear on FSC 50-3; Log of evacuations, FSCs, Isolated Burials, POW Camps; DIA's "389" list; Alphabetical roster of evacuated remains received under Operation Glory as Named Cases; Operation Plan "Glory" 14-54; Isolated burial reconciliation; Official and unofficial POW roster; Allied unrecovered personnel; Unit and division list; CIU case numbers ledger; National Memorial Cemetery of the Pacific, Record of Interment, Section U, Korean War Unknowns.

Field Search Cases (FSC). U.S. Army and Marine Corps, numbered 0001-1061, containing casualty lists, unit battle histories and map overlays. U.S. Air Force, numbered 0001-0826. Contains case check list, an air crew casualty report, witness statements, affidavits and map overlays.

"Mapper" Database. Created from data extracted from Case Status Cards, Casualty Data Cards, Field Search Cases, 293 Files, and other casualty lists. The Mapper data base can be searched and sorted by name, service number, grade, branch of service, casualty status, date of incident, date of death/presumptive finding of death, field search case number, map sheet, UTM grid coordinate, unit, race, height, weight, age, POW camp and temporary cemetery. As of February 17, 1993 Mapper contained 31,027 UNC individual casualty entries, 2,123 U.S. POW(BNR), 6,029 U.S. MIA/KIA(BNR), 3,226 U.S. POW(RMC), 21 U.S. voluntary nonrepatriates, 18,642 U.S. MIA/KIA resolved, 859 U.S. unknowns buried at the National Memorial Cemetery of the Pacific, 134 UN POW/MIA/KIA. Upon completion the Mapper system will contain all U.S./UN Korean War casualties (minus wounded).

CAPMI Dental Base. CAPMI (Computer-Assisted Post Mortem Identification) is a sorting system that can rapidly limit the dental identification process to a few rather than several thousand records. A key file (post mortem record) is compared to the file in question (ante mortem record).

The National Personnel Records Center (NPRC), located in St. Louis, Missouri maintains hundreds of thousands of service and medical records of armed forces personnel. Access to these records is governed by the Privacy Act of 1974. Further restrictions on access and release have been established by individual service branches. NPRC records were savaged by a fire on July 12, 1973. The blaze destroyed about 80 percent of the records for Army personnel discharged between November 1, 1912, and January 1, 1960, and 75 percent of the records for Air Force personnel with surnames Hubbard through "Z" discharged between September 25, 1947, and January 1, 1964. The records damaged in the fire are brittle and difficult to read.

Appendix 3

ROSTER OF VICTIMS FROM REPATRIATED UNC POWS

Found in: Chapter Two, Volume 1
Source of this information: Judge Advocate Section, War Crimes
Division, National Archives, Suitland, MD, Reference Branch.

ROSTER OF VICTIMS WHOSE NAMES ARE MENTIONED IN STATEMENTS FROM U.N. POW RETURNEES

NAME	SERIAL NUMBER	RANK	TYPE OF INCIDENT	SOURCE OF INFORMATION
Abbot Richard	AF 12357185	S/Sgt.	Torture	Capt. Meirer Diercks
Acomsta Reynaldo E.	RA 19312002	Cpl.	Torture	Cpl. Reynaldo E. Acosta
Adair Sammie	RA 13332596	Pfc.	Torture	Pfc. Sammie Adair
Adams Howard G.	RA 38556261	Cpl.	Mistreatment	John Narvin
Adams Joel R.	RA 15259633	Pfc.	Torture	Joel R. Adams
Adams John W.	US 53030697	Pfc.	Mistreatment	John W. Adams
Adams Raymond J.	RA 1723337	Sfc.	Death from Mistreatment	Cpl. Walter Williams
Addesso Harry J.	RA 12304194	Pvt.	Mistreatment	Harry J. Addesso
Aguirre Alfredo	US 55050058	Sgt.	Torture	Sfc. Raymond Cook
Aldeis Manuel A.	RA 18016757	M/Sgt.	Torture	Manuel A. Aldeis
Ales Marion L.	0-1185534	Lt.	Death from Mistreatment	Lt. Col. Fry
Allen James M.	RA 143313064	Cpl.	Mistreatment	Cpl. James M. Allen
Andrews Charles L.	RA 12283792	Pvt.	Death from Mistreatment	Sfc. Ordonio
Andino Perez Emiliano	ER 30429512	Pvt.	Death from Mistreatment	Sgt. Rivera Perez Pedro
Antrome Joseph	RA 13265613	Pfc.	Death from Mistreatment	Charles Edward Massie
Armour James L.	RA 06530402	Sfc.	Death from Mistreatment	Pfc. Glenn Edgar
Backie Donald L.	RA 13346184	Pfc.	Death from Mistreatment	Capt. Bromser
Bailey Lawrence	RA 16314351	Pfc.	Mistreatment	Pfc. Buildo C. Rodriguez
Bak Joseph	ER 36557729	Pfc.	Death from Mistreatment	Capt. Radoszewski

Name	Service No.	Rank	Cause	Name / Notes
Banach Stanley A.	RA 36870187	Pvt.	Death from Mistreatment	Capt. Radoszewski
Barber Julius J.	RA 15297187	Pfc.	Mistreatment	Julius J.Barber
Barcus Floyd A.	RA 15416276	Cpl.	Torture	Sgt. Joseph B. Harbin
Barrick George M.J.	0-0057513	Lt.	Murder	Capt. Wadie Rountree
Barter Charles T.	0-0451624	Maj.	Death from Mistreatment	Sfc. James M. ??gsdale
Batdorff Robert L.	1064220-USMC	Pfc.	Mistreatment	Robert L. Batdorff
Baylis Raymond B.	RA 13280754	Cpl.	Mistreatment	Pfc. Robert L. Jones
Baylow Page T.	RA 13348436	Pvt.	Torture	Pvt. Page T. Baylow
Bean Thomas J.	RA 13317020	Pfc.	Torture	Pfc Lane
Beaulieu Richard J.	RA 11191677	Pfc.	Death from Mistreatment	Capt. Roy Russell
Bednarz Joseph P.	0-1336864	Capt.	Mistreatment	Capt. Joseph P. Bednarz
Bell Charlie	RA 34534863	Cpl.	Death from Mistreatment	Charles Edward Massie
Bemerer Albert L.	RA 15261032	Sgt.	Mistreatment	Sgt. Albert L Bemerer
Bender Ralph	RA 16286478	Pfc.	Death from Mistreatment	Pfc. Gildo C Rodriquez
Beswick Byron Herbert	029003 USMC	Capt.	Torture	Capt. Byron Herbert Beswick
Beverly John E.	RA 13270876	Pfc.	Death from Mistreatment	Sgt. Sherman Cross
Bigan Andrew E.	0-0976291	1st Lt.	Torture	1st Lt. Andrew B Bigan
Billeck Edwin Alfred	?R 3854392?	Pfc.	Mistreatment	Pfc. Edwin Alfred Billeck
Bittner Donald R.	RA 13299?67	Cpl.	Torture	Cpl. Raymond F. Goodburlett
Black Vance E.	0004197A	Lt. Col.	Death from Torture	Thomas D Harrison
Blew Paul R.	0-1169428	Capt.	Murder	Cpl. Charles Taylor
Bley Roy H.	010450 USMC	Maj.	Torture	Maj. Roy H Bley

Name	Service No.	Rank	Offense	Witness
Bobbs John G.	RA 23770?62	Cpl.	Death from Mistreatment	Capt. Bromser
Bonetsky Robert W.	RA 1344403	Pfc.	Mistreatment	Pfc. Robert W Bonetsky
Bonner William N.	RA 46062447	Cpl.	Death from Mistreatment	Vincent G Simonetti
Boody Claude A.	R 18106803	M/Sgt.	Mistreatment	M/Sgt. Katsui Tunigawa
Booker Jessie V.	020617 USMC	Maj.	Mistreatment	Lt. Col. Lan?ron
Boswell Elvin L.	RA 14328476	Cpl.	Death from Mistreatment	Capt. Russell
Boswell William G.	A-02088249	Lt.	Torture	Lt. Robert Howell
Bounds Leonard B.	0-1297174	Capt.	Mistreatment	Capt. Leonard B. Bounds
Bradford Ulysses H.	0-1296645	Capt.	Death from Mistreatment	Capt. Ralph Wardella
Brassfield Harry C.	RA 06804544	M/Sgt	Death from Mistreatment	Pfc. Robert L. Jones
Branch Charles S.	RA 06985252	M/Sgt	Death from Mistreatment	Capt. Roy H. Russell
Bredeson Arlin S.	RA 37753605	Cpl.	Death from Mistreatment	Capt. Roy H. Russell
Breton Joseph E.	0-2002408	Capt.	Mistreatment	Joseph E. Breton
Brooks Robert I.	RA 16261246	Pfc.	Mistreatment	Pfc Robert I. Brooks
Brown Andrew B.	RA 17276004	Sgt.	Murder	Pfc. Simon T. Synum
Brown Billy A.	1108329-USMC	Pfc	Mistreatment	Pfc. Billy A. Brown
Brown Gerald M.	AF-0009625A	Lt. Col.	Torture	Maj. Harry Gibb
Brumbelow Clifton L.	RA 24767249	Pfc.	Torture	Cpl. Ernest T. Jenkins
Buli Bernard	RA 13334990	Sgt.	Torture	Sgt. Bernard Buli
Bulkowiski George	0-2000612	Capt.	Death from Mistreatment	Capt. Ralph Nardella
Bundy Lyonel D.	66423-USMC	Sgt.	Mistreatment	Sgt. Philip N. Latora
Burdue Wayne	0-0485664	Maj.	Death from Mistreatment	Capt Leamon
Burke Stanley A.	1092495-USMC	Cpl.	Torture	Cpl. Stanley A. Burke

Name	Service Number	Rank	Category	Witness
Bunnell Hubert K.	RA 11094837	Sgt.	Death from Mistreatment	Sfc. Raymond Cook
Burrows John K.	0-2014447	2nd Lt.	Death from Mistreatment	Capt. Deakin
Bynum Simon T.	ER 38483279	Pfc.	Mistreatment	Pfc. Simon T. Bynum
Cabello Thomas M.	RA 16262736	Cpl.	Torture	Pfc. Robert W. Bonetsky
Cain Hohn T.	49725-USMC	M/Sgt	Torture	M/Sgt. Hohn T. Cain
Canaan Gerald C.	USW 505807	Ensg.	Mistreatment	Ensg. Gerald C. Cannaan
Carr Baldwin R.	0-2209414	2nd Lt.	Murder	Sfc. William R. Docs
Carrier Charles L.	0-0395468	Capt.	Death from Torture	Sgt. Charles E. Rollins
Carter Bartus	AF 02068183	1st Lt.	Torture	A/1c Travis C. Wendle
Carter Gail W.	RA 16212566	Cpl.	Torture	Pfc. John W. Adams
Ceasor James	RA 15236300	Cpl.	Death from Mistreatment	Cpl. Walter Williams
Chastin Ben	RA 16234438	Pvt.	Torture	James J. Volpon?
Clark Vernon W.	RA 11186440	Pfc.	Mistreatment	Cpl. Robert E Sitler
Cline Charles J.	MR 18260943	Pfc.	Death from Mistreatment	Cpl. Willie A Parker
Clouse Bunhard C.	RA 16297035	Cpl.	Death from Mistreatment	Capt. Roy H Russell
Clubb Charles E.	RA 17264263	Sgt.	Mistreatment	Sgt. Charles E Clubb
Cockfield Graham M.	RA 44092762	M/Sgt.	Mistreatment	M/Sgt. Graham M Cockfield
Coffee Robert J.	659953 USMC	Sgt.	Mistreatment	Sgt. Robert J Coffee
Cogburn James A.	RA 14043351	SFC	Torture	SFC. James A. Cogburn
Combs Charles H.	RA 13333105	SFC	Mistreatment	SFC. Charles H. Combs
Conley Benjamin L.	RA 35221518	Sgt.	Mistreatment	Sgt. Benjamin L Conley
Conley James T.	RA 13289386	Cpl.	Mistreatment	Cpl. James T. Conley
Connacher Kenneth	RA 13315993	Pvt-2.	Torture	James J Volpone

Name	Service Number	Cause	Identified By
Connick Carl F.	RA 12119783	Pfc.	Death from Mistreatment	Cpl. Beecher Monroe Mefford
Conway Henry L Jr	?54354 USMC	2d Lt.	Mistreatment	2d Lt. Henry L Conway Jr
Cope Kenneth E.	RA 14229309	Sgt.	Torture	Cpl. John L. Watters
Cossins Carl V.	RA 35612033	Cpl.	Mistreatment	Cpl. Edward C. Sheffield
Council William W.	RA 24971442	Pvt.	Murder	Cpl. Edward C. Sheffield
Cox Calvin M.	RA 10736287	Sgt.	Murder	Sgt. Bernard Buli
Cox Malcolm Robert Jr.	0-0062690	2nd Lt.	Death from Mistreatment	Lt. Watson
Cox William O.	RA 13320627	Cpl.	Death from Mistreatment	Sgt. Eugene F. Thronson
Culbertson Ralph E.	0-1949515	Capt.	Torture	Capt. Zimmerman
Dansberry Richard	RA 27936689	Pfc.	Death from Mistreatment	Capt. Radoszewald
Darden Roy Jr.	507924USMC	Sgt.	Mistreatment	Roy V. Ratliff
Danjat John	0456188	Maj.	Mistreatment	Maj. John Daujat
Davis Finley J.	RA 33293511	M/Sgt.	Death from Mistreatment	Cpl. Walter Williams
Davis Norman R.	AO-0769262	Lt.	Death from Mistreatment	Lt. Bonnie C. Bowling
Day John W.	RA 18347572	Sgt.	Mistreatment	Sgt. John W. Day
Denmark Iler D.	0-2028560	2nd Lt.	Mistreatment	2nd Lt. Iler D. Denmark
Deyoung Reginald	US 51049665	Cpl.	Death from Mistreatment	M/Sgt. Earl De Fontes
Diaz Donald D.	0-0362090	Maj.	Death from Mistreatment	Capt. Radowszewski
Dibble Donald E.	RA 12291235	Cpl.	Death from Mistreatment	Maxie L. Austin
Didur Alexander	0-0401335	Capt.	Death from Mistreatment	Capt. Deakin

Name	Service Number	Rank	Cause	Reported by
Dillard Floyd	RA 13271469	Pfc.	Death from Mistreatment	Sgt. Roosevelt Powell Jr.
Dillon William K.	US 52064742	Pfc.	Mistreatment	William K. Dillon
Dixon Ralph P. Jr.	058371	1st Lt.	Mistreatment	Ralph P. Dixon Jr.
Dobbs Byron A. Jr.	A00883799	Capt.	Torture	Capt. Meirerdcks
Donahue Jack F.	RA 15279948	Pfc.	Mistreatment	Pfc. Jack F. Donahue
Dohovan Lawrence	RA 13309915	Cpl.	Mistreatment	Sgt. Rudolph A. Pavlik
Dowe Ray M. Jr.	0-0062650	1st Lt.	Mistreatment	1st Lt. Ray M. Dowe Jr.
Dowling Donald F.	1063259USMC	Pfc.	Death from Mistreatment	Sgt. Mickey K. Scott
Dowling Paul E. Jr.	1063264USMC	Pfc.	Death from Mistreatment	Sgt. Mickey K. Scott
Downey Earl D.	654337USMC	Sgt.	Mistreatment	Sgt Earl D. Downey
Drake Robert E.	RA 1621984	Cpl.	Death from Mistreatment	Charles Edward Massie
Drennan Hugh J.	RA 20725573	SFC.	Death from Mistreatment	1st Lt. Teegue
Illegible		Pfc.	Mistreatment	Pfc. Rados Dudukovich
Duncan Wyatt G.	RA 39011059	M/Sgt.	Death from Mistreatment	SFC. Alla?
Dunford Berton E.	RA 13332945	Cpl.	Mistreatment	Cpl. Berton E Dunford
Dungen Benman	RA 18903954	Cpl.	Death from Mistreatment	Charles Edward Massie
Dunn John J.	0-0031385	Lt. Col.	Mistreatment	Lt. Col. John J Dunn
Edens Malcolm E.		Capt.	Death from Mistreatment	Capt. Joseph L Breton
Ebeler Donald ?		Pfc.	Death from Mistreatment	Capt. Kutys
Ellis Emanuel		Cpl.	Death from Mistreatment	Sgt. Sherman Gross
Emerson James L.		Pfc.	Murder	Denny B. Young

Name	Service No.	Rank	Offense	Complainant
Enfinger Edgar		Sgt.	Death from Mistreatment	Pfc. Edgar Glenn
Illegible		Capt.	Death from Mistreatment	1st Lt. Teague
Espelin Oscar L.		Maj.	Death from Mistreatment	Lt. Kopischkie
Ezell Dee E.		Capt.	Torture	Capt. Dee E Ezell
Ezzell De Joyce E.		Cpl.	Death from Mistreatment	Cpl. Ernest T Jenkins
Falls Eino E.	W-0906717	W.O.	Death from Mistreatment	Lt. Col. Fry
Farris Alvin R.	RA 37217412	Pfc.	Death from Mistreatment	Capt. Roy H. Russell
Fastener Michael C.	RA 06933149	M/Sgt.	Death from Mistreatment	Sgt. William F. Evans
Fedenets Andrew	0-1175433	Maj.	Mistreatment	Maj. Andrew Fede?ots
Findlay Edward H.	RA 16264242	Cpl.	Death from Mistreatment	Sfc. Allemand
Fitzgerald John J.	ER 55004505	Pfc.	Death from Mistreatment	Capt. Radoszewski
Flores Nick A.	1091431USMC	Cpl.	Torture	Cpl. Nick A. Flores
Floyd Delmas F.	RA 18281341	Sgt.	Mistreatment	Sgt. Delmas F. Floyd
Fluegel Martin C.	ER 37807416	Cpl.	Death from Mistreatment	Capt. Radowszewski
Flynn John P. Jr.	032419USMC	Capt.	Torture	M/Sgt. John T. Cain
Foreacre Louis K.	1175294USMC	Cpl.	Mistreatment	Cpl. Louis K. Foreacre
Fox Karl M.	RA 15408379	Cpl.	Mistreatment	Robert Y. Kojima
Franklin Richard L.	ER 38471678	Sgt.	Death from Mistreatment	Pfc. Fred Obroff
Freeman Everett	RA 13292502	Cpl.	Torture	Cpl. Everett Freeman
Freeman Russell L.	RA 13268529	Pvt.	Mistreatment	Pvt. Russell L. Freeman
Freeman William D.	ER 44112216	Pvt.	Mistreatment	Cpl. Preece

Name	Service No.	Rank	Category	Reported by
Fringeli Ralph G.	US 52009892	Pvt.	Death from Mistreatment	Pfc. Dudukovich
Furlow Robert D.	RA 12115793	Pfc.	Death from Mistreatment	Cpl. Mefford
Gallagher Donald	NG 23891063	Cpl.	Death from Mistreatment	Cpl. Donald E. Frazee
Gambocurta Henry	RA 13315507	Sgt.	Mistreatment	Sgt. Henry Gambocurta
Geisendolfer Lou	US 55033968	Pfc.	Mistreatment	Pfc Lou Geisesndolfer
Germroth Richard	RA 13229606068	Pvt.	Mistreatment	Sgt. Rudolph A. Pavlik
Ghinazzi Mario R.	ER 57501579	Pfc.	Death from Mistreatment	Capt. Radowszewski
Gibb Harry E.	047853	Maj.	Torture	Maj. Harry E. Gibb
Gibbens Edward M.	A0696226	Capt.	Torture	Lt. Leroy Bond
Glenn Phillip K.	0-1118897	Lt.	Death from Mistreatment	Lt. Col. Fry
Gonzales Jesus G.	RA 38440003	Sgt.	Mistreatment	Cpl. Ernest T. Jenkins
Goodburlett Raymond F.	RA 12283162	Cpl.	Torture	Cpl. Raymond F. Goodburlett
Goodwin Andrew L.	01309547	Capt.	Mistreatment	Capt. Andrew L. Goodwin
Goosby Connie	RA 44154983	Pfc.	Death from Mistreatment	Sgt. Roosevelt Powell Jr.
Graham Alfred P. Jr.	1198510USMC	Cpl.	Mistreatment	Cpl. Alfred P. Graham Jr.
Gramling Roy M.	0-0390536	Maj.	Mistreatment	Capt. Millard J. Butler
Green Marvin W.	0-2055146	Maj.	Mistreatment	Maj. Marvin W. Green
Greenfield Larry L.	RA 17278225	Pfc.	Death from Mistreatment	Cpl Raymond Arias
Gross Walter F.	ER 12262725	Pvt.	Death from Mistreatment	Lt. Col. Paul Liles
Guinter Dorland F.	RA 13278949	Cpl.	Mistreatment	Cpl. Dorland F. Guinter

Name	Service Number	Rank	Offense	Responsible
Gunnell James J.	RA 18197399	Cpl.	Death from Mistreatment	Charles E. Massie
Hall Harold T.	RA 16228726	Cpl.	Death from Mistreatment	Cpl. Calso J. Montoya
Hamill Edward T.	RA 19316662	Pvt.	Death from Mistreatment	Sfc. Ordonio
Hammond Joseph	RA 15284403	Pvt.	Torture	Pvt Joseph Hammond
Hansen Robert M.	0-0262443	Capt.	Death from Mistreatment	Cpl. Booker Johnson
Harbin Joseph B.	1087610USMC	Sgt.	Mistreatment	Sgt. Joseph B. Harbin
Hardage Roy H.	RA 19306271	Cpl.	Mistreatment	Cpl. Jimmy D. Dunn
Haney Marvin A.	0-1913362	2nd Lt.	Death from Mistreatment	Maj. Shirey
Hankey Charles C.	RA15271727	Cpl.	Mistreatment	Cpl. Charles C Hankey
Harlan John C.	0-247463	Maj.	Torture	Maj. John C Harlan
Harris Clarence	RA 16261687	Pvt.	Mistreatment	Russell L Freeman
Harris Theodore R.	A00782261	Capt.	Mistreatment	LtJG. John A. DeMasters
Harris Walter R.	0-16518 USMC	Maj.	Torture	2d Lt. Denmark
Harrison Thomas D.	0009759A	Lt. Col.	Torture	Lt. Col. Thomas D Harrison
Hatcher J.C.	RA 14316137	Pvt.	Torture	Pvt. J.C. Hatcher
Haugen Richard D.	0-0062832	1st Lt.	Death from MIstreatment	Capt. Deakin
Healy Daniel E.	RA 46031097	Sgt.	Death from Mistreatment	Robert A Maclean
Heard Delbert E.	RA 16921929	Sfc.	Death from Mistreatment	Capt. Roy H Russell
Hefta Kenneth	ER 17217130	Cpl.	Death from Mistreatment	Capt. B. Radoszewski
Henderson Jack B.	A01911650	1st Lt.	Mistreatment	Lt. Col. Thomas D Harrison
Herrera Pedro	RA 18253222	Cpl.	Mistreatment	Cpl. Celso J Montoya

Name	Service No.	Rank	Offense	Witness
Hess Edward J Jr	US 52057157	Pvt.	Death from Mistreatment	Pfc. Dudukovich
Hester, James C.	653540 USMC	Pfc.	Death from Mistreatment	Sgt. Mickey K Scott
Hill James F.	0-0038835	Lt. Col.	Death from Mistreatment	Maj. John Harlan
Hicks Kenneth A.	RA 16246409	Sfc.	Death from Mistreatment	Sgt. Gambocurta
Hints Harold	038772USMC	1st Lt.	Death from Mistreatment	Capt Arthur Wagner
Hobart Richard H.	RA 13336297	Cpl.	Death from Mistreatment	Cpl. Billy Joe Cambell
Hodges Carrell T.	AF 19356625	M/Sgt.	Mistreatment	Capt. Robert B. Lipscombe
Holmes Roxie J.	RA 15422192	Cpl.	Mistreatment	Cpl. Ernest T. Jenkins
Howard Charles F.	0-2204038	1st Lt.	Mistreatment	Capt. Millard J. Butler
Hume Thomas	0-0023931	Maj.	Death from Torture	1st Lt. Alan L. Lloyd
Huth William F.	US 52003899	Pfc.	Death from Mistreatment	Sgt. Bemerer
Jackson Clinton H.	0-1310717	Lt.	Death from Mistreatment	Capt. Roy H. Russell
Jackson Herbert	RA 18297462	Cpl.	Death from Mistreatment	Sgt. Sherman Cross
Jacobson Lyle	RA 19350277	Pfc.	Death from Mistreatment	Sgt. Rudolph A. Pavlik
Jeanplong Paul A.	RA 19330301	Pfc.	Death from Mistreatment	1st. Lt. Teague
Jessup Howard L.	RA 15281890	Pfc.	Death from Mistreatment	Pfc. Fred M. Lane Jr.
Johansen Charles V.	AF 19124748	S/Sgt.	Torture	Lt. J.G. John A. De Masters
Johnson Booker T.		Cpl.	Mistreatment	Cpl. Booker T Johnson

Name	Rank	Cause	Reference
Johnson Frank N.	Pfc.	Death from Mistreatment	Cpl. Robert ??
Johnson Joe L.	Sgt.	Death from Mistreatment	Pfc. Charles ? Boulduc
Johnson John N.	Sgt.	Death from Mistreatment	Capt. Roy E. Russell
Johnson Nathaniel	Cpl.	Death from Mistreatment	
Jones Robert L.	Pfc.	Mistreatment	Pfc. Robert L Jones
Joyce William E Jr.	Pfc.	Death from Mistreatment	Lt. Dixon
Jumper ??		Death from Mistreatment	Cpl. Walter Williams
Illegible		Death from Mistreatment	Capt. ??
Illegible		Death from Mistreatment	1st Lt. Joseph ??
Kaschko Harold L.	Maj.	Mistreatment	Maj. Harold L. Kaschko
Keith, John ? Jr.	Lt. Col.	Death from mistreatment	Sgt. Joseph ? Day
Knicley Alfred L.	Pfc.	Torture	Sgt. John ? Day
Knowles Billy C.		Torture	Pfc. ? Coburn
Koslsch John K. 42447 6USM	Lt. J.G.	Death from Mistreatment	Capt. Radowszewski
Kovatch Ernest S. 0-1915397	Lt.	Mistreatment	Lt. Ernest S. Kovatch
King Reginald W. RA 37621549	Sfc.	Death from Mistreatment	Sgt. Charles E. Rollins
King Charles E. RA 18314926	Pfc.	Death from Mistreatment	1st Lt. Taegue
La France D.J. RA 06252159	M/Sgt.	Death from Mistreatment	M/Sgt. Phillip Doerfer
Lane Fred W. RA 14341315	Pvt.	Mistreatment	Pvt. Fred W. Lane
Lanier Claude RA 13270847	Cpl.	Death from Mistreatment	Robert I. Brooks

Name	Service Number	Rank	Cause	Reported by
Lansdell Charles L.	RA 14268563	Pvt.	Death from Mistreatment	Cpl. Thurman Jones
Larson Derfee	0-0269143	Capt.	Death from Mistreatment	Lt. Col Fry
Leach Edward T.	0-1688455	1st Lt.	Death from Mistreatment	Maj. Gibb
Ledger Ernest W. Jr.	RA 11168947	Pfc.	Death from Mistreatment	1st Lt. Taegue
Lee Clarence O.	RA 06557867	M/Sgt.	Death from Mistreatment	Cpl. Thurman Jones
Lee Sunnie S.	RA 30118689	Cpl.	Death from Mistreatment	1st Lt. Taegue
Le Master James E.	RA 15421651	Cpl.	Death from Mistreatment	Capt. Roy H. Russell
Lennox Richard N.	RA 16328282	Pfc.	Death from Mistreatment	Pfc. Nick J. Antonis
Lessman Billy J.	1152336USMC	Pfc.	Mistreatment	Cpl. Alfred P. Graham
Lester Leroy	RA 13337050	Pfc.	Mistreatment	Sgt. Clubb
Lewis Lyman E.	RA 15266324	Pfc.	Death from Mistreatment	Sgt. Sherman Cross
Lewis William J.	01691941	1st Lt.	Torture	1st Lt. William J. Lewis
Linfante Raymond	US 51025511	Pvt.	Mistreatment	James J. Volpone
Little Thomas E.	RA 15422473	Sfc.	Death from Mistreatment	Sfc. Raymond Cook
Longmire Chester	RA 44145686	Pfc.	Death from Mistreatment	Cpl. Walter William
Lorenzo Michael J.	01634085	Maj.	Torture	Maj. Michael J. Loranzo
Lovelady Wallace R.	RA 14224567	Cpl.	Death from Mistreatment	Sgt. William F. Evans
Ludwig Antoony R.	RA 15270543	Pfc.	Mistreatment	Lt. Col. Thomas D. Harrison
Lyke Thomas A.	RA 15274514	Pfc.	Mistreatment	Pfc. John W. Adams

Name	Service Number	Offense	Rank	Witness/Reference
Maadox James	RA 15046510	Death from Mistreatment	Sfc.	Capt. Fred L. Spaer
MacGhee David F.	A0790271	Mistreatment, Torture	Maj.	Maj. David F. MacGhee
Metz Henry X.	AF 11027011	Mistreatment	Sgt.	Capt. Luther Jones
Mefford Beecher Monroe	RA 15261779	Mistreatment	Cpl.	Cpl. Momroe Beecher Mefford
		Death from mistreatment	Cpl.	Capt. Roy E. Russell
		Death from mistreatment	Pvt.	
		Torture	Capt.	Capt. Herbert ??
		Murder	Capt.	Capt. ?? Speer
		Mistreatment	Cpl.	Cpl. ? ?-Alvarez
Martin J.D.		Torture	Cpl.	Cpl. J.D. Martin
McCabe Roger		Mistreatment	Pfc.	Robert Y. Kajima
McCall Rufus ?		Death from MIstreatment	Pfc.	Cpl. ?? Taylor
McCracken Kenneth		Murder	Pfc.	William ? ?
McElroy Jess H.		Torture		? Jess ? McElroy
McGee Marcus		Torture	Cpl.	Cpl. Marcus McGee
McKinney Dan L.		Torture	Cpl.	Loyd L. Osborn
McClain William A.		Mistreatment	Capt.	Capt. John ? Caldwell Jr.
Medlin John William		Torture	Pfc.	Pfc. John William Medlin
		Torture		
Menzia Conrad C.	ER 37775204	Mistreatment	Pfc.	Edwin A. Billeak
Milantoni Patsy A.	0-1882208	Torture	2nd Lt.	2nd Lt. Patsy A. Milantoni
Miller H.P.	A01910262	Death from Mistreatment	1st Lt.	Lt. Col. Thomas D. Harrison
Mitchell Harvey O.	RA 17233968	Torture	Pfc.	Cpl. Allen Washington

Name	Service No.	Rank	Cause	Witness
Monroe Napoleon	RA 19369510	Pfc.	Death from Mistreatment	Cpl. Booker Johnson
Monrowe Billy J.	RA 17252011	Cpl.	Murder	Cpl. Edward C. Sheffield
Montgomery James H.	RA 24416174	Pfc.	Torture	Pfc. James H. Montgomery
Montoya Celso J.	RA 25637810	Cpl.	Torture	Cpl. Celso J. Montoya
Nava Adolphus	W-2141394	WO	Death from Mistreatment	Cpl. Dunford
Morris Stafford L.	RA 132266178	Cpl.	Death from Mistreatment	Charles Edward Massie
Moss Lawrence D.	0-2262077	2nd Lt.	Death from Mistreatment	Capt. Curtiss
Newman Cecil E.	0-0059249	2nd Lt.	Death from Mistreatment	Sgt. Escobar Torres Vicente
Nieman R.C.	0-0974393	2nd Lt.	Death from Mistreatment	Maj. Nugent
Nix Henry E.	RA 14225117	M/Sgt.	Mistreatment	Msgt. Tanigawa Katsoki
O'Conner Edward M.	128651USMC	Pfc.	Death from Mistreatment	Cpl. Robert J. Chester
O'Keefe Arthur	RA 20214477	Cpl.	Mistreatment	Cpl. Chester J. Gorski
O'Leary James P.	RA 11183498	Cpl.	Death from Mistreatment	Cpl. Celso J. Montoya
Osborn Loyd E.	670828USMC	Pfc.	Mistreatment	Pfc. Loyd E. Osborn
Palmer Duncan	AF 0015921A	Maj.	Mistreatment	Maj. Duncan Palmer
Parker Jerry W.	RA 17257884	Sgt.	Death from Mistreatment	M/Sgt. Phillip Doerfer
Parker Willie A.	RA 57301086	Pfc.	Mistreatment	Pfc. George M. Sayre
Patton Gene R.	RA 18350661	Pvt.	Mistreatment	Sgt. Guy Lewis
Pavlik Rudolph A.	RA 35082583	Sgt.	Torture	Sgt. Rudolph A. Pavlik
Pearson Raymond E.	0-2014734	Lt.	Death from Mistreatment	Maj. Marvin W. Green
Peart Edwon A. Jr.	0-1913203	2nd Lt.	Death from Mistreatment	Capt. Jones

Name	Service No.	Rank	Cause	Witness
Penn Edward L.	RA 15199811	Sgt.	Death from Mistreatment	1st Lt. Taegue
Perry Jackie L.	RA 13332872	Pvt.	Torture	Cpl. Donald E. Frazee
Petroff John Jr.	RA 19255403	Cpl.	Death from Mistreatment	Pfc. Fred Obroff
Pettigrew John Bob	ER 38633783	Pfc.	Death from Mistreatment	Pfc. Eddie G. Barnes
Phillips Raymond E.	RA 18352160	Pfc.	Mistreatment	Pfc. Raymond E. Phillips
Pickering Fred R.	0-0417252	Capt.	Death from Mistreatment	Capt. Radowszewski
Plunkett Waitcell	RA 38303199	Sfc.	Death from Mistreatment	Sfc. Raymond Cook
Polk Warren F.	A01910005	Lt.	Death from Mistreatment	Antonio Sanchez
Pool Edward	RA 18342185	Pfc.	Death from Mistreatment	Capt. Thurman Jones
Porter Arelious	RA 33646108	Sgt.	Torture	Sgt. Arelious Porter
Preece Ellas J.	RA 18363793	Cpl.	Torture	Cpl. Ellas J. Preece
Prestridge Wyatt E.	RA 34337233	Sgt.	Torture	Sgt. Wyatt E. Prestridge
Pritchett Willie G.	RA 18264084	Cpl.	Murder	Cpl. Buster White
Pucirilli Felix	RA 12345876	Pvt.	Mistreatment	Pvt. Felix Pucirilli
Ragsdale James N.	RA 07081039	Sfc.	Mistreatment	Sfc. James N. Ragsdale
Ray Donald R.	RA 14313140	Cpl.	Mistreatment	Sgt. Billy J. Buchanan
Reiley Thomas P.	RA 06070125	Sgt.	Death from Mistreatment	Maj. Koschko
Rice Glen W. Jr.	NG 25033410	Pfc.	Mistreatment	Sgt. Robert A. Strachan Jr.
Ritter John R.	RA 23743661	Pfc.	Mistreatment	John Narvin
Roberts Gaines C.	RA 14330743	Sfc.	Mistreatment	Sfc. Gaines C. Roberts
Robinson Joseph C.	RA 13344449	Pfc.	Death from Mistreatment	Charles Edward Massie

Name	Service No.	Rank	Offense	Witness
Robinson Marshall	RA 15266644	Pfc.	Mistreatment	Russell L. Freeman
Rodeski William	US 55024012	Pfc.	Death from Mistreatment	Lt. Dixon
Rodriguez Gildo C.	RA 42211386	Pfc.	Torture	Pfc. Gildo C. Rodriguez
Rogers George P.	RA 18275475	Pvt.	Torture	Pvt. George P. Rogers
Rogers Lloyd G.	RA 17093165	Pvt.	Death from Mistreatment	M/Sgt. Phillip Doerfer
Rollins Charles E.	RA 142817767	Sgt.	Torture	Sgt. Charles E. Rollins
Rothlauf Donal G.	RA 17264716	Cpl.	Death from Mistreatment	Lt. Delashment
Rowden Thomas	AF12353529	S/Sgt.	Attempted Murder	Lt. Col. Newton Lantron
Ruddell James C. Jr.	0-0057177	Lt.	Death from Mistreatment	Maj. Marvin W. Green
Ruff Wilfred J.	RA 19360257	Sgt.	Torture	Cpl. Goodburlett
Russell Roy H.	0-1102027	Capt.	Torture	Capt. Roy H. Russell
Sayre George M.	RA 29005106	Pfc.	Mistreatment	Pfc. George M. Sayre
Schade James	RA 13168071	M/Sgt.	Mistreatment	M/Sgt. James Schade
Schahill James P.	RA 12286061	Cpl.	Mistreatment	Cpl. Ernest T. Jenkins
Sedotal Junius J.	RA 18353184	Pfc.	Attempted Murder	Pfc. Junius J. Sedotal
Sellers Lonnie J.	ER 33388512	Pfc.	Death from Mistreatment	Capt. Jones
Shaw James P.	RA 44146318	Pvt.	Death from Mistreatment	Pfc Nick J. Antonis
Sheriff Louis	US 52035484	Pvt.	Death from Mistreatment	Capt. Goodwin
Shoremen James G.	RA 06882298	M/Sgt.	Death from Mistreatment	Pfc. Jose A. Marques
Simmons Tyson	RA 13348286	Pfc.	Mistreatment	Cpl. Allan Washington
Simpson Robert L.	A00763757	1st. Lt.	Death from Mistreatment	Lt. J.G. John Thornton

Name	Service Number	Rank	Cause	Reported By
Sirman Donald S.	A00686024	1st Lt.	Murder	Maj. Nugent
Slaughter Lum L.	RA 14289884	Cpl.	Death from Mistreatment	Cpl. Dunford
Smith Bob T.	RA 44127929	Sfc.	Torture	Sfc. Bob T. Smith
Smith Clyde R.	RA 14352795	Pvt.	Mistreatment	Cpl. Ernest T. Jenkins
Smith Jerrold R.	ER 16233015	Pfc.	Death from Mistreatment	Sgt. Bemerer
Smith Mercer R.	024054USMC	Capt.	Mistreatment	Capt. Mercer R. Smith
Smoak Harvey	RA 1412394	M/Sgt.	Death from Mistreatment	Sgt. Ira D. Smith
Snock Joseph	RA 13236645	Cpl.	Death from Mistreatment	Pfc. Rex Dodge
Soriano Fred D.	0-1896563	1st Lt.	Mistreatment	1st Lt. Fred D. Soriano
Spano Joseph	RA 44109533	Cpl.	Mistreatment	Cpl. Ernest T. Jenkins
Sparks James R.	RA 19329460	Pfc.	Death from Mistreatment	1st Lt. Taegue
Speer Fred L.	01172293	Capt.	Mistreatment	Capt. Fred L. Speer
Spoon Manuel J.	RA 17003172	Sfc.	Death from Mistreatment	Pfc. Edgar Glenn
Stai Melvin R.	0-2035983	Capt.	Killed in Air Attack on unmarked PW Camp	Maj. Shirey
Stanley James L.	A00591426	1st Lt.	Torture	1st Lt. Kenneth W. Henry
Stein Robert A.	RA 12002299	M/Sgt.	Killed in Air Attack on unmarked PW Camp	Pfc. Gildo C. Rodriguez
Storey Dallas R.	RA 16267669	Pfc.	Death from Mistreatment	Cpl. Walter Williams
Story Leroy A.	RA 19242321	Pfc.	Death from Mistreatment	Cpl. Taylor
Sund Roland V.	0-2037738	Lt.	Death from Mistreatment	CWO Dwight E. Coxe
Sutton Frederick G.	RA 18145803	Pfc.	Death from Mistreatment	Cpl. Booker Johnson

Name	Service Number	Rank	Cause	Witness/Other
Swartz Donald L.	RA 16306764	Cpl.	Torture	Sgt. Ira D. Smith
Swain Vincent Jr.	RA 17280635	Pfc.	Death from Mistreatment	Capt. Radoszewski
Tadaki Tomio	RA 10103759	Cpl.	Mistreatment	Cpl. Tadaki
Taliaferro Dennis L.	1115829USMC	Pfc.	Murder	Cpl. Sidney ?ehl
Taylor Charles E.	RA 15441754	Cpl.	Torture	Cpl. Charles E. Taylor
Taylor Rafe M.	RA 18342382	Cpl.	Torture	Cpl. Rafe M. Taylor
Thomas George H.	27326USMC	Cpl.	Death from Mistreatment	Loyd E. Osborn
Thompson, Elmore M.	RA 13270927	Cpl.	Death from Mistreatment	Sgt. Sherman Cross
Thompson James	RA 36101834	M/Sgt.	Mistreatment	M/Sgt. Tanigawa
Thornton Cordus H.	0-2055242	2nd Lt.	Murder	Lt. Col. Lantron
Thronson Eugene F.	RA 14300927	Sgt.	Mistreatment	Sgt. Eugene F. Thronson
Thurman Ruben Jr.	RA 34745157	Cpl.	Death from Mistreatment	Sgt. Roosevelt Powell Jr.
Tilch Philip W.	AF 13327852	A/1c	Death from Mistreatment	Maj. Gibb
Tompkins Daniel D.	RA 13386788	Pfc.	Mistreatment	Cpl. Ernest T. Jenkins
Toomey Robert L.	A1911004	1st Lt.	Mistreatment	A/1c Weldon
Trail Joseph J.	RA 13294088	Pfc.	Death from Mistreatment	1st Lt. Teague
Trash William G.	06141USMC	Lt. Col.	Torture	Capt. Gerald Fink
Treat Francis L.	A00813257	Capt.	Mistreatment	Lt. J.G. De Masters
Trexler Tommy P.	02014531	2nd Lt.	Torture	2nd Lt. Tommy P. Trexler
Underwood Raymond C.	RA 44042044	Sgt.	Murder	Cpl. Robert E. Sitler
Uurtamo Stephen T.	0-1285146	Capt.	Death from Mistreatment	CWO Coxe
Vanderkoy Charles	RA 15295500	Cpl.	Death from Mistreatment	James Volpone

Name	Service Number	Rank	Category	Responsible
Vallancourt John	RA 16279774	Sgt.	Death from Mistreatment	Sfc. Allemand
Vails Maxwell W.	O-1295462	Capt.	Death from Mistreatment	1st Lt. Louis Wilson
Vaughan James V.	RA 25986824	Sgt.	Torture	Sgt. Vaughan
Wailes Ardean R.	RA 17273525	Pvt.	Death from Mistreatment	Sgt. Roosevelt Powell Jr.
Warren Samuel	RA 33120547	Sgt.	Death from Mistreatment	Sgt. Roosevelt Powell Jr.
Wells James R.	RA 57400787	Pfc.	Mistreatment	Pfc. James R. Wells
Wesley Walter H.	RA 14212597	Cpl.	Death from Mistreatment	Sgt. Roosevelt Powell Jr.
Whaley Elwin I.	O-0453764	Maj.	Death from Mistreatment	Maj. Gibb
Whitaker Charles L.	RA 15280639	Cpl.	Mistreatment	Cpl. Sheffield Edward C.
White Charles A.	RA 15296548	Pfc.	Death from Mistreatment	Franklin D. Richesson
Woodson Ralph	RA 18335548	Sgt.	Torture	Charles Edward Massie
Woolford William L.	ER 33723258	Cpl.	Death from Mistreatment	1st Lt. Bailey
Wilson William D.	A00735720	Maj.	Torture	Lt. J.G. De Masters
Winters William W.	O-0942161	Lt.	Death from Mistreatment	Capt. Kutya
Wright William J.	AF 00941586	Lt.	Mistreatment	Lt. William J. Wright
Wright Vernon L.	A0191O299	Lt.	Torture	Lt. Col. Zacherle
Yarrish Gerald V.	RA 1194666	Cpl.	Death from Mistreatment	1st Lt. Taegoe
Zumar Charles	RA 13335462	Pvt.	Death from Mistreatment	Capt. Radowszowski

BRITISH:

Name		Category	
Ahearn Jerry		Death from Mistreatment	1st Lt. James Slavrakes
Aldrich James		Death from Mistreatment	Maj. Shirey
Cabrow Henry		Torture	Lt. Henry H. Osborne
Craig Bobby		Death from Mistreatment	Cpl. Preece
Lyons Edward		Death from Mistreatment	Lt. Col. Paul Liles
Gabriel Henry		Death from Mistreatment	Lt. Conley Clarke
Washbrook Ronald		Death from Mistreatment	Lt. Col. Thomas D. Harrison
Wheller Henry		Torture	Lt. Henry Osborne
Lankford Dennis		Torture	Ensg. Garald C. Canaan
May Patrick		Mistreatment	Cpl. Preece

AUSTRALIAN

Name		Category	
Digger		Death from Torture	Cpl. Delbert L. Marks
Harvey Gordon		Mistreatment	Lt. J.G. John W. Thornton

Appendix 4

ROSTER OF VICTIMS FROM U.S. 8TH ARMY SOURCES

Found in: Chapter Two, Volume 1
Source of this information: Judge Advocate Section, War Crimes Division records, National Archives, Suitland, MD, Reference Branch.

VICTIM LIST FROM 8TH ARMY FILES

NAME	RANK	SERIAL NO.	KWC NO.	DATE OF INCIDENT	TYPE OF INCIDENT
Abbott, Leroy	Pvt	RAI5381689	16	17 Aug 50	Murder
Abbott, Richard F.	PFC	RA11177760	1826	31 Dec 50	Death from Mistreatment
Abbott, Robert	LT Col	0-1285369	1827D	26 Nov 50	Mistreatment
Ackerman, Jack M.		RA16266426	76	20 Oct 50	Murder
Adams, William R.	2d Lt	0-2262254	1827D	30 Nov 50	Death from Mistreatment
Addington, Harold J.	Cpl	13333084	1817	29 Aug 53	Mistreatment
Agnew, Robert M.	Sgt	RA6393412	66-B		Mistreatment
Allemand, Leland D.	PFC	RA18256567	1819a	Dec, Jan 58	Mistreatment
Allen, Clifford	Capt	01311959	1821,1819A	1 Dec 50	Mistreatment
Ambrose, Thomas		RA14281064	76	20 Oct 50	Mistreatment
Anderson, Clarence	Capt	0-61069	1819A	2 Sep 53	Mistreatment
Anderson, James F.	PFC	RA14300794	28	26 Sep 50	Murder
Andino, Fonseca	Pvt	U850115241	1819A	24 Sep 52	Death from Mistreatment
Appenfeiner, James	Lt	0-0514946	1821	16 Jun 51	Death from Mistreatment
Aitkins, Virgil F.		RA16315705	76	20 Oct 50	Murder
Alberty, Estelle	Pvt	RA13304667	2	10 Jul 50	Murder
Alexander, John	Cpl	RA11156537	313	16 Feb 51	Murder
Allen, John F.	PFC	RA11191221	66		Mistreatment
Allison, William	Sgt		75	Sep 50	Mistreatment
Amerose, Thomas	Cpl	RA14281064	76	20 Oct 50	Murder
Amerson, Eldred J.	Pvt	RA17226293	66		Mistreatment
Anderson, John	M/Sgt	RA06267477	1821	25 Dec 50	Mistreatment
Anderson, Raymond O.	PFC	RA13285998	21	2 Sep 50	Murder
Armstrong, Wilson C.	Pvt	RA13347921	358	15 Feb 51	Murder
Arkins, Clifford	PFC	RA158	79	Oct 50	Death from Mistreatment
Aulde, Opal D.	Sgt	RA38185655	1260, 1243	11 Jul 50	Murder

Name	Rank	Serial Number		Date	Cause
Bailey, Otis	Cpl		1819A	26 Nov 50	Death from Mistreatment
Bailey, Paul R.		RA13285855	76	20 Oct 50	Murder
Baxter, L. Jr.	Capt	0-0402619	1823, 1831	30 Jul 51	Death from Mistreatment
Ball, James L.	Cpl	RA15288515	1819A	30 Nov 50	Mistreatment
Barcus, Floyd	Sgt	RA15416276	1815		Mistreatment
Barfield, David D.	PFC	RA14337753	1260		Murder
Barnes, Mathew J.	Capt	0-1171042	67, 88		Mistreatment
Bass, William T. Jr.	PFC	RA14313568	76	20 Oct 50	Murder
Baylor, Page T., Jr.	PFC	RA13348436	18270	10 Aug 53	Murder
Beck, Earl L.	Cpl	RA13309481	1819A	1 Dec 50	Mistreatment
Behrs, William F.	Cpl	US55167130	1673		Murder
Bell, Christian A.	PFC	12318322	21	3 Sep 50	Murder
Bell, Alton R.	PFC	RA18363838	151	2 Dec 50	Mistreatment
Bell, Joseph T.	Cpl	RA13265544	76	20 Oct 50	Murder
Bennett, William	PFC	RA24634632	166	16 Jan 51	Murder
Bernal, Joe M.	PFC	RA39597793	119	21 Oct 50	Murder
Bevilock, Ersel	PFC	RA06883691	76	20 Oct 50	Murder
Binsterveldt, Thomas C.	Ens	N-0506698	1831	14 May 51	Death from Mistreatment
Blackwood, Remus M.	PFC	RA14300498	66	29 Aug 50	Mistreatment
Blair, Elsie L.		RA14338197	76	20 Oct 50	Murder
Blake, Dale D.	Cpl	RA27356461	76	20 Oct 50	Mistreatment
Blalock, Douglas W.	1st Lt	0-947892	75,76,87,129	Sep,Oct 50	Mistreatment
Blanchett, Arnie	Sgt	RA14331351	26	22 Sep 50	Murder
Blanton, Emory M.	PFC	RA14252969	76	20 Oct 50	Murder
Bilby, Joseph		RA23753660	66	1 Sep 50	Murder
Bishop, Theodore	1st Lt	0-0970056	1824	11 Feb 51	Death from Mistreatment
Bivens, William F.	Lt	0-1010525	1821	30 Nov 50	Death from Mistreatment
Boldon, William M.	Major	0-0398864	1824	13 Feb 51	Death from Mistreatment
Bomberry, Robbie O.	Sgt	RA6285896	76	20 Oct 50	Mistreatment
Bo??, Leroy	Pvt	RA19348488	16	17 Aug 50	Murder

Name	Rank	Service Number			Date	Cause
Bourgeois, James	PFC	RA18303186	1818		12 Aug 53	Murder
Illegible, Claud W.	Capt	01300444	1821,	1819A	28 Nov 50	Mistreatment
Borst, Arthur W.	Pvt	RA12349274	16		17 Aug 50	Murder
Bourdeau, Philip	SFC	RA11017203	1817			Mistreatment
Bowling, Bonnie C.	Lt	02212078	1817		3 Jan 51	Mistreatment
Bowman, Herbert L.	1st Lt	0-1338435	143		6 Nov 50	Murder
Boydefon, James L.	Lt	0-2208321	75		5 Oct 50	Murder
Bracken, Russel	SFC	RA06946198	163		19 Jul 50	Murder
Brady, Thomas L.	PFC	RA18276760	75, 76		Sep, Oct 50	Mistreatment
Brandt, Arnold	Lt Col	0-0031955	1827D		27 Nov 50	Death from Mistreatment
Bradley, Thomas B.	Cpl	RA13316945	1818		30 Nov 50	Death from Mistreatment
Illegible, Morris W.		RA17265257	1444		8 Sep 50	Murder
Brewer, John H.	Capt.	0-390791	67		13 Oct 50	Mistreatment
Briggs, Raymond	SFC	RA15294902	1818		30 Nov 50	Death from Mistreatment
Briley, Ray A.	Sgt	Ra16264212	16		17 Aug 50	Murder
Bristow, Benjamin	PFC	RA15257989	16		17 Aug 50	Murder
Brockes, John T.	SFC	RA37185587	1824			Mistreatment
Brothers, Richard D.	PFC	RA16310529	166		16 Jan 51	Murder
Broussard, Horace	SFC	RA18212250	1815			Mistreatment
Brower, William J.	PFC	RA17265403	66-A		29 Jul 50	Death from Mistreatment
Brown, Donald	PFC	RA13211702	358			Murder
Brown, Doyle	PFC	RA14298574	28		26 Sep 50	Murder
Brumer, Riley R.	1st Lt	0-2262349	1821		28 Nov 50	Mistreatment
Bryant, Charles R.	PFC	RA15431341	67		13 Oct 50	Mistreatment
Bryant,	SFC	RA18320077	67		20 Sep 50	Murder
Bullock, James W.	Cpl	RA44047611	1819A			Mistreatment
Burks, John M.	Capt	01288175	167		14 Jan 51	Murder
Burkmeimer, Raymond	PFC	ER57222027	219		29 May 51	Murder
Burkit, William C	1st Lt	0-041304	26		22 Sep 50	Murder
Burt, J.C.	PFC	RA19323138	23		5 Sep 50	Murder

Name	Rank	Serial No.	No.	Date	Cause
Butler, Melvin	Cpl	RA16312004	403		Mistreatment
Buttrey, Linton J.	Capt	0-407113	10	17 Jul 50	Mistreatment
Byrd, James W.	1st Lt	0-0061913	1824	12 Feb 51	Death from Mistreatment
Bywater, William D.	Cpl	ER37784485	193	31 Mar 51	Murder
Cables, Myles A.	Cpl	RA6738834	75	20 Oct 50	Mistreatment
Caldwell, Howard O.	1st Lt	0-1108530	1821	30 Nov 50	Death from Mistreatment
Calendar, George D.	Sgt	RA36174869	66	27 Jul 50	Mistreatment
Illegible, William A.	Cpl	RA11187371	1819A	3 Nov 50	Mistreatment
Cameron, John L.	PFC	RA19364093	151		Mistreatment
Campbell, Clark G.	Lt Col	0-0038774	1891A	6 May 51	Death from Mistreatment
Canterbury, Roy W.	Pvt	RA3534106	167	14 Jan 51	Murder
Cardwell, Clarence A.	PFC	RA13234554	1815	3 Sep 53	Mistreatment
Carlson, Dale W.	1st Lt	0-1308923	793		Mistreatment
Carroll, Peter J.	Pvt	RA16309801	167	14 Jan 51	Murder
Castana, Pete	Pvt	RA19357353	76	20 Oct 50	Murder
Castleberry, Wm R.	PFC	RA19328437	28	26 Sep 50	Murder
Catchings, Junior	Sgt	RA16266349	75	8 Oct 50	Mistreatment
Causey, Billie J.	Pvt	RA14318964	16	17 Aug 50	Murder
Cerino, Joseph Jr.	PFC	RA12313845	75	Oct 50	Mistreatment
Chase, John L.	Pvt	RA2813066	66	5 Sep 50	Death from Mistreatment
Cherry, Richard F.	PFC	RA18011625	104	26 Sep 50	Murder
Chestnut, Fred D.	Maj	0-0045795	1819A	30 Nov 50	Death from Mistreatment
Christian, Roland	PFC	RA1196016	166	16 Jan 51	Murder
Christin, Gilbert	M/Sgt	RA6642959	134	2 Nov 50	Mistreatment
Cisco, Boyd Jr.	Cpl	RA15272077	151		Mistreatment
Cisneros, Rudolph		RA38701092	76	20 Oct 50	Murder
Clarifi, George B.	Cpl	RA14002580	915	9 Jul 50	Murder
Clarno, Edward W.	Pvt	ER55011452	1824	14 Feb 51	Death from Mistreatment
Clements, Elsie G.		RA16260507	1444	6 Sep 50	Murder
Clements, Paul	Pvt	RA15210053	1817	30 Nov 50	Mistreatment

Clear, David F.	Cpl	RA36488164	67	13 Oct 50	Murder
Cleveland, Jarrell	PFC	RA14294724	26	22 Sep 50	Murder
Cloutman, Rodney F.	Capt	0-0887605	1821	26 Nov 50	Death from Mistreatment
Cobalis, Vincent J.	WOJG	W-0906667	1817	15 Feb 51	Mistreatment
Cochran, Sam L. Jr.	Cpl	RA6965328	66	27 Jul 50	Mistreatment
Cohan, Frank	PFC	RA16303244	28	26 Sep 50	Murder
Coke, Richard B.	1st Lt	0-1540946	1824	28 Nov 50	Death from Mistreatment
Cole, William H.	PFC	RA14324001	142		Mistreatment
Colson, Joseph	Cpl	AF12777847	164	13 Dec 50	Murder
Coleman, Norris	Capt	0-1106651	1819A		Death from Mistreatment
Collins, John W.	Pvt	RA35240519	16	17 Aug 50	Murder
Conte, Salvatore			1819A		Mistreatment
Conley, Ulysses	M/Sgt	RA38355200	1821	1 Dec 50	Death from Mistreatment
Contrearas, Ernest E.	Cpl	RA17101200	1815		Mistreatment
Coogan, James J.	Pvt	RA43015027	1823		Mistreatment
Cooke, Bobby G.	Cpl	RA13348627	167	4 Jan 51	Murder
Cook, Howard D.	Pvt	RA15424004	143	6 Nov 50	Murder
Cordero, Hester	Capt	0-927409	1819A	9 Dec 50	Torture
Correa, Jesus D.	PFC	RA38025785	75	21 Jul 51	Death from Mistreatment
Corey, Ervin L.		RA35128168	110		Mistreatment
Counts, Woodrow W.	Cpl	RA15215302	76	20 Oct 50	Murder
Cox, James	PFC	RA19326199	10	17 Jul 50	Murder
Cox, Embry V.	PFC	RA14354254	151		Torture
Coin, Dwight	CWQ	W-2142515	1822, 1819A	1 Dec 50	Mistreatment
Craig, Arlton B.	Cpl	RA13231396	75	26 Jul 50	Torture
Crawford, Garland D.	Capt	0-0366812	1821	28 Feb 51	Death from Mistreatment
Crissky, Elmer	PFC	RA13270894	66	27 Jul 50	Attempted Murder
Culley, Wallace H.	Cpl	RA13255708	313	19 Feb 51	Attempted Murder
Curry, James B.	1st Lt	0-1533041	1819A	6 Aug 53	Attempted Murder
Custer, Vernon C.	PFC	RA13292162	28	26 Sep 50	Murder

Curtiss, Homer A.	Capt	0-1303860	1831	19 May 51	Mistreatment
Crockett, John D.	2nd Lt	0-2262332	1817	6 Jul 51	Death from Mistreatment
Crow, Richard W.	Pvt	RA17277731	66		Mistreatment
Cunningham, John F.	PFC	RA12305730	66	1 Sep 50	Mistreatment
Cutting, Harry A.	Sgt	RA37749151	1822		Mistreatment
Dartel, James E.	Sgt	RA34972473	1819A	1 Dec 50	Mistreatment
Dartels, Willie L.	PFC	RA38136347	1815		Torture
David, Edward	Pvt	RA36313062	143	6 Nov 50	Murder
Davis, Henery L.		RA14281714	76	20 Oct 50	Murder
Davis, George T.	Cpl	31493724	76	20 Oct 50	Attempted Murder
Davis, Richard J.	PFC	RA11194845	66	24 Jul 50	Torture
Day, Roy L.	Cpl	RA06270236	16	17 Aug 50	Attempted Murder
Dean, Duane M.	PFC	RA16290150	66		Torture
Deanda, Marcello C.	PFC	RA18254151	76	10 Oct 50	Murder
Deaton, Vernon D.	Cpl	RA15225819	145		Torture
Dent, Wm. A. Jr.	Pvt	RA15288340	28	26 Sep 50	Murder
Desilva, Rudolph H.	Capt	0-1329102	1819A	Jan 51	Mistreatment
Dick, Charles E.	PfC	RA15379078	1823		Mistreatment
Digardi, Anton	Pvt	RA21936768	151		Mistreatment
Doherty, Joseph A.	PFC	RA11133467	142		Attempted Murder
Dooley, Johnny K.	Pvt	RA34338488	16	17 Aug 50	Murder
Donnel, Donald W.	PFC	1137273	185	5 Feb 51	Murder
Dorsey, Harold R.		RA15281637	76	20 Oct 50	Murder
Dotson, Robert F.	Sgt	RA16281337	1815		Mistreatment
Doty, Marion R.	PFC	RA15296207	143	6 Nov 50	Murder
Illegible, Ray M. Jr.	Lt	0-0062650	1821	Dec 50	Torture
Illegible, Norman L.	Lt	0-2206055	1817	6 Jul 50	Murder
Illegible, Edmund J.	Sgt	RA12313255	1815	1 Sep 53	Mistreatment
Illegible, Illegible	PFC	RA14369490	1823		Mistreatment
Durham, Charles H.	Pvt	RA19323651	76	1 Nov 50	Murder

Name	Rank	Serial Number		Date	Offense
Dutcher, Lee E.	PFC		185	5 Feb 51	Murder
Edwards, Cecil C.	Pvt	RA18349454	16	17 Aug 50	Murder
Edwards, Clayton O.	PFC	1084622	75		Attempted Murder
Illegible, Burdett W.	PfC	RA19359501	76	O/A 20 Oct 50	Attempted Murder
Eichelsdoerfer, Howard	Capt	0-60718	1821		Mistreatment
Ellis, Alfred O.	Maj	01049140	1821, 1819A		Mistreatment
Ellis, John F.	Capt	0-2017224	1821	Dec50-Jan51	Death from Mistreatment
Ellison, John Y.		RA20951322	76		Attempted Murder
English, Illegible L.	Lt	0-2262261	1821	O/A 10 Feb51	Death from Mistreatment
Erickson, Richard A.	1st Lt	01184816	88		Attempted Murder
Erwin, Jefferson D.	1st Lt		1827D	1 Dec 50	Mistreatment
Eurich, George S.	Sgt	RA20909803	66		Mistreatment
Evans, Conley G.	PFC	RA18281326	23	O/A 27 Aug50	Murder
Evans, Jess E.	Maj	0-0365336	1819A	Apr 51	Death from Mistreatment
Ewing, John D.	PFC	RA17254987	2		Murder
Exuer, William J.	Cpl	AF14248755	164	13 Dec 50	Death from Torture
Farler, Hugh	Capt		1846	Dec 51	Death from Mistreatment
Faudskar, Donald L.	PFC	RA17281790	487		Mistreatment
Farthing, Robert J.	Maj	0-1030875	1817-1846	5 Dec 51	Death from Mistreatment
Fawley, Richard R.		RA19330057	432		Murder
Feihgelter, Herman	Capt	0-549715	10	16-17 Jul 50	Murder
Fernandez, Joseph	SFC	RA33559586	66-18	1-28 Sept 50	Mistreatment
Illegible, Harlon C.	PFC	RA15121670	16	17 Aug 50	Mistreatment
Illegible, Robert F.		RA_0599	76	20 Oct 50	Murder
Illegible, Clemon W.		RA19326496	76	20 Oct	Murder
Illegible, Joseph P.	PFC	RA1628_886	91	Oct 50	Murder
Illegible, Howard W.	Pvt	RA45045498	76	20 Oct 50	Murder
Illegible, Richard T.	Pvt	RA13317554	16	17 Aug 50	Murder
Illegible, John A.	Pvt	RA1334039	75	Sept-Oct 50	Mistreatment
Illegible, William R.	Capt	0-740692	346-B		Attempted Murder

Name	Rank	Service Number			Charge
Illegible, George F.	Cpl	RA13278671	66		Mistreatment
Illegible, John R.		ER1722873	1815	12 Feb 50	Mistreatment
Fletke, Kenneth G.	Pvt	RA16295160	16	17 Aug 50	Murder
Flores, Willie	Cpl	RA13031261	20	O/A 1 Sep 50	Murder
Forbord, Wesley O.	Pvt	RA17218487	487		Murder
Foster, David W	Sgt	RA06297610	88	13 Oct 50	Murder
Fourboard, Wesley	Pvt	RA17218487	487	2 Mar 51	Murder
Fox, John A.	1st Lt	0-2012477	1842		Mistreatment
Franco, Julio E.		US56000485	76	20 Oct 50	Murder
Franklin, Edwin J	1st Lt	0-1303701	1819A	May 51	Mistreatment
Franklin, James L.	Cpl	RA14331297	143	6 Nov 50	Murder
Franklin, James M.	Pvt	RA13318058	1819A	23 Apr 51	Mistreatment
Francoeur, Benoit R.	PFC	RA11190469	21	2 Sep 50	Murder
Freede, Frank P.	SFC	RA18000869	66		Mistreatment
Froehlich, William E.	Sgt	RA15402866	1815		Mistreatment
Funkhouser, Marvin	SFC	RA17204405	1815		Death from Mistreatment
Galing, Bernard W.	Capt	060574	1824		Mistreatment
Garcia, Arthur S.	Pvt	RA19339453	16	17 Aug 50	Murder
Garcia, Ernesto , Jr.	PFC	RA18255745	76	20 Oct 50	Murder
Garcia, Leonard P., Jr.	Cpl	RA1834427	76	20 Oct 50	Murder
Gardner, Charles E.	Cpl	RA14300642	166		Murder
Garner, Lester R.	Pvt	RA15379828	28	O/A 27 Aug50	Murder
Garrett, Jodie H.	SFC	RA70077200	66		Mistreatment
Gentry, Robert E.	M/Sgt	RA06569572	28&66	O/A 27 Aug50	Murder
Gifford, Allen J.	PFC	RA13282225	76	20 Oct 50	Attempted Murder
Gilbert, Donald E.	Pvt	RA19303095	66		Mistreatment
Goering, Carl G.	Maj	0-0225202	1817	Jan 51	Death from Mistreatment
Goodwin, John E.	SFC	RA14005297	66		Mistreatment
Gossar, Edward	PFC	Illegible	75-76-63	Oct 50	Murder
Gothard, Clifford E.	SFC	RA14293417	167		Murder

Goyette, Joseph T.	M/Sgt	RA0681106	915	19 Jul 50	Murder
Gracey, Burton A.	Sgt	RA12224863	1827D	Feb 51	Death from Mistreatment
Granberry, Carl F.	PFC	RA14289888	76	20 Oct 50	Murder
Graveline, Ernest L.	Capt.	0-0975954	1819A, 1823, 1840	15 Oct 51	Death from Mistreatment
Gray, George W.	PFC	RA19352401	1819A		Mistreatment
Gregory, Edward W.	PFC	RA21275734	66		Mistreatment
Greis, Raymond C.	Maj	0-0033880	1824		Death from Mistreatment
Gresier, Donald T.	Pvt	RA21724933	75	Sep-Oct 51	Death from Mistreatment
Griffiths, Jack D.	Maj	0-0036376	1827D	Jul 51	Death from Mistreatment
Gri??ig, William O.	PFC	RA26362768	67	13 Oct 50	Murder
Illegible, John E.	PFC	RA13273580	28	27 Aug 50	Murder
Grubisch, Michael C.	Cpl		185	5 Feb 51	Murder
Illegible, Merrill L.	PFC	RA12115999	151		Mistreatment
Goetz, George R.	M/Sgt	RA35800374	113	8 Nov 50	Murder
Hager, William A.	Pvt	RA13314837	23	O/A 27 Aug 50	Murder
Halcomb, Edward G.	PFC	RA15256370	75	Sep-Oct 50	Mistreatment
Hall, Hedrey D.	PFC	RA14315942	76	20 Oct 50	Murder
Hall, Raymond E.	SFC	RA6358843	76	20 Oct 50	Murder
Hamilton, Raymond D L	Pvt	RA16323889	75	17 Oct 50	Mistreatment
Hanchey, Ray H.	Pvt	RA25014239	75-76	20 Oct 50	Attempted Murder
Hannen, Clarence E.	Pvt	RA13327794	143	6 Nov 50	Murder
Harmon, John W.	Cpl	RA16235441	23	O/A 27 Aug 50	Murder
Harmon, Hubert	PFC	RA15233595	75	Sep-Oct 50	Death from Mistreatment
Harris, Eugene S.	Cpl	RA06997157	28	O/A 27 Aug 50	Murder
Harris, William R.	1st Lt	0-0961860	1821	O/A 10 Apr 51	Death from Mistreatment
Harrison, Joe T.	Capt	01333970	1819A	Nov 50	Mistreatment
Hartlies, Lawrence J.	Pvt	RA15292726	28	O/A 27 Aug 50	Murder
Hartman, Roger W.	2nd Lt	01685689	1842	28 Feb 51	Murder
Hartwig, Vernon G	PFC	RA14344720	26	O/A 22 Sep 50	Murder

Name	Rank	Serial Number	Unit	Date	Charge
Haskin, Ernest E.	Pvt-2	RA35772472	1822		Mistreatment
Hastie, John C.	Capt	0-0027332	16	Jan 51	Death from Mistreatment
Hastings, Charles	Pvt	RA13331052	1817	17 Aug 50	Murder
Heath, Joe T.	Cpl	US58096863			Mistreatment
Hembree, Frank R.	PFC	RA19348384	915	19 Jul 50	Murder
Henderson, Andrew J.	PFC	RA44108109	76	20 Oct 50	Attempted Murder
Hendricks, Charles H.		RA16294533	76	20 Oct 50	Murder
Illegible, William F.	PFC	RA37552980	76	20 Oct 50	Attempted Murder
Henry, Roy J.	Cpl	RA10732588	142B		Attempted Murder
Hefhner, Clayton F.	Pvt	RA16264666	91	Oct 50	Murder
Hernandez, Florenti		NG30436729	1819A		Death from Mistreatment
Herndon, Joseph M.	Pvt	RA13273433	16	17 Aug 50	Murder
Herndon, Rogers	PFC	RA14353051	1819A	21 Dec 50	Attempted Murder
Herrera, Pedro A	Cpl	RA18253222	1819A	June 1952	Mistreatment
Hickok, Robert H.	PFC	RA12284788	1819A		Mistreatment
Hickman, Evans	PFC	RA21697779	113	8 Nov 50	Murder
Higgins, John H.	1st Lt	01048407	26&66	31 Aug 50	Murder
Hilgerson, John J. Jr.	Pvt	RA14279507	16	17 Aug 50	Murder
Hill, Nathan			10		
Hill, Wayne W.	PFC	RA16304101	76	20 Oct 50	Murder
Hines, Leonard	Sgt	RA33180282	76	20 Oct 50	Murder
Hinckley, James	Lt Col	0-0052289	1819A	30 Jan 51	Death from Mistreatment
Hires, Ansel C	Sgt	RA44108833	1818	12/50-1/51	Death from Mistreatment
Hluboky, Edward L.		RA42176417	1260	11 Jul 50	Murder
Hodge, William M.	Pvt	RA15258056	75	Sep-Oct 50	Death from Mistreatment
Hodges, William E.		RA19357873	76	20 Oct 50	Murder
Illegible, George M.	Sgt	RA37866756	75	20 Jul 50	Death from Mistreatment
Illegible, Frederick III	Lt		1821	O/A 1 Mar 51	Death from Mistreatment
Hogan, Billy R	Pvt	RA25413285	16	17 Aug 50	Murder

Name	Rank	Service Number		Date	Charge
Hogston, Kenneth R.	Cpl	RA13263679	26	O/A 22 Sept 1950	Attempted Murder
Illegible, Marion O.	PFC	RA14834912	186		Mistreatment
Horning, William J.	Cpl	RA19264350	166	16 Jan 1951	Murder
Horton, Duane	PFC	RA16315359	516	1 Jan 51	Murder
Howell, Robert P.	1st Lt	0-2020994	1819A		Mistreatment
Horenger, Wayne E.	PFC	RA11196288	1815		Mistreatment
Hook, Raymond E	Sgt	ER37737968	313	O/A 17 Feb 51	Murder
Hoffman, Glenn E.	Pvt	RA15281256	16	17 August 50	Murder
Hull, Leonard C.	Cpl	RA12242197	75	Sep-Oct 50	Murder
Hume, Thomas	Maj	0-0023931	1821	May 51	Death from Torture
Humes, Robert A.	Sgt	RA15260371	16	17 Aug 50	Murder
Hunsicker, Kenneth P.		RA15353745	76	20 Oct 50	Murder
Hershmann, Frederick C.	Cpt	RA12184021	67	13 Oct 50	Attempted Murder
Hurt, Garrison	PFC	RA18277750	67	13 Oct 50	Murder
Hyslop, Kenneth C.	Capt	0-0543377	1835	Dec50-Jan51	Death from Mistreatement
Ivanushka, Michael	Capt	0-1322155	1821		Mistreatment
Ikamekona, William	Cpl	RA29044887	313	O/A 17 Feb 51	Murder
Jackson, Clinton	1st Lt	0-1310717	1821	O/A 18 Jan 51	Death from Mistreatment
Jackson, Theodore	Cpl	RA38416335	1819A		Mistreatment
Jacobson, Lyle N	Cpl	RA19350277	1819A		Mistreatment
Jacques, Leo W.	Pvt	RA11199247	16	17 Aug 50	Murder
Jamison, Allen H.	SFC	RA39001766	66		Mistreatment
Jaramillo, Arturo	Cpl	RA17263232	403		Attempted murder
Jarrell, Cleveland	PFC	RA14294724	26	22 Sept 50	Murder
Jenkins, Timothy	PFC	RA18281108	133		Attempted Murder
Jewell, Joe L.	Cpl	RA15259751	1815		Mistreatment
John, Valdor W.	PFC	RA16282077	76	20 Oct 50	Attempted Murder
Johns, Lewis D.	Pvt	RA3454783	66		Mistreatment
Johnson, Harlan W.	PFC	RA16288743	21		Attempted Murder

Johnson, Samuel	Cpl	RA34057128	1819A	31 Jan 51	Death from Mistreatment
Jones, Donald J.	Sgt	RA37656330	1818	Mar 51	Death from Mistreatment
Jones, Eugene G.	Pvt	RA17274614	76	20 Oct 50	Attempted Murder
Jones, Frank L.		RA17255472	432		Murder
Jones, William H.	Sgt	RA34706220	66		Mistreatment
Jones, Wilbur G. Jr.	Lt	0-0050863	1819A		Mistreatment
Jordan, Frank	PFC	RA11181128	66		Mistreatment
Joyce, Thomas Jr.	Capt	0-1825961	1815	23 May 51	Death from Mistreatment
Justus, Bert W. Jr.	1st Lt	0-1178205	1824		Death from Mistreatment
Justice, Alvis		RA35999290	76	20 Oct 50	Murder
Kamoku, Benjamin S.	Pvt	RA29030855	76	20 Oct 50	Murder
Karaiseky, Raymond J.	PFC	RA12305545	16	17 Aug 50	Murder
Karnos, Richard J.	Capt	0-1181320	1824		Death from Mistreatment
Kayer, Virgil A.	Cpl	ER57502732	1823		Mistreatment
Kearney, James A.	Pvt	RA13343283	28	O/A 27 Aug 50	Murder
Kreman, William P.	Capt.	02017072	1812A		Mistreatment
Keith, John W., Jr.	Lt Col	0-0032482	1827D	6 May 51	Death from Misatreatment
Kellum, William H.	1st Lt.	0-0062736	1821		Death from Mistreatment
Kelly, Edward J.	PFC	RA12119061	21	2 Sep 50	Murder
Kelly, James C.	SFC	RA12264774	1819A	Feb-Mar 50	Death from Mistreatment
Kennedy, Gilbert C	Sgt	RA19294578			Death from Mistreatment
Kephart, George W.	Pvt	RA16296456	66		Mistreatment
Kerns, John A., Jr.		RA14244936	76	20 Oct 50	Murder
Killion, William J.	1st Lt	02262191	1819A		Mistreatment
Ki?brell, Roy	Pvt	RA17259644	151		Mistreatment
Kinard, Charles E.	Cpl	RA14263806	507		Mistreatment
King, Edmund	2d Lt	0-1913399	1824		Death from Mistreatment
King, James R.	SFC	RA39336890	66		Attempted Murder
King, Ralph	PFC	RA35685568	76	20 Oct 50	Murder
Kirchcker, Robert B.	1st Lt.	0-0929076	1823	Jun-Dec 51	Death from Mistreatment

Name	Rank	Service No.	63-75-76	Date	Charge
Kirwin, John W.	Pvt	RA18282785	63-75-76	Oct 50	Death from Mistreatment
Kistler, Charles R.	PFC	RA13304076	66		Mistreatment
Kling, Eugene H	PFC	RA16304082	193		Murder
Knapp, Donald W.		RA16320716	76	20 Oct 50	Murder
Knight, Sam	M/Sgt	RA34620991	403		Attempted Murder
Kopischkie, Carl E	Lt Col	0346614	1827D		Mistreatment
Kornig, Fred	Lt.		1821	O/A 9 Mar 51	Death from Mistreatment
Krasko, John	Lt.	059406	1819A		Mistreatment
Kreider, Lloyd D.	PFC	RA13266788	76	20 Oct 50	Attempted Murder
Krobath, William F.	PFC	RA13296790	1819A	Feb 52	Torture
Kubinek, Roland W.	Capt	0-0977699	1822	31 May 51	Death from Mistreatment
Kumagai, Takeshi	Sgt	RA10733734	75&132	20 Jul 50	Attempted Murder
Kunkle, William H.	M/Sgt	RA37157664	1827D	Feb 51	Death from Mistreatment
Lackner, Joseph C.	WOJG	W-2142973	1821	15 Apr 51	Death from Mistreatment
LaCourse, Gerald Floyd	PFC	RA11168863	26	O/A 22 Sept 50	Murder
Landers, Lawrence E.	Cpl	RA15208600	1821	28 Feb 51	Death from Mistreatment
Lantron, Newton W	Lt Col		1842		Mistreatment
Larios, Martin	PFC	RA18354517	75		Mistreatment
Laroue, Billy J	Cpl	RA18281230	1818	Dec 50-Jun 51	Death from Mistreatment
Latanation, Mike		RA13013045	76	20 Oct 50	Murder
Lawley, Odie N	Sgt	RA6365221	1815		Mistreatment
Lavell, Geoffrey	Maj	0-0022049	1817	8 Feb 51	Death from Mistreatment
Leach, Edward T.	Lt	0-1688455	1817		Death from Mistreatment
Leamon, Nickolas J.	Capt	0-1102814	1822		Mistreatment
Ledford, Vernon S.	Sgt	RA665393	28	O/A 27 Aug 50	Murder
Lee, James O.	Sgt	RA15423171	26	O/A 22 Sept 50	Murder
Lee, Robert A.	SFC	RA7080656	1822		Mistreatment
Lemmen, John R.	Pvt	RA16343767	219	29 May 51	Murder

Name	Rank	Service Number	Number	Date	Offense
Leonberger, Karl	Capt	O-1176106	1827D	2 Jan 1951	Death from Mistreatment
Lindsay, Homer F.	Capt	O-1173353	1824	1 June 51	Death from Mistreatment
Liles, Paul V. S.	Lt Col	O-0023876	1820		Mistreatment
Illegible	1st Lt	O-1331524	1824		Mistreatment
Littlefield, Gary	Cpl	RA18282616	1818	Jan 51	Mistreatment
Lobo, Illegible F.	PFC	RA19336901	28	O/A 27 Aug 50	Murder
Locke, William D.	Capt	12455A	75	14 Oct 50	Mistreatment
Lockett, William	Cpl		1819A		Death from Mistreatment
Loomis, Joseph M.	2d Lt	O-2262289	186		Mistreatment
Loe, Aaron	Sgt		10		Death from Mistreatment
Lott, George M.	2d Lt	O-2204398	1817	6 Jul 51	Death from Mistreatment
Loving, Charles R.	Cpl	RA13290631	76	20 Oct 50	Murder
Lowery, William T.	Cpl	ER14172474	313	O/A 17 Feb 51	Murder
Ludlum, David W.	Cpl	RA19361682	1823		Mistreatment
Lusk, Jessee M.	Sgt	RA38507751	1819A	May 51	Death from Mistreatment
Lynch, Harold M.	Pvt	RA37582980	76	20 Oct 50	Murder
Hackrall, Blaine E.	SFC	RA6573917	66		Mistreatment
Maddock, Robert L.	SFC	RA38414108	1818		Mistreatment
Magnant, Joseph A.	1st Lt	O-2262255	1821		Mistreatment
Mamegre, Leo J.	WOJG	W-0906876	1822	Feb 51	Death from Mistreatment
Mannig, Billy Dean	PFC	RA16319812	26	O/A 22 Sept 50	Murder
Mamring, Roy	Pvt	RA16327603	16		Attempted Murder
Magnant, Joseph V.	Capt	O-2001784	1819A		Mistreatment
Martin, James E.	Pvt	RA19341720	66		Mistreatment
Martin, John D.	PFC	RA19290302	1819A		Mistreatment
Martin, John Ervin	Pvt	RA16322959	75&76	20 Oct 50	Attempted Murder
Massey, Edward D.	Pvt	RA20468807	1260		Murder
Masterson, Harold A.	M/Sgt	RA39195677	18270	Mar 51	Death from Mistreatment
Matta, George J.	SPC	RA31208295	1818		Mistreatment

Name	Rank	Serial No.	No.	Date	Charge
Maxwell, Herbert	Pvt	RA57509059	1823		Death from Mistreatment
Mayo, Gene R.	Cpl	RA19348436	143	6 Nov 50	Murder
Mayrand, Charles	2d Lt	0-0060922	1821	O/A 1 Apr 51	Death from Mistreatment
McAbee, Filmore W.	Maj	01294507	1819A	May&Jun 51	Murder
McArdle, John G.	PFC	RA293981	10		Death from Mistreatment
McClaim, William A.	Capt	0-2001746	1821	May 51	Torture
McClury, Gilbert Nilon	PFC	RA18255025	219	29 May 51	Murder
McDermott, Thomas	PFC	RA13342355	219	29 May 51	Murder
McDougle, Charles	2d. Lt	0-1685564	66	O/A 5 May 51	Death from Mistreatment
McGrady, Elmer J.	Sgt	RA1945470	66		Mistreatment
Illegible, Harbert T.	Pvt	RA18340126	16	17 Aug 50	Murder
McKittrick, Paul L.	Pvt	RA16321907	119	Sep-Oct 50	Death from Mistreatment
McLaughlin, Joseph E.		ER12304440	487	2 Mar 51	Murder
McMullan, Patrick J.	1st Lt	0-2021034	1824	23 April 51	Death from Strafing of Unmarked PW Camp
McNicholas, Henry J.	1st Lt	0-2208401	24	O/A 21 Sept 50	Attempted Murder
Meader, Roy T.	Pvt	RA14269993	151		Mistreatment
Melvold, Charles W.	PFC	USMC1102823	185	5 Feb 51	Murder
Merrill, Gerald F.	Cpl	RA16284501	166	16 Jan 51	Murder
Mesa, Rudy V.	Pvt	RA18310994	76	20 Oct 50	Murder
Metzgar, Maurice R	Lt	0-1059560	1819A	Jul-Aug 51	Death from Mistreatment
Michael, Marion W.	M/Sgt	RA15104339	75&76	20 Oct 50	Attempted Murder
Mikesell, Harold E.	PFC	RA3642359	76	20 Oct 50	Murder
Miland, William L.	Cpl	RA13283113	136&143	6 Nov 50	Attempted Murder
Miller, Donald G.	Pvt	RA19358749	75&76	20 Oct 50	Murder
Kingley, Harry F.	Pvt	RA15431745	1819A		Mistreatment
Minietta, Charles	Capt	0-1179545	1842		Mistreatment
Mistretta, Joseph L.	PFC	RA31230077	76	Aug-Sep 50	Mistreatment
Mitchell, Everett L.	PFC	RA39483327	28	O/A 27 Aug 50	Murder

Name	Rank	Serial Number		Date	Offense
Mitchell, Don	Cpl	RA15251692	1817		Mistreatment
Mitchell, John William	Pvt	RA13269091	26	O/A 22 Sept 50	Murder
Mlaseac, Milton J.	Pvt	RA16325297	16	17 Aug 50	Murder
Mosley, Willis W.	PFC	RA15378228	28	O/A 27 Aug 50	Murder
Mohr, Harry A.	Pvt	RA13309024	66	13 Sept 50	Death from Mistreatment
Mouscvitz, Joseph T.	PFC	Illegible	16	17 Aug 50	Murder
Montfort, Houston E.	Pvt	RA18281328	16	17 Aug 50	Murder
Montgomery, James H.	Cpl	RA24416174	1823		Mistreatment
Montgomery, Robert W.	Cpl	RA19315597	219	29 May 51	Murder
Moore, Claude F	Pvt	RA14279874	76	20 Oct 50	Murder
Moore, Frank	M/Sgt	RA06241287	1827D	Mar 51	Death from Mistreatment
Moore, James R.	PFC	RA17259199	76	20 Oct 50	Murder
Mordan. Melvin W.	Pvt	RA16317426	16	17 Aug 50	Murder
Morris, Milton Jr.	Cpl	RA14293576	76	20 Oct 50	Murder
Morris, Prince H.	Sgt	RA14287102	1821		Death from Mistreatment
Morris, Robert L.	SFC	RA33935311	75		Mistreatment
Morris, Ronald R.	PFC	RA13340506	66	19 Sep 50	Death from Mistreatment
Morrison, Richard O.	Cpl	RA17255458	1819A		Mistreatment
Mosslander, Charles R.	PFC	RA16330250	167	14 Jan 51	Murder
Mounce, Aaron W.	Sgt	RA35787273	75&76		Mistreatment
Muldrow, Frederick N	Cpl		1819A		Mistreatment
Mullins, Orville R.	Sgt	RA43013189	1817		Mistreatment
Munger, Clyde O.	Sgt	RA14220020	66		Mistreatment
Murphy, Edmund J.	Maj	O-1168389	1819A	Jul 51	Death from Mistreatment
Mose, Earl L.	Cpl	RA25742057	158	4 Nov 50	Murder
Mosser, Alvin D.	Cpl	RA16307192	76	20 Oct 50	Murder
Myers, Ray A.	Cpl	RA25129531	435		Mistreatment
Mylnarski, Joseph A.	Sgt	RA06562041	28	O/A 27 Sep 50	Murder
Nardella, Ralph A.	Capt	01337073	1821	Feb 52	Torture

Name	Rank	Service No.	No.	Date	Offense
Naylor, Clifford M	PFC	RA16307293	76	20 Oct 50	Murder
Neighbors, Gerald W.	Sgt	RA18316846	1819A		Mistreatment
Nelson, John H.	SFC	RA17233488	1824		Death from Mistreatment
Newman, Charles P.	Cpl	RA17229325	66		Mistreatment
Newman, George	PFC	RA15411542	119	Sep-Oct 50	Death from Mistreatment
Narison, Robert R	Cpl	RA16278731	66		Mistreatment
Niemann, R. C.	2d Lt	0-0974393	1842	O/A 1 Sep 50	Death from Mistreatment
Newman, Jack D.	PFC	RA15259900	28	O/A 27 Aug 50	Murder
Nixon, Charles L.	2d Lt.	0-2262303	435	29 Apr 51	Murder
Nolan, Almond L.	Cpl	RA12115667	1819A		Mistreatment
Nolan, Lawrence T.	Sgt	RA123319287	142	16 Nov 50	Death from Mistreatment
O'Brien, Raymond J.	PFC	RA18303460	63-75-76	Sep-Oct 50	Death from Mistreatment
O'Brien, Robert J.	Pvt.	RA12342536	16	17 Aug 50	Murder
Cernoff, Fred O.	PFC	RA15429983	1823		Mistreatment
O'Connor, Joseph L.	Capt		1835		Mistreatment
O'Dowd, Paul T. R.	1st Lt	0-0955768	1819A		Mistreatment
Oliver,	Sgt		66		Murder
Olfis, Leonard K	1st Lt	0-0030434	1822	Jan-Feb 51	Death from Mistreatment
Orland, David A., Jr.	PFC	RA25183501	66		Mistreatment
Ormand, Robert J.	Maj	0-0040192	1819A	O/A 5 Nov 50	Death from Mistreatment
Ortega, Jose H.	PFC	RA18254008	76	O/A 20 Oct 50	Attempted Murder
Osborne, Chester	Capt		1821	Jul-Aug 52	Torture
Overton, Lawrence S.	1st Lt	0-0439459	1819A		Death from Mistreatment
Owens, Raymond E.	PFC	RA1814549	28	20/A 7 Aug 50	Murder
Illegible, Rufus D.	PFC	RA14290069	28	O/A 27 Aug 50	Murder
Palmer, Willie Jr.	Cpl	RA34953713	26	O/A 22 Sep 50	Attempted Murder
Parenti, Glendon	SFC	RA38662770	76	20 Oct 50	Murder
Parke, Robert E.	Capt	0-1177928	1827	Feb 51	Death from Mistreatment
Parker, F.D.	Pvt	RA14315198	166	16 Jan 51	Murder
Parks, Jack F.	PFC	RA13275808	2	11 Jul 50	Murder

Name	Rank	Serial Number	No.	Date	Cause
Parsell, John A. Jr.	Sgt	RA16284903	75		Mistreatment
Parris, Harold G.	1st Lt	0-1183940	143	6 Nov 50	Murder
Patchoski, Edmund J.	Sgt	RA13278051	1815		Mistreatment
Patterson, Arthur J.	1st Lt.	0-1651559	10	16 Jul 50	Murder
Patterson, Ithal T.	Pvt	RA25638377	76	20 Oct 50	Murder
Patterson, Orlando R.	Pvt	RA16293916	76	20 Oct 50	Murder
Payne, Murray L.	2d Lt	0-1688548	194	14 Feb 51	Murder
Pattes, John D.	PFC	RA15415327	75	16 Jul 50	Death from Mistreatment
Peckham, Charles L.	Capt	0-1287938	1826		Mistreatment
Peccraro, Anthony	Capt	059373	1821		Mistreatment
Pedicome, Henry A.	Capt	0-1176760	1819A		Mistreatment
Peters, Ralph E.	PFC	RA15413979	28	O/A 27 Sep 50	Murder
Peterson, John H.	SFC	RA31464958	25	O/A 27 Aug 50	Murder
Phillipen, Robert J.	PFC	RA12324709	136		Death by burning or burying
Phillips, Howard D.	Cpt	RA1431361	76	20 Oct 50	Murder
Phillips, Kenneth W.	PFC	RA37145634	66		Death from Mistreatment
Philpot, Robert F.	PFC	RA14355426	1815		Mistreatment
Picerno, Joseph	PFC	US51105429	1817		Mistreatment
Pierce, Orville W.	Maj	0-0380112	1827D	Apr 51	Death from Mistreatment
Pinkston, James L.	Cpl	RA14310890	1819A		Mistreatment
Plocha, Frank L	Pvt	RA45024272	1831	10 June 51	Death from Mistreatment
Poston, John D.	Pvt	RA44109913	1819A		Mistreatment
Poole, Jack E.	Pvt	RA16286184	119	30 Oct 50	Death from Mistreatment
Porter, John P.	M/Sgt	RA38262545	1619A		Mistreatment
Postlethait, Clare	Sgt	RA06898582	1819A	O/A 22 Nov 50	Death from Mistreatment
Potorski, John S.		RA33941745	189	28 Mar 51	Murder
Potts, Hubert S.	2d Lt.	0-2014804	191	31 Mar 51	Murder
Potts, Roy H.	PFC	RA19304202	21	3 Sep 50	Murder
Poulin, Thomas J.	PFC	RA31505226	26	22 Sep 50	Murder
Powell, Brook T.	PFC	RA15412678	16	17 Aug 50	Murder

Name	Rank	Service Number		Date	Offense
Prabucki, William J.	Cpl	RA13300047	1817		Mistreatment
Preston, Cecil V.	Cpl	RA19358887	1819A		Mistreatment
Pritchett, Willis G.	Cpl	RA18264084	1619A	Jul 51	Murder
Pryor, George T.	PFC	RA15045114	63-75-76	11 Oct 50	Murder
Purger, Tremon E.	PFC	RA14291324	16	17 Aug 50	Attempted Murder
Rae, George W.	PFC	USA01126123	135	5 Feb 51	Attempted Murder
Ramirez, Domingo	Cpl	RA18356250	793		Mistreatment
Ramsier, James H.	Cpl	ER57149266	487		Mistreatment
Ramson, Waymon	M/Sgt	RA16148573	133		Attempted Murder
Rarick, Roland D.	Sgt	RA16265462	63-75-76	Sep-Oct 50	Death from Mistreatment
Raskin, Alfred J.	2d Lt	0-0061817	1821	O/A 15 Feb 51	Death from Mistreatment
Ratcliffe, Griffith, III	Sgt	RA13259086	75	14 Oct 50	Murder
Ray, Harold	SPC	RA35411588	119	20 Oct 50	Killed by Strafing from U.S. Planes
Rean, Bruce A	Pvt	RA13280781	16	17 Aug 50	Murder
Reese, Jodie S. Jr.		RA18139391	76	20 Oct 50	Murder
Reefe, Harry J.	PFC	RA13344137	142	16 Nov 50	Murder
Reeves, Clifford	Sgt	RA37215138	76	20 Oct 50	Murder
Reoney, Earnest Sr.	Cpl	RA13268079	16	17 Aug 50	Murder
Reid, Kenneth R.	2d Lt	0-948802	66		Mistreatment
Remtschler, James D.	PFC	RA13300842	143	6 Nov 50	Murder
Reynolds, James H.	PFC	RA1925552	1821		Death from Mistreatment
Rhoden, Berry F.	Cpl	RA14329093	20		Attempted Murder
Rhodes, Don Jr.	PFC	RA15210561	163		Torture
Richardson, Calvin W.	Cpl	US53007937	219	29 May 51	Murder
Richards, Donald R.	PFC	RA11178438	143	6 Nov 50	Murder
Rindels, Raymond M.		RA18322015	76	20 Oct 50	Attempted Murder
Rivera, Floyd		RA37720948	76	20 Oct 50	Murder
Roach, Paul A. Jr.	1st Lt.	0-062605	1829		Mistreatment

Roberson, Allen M.	Pvt	RA14325062	28	26 Sep 50	Murder
Robertson, James P.	Pvt	RA17274652	28	26 Sep 50	Murder
Robertson, Marshall	Cpl	RA13232210	1819A		Mistreatment
Robertson, Paul E.	Pvt	RA13294064	66		Mistreatment
Rocenerk, Louis	Caot	01398378	1819A		Mistreatment
Roffe, Adolphes W.	1st Lt	0-0027848	1821		Death from Mistreatment
Rogers, George W.		RA18288807	1819A		Mistreatment
Rogerson, Thomas G.	Cpl	AF12237987	164	13 Dec 1950	Death from Torture
Roney, Gordon R.	Pvt	RA14300892	75		Mistreatment
Rooks, Daniel F.	Maj	0-0379979	1824	22 Apr 51	Death from Mistreatment
Rooks, John M. Jr.	Sgt	RA14334723	162		Mistreatment
Rookstool, Melvin Dale	PFC	RA19361991	76	20 Oct 50	Attempted Murder
Rose, Jack L.		RA16293510	113	8 Nov 50	Attempted Murder
Rose, Leo C	Cpl	RA37007685	76	20 Oct 50	Attempted Murder
Illegible, Robert P	PFC	RA15274055	76	20 Oct 50	Attempted Murder
Roth, Bernard F.	2d Lt	0-2202317	1819A O/A	15 Jan 51	Death from Mistreatment
Illegible, Louis	Sgt	RA35467082	76	20 Oct 50	Murder
Robin, Tibor	Cpl	RA19363581	1819A		Mistreatment
Rudd, James H.	Pvt	RA15257595	16	17 Aug 50	Attempted Murder
Ruffato, Barney P.	M/Sgt	RA6520124	76	20 Oct 50	Attempted Murder
Ruffles, Anthony R.	Cpl	RA16269173	66		Mistreatment
Rummer, Leroy Jr.	Pvt	US55031544	219	29 May 51	Murder
Ruthstrom, Carroll O.	Pvt	RA18358805	76	20 Oct 50	Murder
Ryan, Frederick M.	Pvt	RA15380630	16	17 Aug 50	Attempted Murder
Ryan, Robert W.	Sgt	RA20616966	143	6 Nov 50	Murder
Salvie, Robert J.	Cpl	RA13300064	76	20 Oct 50	Murder
Samolinski, Stanley	PFC	RA16303975	75	30 Oct 50	Death from Mistreatment
Santora, Bert	Lt. Col	0-0031758	1817		Mistreatment
Sara, John	SFC		1818		Death from Mistreatment
Sanders, Jack J.	1st Lt.	0-0963472	1824	20 Apr 51	Death from Mistreatment

Name	Rank	Service Number		Date	Charge
Scarborough, Billy W.	Pvt	RA13353081	66		Mistreatment
Schuman, Walter	Pfc	RA16260759	16	17 Aug 50	Murder
Scott, Fred R.	Pfc	RA24613012	66		Mistreatment
Segura, George P.	Pvt	RA19358076	76	20 Oct 50	Murder
Semosky, George Jr.	PvtO/A	RA13313405	16	17 Aug 50	Murder
Illegible, Robert B.	Sgt	RA31215310	28	26 Sept 50	Murder
Illegible,	1st Lt	0-0959727	1821	12/50 1/51	Death from Mistreatment
Sewell, William G.	Pvt	RA19341905	28-75	27 Jul 50	Murder
Shaffron, Paul	Pvt	RA23764736	76	20 Oct 50	Murder
Sharpe, Robert L.	Pvt	RA14333128	75	20 Oct 50	Murder
Sharver, James A	Cpl	RA15410598	76	20 Oct 50	Murder
Shepard, Harold R.		RA14339752	76	20 Oct 50	Murder
Shepard, Tony J.	Pvt	RA19362010	28	26 Sep 50	Murder
Sherman, Harry H., Jr.	Lt.	A00591055	1817	3 June 51	Murder
Shimagawa, Susuman	Cpl	RA10103695	63-75-786	1817	Mistreatment
Illegible, Robert M.	Sgt	RA39084228	76	20 Oct 50	Murder`
Illegible, William M.	Maj	026 635	1824		Mistreatment
Shock, Howard R.	Sgt	RA37121258	28	26 Sep 50	Murder
Shur, Lee J.	PFC	RA16259854	22	4 Jul 50	Murder
Shurtz, Robert W	Lt. Col	0-0042967	1827D	Dec 51	Death from Mistreatment
Simmons, Albert E.	Cpl	RA12285683	66	26 Sep 50	Murder
Simmons, John W.	PFC	RA192936363	16	17 Aug 50	Murder
Simms, Clemmie	M/Sgt	RA06247268	1821	12/50-1/51	Death from Mistreatment
Slater, Edward M.	Pvt.	RA16280381	63-76	21 Oct 50	Attempted Murder
Smith, Albert W.	Lt	Illegible	1821 O/A	25 Apr 51	Death from Mistreatment
Smith, Charles M.	PFC	RA13348375	1819A		Mistreatment
Smith, Clifford H.	PFC	RA19326591	1818		Torture
Smith, Edwin S.	WOJG	W-2141446	1819A	30 Nov 50	Attempted Murder
Smith, Frederick A.	Maj	0-364183	1827D		Mistreatment
Smith, Harold E.	Pvt	RA17232970	75		Mistreatment

Name	Rank	Service No.	No.	Date	Charge
Smith, Harry J.	Cpl	RA12290732	21	3 Sep 50	Attempted Murder
Smith, Joseph W.	2d Lt	0-2262370	1821		Death from Mistreatment
Smith, Roy T.	PFC	RA17265588	10		Death from Mistreatment
Smith, Russel G.	PFC	RA44023761	161		Attempted Murder
Smith, William W.	PFC	RA16308504	1819A		Mistreatment
Snodgrass, George L.			75		Mistreatment
Snyder, Raymond A.	Pvt	RA16329915	20	16 Sep 50	Murder
Spencer, Grover. Jr.	PFC	RA7002463	76	20 Oct 50	Murder
Stahlman, Harold E.	1st Lt.	02033936	1827D		Torture
Stanley, Milford W.	Capt	0410674	1819A		Mistreatment
Stark, William F.	PFC	US52000677	75	16 Sep 50	Murder
Starkey, Clyde M.	M/Sgt	RA06836312	76	20 Oct 50	Murder
Stein, Robert J.	PFC	RA16322301	28	26 Sep 50	Murder
Still, Robert C.	Cpl	RA13271723	1819A		Mistreatment
Stephens, Elmore J.	Pvt	RA12349407	123	20 Jul 50	Murder
Stephens, Harvey Jr.	PFC	US53016126	219	29 May 51	Murder
Stefima, George	SFC	RA36947644	1817-1819	Jul 51	Death from Mistreatment
Stevens, James E.	WOJG	W-0907007	1821 O/A	25 Apr 51	Death from Mistreatment
Stevens, Simon J.	Capt	0-1826111	1822	Mar-Apr 51	Death from Mistreatment
Stevens, Victor S.	Cpl	RA14236796	75		Mistreatment
Stidham, Henry	Cpl	RA35659422	75-119	20 Oct 50	Murder
Stockham, Richard W.	Pvt	RA28770173	63-75-76	O/A 18 Sep 50	Murder
Stone, Oliver Jr.	Pvt	RA14283603	76	20 Oct 50	Murder
Stovall, John R. Jr.	PFC	RA19338826	28	26 Sept 50	Murder
Strother, Armour D.	Sgt	RA34070619	28	5 Sep 50	Murder
Sullivan, James F.	2d Lt	0-2021061	1821	O/A 25 Apr 51	Death from Mistreatment
Sullivan, Peter	Cpl	RA31389187	10	16 Jul 50	Murder
Sund, Roland V.	1st Lt	0-2037738	1822		Death from Mistreatment
Sutterfield, Roy G.	Pvt	RA13333512	76	20 Oct 50	Attempted Murder

Name	Rank	Serial Number		Date	Offense
Sweet, Lawrence H.	Cpl	RA11188306	66		Mistreatment
Tabor, Stanley E.	1st Lt.	0-0060663	75	8 Oct 50	Death from Mistreatment
Takamara, Sam O	1st Lt	02030706	132-75	20 Jul 50	Murder
Takvam, Bernard D	PFC	US55084546	1673	24 Oct 52	Murder
Tamaye, Guichi	PFC	RA10103601	1817		Mistreatment
Tamsey, Roger M.	Pvt	RA13319528	166	16 Jan 51	Murder
Tarnipol, Herbert	SFC	RA06709773	28	26 Sep 50	Murder
Tatem, Joseph T.	PFC	RA12312654	66		Mistreatment
Tavarks, Tony	PFC	RA39760931	16	17 Aug 50	Murder
Taylor, Oscar L.	Pvt	RA19341654	76	20 Oct 50	Murder
Todd, Lester R.	PFC	RA17280565	1817		Mistreatment
Tinsley, Earl G.	Cpl	RA14346156	67	14 Oct 50	Murder
Tomey, John R.	Pvt	RA17271539	76	20 Oct 50	Attempted Murder
Toomey, Joseph D	1st Lt	0-0059248	1821	28 Feb 51	Death from Mistreatment
Torigian, Frank W.	Sgt	RA37580885	76	20 Oct 50	Murder
Trammel, William O	PFC	RA14337466	16	17 Aug 50	Murder
Traverso, Arthur H.	Pvt	US51018884	219	29 May 51	Murder
Traecy, Edgar J. Jr.	Lt Col	0-0019892	1827D	May 51	Death from Mistreatment
Treffery, Wendell H.	Cpl	RA11165660	1815		Mistreatment
Tremblay, Tellesphor C.	M/Sgt	RA6562051	66		Mistreatment
Tremblay, Aurel Norman	SFC	RA18367046	76	20 Oct 50	Murder
Truett, Raymond E	PFC	RA13366639	1817	30 Jun 52	Death from Mistreatment
Urquhart, Leroy G.	Pvt	RA13341365	26	O/A 22 Sep 50	Murder
Uptegraph, Harold L.	PFC	RA18343400	20		Attempted Murder
Van Harn, Henry W.	Pvt	RA19354218	76	20 Oct 50	Murder
Van Newhouse, Richard		RA15295457	1815		Death from Mistreatment
Veochrone, John R.	Pvt	RA15292710	66		Mistreatment
Vester, John W.	Capt	0-0028280	1824	29 Feb 51	Death from Mistreatment
Villa, Paul	Cpl	RA19305724	1292	8 Jul 50	Murder
Villages, Elima D.	Cpl	RA16203023	1815	5 Oct 52	Torture

Name	Rank	Service Number		Date	Charge
Volturo, Sylvester S	PFC	RA19079921	76-66	20 Oct 50	Attempted Murder
Voyles, Eugene R.	PFC	RA15418780	76	20 Oct 50	Murder
Wagner, Kenyon J.	Cpl	RA16291949	1819A		Mistreatment
Walk, Arnold E.	Cpl	RA16018362	76	20 Oct 50	Murder
Wallace, Clyde L. Jr.	Lt	0-1018859	1815	19 May 51	Death from Mistreatment
Walker, John H	Maj	0268569	1821		Mistreatment
Warren, Leonard A.	Pvt	RA14349523	75		Mistreatment
Illegible, Paul E.	PFC		185	5 Feb 51	Murder
Waters, John L.	Cpl	RA6394755	1819A		Mistreatment
Webb, St. Clair	Lt	0-0541329	1821	Dec 50	Death from Mistreatment
Webster, Walter J.	Pvt	RA13391069	66		Mistreatment
Weinel, Carey H.	SFC	RA37309511	28	O/A 7 Sep 50	Attempted Murder
Wells, Burton	SPC		5		Death from Mistreatment
Wells, Harry L.	PFC	RA34023695	915	19 Jul 50	Murder
West, Roy L.	Cpl		185	5 Feb 51	Murder
Westbrooks, David C.	Cpl	RA14325704	143	6 Nov 50	Murder
Whelden, Don M	Pvt	RA19351445	66		Mistreatment
Whitcomb, Walter R.	Pvt	RA12349858	63-76	O/A 1 Oct 50	Attempted Murder
White, Elvis J.	PFC	RA18293397	75	20 Oct 50	Death from Mistreatment
White, Frank M.	Capt	0-2033271	1827D	Feb 51	Death from Mistreatment
Whited, Roy N.	Sgt	RA170096685	75	17 Jul 51	Murder
Whitehead, Joseph C.	Capt	0-1321272	1822	Dec 50	Death from Mistreatment
Wick, Leander F.	SPC	RA37297932	66		Mistreatment
Williams, James R.	Cpl.	RA15277924	151		Mistreatment
Williams, Johnny Jr.	PFC	RA18280239	76	20 Oct 50	Murder
Williams, Roosevelt	Sgt	ER38234639	1815		Mistreatment
Williams, William M.	Cpl	RA3456838	16	17 Aug 50	Murder
Willis, Doyle D.	PFC	RA19294267	76	20 Oct 50	Murder
Wilson, Gilmar W.	PFC	RA13305392	28	26 Sep 50	Murder
Wilson, Louis	1st Lt	061384	1820-1819A		Mistreatment

Name	Rank	Service Number		Date	Offense
Winiarski, William A.		ER13209377	435		Mistreatment
Winkler, Marvin J.	Pvt	RA13304302	76	20 Oct 50	Murder
Winter, George	Sgt	RA13260189	66		Mistreatment
Winters, Frederick W.	Maj	0-1287100	1819A	10 Jul 51	Death from Mistreatment
Winthrop, Ralph E.	Cpl	RA16205477	28	26 Sep 50	Murder
Wirt, Frederick B.	Capt	C-1104016	75-76-87-129	20 Oct 50	Murder
Wirtz, Harold D.	Pvt	RA17270373	119	30 Oct 50	Death from Mistreatment
Wise Robert H.	Capt	0-1319372	1821-1819A		Mistreatment
Illegible,	Cpl	RA32933577	76	20 Oct 50	Murder
Wist, Harld L.	PFC	RA18311579	1817		Mistreatment
Wolf, Thomas W.	PFC	ER16233784	192	25 Mar 51	Murder
Wood, Lyle E.	Cpl	RA17247032	75-76-87-129		Mistreatment
Woodhouse, Melvin J.	Pvt	RA13318164	1815		Mistreatment
Wooldridge, Claude C.	Pvt	RA19329889	76	20 Oct 50	Murder
Wooldridge, Larry	PFC	RA13322938	1817		Mistreatment
Wootan, Cecil L.	SFC	RA06321967	110	3 Sep 50	Death from Mistreatment
Wright, Raymond S	Pvt	RA18283881	75		Mistreatment
Wynne, A. D.	Sgt		1817	Nov 51	Death from Mistreatment
Wright, Lester J.	Pvt	RA23763269	66		Mistreatment
Yarnell, William F.	Cpl	AF17259912	164	13 Dec 50	Death from Torture
Yde, Erik F	Capt	0-0038396	1824	30 Jun 51	Death from Mistreatment
Yeager, James W.	Pvt	RA26240545	76	20 Oct 50	Attempted Murder
Yesenko, Thomas	Sgt	USMC551510	185	5 Feb 51	Murder
Young, Oliver	Cpl	RA18349993	1824		Mistreatment
Zacherle, Alerich L. E.	Lt Col	042817	1821	Oct-Nov 52	Torture
Zawaki, Frank	Cpl		75-76-87-129		Mistreatment
Zimmerman, Stanley G.	Capt	0-1015360	1824		Mistreatment
Zmeskall, Charles Lt	Lt	0-1120624	1821	Dec 50	Death from Mistreatment

Australian Personnel					
Madden,	Pvt		1824	Nov 51	Death from Mistreatment
Harvey, Gordon	Lt	AF	1821		Mistreatment
British Personnel					
Harding,	Maj.		1819A		Torture
Cabral, Henry	Lt.		1824	Stp-Dec 51	Death from Mistreatment
Garner,	Col		1819A		Torture
Eastgate,	Lt		639		Murder
Probin,	Lt		1817		Death from Mistreatment
Tomlinson, David A		2250187	639	23 Apr 51	Murder
Tucker, Thomas			639		Murder
Philippine Personnel					
Salting, Bienvenide	Lt		1817		Mistreatment
Belgium Personnel					
Clarys,			639	23 Apr 51	Murder
Civilian Personnel					
Collier, Anthony	Rev		1512		Murder

Appendix 5

LETTER FROM THE SECRETARY OF THE ARMY

Found in: Chapter Three, Volume 1
Source of this information: Assistant Secretary of the Army Letter to the Secretary of the Army, December 22, 1953, "a brief synopsis of past actions and future plans concerning 3,404 United Nations and Republic of Korea personnel previously listed as prisoners of war and still unaccounted for by Communist forces."

2.   On 6 September 1953 both the Communist and the United Nations Command announced that repatriation had been completed for all individuals who had elected to be returned. On 9 September 1953 the United Nations Command presented to the Communists a list of 3,404 United Nations and Republic of Korea personnel still unaccounted for (this list included the names of 944 United States personnel, of which 610 were Army). On 21 September 1953 the Communists made their first reply concerning the list furnished on 9 September. The reply stated that 518 of the persons included had already been repatriated and that 380 had previously been reported to us as dead, escaped, or already returned. No identification by name or nationality was made.

3.   On 25 September 1953 the second United Nations demand for an accounting of these people was made. The Communists were told that the first reply was completely unsatisfactory. On 3 October 1953 the Communists countered this demand by submitting a list of 98,783 names of Communists who they claimed were being held in United Nations custody. No further accounting was made of the personnel included on our original list.

4.   On 23 November 1953 three Koreans, former members of the Republic of Korea Army, escaped through the demilitarized zone and reported to the United Nations Command that Communists still held large numbers of prisoners of war. The Communists refused joint interrogations of the 3 Koreans on this charge and on 1 December 1953 the Neutral Nations Supervisory Commission declined to conduct an investigation of the allegations made by the 3 Koreans.

5.   On 10 December 1953 the senior United States member of the Military Armistice Commission again charged the Communists with violation of the Armistice by retaining custody of prisoners of war who desired repatriation. The Communists countered by a demand for accounting of 27,000 prisoners of war "illegally released by President Rhee with assent of the United Nations Forces."

6. On 14 December 1953 two additional Koreans escaped to South Korea and confirmed the allegations made by the first 3 defectors. General Hull directed the Military Armistice Commission to request unilaterally a mobile inspection team from the Neutral Nations Supervisory Commission to proceed to Munsan-ni to determine whether the 2 Korean defectors were actually prisoners of war impressed into the North Korean Army. This request was not to be submitted to the Neutral Nations Supervisory Commission until after a positive identification of the 2 Koreans was established. Verification of the 2 Koreans as bona-fide members of the Republic of Korea Army was made on 16 December 1953.

7. The State Department is notifying the Commander-in-Chief, United Nations Command, that the British through their Foreign Office in Peiping will seek to confirm through unofficial reports that Communist China is holding in custody United Nations personnel in China. Also in accordance with the personal desires of Secretary Dulles, as expressed in a message received from him this morning, the Commander-in-Chief, United Nations Command will be instructed to press continuously Communist members of the Military Armistice Commission to account for missing personnel. Repeated demands will be made. Close liaison between the Department of State and the Department of Defense concerning this matter has been in operation since July 1953 and will continue.[1]

---

[1]Memorandum to Army Chief of Staff (Confidential), from Hugh M. Milton II, Assistant Secretary of the Army, December 22, 1953, OSA 383.6, located in RG319 "RECAP-K."

Appendix 6

CHRONOLOGY OF UNC POW/MIA/REMAINS EFFORTS

Found in: Chapter Three, Volume 1
Source of this information: United Nations Command Military Armistice Commission, Seoul, Republic of Korea

MAC: Military Armistice Commission
SEC: (MAC) Secretaries
KPA: (North) Korean People's Army
CPV: Chinese People's Volunteers
SM: (MAC) Senior Member
AA: Armistice Agreement
JDO: Joint Duty Officer
NNSC: Neutral Nations Supervisory Commission

	ACTION	DATE	DESCRIPTION
1.	18th MAC	9 Sep 53	Original list of 3,404 unaccounted for POWs passed.
2.	54th SEC	24 Sep 53	List amended: US-add 41, delete 27; UK-add 2; Canada-add 1.
3.	85th SEC	2 Nov 53	List amended: US-add 10, delete 2.
4.	105th SEC	19 Feb 54	List amended: US-add 1, delete 23; UK-delete 1.
5.	47th MAC	17 Aug 54	List passed.
			Note: - KPA in 1954 provided the UNC with reports containing the burial sites of 1,399 deceased UNC POWs. - UNC in 1954 provided a record of 2,488 deceased UNC military personnel buried in ten (UNC) cemeteries in NK. - KPA in 1954 returned a total of 4,023 remains, including POWs, of deceased UNC military which included 1,869 Americans.
6.	67th MAC	26 Nov 55	List passed.
7.	69th MAC	25 Feb 56	KPA/CPV returned 67th MAC list giving accounting. Final revisions result in UNC list of 2,233 unaccounted for POWs.
8.	SEC Ltr	7 Jul 58	List passed.
9.	94th MAC	22 Jan 59	Inquiry by Senior Member.

ACTION	DATE	DESCRIPTION
10. SM Ltr	24 Jun 60	List passed.
11. SM Ltr	16 Jan 62	List passed.
12. SM Ltr	23 Feb 63	List passed.
13. SEC Ltr	11 Aug 64	List passed.
14. 210th MAC	4 Jun 65	Senior Member referred to 11 Aug 64 list asking for accounting.
15. 229th MAC	11 Oct 66	UNC Senior Member referred to 11 Aug 64 list asking for accounting.
16. 257th MAC	7 Nov 67	UNC Senior Member raised the matter of the 2,233 unaccounted for UNC POWs. KPA ignored this request.
17. UNC SM Ltr	26 May 69	UNC Senior Member sent a letter to Senior Member, KPA/CPV requesting information on unaccounted for UNC POWs. No response from KPA Senior Member.
18. UNC SM Ltr	10 Apr 70	UNC Senior Member sent a letter to Senior Member, KPA/CPV requesting information on unaccounted for UNC POWs. No response from KPA Senior Member.
19. UNC SM Ltr	16 Apr 71	UNC Senior Member sent a letter to Senior Member, KPA/CPV requesting information on unaccounted for UNC POWs.
KPA SM Reply	5 May 71	KPA/CPV Senior Member's reply to UNC Senior Member's letter of 16 Apr 71, which stated that they repatriated all prisoners to UNC side and that the UNC must return KPA POWs.
20. UNC SM Ltr	25 Apr 72	UNC Senior Member sent a letter to Senior Member, KPA/CPV requesting information concerning unaccounted for UNC POWs.

	ACTION	DATE	DESCRIPTION
	KPA SM Reply	26 May 72	KPA/CPV Senior Member's reply similar to that of the previous year's.
21.	UNC SM Ltr	31 May 73	UNC Senior Member sent a letter to Senior Member, KPA/CPV requesting information concerning unaccounted for UNC POWs.
	KPA SM Reply	18 Jun 73	KPA/CPV Senior Member's reply similar to that of the previous year's.
22.	UNC SM Ltr	17 May 74	UNC Senior Member sent a letter to Senior Member, KPA/CPV requesting information concerning unaccounted for UNC POWs.
	KPA SM Reply	28 May 74	KPA/CPV Senior Member's reply similar to that of the previous year's.
23.	UNC SM Ltr	19 Jun 75	UNC Senior Member sent a letter to Senior member, KPA/CPV requesting information concerning unaccounted for UNC POWs.
	KPA SM Reply	28 June 75	KPA/CPV Senior Member's reply similar to that of the previous year's.
24.	UNC SM Ltr	2 Jul 76	UNC Senior member sent a letter to Senior Member, KPA/CPV requesting information concerning unaccounted for UNC POWs.
	KPA SM Reply	12 Jul 76	KPA/CPV Senior member's reply similar to that of the previous year's.
25.	UNC SM Ltr	17 Aug 77	UNC Senior Member sent a letter to Senior Member, KPA/CPV requesting information concerning unaccounted for UNC POWs.
	KPA SM Reply	22 Aug 77	KPA/CPV Senior member's reply similar to that of the previous year's.

ACTION	DATE	DESCRIPTION
26. UNC SM Ltr	17 Aug 78	UNC Senior Member sent a letter to Senior Member, KPA/CPV requesting information concerning unaccounted for UNC POWs.
KPA SM Reply	24 Aug 78	KPA/CPV Senior Member's reply similar to that of the previous year's.
27. UNC SM Ltr	20 Aug 79	UNC Senior Member sent a letter to Senior Member, KPA/CPV requesting information concerning unaccounted for UNC POWs.
KPA SM Reply	29 Aug 79	KPA Senior Member simply referred to his previous letters.
28. UNC SM Ltr	8 Aug 80	UNC Senior Member sent a letter to Senior Member, KPA/CPV requesting information concerning unaccounted for UNC POWs.
KPA SM Reply	13 Aug 80	KPA Senior Member simply referred to his previous letters.
29. UNC SM Ltr	3 Sep 81	UNC Senior Member sent a letter to Senior Member, KPA/CPV requesting information concerning unaccounted for UNC POWs.
KPA SM Reply	17 Sep 81	KPA Senior Member simply referred to his previous letters.
30. UNC SM Ltr	11 Aug 82	UNC Senior Member sent a letter to Senior Member, KPA/CPV requesting information concerning unaccounted for UNC POWs.
KPA SM Reply	17 Aug 82	KPA Senior Member simply referred to his previous letters.
415 MAC	21 Dec 82	UNC Senior Member requested the KPA/CPV to conduct a search of the burial sites of UNC POWs at UNC POW Camp No. 5 for possible UNC remains and passed a map depicting the burial site. KPA ignored the request.

ACTION	DATE	DESCRIPTION
31. UNC SM ltr	17 Aug 83	UNC Senior Member sent a letter to Senior Member, KPA/CPV requesting information concerning unaccounted for UNC POWs; also asked for the return of remains.
KPA SM Reply	22 Aug 83	KPA Senior Member simply referred to his previous letters.
32. UNC SM Ltr	17 Aug 84	UNC Senior Member sent a letter to Senior member, KPA/CPV requesting information concerning unaccounted for UNC POWs; also asked for the return of remains.
KPA SM Reply	24 Aug 84	KPA Senior Member simply referred to his previous letters.
33. UNC SM Ltr	28 Aug 85	UNC Senior Member sent a letter to KPA/CPV requesting information concerning unaccounted for UNC POWs; also asked for the return of the remains.
34. NK Foreign Minister in N.Y.	20 Oct 85	NK Foreign Minister tells Frank Kerr of the Chosin Few that NK will cooperate in returning military remains if the U.S. Govt formally requests a search for and recovery of US war dead.
KPA Staff Officers's comments	Oct 85	KPA staff officer comments informally at Panmunjom that NK might start looking for military remains if asked to do so.
35. UNC SM Ltr	23 Nov 85	UNC requests KPA search for and repatriate UNC remains.
36. Comments by UNC and KPA officers	Jan-Feb 86	UNC position: - The subject of military remains is a humanitarian issues. - Remains should be returned through the MAC. KPA position:

ACTION	DATE	DESCRIPTION
		- Armistice does not cover search and exhumation.
37. UNC Ltr to UNC Members	11 Feb 86	UNCMAC Senior Member sent letters to 16 UNC Member nations requesting all available information regarding the status of MIAs. Eleven nations responded to this query; some with additional info on MIAs.
38. UNC SM Ltr	14 Feb 86	Remains issue involves the UNC, not just U.S. CINCUNC, signatory to the AA, represents all UN/ROK forces. MAC, not a new agency, should handle remains issues. UNC is prepared to discuss details involving the process of searching for military remains.
39. KPA SM Ltr	4 Mar 86	Military remains will be returned when recovered, but AA does not require search and exhumation.
40. UNC SM Ltr	5 Apr 86	Both sides have a moral and humanitarian obligation to search for, disinter, and deliver military remains. Proposed exchange of info on possible location of remains. UNC recommended KPA call a no-press Secretaries' meeting to discuss remains issue.
41. KPA SM Ltr	28 Apr 86	NK position remains the same, will return military remains when discovered, but not obliged to search for remains.
42. 479th SEC	19 Aug 86	Provided KPA with available information regarding remains.

	ACTION	DATE	DESCRIPTION
43.	KPA SEC public release	11 Sep 86	NK position remains the same, info passed to "appropriate agencies."
44.	UNC SEC Ltr	22 Oct 86	Asked if KPA recovered any remains based on info provided at 19 Aug 86 SEC meeting; provided additional info on three Colombian MIAs.
45.	Meeting with Chosin Few	11 Dec 86	Briefed UNC actions/position on remains negotiations.
46.	UNC SEC Ltr	18 Dec 86	A follow-up ltr asking if they have had any success in discovering remains; provided additional info on KPA discovery of UNC remains in DMZ in 83 and 85.
47.	KPA/CPV SEC Ltr	29 Dec 86	Responded to UNC 18 Dec 86 ltr: Maintained same position; info passed to "relevant organs."
48.	UNC SEC Ltr	12 Jan 87	Notified KPA of 25 remains searched for and recovered vic. Obong-ni; offered to return remains.
49.	KPA/CPV SEC Ltr	20 Jan 87	Acknowledged UNC's 12 Jun 87 letter and requested evidence and CIL Rpt. (Both passed at JDO Mtgs.)
50.	KPA/CPV SEC Ltr	3 Mar 87	Declined to accept Obong-ni remains "due to lack of evidence."
51.	UNC SEC Ltr	11 Mar 87	Asked north to review all available info once more before rejecting the remains.
52.	482nd SEC	26 May 87	Offered to return 25 KPA remains; provided info on burial sites at the KPA APEX Camps; and requested the return of UNC remains. The KPA again rejected the offer.
53.	Burial of NK remains	9 Jun 87	Buried 25 KPA remains near Uijongbu.

ACTION	DATE	DESCRIPTION
54. 438th MAC	30 Jul 87	UNC position:

- The KPA has an obligation to return UNC remains which NK officials have told US veterans that they have discovered.

- The remarks made by KPA staff officers led the UNC to believe NK may have already discovered UNC remains.

- The question of remains is not only an Armistice issue but also humanitarian issue. The MAC is the appropriate agency to deal with the remains issue.

- The UNC is prepared to negotiate a subsequent agreement similar to the one of 1954 to eliminate any technical problem involving the question of searching for and discovery of remains.

- The UNC is prepared to dispatch a multinational team, accompanied by the NNSC representatives, to assist NK in locating UNC remains.

The KPA must return the UNC remains thru the MAC.

KPA position:

- Search for and recovery of remains is not an armistice issue.

- KPA would not discuss the remains issue at the future MAC meeting.

- KPA ignored the UNC proposal for dispatching a multinational team.

| 55. SM Press Conference | 30 Jul 87 | Following the 483rd MAC mtg, UNC SM held a press conference and made the following points. |

ACTION	DATE	DESCRIPTION
		- The UNC must and will continue its efforts to resolve the remains issue.
		- The UNC multinational team proposal offers the capability the KPA say they do not have within the MAC to look for remains.
		- The UNC hs been working diligently on this issue over the years, but is being stopped by the other side.
		- The KPA is using the remains issue in an attempt to force bilateral negotiations with nations that currently do not recognize NK.
56. UNC SM Ltr	14 Nov 87	Korean war remains is an Armistice and a humanitarian issue. MAC is the most appropriate agency to handle the issue. A multinational team may be sent to NK to assist searching for UNC remains. Requested the KPA return UNC remains which NK already has in its possession.
57. KPA SM Ltr	21 Nov 87	Responded to the 14 Nov 87 UNC Ltr, repeating its standard position that Korean war remains issue is outside the purview of the Military Armistice Commission.
58. UNC SEC Msg	9 Jan 88	Proposed the 490 SEC meeting for 15 Jan 88 to deliver and receive UNC (U.S.) remains which NK indicated to numerous individuals that they have in their possession. Advised the KPA that three U.S. Congressmen will participate in receiving UNC remains.

ACTION	DATE	DESCRIPTION
59. KPA SEC Msg	14 Jan 88	Responded that the MAC Secretaries meet informally on 20 Jan 88 to discuss the procedures for the return of "U.S. Army" remains they have "recently disinterred." Suggested that the three U.S. Congressmen attend the meeting on 20 Jan 88.
60. KPA SEC Msg	22 Jan 88	KPA accepted the UNC counterproposal to delay the informal meeting until 27 Jan 88.
61. UNC SEC Msg	26 Jan 88	Proposed the 490th SEC meeting be held at 1500 hrs, 27 Jan 88 to receive the UNC remains which the KPA discovered (following the informal meeting planned for 1000 the same day).
62. KPA SEC Msg	26 Jan 88	Cancelled the 27 Jan 88 SEC meeting under the pretext of the U.S. "sanctions" against the NK bombing of a KAL plane.
63. UNC SEC Msg	28 Jan 88	Pointed out the NK misuse of the remains issue for their irrelevant propaganda, and requested the return of UNC remains.
64. KPA SEC Msg	2 Feb 88	- Repeated its excuse for cancelling the meeting and specifically mentioned the names of two "U.S. Army men" whose remains they have discovered "among the remains of U.S. Army men in our possession." - Reiterated its standard position that they don't have to return the remains "disinterred." - NK radio (KCNA) broadcast this KPA message.
65. UNC SEC Msg	3 Feb 88	Proposed the 490th SEC meeting for 1400 hrs, 5 Feb 88 to receive the remains of the two U.S. Army men they have discovered.

ACTION	DATE	DESCRIPTION
66. KPA SEC Msg	4 Feb 88	- Rejected the UNC request for the 490th SEC meeting saying that the subject of the remains "disinterred" is outside the purview of the MAC. - NK radio (KCNA) broadcast the KPA message.
67. UNC SM Ltr	16 Feb 88	Called for return of all UNC remains that KPA has publicly announced they are holding.
68. KPA SM Ltr	29 Feb 88	- Rejected UNC SM request of 16 Feb 88.
69. 490th SEC	23 Mar 88	- UNC side asked KPA to reconsider their decision to not return remains.
70. 492nd SEC	27 Apr 88	- The KPA continue to refuse to return remains they publicly state they have in their possession. - The KPA have a humanitarian obligation to search for, disinter, and deliver remains; especially remains which have previously been discovered. - The UNC again asked the KPA to return all remains they presently have in their possession.
71. 443rd MAC	26 May 88	UNC position: - The KPA has a humanitarian obligation to return the remains of UNC military personnel they officially and publicly admitted to have already discovered. - Such a humanitarian act would help create a more positive atmosphere on which to base progress in other areas of concern to both sides.

ACTION	DATE	DESCRIPTION
72. 494th SEC	23 Jun 88	UNC position: - The KPA continue to refuse to return remains they publicly state they have in their possession. - The KPA have an Armistice and humanitarian obligation to search for, disinter, and deliver remains; especially remains which have previously been discovered. - The UNC again asked the KPA to return all remains they presently have in their possession. KPA response: - The issue of the return of remains is not an Armistice issue and the reason the issue has not previously been resolved is due to the unreasonable attitude of the U.S. Gov't; i.e., imposing sanctions againt NK over the KAL Flt 858 bombing.
73. Meeting with Chosin Few	30 Jun 88	- Briefed UNC actions/position on remains negotiations.
74. 444th MAC	15 Jul 88	- UNC side asked the KPA to discuss the return of UNC remains they publicly acknowledged holding.
75. 446th MAC	13 Feb 89	- UNC Closing Statement mentioned that an easy confidence building/tension reduction measure requiring only unilateral KPA action is to return the remains they have publicly admitted holding and those they are holding but not publicly acknowledged. - UNC pointed out their humanitarian and legal responsibilities to return all UNC remains.

ACTION	DATE	DESCRIPTION
76. 448th MAC	9 May 89	- UNC asked the KPA/CPV to return the Korean War Remains they've publicly stated they're holding and pointed out it would be a very easy, unilateral confidence building measure on their part.
77. 495th SEC	12 May 89	- UNC returned to the KPA/CPV the partial sets of remains of 19 CPV soldiers recently discovered at two locations at the Chipyong-ni Korean War Battle site.
78. UNC SM Ltr	16 May 89	- Noted KPA/CPV identified by name on 2 Feb 88 the remains of 2 UNC soldiers they're holding. - Stated UNC continues to honor the AA as the 12 May 89 CPV remains return demonstrates. - States remains return is a confidence building measure which will reduce tension on the peninsula. - Requested the return of all UNC remains the KPA/CPV publicly stated they're holding.
KPA SM Reply	5 Jun 89	- Not obligated by AA to disinter remains. - Willing to return remains due to humanitarian reasons if US sanctions are lifted.

Appendix 7

RAND LIST OF USAF PERSONNEL IN SOVIET RECORDS

Found in: Chapter Four, Volume 1
Source of this information: Noted in table legend.

? = Unmatched or unidentified

Italics = Held on territory of PRC (confirmed or suspected)

List = Name appears on the following lists:

    V = Name appears on Volgovonov/Senate Select Committee list
    UNC = Name appears on UNCMAC 389 list
    TFRM = Name appears on Task Force Russia (TFR) May 1992 list
    TFRS = Name appears on Task Force Russia September 1992 list
    RANDM = Name appears on RAND May 1992 list
    RANDS = Name appears on RAND September 1992 list
    ## = Name on TFRS and RANDM, not included on TFRM or RANDS

FSC = Field Search Case number

Sta = Status as reported in FSC or 293 casualty file or on casualty card:

    RMC = Returned to military control, presumably repatriated
    MIA = Missing In Action
    KIA = Killed In Action (Soviet determination)
    BTB = Believed to be POW
    ? = No information or unknown
    D = Reported deceased in Soviet records

Last Name Craft/Duty	First	Rank/Service No. Unit No. and Name	Captured	List	FSC #	Status
Stahl ?/?	Charles Eugene	2Lt/253981	7 Jan 1952	TFRM TFRS RANDM RANDS		RMC
Maultsby F-80/Pilot	Charles Weine	2Lt/AO-1910993 35 F-B/8 F-B Grp	5 Jan 1952	TFRM TFRS RANDM RANDS		RMC
Green F-84E/Pilot	Joseph F.	2Lt/20803A ?	11 Jan 52	TFRS RANDM RANDS ##		RMC
Eyres B-29/?	Thomas Llewellyn	1St/AO-0695638 93rd Bomb Sq Med	??	TFRM TFRS RANDM RANDS	A426	RMC
Henderson ?/?	Jack E.	Captain/?	31 Aug 51	TFRM TFRS RANDM RANDS		RMC
Wilkens ?/?	James V.	Captain/?	3 July 51	TFRM TFRS RANDM RANDS		RMC
MacLelland B-26B/Pilot	Donald J.	LtCol/AO-790369 729 Bomb Squad	8 May 51	TFRM TFRS RANDM RANDS	A187	RMC
Smith ?/?	J. B.	Captain/?	8 May 51	TFRM TFRS RANDM RANDS		RMC
Wright F-86E/Pilot	Vernon	1Lt/A0-1910299 25 Ftr Intcp Sq	16 Jan 52	TFRM TFRS RANDM RANDS		RMC
Peterson F-86E/Pilot	Daniel Delong	2Lt./2221743 25 F-I Sq/51 F-I	17 Jan 52	TFRM TFRS RANDM RANDS		RMC
Enoch B-26/?	Kenneth Lloyd	1Lt/A0-2069988 ?	13 Jan 52	TFRM TFRS RANDM RANDS	A415	RMC
Quinn B-26/?	John S.	1Lt/17993A ?	13 Jan 52	TFRM TFRS RANDM RANDS	A415	RMC

Thrash ?/?	William Gay	LtCol/?	12 Dec 51	TFRM TFRS RANDM RANDS		RMC
Richardson ?/?	Judson C.	?/?	14 Dec 51	TFRM TFRS RANDM RANDS		RMC
Kubicek B-29/Pilot	Harold Bratislav	Cpt/12108A 93rd Bomb Sq Med	4 July 52	TFRM TFRS RANDM RANDS	A426	RMC
Frick F-86A/Pilot	Vance R.	2Lt/? 336 F-I/4 F-I Grp	21 Apr 52	TFRM TFRS RANDM RANDS		RMC
DeArmond F-86/Pilot	Michael Edward	1Lt/20161A 335 F-I/4 F-I Grp	21 Apr 52	TFRM TFRS RANDM RANDS		RMC
Parks F-86E/Pilot	Roland William	2Lt/23197A 51st Ftr Intcp Wg	4 Sept 52	TFRM TFRS RANDM RANDS	A590	RMC
Ellis F-86A/Pilot	John G.	1Lt/A0-1862790 336 F-I/4 F-I Grp	20 July 52	TFRM TFRS RANDM RANDS		RMC
Zwiacher F-80/Pilot	John Wesley	1Lt/A0-2222083 36 F-B/8 F-B Grp	30 Apr 52	TFRM TFRS RANDM RANDS		RMC
Tenney F-86E/Pilot	Gilbert 51 F-Int Grp	Cpt/803490, 289613	3 May 52	TFRS RANDM RANDS ##	A784	MIA /D
Reid B-29/Left gnr	Elbert J. Jr.	A1C/A0-14382534 19th Med Bomb Gp	10 June 52	TFRS RANDM RANDS ##	A580	MIA
Kniss F-51/Pilot	Paul R.	2nd Lt/491936 12 F-B Sq/18 F- B	31 May 52	TFRS RANDM RANDS ##		MIA
?Jiliam ?Gilliam ?/?		Major/?	14 Apr 52	TFRS RANDM RANDS ##		D
Arnold B-29/Pilot	John Knox, Jr.	Col/1212A 91st Strat Recon	12 Jan 53	V TFRM TFRS RANDM RANDS	A654	RMC

Thompson B-29/?	*John Walker*	A2C/AF-13361707 581 Resupply Cmd	13 Jan 53	TFRM TFRS RANDM RANDS	A654	RMC
Buck B-29/AOBomber	*John W.*	1Lt/A0-787245 91st Strat Recon	13 Jan 53	V TFRM TFRS RANDM RANDS	A654	RMC
Llewellyn B-29/Navigtr	*Elmer Fred*	Cpt/A0-2072360 91st Strat Recon	13 Jan 53	TFRM TFRS RANDM RANDS	A654	RMC
Vaadi B-29/ACCmdr	*Eugene J.*	Cpt/A0-825008 91st Strat Recon	13 Jan 53	TFRM TFRS RANDM RANDS	A654	RMC
Schmidt B-29/?	Daniel C.	A2C/AF-19391475 91st Strat Recon	13 Jan 53	V TFRM TFRS RANDM RANDS	A654	RMC
Benjamin B-29/Scanner	*Harry* *Martin*	A1C/AF-27345828 91st Strat Recon	13 Jan 53	V TFRM TFRS RANDM RANDS	A654	RMC
Kiba B-29/Radio Op	*Steve E.*	A1C/15426310 91st Strat Recon	13 Jan 53	V TFRM TFRS RANDM RANDS	A654	RMC
Baumer B-29/Inst Plt	*William H.*	Maj/A0-733786 91st Strat Recon	13 Jan 53	TFRM TFRS RANDM RANDS	A654	RMC
Brown B-29/Flt Eng	*Howard W.*	TSg/AF-36809947 91st Strat Recon	13 Jan 53	TFRM TFRS RANDM RANDS	A654	RMC
Brown B-29/Pilot	*Wallace L.*	2Lt/A0-2221928 91st Strat Recon	13 Jan 53	TFRM TFRS RANDM RANDS	A654	RMC
Moreland B-29/Navigatr	Joseph E.	1Lt/AO-2070097 91st Strat Recon	4 July 52	TFRS RANDM RANDS ##	A611	RMC
Strieby B-29/Co-pilot	Francis Allen	2Lt/AO-1912123 91st Strat Recon	4 July 52	TFRS RANDM RANDS ##	A611	RMC

Name / Aircraft	First name	Rank/Serial / Unit	Date	Status	Code	Remarks
Brazil B-29/?	Kenneth S.	1Lt/AO-772819 91st Strat Recon	4 July 52	TFRS TFRM RANDM RANDS	A611	RMC
Combs B-29/Radio op	Edwin D.	A1C/AF-18359624 91st Strat Recon	4 July 52	TFRS RANDM RANDS ##	A611	RMC
Koski B-29/?	William Emile	A1C/17299984 91st Strat Recon	4 July 52	TFRS RANDM RANDS ##	A611	RMC
Johansen B-29/Photo op	Charles Vernon	SSgt/AF-19124748 91st Strat Recon	4 July 52	TFRM TFRS RANDM RANDS	A611	RMC
Rivers B-29/Engineer	Bernard Francis	SSgt/AF-11158439 91st Strat Recon	4 July 52	V TFRS RANDM RANDS ##	A611	RMC
Bass B-29/Tail gnr	Kenneth H.	A1C/AF-14357650 91st Strat Recon	4 July 52	V TFRS RANDM RANDS ##	A611	RMC
Hand B-29/R gunner	Donald L.	A2C/19371141 91st Strat Recon	4 July 52	V TFRS RANDM RANDS ##	A611	RMC
Fisher F-86F/Pilot	*Harold Edward*	Cpt/445018 R# /AO2204126 actual 39th Ftr Intcp Sq	7 Apr 53	TFRM TFRS RANDM RANDS	A672	RMC
Harker F-84G/Pilot	Charles A.	1Lt/640924-R# /AO2224102- actual 311th Ftr Bmr Sq	4 May 53	UNC TFRS RANDM RANDS ##	A692	MIA KIA
Niemann F-86E/Pilot	Robert	1Lt/989294/*2228 7A* 334 Ftr-Intcp Sq	12 Apr 53	TFRS RANDM RANDS ##	A678	MIA **/D**
Osburn F-84D/Pilot	John Arthur	Cap/796188 311 F-B/58 F-B Gp	19 Sept 52	TFRS RANDM RANDS ##		MIA
Heller F-86/Pilot	*Edwin Lewis*	LtCol/9900A 16th Ftr-Intcp Sq	23 Jan 53	TFRM TFRS RANDM RANDS	A648	RMC

Izbiky F-86E/Pilot	Edward G.	2Lt/AO-2223853	19 Feb 53	TFRM TFRS RANDM RANDS		RMC
Pape ?/?	Donald L.	1st Lt/?	15 May 53	TFRM TFRS RANDM RANDS		RMC
Giraudo F-86/Pilot	John	Col/A-16292	16 June 53	TFRM TFRS RANDM RANDS		RMC
Bettinger ?/?	Stephen L.	Maj./AO-816087	20 July 53	TFRM TFRS RANDM RANDS		
Coury F-86F/Pilot	Robert A.	Capt./AO-687678 12 F-B Sq 18 F- B	10 June 53	TFRM TFRS RANDM RANDS		MIA BTB
Hodges F-86/Pilot	Albert V.	1Lt/AO-2224077	19 June 53	TFRM TFRS RANDM RANDS		MIA
Dillon F-86F/Pilot	Edward	2nd Lt/AO- 2225448 12 F-B Sq 18 F- B	15 June 53	TFRM TFRS RANDM RANDS		MIA BTB
Pinkstone Meteor/Pilot	Donald William	Sgt/A-2925 77 I/F Sqd RAAF	15 June 53	TFRM TFRS RANDM RANDS	A719	RMC
Fornes ??/Pilot	William L.	1Lt/ 69 AS 58 IBG	6 Aug 52	TFRM RANDS		RMC
Schwable ?/?	Fran H.	Col/ 1st Marine Wing	8 Jul 52	TFRM RANDS		RMC
Johanson B-29/?	Charles Vernon	Sgt/??	4 Jul 52	TFRM RANDS		RMC
Bartholomew ?/?	Gabriel P.	Maj/334 AS	18 Oct 52	TFRM RANDS		RMC
Johnson ?/?	Johnny M.	Sgt/ 307 Bomber Wing	18 Oct 52	TFRM RANDS		MIA KIA
Abrahamson ?/?	Gerald	?/? 28th BAS	29 Jan 53	TFRM RANDS		RMC
Van Slyke ?/Radio Oper.	Leland H.	A2C/? 28 AS, 19 BAG	30 Dec 52	TFRM RANDS		RMC
Shawe ?/Pilot	Hamilton	2Lt/ 8 Res 5th AA	1 Dec 50	TFRM RANDS		RMC
McDonough RB-45/Pilot	Charles	Capt/? 5th AS, 363 Det	4 Dec 50	TFRM RANDS		MIA KIA
?Denstech B-29/Pilot	Frank S.	Capt/?	10 Nov 50	TFRM RANDS		?
?Hern B-29/?	Joseph S.	?/? 371 AS, 307 AG	12 Apr 51	TFRM RANDS		RMC

Oldewage B-29/?	Daniel Henry.	Sgt/?	12 Apr 51	TFRM RANDS		RMC
Metz B-29/?	Henry X.	Sgt/?	12 Apr 51	TFRM RANDS		RMC
King B-29/Gunner	Marvin E.	A1C/?	4 Dec 51	TFRM RANDS		RMC
Knego B-29/Nav.	George J.	Lt/?	4 Dec 51	TFRM RANDS		RMC
Moree ?/?	Leonard Levi	Sgt/? 371 AS, 307 AG	4 Dec 51	TFRM RANDS		RMC
Gant d. May 2, 92 in USA B-29/Gunner	**John K.**	Sgt/AF14051878 93 AS, 19th AG	4 Dec 51	TFRM RANDS	A180	RMC
Millward d. Oct 16, 91 in USA ?/Gunner	George E.	Sgt/? 93		TFRM RANDS	A180	RMC
Bergmann ?/Radio Op.	Louis H.	Sgt/ 93 AS, 19 AG		TFRM RANDS	A180	P MIA KIA
Unruh B-29/Pilot	Halbert C.		4 Apr 51	TFRM RANDS		MIA KIA
Dean ?/?	Zach Wesley	Capt/ 39 AS. 35 AG	22 Apr 51	TFRM RANDS		RMC
?Obney ?/?		Major 40th AS, 35th AG	13/4 Aug 51	TFRM RANDS		
Miller Buried in MT ?/Pilot	Howard P. Jr.	1Lt/AO1910262 336th AS, 4th AG	22 Jun 51	TFRM RANDS	A224	RMC rem ain
??Harm B-29/Gunner		?/? 307th BAG	?? Sept 52	TFRM RANDS		??
Weese B-29/?	*Henry D.*	1Lt/A0091871	12 Jan 53	TFRM RANDS	A654	MIA D
Van Voorhis B-29/?	*Paul E.*	1Lt/A0291867	12 Jan 53	TFRM RANDS	A654	MIA D
MacKenzie ?/Pilot	*Andrew* *Robert* R Canadian AF	Squad Leader/?	15 June 52 *5 Dec 52*	TFRM		RMC

Appendix 8

ADDITIONAL EVIDENCE CONCERNING TRANSPORT OF AMERICAN POW/MIAs
FROM KOREA TO USSR TERRITORY

Found in: Chapter Five, Volume 1
Source of this information: Senator Bob Smith (R-NH), Army Task Force
Russia (TFR), and Paul M. Cole

HISTORICAL REPORTS COLLECTED BY PAUL M. COLE

Assertions that Americans were transferred to Soviet territory from
Korea or China can be found in official sources, academic articles, and
the popular press. These sources tend either to assert or assume that
American servicemen were transported to Soviet territory. Perhaps the
best known assertion was made in 1955 by an unidentified refugee who
reported to the U.S. military attaché in Hong Kong that hundreds of
American servicemen had been transferred from North Korea through China
to USSR territory.

> The attaché's source was a Polish citizen who reportedly
> witnessed about 700 soldiers getting off a train on the Sino-
> Soviet border while the train's undercarriages were changed
> from standard-gauge to broad-gauge width.[1]

A magazine article in May 1953 asserted, based on alleged Soviet
sources, that "our best information is that large numbers of Americans
are now living in camps scattered in the various Republics of Russia."[2]

On September 8, 1955, Walter J. Stoessel, Jr., Officer in Charge,
USSR Affairs wrote to the Chief of the Casualty Branch, Department of
the Air Force, requesting

> information contained in the records of the Department of
> Defense concerning Captain David H. Grisham, who was reported
> missing in action in Korea on September 3, 1950. A recently
> released foreign prisoner-of-war has reported seeing in the
> Soviet Union an American named "Grisham." The Honorable

---

[1]*POW-MIA Fact Book* (Washington, D.C.: Department of Defense,
1991), "Missing and Unaccounted for Americans from World War II and the
Korean War," pp. 35-36.
[2]Zygmunt Nagorski, Jr., "Unreported GI's in Siberia," *Esquire*, May
1953.

Overton Brooks, United States Representative from Louisiana, has requested the Department of State to make an investigation to learn whether the person referred to could be Captain David. H. Grisham. In determining this question, it would be helpful to know the circumstances in which Captain Grisham's airplane disappeared or crashed, the territory in which it is believed the plane might have landed or crashed, and the names of other crew members, if any, who died or disappeared at the same time.[3]

The DoS notified the American Embassies at Moscow and Vienna on September 19 that "the family and Congressman of Captain David H. Grisham, missing during a combat mission in Korea 1950, have inquired about the possibility that he is in the USSR. Attempt to find the POW sources of the story and interrogate them with a view of learning whether an American named Grisham is in the USSR or if the AP report incorrectly reported the name."[4]

On September 8, Representative Carl Elliott wrote to the Secretary of State on behalf of the parents of Airman 2nd Class Robert Q. Hopkins who had read a newspaper account that a "Mr. Hopkins" was recently released by the Russians. Airman 2nd Class Hopkins was a gunner aboard a USAF B-29 which ditched nine miles north of the Kadena Air Force Base while returning from a combat mission over North Korea. Three survivors were picked up from the crash site. Airman 2nd Class Hopkins was not among them. Congressman Elliott "gathered it had been determined that the Hopkins released by the Russians is of German nationality."[5] The DoS responded on September 26 that "it became apparent soon after questioning by United States authorities in Germany, that the Mr. Hopkins released by the Soviet Union is not an American citizen. In fact, it has been established that he is a German national by the name of [name deleted] and has since been turned over to the German Red Cross for repatriation." Further, the DoS reported, the Department of Defense

---

[3]Letter from Walter J. Stoessel, Jr., to Lt. Colonel Richard A. Steele, Chief of the Casualty Branch, Department of the Air Force, September 8, 1955.

[4]From State #921 to Vienna (Official Use Only), September 19, 1955, 611.61241/9-1955.

[5]Letter from Congressman Carl Elliott to the Secretary of State September 8, 1955, 611.61241/9-855.

had informed them that "none of the survivors of the aircraft accident indicated that they had seen Airman Hopkins after the time of the emergency. The remainder of the crew were declared dead by the Far East Air Forces inasmuch as the statements of the survivors indicated that the prevailing circumstances precluded the chance of survival of the other men."[6]

On December 21, 1955, the American Embassy at Vienna reported to the DoS:

> The investigations which have been conducted by the Ministry of the Interior and the Austrian police among the nine Austrian prisoners who have returned from the Soviet Union on September 1 have failed to substantiate the AP Vienna report concerning GRISHAM or GRISHMAN. Indirect contact which the Embassy has also had with these returnees has been equally unsuccessful. None of the returnees appear to have any knowledge, personal or hearsay, of anyone named Grisham or Grishman. The Austrian AP reporter who interviewed the returnees at the Bad Voeslau railroad station cannot remember which of the men told him about "Grishman" although he asserts that he is sure the name was "Grishman." The Embassy believes that there may have been some linguistic confusion over the name, since the names of alleged Americans reported to the Embassy have been frequently garbled.[7]

Letters forwarded from Congress to family members of servicemen unaccounted for after the Korean War received serious consideration by the Departments of State and Defense. In one case, which is worth noting at length to reveal how decisions were made on similar cases in light of prevailing policy and procedures, the sister of a missing U.S. Marine wrote to Secretary Dulles in February 1956. She had read an article in *Reader's Digest* that asserted American servicemen who had served in Korea were being held alive in the Soviet Union. The sister wrote to inquire whether her brother had been transported from North

---

[6]Letter from Florence Kirlin, Acting Assistant Secretary, to Congressman Carl Elliot, September 26, 1955, 611.61241/9-855. Letter from Lt. Col. Richard A. Steele, Chief, Casualty Branch, Personnel Services Division, Directorate of Military Personnel, to Miss Mary R. Wilson, Public Services Division, Department of State, September 16, 1955, 611.61241/9-1655.

[7]From Vienna #555 to State (Official Use Only), December 21, 1955, 611.61241/12-2155.

Korea to the Soviet Union.[8] The first reply came from an assistant
secretary of state three weeks later. Noel Hemmendinger, Acting
Director of the Office of Northeast Asian Affairs, wrote that "the
Department of State started an investigation to determine the accuracy
of . . . statements concerning the possible presence in the Soviet Union
of American flyers and soldiers. Our representatives abroad have
investigated these reports, have interviewed persons who supposedly have
information concerning the reports, and have followed up all other leads
which might result in information indicating that American military
personnel are in the Soviet Union. The Department of State is actively
investigating all reports which might contribute information pertaining
to this question."[9]

The sister's letter was then forwarded to the Department of Defense
for a more complete reply.[10] The Headquarters of the United States
Marine Corps wrote to the sister

> I am sincerely sorry there is no information I can give you
> which would encourage you and your family in your hope that
> [your brother] is alive. The fact that your brother's remains
> were not identified among those returned to us by the
> Communists is not an indication he is alive. There were many
> remains of Marines declared nonrecoverable who were actually
> buried by our forces in United Nations temporary cemeteries
> and isolated graves in North Korea, even though the location
> of the cemeteries and graves were furnished the Communists.[11]

Another letter was sent to the sister by the Director of Personnel.
This letter summarized the events leading up to the crash of the
aircraft piloted by the Marine in question. The letter goes on to say,

---

[8]For privacy reasons, names of family members and some private
individuals will not be given in this report. The National Archive
decimal number provides adequate identification. 611.61241/2-2456.

[9]Letter from Noel Hemmendinger, Acting Director, Office of
Northeast Asian Affairs, Department of State, March 14, 1956.

[10]Letter from Noel Hemmendinger, Acting Director, Office of
Northeast Asian Affairs, to Lt. Colonel James Monroe, USAF, Subsidiary,
Plans Division, Directorate of Plans, DSC/G, Headquarters United States
Air Force, March 14, 1956, 611.61241/2-2456.

[11]Letter from F. B. Nihart, Lt. Colonel, U.S. Marine Corps, Head,
Personal Affairs Branch, by direction of the Commandant of the Marine
Corps, March 22, 1956, FW611.6/241-3-2556.

He was carried on our rolls as missing in action from 29 September 1950 until his status was administratively changed on 2 December 1952 to killed in action. This finding was made by a board of officers who, after an exhaustive analysis of the investigative report and interrogations of prisoners returned to us, could find no evidence that he was held prisoner. In view of the circumstances of his disappearance and the lapse of time without word of his whereabouts, the fact that he lost his life in Korea seems conclusive and inescapable. [Your brother's] remains have recently been declared nonrecoverable.[12]

In addition to other letters, the mother of the Marine in question received the following letter from Marine Headquarters in 1956.

I must disappoint you in your belief that your son is not dead until you receive his tags. The return of identification tags is not considered evidence that a man is dead. Firstly, even the presence of tags on a body, while helpful in determining an association, does not constitute positive identification. Secondly, identification tags are considered Government property and, even if found, are generally returned to the next of kin only in company with remains. I join Captain Witherspoon in his hope that in time you will be able to accept the fact of [your son's] death, as hard as it is to bear, and thereby lessen the grief and disappointments which accompany the vain hope for the return of your son.[13]

Another sister of the dead Marine received a reply to her letter of February 25 from George H. Haselton, Acting Assistant Director, Office of Special Consular Services, on June 28, 1956. Haselton wrote in reference to the assertion that the Marine

was lost in the Korean war and your belief that he may be alive in Communist hands. We are sorry that the Department of Defense which is constantly on the alert for information on this subject, has not been able to obtain any evidence whatever to support your belief that, contrary to the official findings, your brother may be alive in Communist hands. Had there been any such evidence this Government would have immediately taken energetic action based on the evidence.[14]

---

[12]Letter from R. O. Bare, Major General, U.S. Marine Corps, Director of Personnel, March 22, 1956, FW611.612441/3-2256.

[13]Letter from F. B. Nihart, Lt. Colonel, U.S. Marine Corps, Head, Personal Affairs Branch, by direction of the Commandant of the Marine Corps, March 22, 1956, FW611.61241/3-2256.

[14]611.61241/6-2856.

In a letter from Usher L. Burdick, Member of Congress, to Thomas S. Gordon, Chairman, House Committee on Foreign Affairs, it is asserted that "while the Defense Department has listed as dead some 450 American men serving with the Armed Forces of the United States in Korea, from time to time it is reported that one here and there is still living and a slave in Russian labor camps, or in Communist China."[15]

On January 2, 1957, the Department of State notified the American Embassy at Tokyo:

> Press reports state that returning Japanese POW's have reported seeing Americans in Soviet prison camps. The Department has promised the Senate Foreign Relations and Armed Forces Committees as well as individual Congressmen to keep them currently informed on the subject of American military personnel detained in Soviet prisons. It is essential, therefore, that the Department have soonest the fullest possible detailed report on this subject, interrogators concentrating on closest details of the identification of Americans, scene, place, time, etc. The Department is already informed of the statement by repatriate Naito to *Asahi Evening News* re presence of Americans Oggins and Cumish; the latter is already repatriated and the Department is reconsidering the former case.[16]

American Ambassador to the United Nations Henry Cabot Lodge, Jr., wrote to the DoS On January 21, asking to be kept informed as to "what the Department is saying and thinking" on the subject of "American military personnel detained in Soviet prisons." Ambassador Lodge asked also to "receive the Department's own classified estimate of the probable situation of the missing men, including specifically the possibility that some of the men captured in the Korean war may be alive in the Soviet Union."[17] Ambassador Lodge received the following reply on

---

[15]U.S. Congress, House, Subcommittee on the Far East and the Pacific, "Return of American Prisoners of War Who Have Not Been Accounted for by the Communists" (Washington, D.C.: U.S. Government Printing Office, 1957), p. 21.

[16]From State #1391, to Tokyo (Confidential), January 2, 1957, 611.61241/1-257.

[17]Letter from the United States Representative to the United Nations, Henry Cabot Lodge, Jr., to Assistant Secretary of State Francis O. Wilcox, January 21, 1957, 611.61241/1-2157.

February 6 that refers to the DoS's telegram No. 1391 to Tokyo sent on
January 2:

> That particular telegram resulted, as it stated, from press
> reports that Japanese prisoners of war repatriated last year
> from the USSR had seen Americans in Soviet prison camps. Its
> purpose was to ensure that these recent repatriates should be
> interrogated so far as possible by appropriate authorities to
> obtain information that might shed light on the fate of
> unaccounted for American military personnel.
>
> As you know, the primary responsibility in this area lies with
> the Department of Defense which is the only agency in this
> Government that maintains a detailed classified estimate
> regarding missing military personnel, including any reports
> relating to their fate and their evaluation in the light of
> known facts. (Possibly our representatives on the Military
> Staff Committee have the latest Defense estimate.) Any
> information that the Department receives is simply passed on
> for evaluation to Defense.
>
> As you are aware, all the American military personnel missing
> in the course of the Korean hostilities have been declared
> legally dead, and there is no evidence suggesting that any of
> them now remain alive in Communist hands. At the same time we
> are continuing to press the Communists in every feasible way
> for an accounting as to the actual fate of these individuals.
>
> I have asked the Bureaus of European and Far Eastern Affairs,
> respectively, to keep this office fully informed with respect
> to any new information that may be received or any statements
> that may be made to interested Congressional committees with
> respect to Americans in Communist custody, whether in the
> Soviet Union or elsewhere, informing them, incidentally, of
> our special interest in this problem. Any such information
> received will be promptly transmitted to you. In the
> meantime, I believe that your letters to any individuals who
> write to you with respect to unaccounted for military
> personnel should remain unchanged.[18]

These efforts either did not reach or did not satisfy representatives of
the American Legion.

An American Legion Post in New York state wrote to Congressman
Steven B. Derounian:

> The American Legion of Nassau County believes the problem of
> the American servicemen held behind the Iron Curtain is a

---

[18]Wilcox to Lodge letter, January 21, 1957.

national disgrace and that the attempts to solve it to date
have been feeble, unavailing, and hardly in keeping with
American tradition. These veterans have been virtually
abandoned by the country for which they offered their lives.
It is the opinion of the American Legion of Nassau County that
responsibility for this situation should be fixed and once
fixed, remedied. It is apparent that when this problem is
presented, it invariably results in buck-passing procedure
that is second to none. The Legislative branch disavows
responsibility and presents it as an Executive problem. This
Executive, by some mysterious reasoning, presents the matter
as a United Nations question. It gets no further.[19]

The DoS response was consistent with its efforts. Congressman Derounian
was told:

Since the end of the Korean conflict, numerous rumors have
persisted alleging that American servicemen are being held as
prisoners of war in Communist China. However, the Communists
do not admit holding any prisoners of war taken in the Korean
hostilities. In fact they have asserted, both in talks with
United States Ambassador Johnson at Geneva and in the Military
Armistice Commission at Panmunjom that they hold no prisoners
of war.

However, there are American military personnel and a large
number of individuals from the forces contributed to the
United Nations Command by other countries and from the
Republic of Korea for whom the Communists have never
satisfactorily accounted. The United States Government and
the United Nations have made and will continue to make every
effort to secure an accounting from the Communists for these
individuals, of whom there is reason to believe the Communists
should have some knowledge. The Department of Defense, which
has primary responsibility for the United States personnel,
makes a continuing examination of all reports and evidence
available to the United States Government on them. Under the
provisions of Public Law 490 (Missing Persons Act) the
Department of Defense has made findings that these men are
presumed dead. The Department of State knows of no facts
controverting these findings.

Your constituents state that the responsibility for these
servicemen has been presented as a United Nations matter.
Since the action in Korea was undertaken on the recommendation
of the United Nations, that organization has expressed its
concern and demanded that the Communists fulfill the
obligation they undertook at the time of the Korean Armistice

---

[19]Letter from Congressman Steven B. Derounian to Assistant
Secretary of State Robert C. Hill, April 22, 1957, 611.61241/4-2257.

Agreement to furnish whatever information they could about our missing men.

You may assure your constituents the United States Government will continue to press most vigorously in Panmunjom and Geneva, and through other channels, for a satisfactory accounting for missing personnel. Every report of detention of American personnel in Communist areas is carefully investigated and every practical action taken to bring about the release of Americans who may be held by the Communists.[20]

An almost identical letter was sent by Assistant Secretary Hill to Senator Henry M. Jackson on April 23.[21]

The article "Yanks Held in Slavery," which appeared in the *New York Journal American*[22] in spring 1958, alleged that "American soldiers who survived the Korean campaigns as war captives" were being held in China and "another class of hapless Americans who, if still living, are detained in the slave-labor camps of the Soviet Union." The article focused on statements by released prisoner John Noble such as "Many other Americans are still in the Soviet, working as slave laborers." "The author encountered few of them personally," the article states, "but that is hardly significant." Noble was quoted as saying, "Prisoners being funneled into Vorkuta . . . said there were many Americans, including veterans of the Korean War, both GIs and officers, and South Korean soldiers, working as slave laborers in their camps. From what I learned, they were PWs captured by the Communist Chinese and North Koreans who were shipped to the Soviet for safe keeping."

These assertions prompted inquiries about Americans in Soviet prisons to be sent to various Members of Congress. Congressman Clement Zablocki, who asked the DoS for comments on the assertions made by John Noble,[23] received a reply coordinated with the Department of Defense

---

[20]Letter from Assistant Secretary Robert C. Hill to Congressman Steven B. Derounian, May 3, 1957, 611.61241/4-2257.

[21]Letter from Assistant Secretary Robert C. Hill to Senator Henry M. Jackson, April 23, 1957, 611.61241/4-2357.

[22]E. F. Thompkins, "Yanks Held in Slavery," *New York Journal American*, March 11, 1958.

[23]Letter from Congressman Clement J. Zablocki to William B. Macomber, Jr., Assistant Secretary of State, March 25, 1958, 611.251/3-2558.

"through Mr. Kelleher of Office of Special Operations." Zablocki was informed "with regard to American servicemen missing and unaccounted for after the Korean War and reported to be held in Soviet slave labor camps, Mr. Noble stated that his information about these men was based solely and entirely on brief conversations he had had with western European prisoners transferred from other camps in Siberia. He was able to furnish only general information as to the time or place that American servicemen were reported seen by those other prisoners. *The Departments of State and Defense after exhaustive efforts in analyzing the information Mr. Noble contributed have not been able to identify any American servicemen reported to be so held.*"[24]

> After his release and return to the United States, Mr. John Noble was questioned by the Department of State regarding his experience in slave labor camps of the Soviet Union. In regard to the American servicemen missing and unaccounted for as a result of the Korean hostilities, Mr. Noble stated under oath that in his ten years of imprisonment he had seen only three Americans, none of whom was a prisoner of war from Korea. He further stated that his information was based solely on brief conversations with European prisoners transferred from other camps. And he was able to furnish only general information as to the time and place concerning servicemen reported seen. After exhaustive efforts in analyzing the information passed on by Mr. Noble, the Departments of State and Defense have so far been unable to identify any American servicemen allegedly so held.[25]

On March 13, 1958, Assistant Secretary of State for Congressional Relations William B. Macomber, Jr., wrote to Congressman Edmund P. Radwan in response to the latter's inquiry on behalf of a constituent "regarding American servicemen who are being held as prisoners in Siberia."[26] Macomber cited testimony by Ambassador Johnson and enclosed

---

[24]Letter from Assistant Secretary William B. Macomber, Jr., to Congressman Clement J. Zablocki, April 18, 1958. Emphasis added.

[25]Letter from Stephen S. Jackson, Deputy Assistant Secretary of State, to Congressman Clement J. Zablocki, April 9, 1958, attached to memo from Mr. Ayleward, Office of Chinese Affairs, Department of State, to Col. John F. P. Hill, USA, Office of Personnel Policy, April 10, 1958.

[26]Letter from Congressman Edmund P. Radwan to Assistant Secretary William B. Macomber, Jr., February 14, 1958, 611.61241/2-1458, and letter from Assistant Secretary of State William B. Macomber to Congressman Edmund P. Radwan, March 13 1958, 611.61241/2-1458.

a background statement entitled, "The Detention of Americans in Certain Eastern European Countries Under Soviet Domination" which was intended to present an "understanding of the problems relating to persons having claim to American citizenship who are presently residing in the Soviet Union or its satellites."

On April 28 a similar inquiry was sent to Assistant Secretary Macomber by Senator Richard L. Neuberger. The Senator asked, on behalf of a constituent, whether "citizens of the United States are being held as prisoners and slaves in the Soviet Union at this time."[27] The Department responded with a letter similar in content to the one sent to Congressman Zablocki.[28] On June 2 the DoS received a letter from Senator Charles E. Potter who quoted a constituent's request for information. The constituent wrote that John Noble knew of "3,000 American nationals who are still in slave camps behind the Iron Curtain. He met many of them personally and he also has seen the list of names our State Department has of these people. We would appreciate your doing what you can to have these horrifying facts investigated."[29] Macomber acknowledged the Senator's letter by phone on June 5th then replied by letter on June 6th. The letter repeated the information forwarded on this subject to Congressman Zablocki and Senator Neuberger.[30] Another inquiry on this subject was made by Congressman George Mahon on July 23.[31] He received a similar reply from the Department.[32]

_____

[27]Letter from Senator Richard L. Neuberger to William B. Macomber, April 28, 1958, 611.61251/4-2858.

[28]Letter from William B. Macomber to Senator Richard L. Neuberger, May 8, 1958, 611.61251/4-2858.

[29]Letter from Senator Charles E. Potter to William B. Macomber, Assistant Secretary of State for Congressional Relations, May 28, 1958, 611.61241/5-2858.

[30]Letter from William B. Macomber, Jr., to Senator Charles E. Potter, June 6, 1958 611.61241/5-2858.

[31]Letter from Congressman George Mahon to William B. Macomber, July 23, 1958, 611.61241/7-2358.

[32]Letter from William B. Macomber to Congressman George Mahon, July 30, 1958, 611.61241/7-2358.

Senator Charles E. Potter, who inquired about Noble's charges on August 7,[33] received a reply from the DoS on August 22.[34] One day later the DoS sent a letter on the same subject to Congressman Charles E. Brownson.[35] A similar letter from the DoS went to Senator Wayne Morse[36] on this subject and one was sent to Senator Lyndon Johnson who had inquired on behalf of a constituent whether "it is true that three thousand Americans are imprisoned in the Soviet Union."[37]

Former Assistant Secretary of State Thruston B. Morton, now a United States Senator from South Carolina, asked his successor to comment on a request by a constituent for information concerning "American citizens allegedly imprisoned in Soviet slave labor camps." In addition to the standard body of information included in DoS replies to such inquiries, Senator Morton was informed:

> During the dictatorship of Stalin, and during the earlier days when the Communists were consolidating their power in the Soviet Union, there were great numbers of prisoners whose ranks were swollen by political offenders and those apprehended upon suspicion of a lack of sympathy with the regime. Soviet authorities disposed of such "undesirable" persons by forcing them to work on projects that served the economic program of the State. Reliable estimates of the total forced labor population during the period of its greatest growth in the nineteen-forties varied from 3.5 to 8 million, and other estimates ran higher. . . . Soviet authorities have not publicly admitted that free labor is more profitable than forced labor. . . . As a result, . . . forced labor now constitutes a very small portion of the total Soviet labor force.[38]

---

[33]Letter from Senator Charles E. Potter to William B. Macomber, August 7, 1958, 611.61241/8-758.

[34]Letter from William B. Macomber to Senator Charles E. Potter, August 22, 1958, 611.61241/8-758.

[35]Letter from John S. Hoghland 2nd, Acting Assistant Secretary for Congressional Relations, to Congressman Charles B. Brownson, August 23, 1958, 611.61241/8-2358.

[36]Letter from Acting Assistant Secretary for Congressional Relations Florence Kirlin to Senator Wayne Morse, October 30, 1959, 611.61241/10-1559.

[37]Letter from Assistant Secretary William B. Macomber to Senator Lyndon B. Johnson, July 27, 1959, 611.61251/7-1059.

[38]Letter from Acting Assistant Secretary for Congressional Relations Florence Kirlin to Senator Thruston B. Morton, October 27, 1959, 611.61241/10-1959.

On July 9, 1959, the DoS noted in a letter to Senator Hubert Humphrey that "representations by the American Embassy at Moscow in recent years have brought about the release from Soviet custody of eight American citizens, six of whom were American soldiers absent without leave from their stations in Europe. In addition, the release has been obtained through negotiations on a local level between United States and Soviet military officials of a number of United States soldiers who were arrested in the Soviet Zone of Germany while absent without leave." John Noble, who was released after a decade in Soviet prisons, "stated under oath that in his ten years' imprisonment he had actually seen three Americans. Of these three, two have since been released and the third, upon investigation, was found to be a national of a Scandinavian country. The Department of State and other agencies of the Government, after exhaustive efforts in analyzing other information that Mr. Noble contributed, have not been able to identify any further Americans."[39]

The Department of State prepared an analysis of John Noble's book, *I Was A Slave In Russia* dated July 1, 1959. In the view of one officer at the DoS, "the book contains no indictment of our Government, our efforts to secure the release of Americans possibly imprisoned in the Soviet Union, or our policy toward the U.S.S.R. In fact some of the statements could be considered rather favorable to our Government and this Department."[40] Relatives of unaccounted for servicemen had their hopes raised anytime an American was allegedly seen in a Soviet camp or when an American was released. Too often the response from the State Department revealed, after investigation, that "we are unable to give you good news."[41]

Senator Frank J. Lausche asked the DoS for "a list of the American citizens, civilian as well as military, jailed or held by Russia and its satellites" on January 5, 1959. A follow up telephone call clarified that Senator Lausche was interested in the satellite countries of

---

[39]Letter from Assistant Secretary William B. Macomber, Jr., to Senator Hubert H. Humphrey, July 9, 1959, 611.61251/6-1359.

[40]Memorandum from SEV: D. H. Meyers to SOV: Miss James, July 1, 1959, 611.61251/7-159.

[41]Letter from Thruston B. Morton, Assistant Secretary of State, to Congressman Overton Brooks, February 15, 1956, 611.61241/2-1556.

Eastern Europe, not Communist China.[42] Senator Lausche was informed by
letter one week later that "at the present time, as far as the
Department is aware, there are no cases of American citizens imprisoned
in Albania, Bulgaria, Hungary, Poland, or Rumania."[43] The following
four Americans were listed as being imprisoned in Czechoslovakia:

> **Jaromir Zastara.** Sentenced in 1949 to 18 years imprisonment
> by the Czechoslovak Government on charges of treason,
> espionage and other anti-State charges. Mr. Zastara has
> American citizenship but never resided in the United States.

> Private First Class **Andrew A. Ballrichard.** On July 1, 1958,
> while apparently emotionally disturbed, Private Ballrichard
> crossed the Czechoslovak border. On August 15 he was
> sentenced to two years imprisonment for illegal border
> crossing.

> Private **Cole Youngert** and Specialist **John R. Kennedy.** These
> American citizens were arrested in Czechoslovakia for
> unauthorized border crossing. On October 28 the Embassy was
> informed that Kennedy had been sentenced to 14 months and
> Youngert to 10 months imprisonment.

The DoS noted that the American Embassy at Prague was permitted to visit
these Americans. Efforts were being made as well to obtain their
release.

The Department reported that it was "pressing the cases of two
American citizens who were held under confinement in the Soviet Union."

> One of these prisoners is an American citizen of dual national
> status who in 1933 at the age of eleven was taken to the
> Soviet Union by her parents. Holding herself to be an
> American citizen, she failed to pay Soviet income tax. She
> was arrested in 1950 for non-payment of Soviet income taxes.
> At a trial attended by a representative of the American
> Embassy at Moscow she was sentenced to two years imprisonment.
> Despite the apparent expiration of her sentence, she has not
> been released. The Department has sent a series of notes in
> her behalf seeking to obtain her release from imprisonment and
> repatriation to the United States.

---

[42]Letter from Stanley M. Andrews, Staff Member, Office of Senator
Frank J. Lausche, to William B. Macomber, Assistant Secretary for
Congressional Relations, January 5, 1959, 611.61251/1-559.

[43]Letter from William B. Macomber, Jr., to Senator Frank J.
Lausche, January 13, 1959, 611.61251/1-559.

The other American citizen imprisoned in the Soviet Union
entered that country in 1940 and soon thereafter was arrested.
His imprisonment was made known to the United States
Government in 1955 by foreign repatriated prisoners-of-war.
In reply to a series of strong representations in his behalf,
the Soviet Government informed us that he was arrested for
violation of Soviet law and for bearing the documents of a
non-existent Soviet citizen. The Department will continue its
efforts in his behalf.[44]

The DoS noted that no information had been released to the general
public on these cases so as to avoid publicity that might complicate
progress toward the release of these two Americans. In addition, four
persons, one Army officer and three enlisted men, were listed as being
detained in the Soviet Zone of Germany. "The circumstances under which
these men came into Soviet or East German custody is not clear; nor is
it clear on what grounds they are being held." There were also several
cases in which members of the American forces in Germany went AWOL and
ended up, voluntarily or involuntarily, in the Soviet Zone. "Judging by
experience in other cases," the DoS noted, "these persons would probably
be permitted to return to West Berlin and American control if they
wished to do so."[45]

From: Amemb Brussels # 23[?] To: DoS (Confidential)
September 8, 1960

Subject: Korean War Prisoners Reported in Soviet Union

On Labor Day, September 5, the Embassy Duty Officer, James W.
White, met with a "walk-in" Polish refugee. [Deleted] said
that he was released on May 1, 1960, after seven and one-half
years detention, from Soviet prison Camp No. 307 near Bulon,
supposedly about [?] kilometers from [?]kutsk. He stated that
he later escaped from Poland via East and West Germany and
entered Belgium on August 9, 1960. He is now a political
refugee in Belgium and he is attempting to emigrate to
Australia.

[Deleted] said that he became acquainted in the Soviet camp
with two American Army prisoners who were captured in Korea in
1951: [Deleted] an infantry Lieutenant, and [Deleted], a
commando or paratrooper Sergeant. They had asked him to
report their presence to the American Embassy in Warsaw, but

---

[44]Macomber to Lausche, January 13, 1959.
[45]Macomber to Lausche, January 13, 1959.

[Deleted] indicated he was afraid to do so. Consequently, he
was taking this opportunity to report the facts to the
American authorities. However, he asked that his name be kept
confidential as its revelation might jeopardize the safety of
his relatives in Poland.

A full memorandum of conversation is enclosed. The Office of
the Army Attaché is separately reporting on this matter
through military channels, which is also attempting to check
further on [Deleted] story and *bona fides*.[46]

The willingness of the U.S. government to pursue information concerning

Americans held illegally in the Soviet Union was exploited by

unscrupulous people. In June 1951 the Defense Department warned

families of American POWs held in Korea against a "heartless extortion

racket" that was being operated by people who claimed to have

information concerning POWs.[47] The families were asked to contact the

Federal Bureau of Investigation in the event they were approached by

anyone fitting this profile. At the time of this warning, when over

10,211 men were listed as missing, 153 as POW in Korea, the Defense

Department noted that efforts were being made to verify any information

concerning the status of missing servicemen. The job was made difficult

because of the refusal of the Communists to release names of prisoners.

The Communists also engaged in deliberate deception. In August 1950,

for example, a photograph released by the Communists was said to depict

American POWs in Korea. In reality the photograph, taken in France in

1944, showed Europeans freed from a German labor camp.[48] One place

where false POW information was generated in the 1950s was Macao. The

U.S. government's willingness to investigate leads created opportunities

for the unscrupulous.

---

[46]611.61241/9-860.

[47]"U.S. Seeks Identities of G.I.'s Held Captive," *New York Times*,
June 20, 1951.

[48]"'U.S. Prisoner' Photo Held Faked by Reds," *New York Times*,
August 8, 1950.

SENATOR SMITH AND TFR EVIDENCE

Army Task Force/Russia (TFR) and Senator Bob Smith[49] compiled additional reports from U.S. sources consistent with the transfer of Americans from North Korea to the territory of the USSR during the Korean War. The following is a summary of this material, identified by source as Army Task Force Russia (TFR) or Senator Bob Smith (SBS). These reports complement those discussed in previous sections of this report.

January, 1952: Army Captain Mel Gile of the Far East Command Liaison Group reports that one of his agents had found that 63 U.S. POWs were being shipped by truck and rail from Pyongyang, North Korea, to Chita in the Soviet Union. Gile states the U.S. command cancelled air strikes on the railway he reported would be carrying the POWs. (SBS citing "1990 Wash. Times and USA Today interviews with Gile.")

January 2, 1952: U.S. Army Intelligence receives information that more than 500 U.N. prisoners were in a camp in Tun Kuan Ying, ten miles east of Mukden, Manchuria "to be given short-term training pending transfer to the Soviet Union on order of central authorities." (SBS with no reference to the source of the document.)

September 2, 1952: CIA report quotes multiple Soviet sources as providing extensive information on transport of Korean War POWs of many nationalities, including Americans, to the USSR. Highlights: In December 1951, it was known that transit camps for prisoners of war captured by the Communists in Korea had been established in Komsomolsk on the River Amur, Magadan, Chita, and Irkutsk. Through these camps passed not only Korean POWs, but also American POWs. From December 1951 to the end of April 1952 several railway transports of American and European (probably British) POWs were seen passing at intervals of ten to 20 days through the Komi-Permyak National District in Northwest Siberia. These transports were directed to Molotov, Gubakha (northwest of Molotov), Kudymkar, and Chermoz on the Kam River north of Molotov. The prisoners were clad in cotton-padded, gray tunics and pants and wore

---

[49]"Chronology of Policy and Intelligence Matters Concerning Unaccounted For U.S. Military Personnel At The End Of The Korean Conflict And During The Cold War," Press release, November 10, 1992.

civilian caps, so called "Sibirki." They had no military insignia. They spoke among themselves in English and they know no other language, except a few words of Russian. . . . According to information from April 1951, a certain number of American POW officers, among who was a group referred to as the "American General Staff," were kept at that time in the command of the Military District of Molotov. Some of the POWs were accommodated in the building of the MVD in Molotov, having been subjected most probably to interrogations. In the town of Gubakha and in the industrial regions of Kudymkar and Chermoz, there were three isolated camps and one interrogation prison for American POWs from Korea, according to information dated February to April 1952. Prisoners kept in the three labor camps were employed in the construction of a new railway line. In one of these camps, called Gaysk, about 200 Americans were kept. There were employed in workshops assembling rails and doing various technical jobs. In some camps near the Gubakha railway, called "Zaprotchdelanki," about 150 Americans were kept, probably soldiers and NCS. Every few days, one to three POWs were taken by officers of the MVD for transportation to Gubakha or Molotov, who never returned to their camps. (TFR, no citation.)

February 24, 1953: An Army Combined Command for Reconnaissance Activities Korea memorandum states: The following information was received from Ministry of Foreign Affairs, Republic of Korea Government. Report originally came from Nationalist Chinese Embassy--According to reliable information, the Communist Chinese Forces have transferred UN POWs to Russia in violation of the Geneva Conference. These POWs will be specially trained at Moscow for espionage work. POWs transferred to Moscow are grouped as follows: British 5, Americans 10, Canadians 3, and 50 more from various countries. Russia has established a Higher Informant Training Team at Uran, Hodasong (phonetic) in Siberia in October 1952. 500 persons are receiving training, one third of them women. Japanese constitute the largest group and the others are Korean, Filipinos, Burmese and American. The date of this information is given as October - 22 December 1952. Comments in this report by the U.S. Army Combined Command for Reconnaissance Activities, Korea state: This office has received sporadic reports of POWs being moved to the USSR since the very inception of the hostilities in Korea. These reports came in great volume through the earlier months of the war, and then tapered off to a standstill in early 1951, being revived by a report from January of this year (1953). It is definitely possible that such action is being taken as evidenced by past experience with Soviet authorities. All previous reports state POWs who are moved to the USSR are technical specialists who are employed in mines, factories, etc. This is the first report that they are being used as espionage agents that is carried by this office. (SBS citing U.S. Army Combined Command Report, February 24, 1953.)

August 10, 1953: Report from the Headquarters, Combined Command for Reconnaissance Acvitity in Korea, 8242nd Army United, Subject: UN PW Camps in Manchuria and China. The report states: A compilation of reports indicates that during the past two years several POW have been transferred from PW camps in North Korea to points in Manchuria, China and Siberia. (TFR, no citation.)

December 31, 1953: CIA report states that Japanese prisoners repatriated from Communist China reported that, as of 1951, the USSR had an interrogation center for U.S. Korean War POWs, mostly aviators, located in the Chang-pai Shan area on the upper Yalu River. When the North Korean forces were pushed north in Korea, this center was moved to An-tu. The Japanese reported that the natives stated that the POWs passed through Mutanchiang, were brought down the Sungari river by boat and, after interrogation, were taken to the USSR. (TFR, no citation.)

January 27, 1954: U.S. Air Force Report No. 1835. A Japanese repatriate from POW Camp #12 at Khabarovsk from 1950-53 reports the following to the U.S. representatives in Tokyo. He states that during the period April-May 1953, he "heard from Soviet guards, prisoners and laborers that the crew of a military plane shot down by Soviets was in Khabarovsk prison." (TFR, no citation.)

March 16, 1954: The Air Force Liaison Office in Hong Kong sent a report to G2, USAF, in Washington. The report is filed by Colonel Delk Simpson, the Assistant Air Liaison officer who had arrived in Hong Kong for duty on November 3, 1953. The report reads, in pertinent part: This office has interviewed refugee source who states that he observed hundreds of prisoners of war in American uniforms being sent into Siberia in late 1951 and 1952. Observations were made at Manchouli on USSR-Manchurian border. Source observed POWs on railway station platform loading into trains for movement into Siberia. In railway restaurant source closely observed three POWs who were under guard and were conversing in English. POWs wore sleeve insignia which indicated POWs were Air Force noncommissioned officers. Source states that there were a great number of Negroes among POW shipments and also states that at no time later were any POWs observed returning from Siberia. Source does not wish to be identified for fear of reprisals agains friends in Manchuria, however is willing to cooperate in answering further questions and will be available in Hong Kong for questions for the next few days. (SBS, no source indicated.) This information was repeated from Hong Kong on March 23, 1954. The source is reported to be "of unknown reliability."

April 19, 1954: Secretary of State John Foster Dulles sends a cable to the American Embassy Moscow instructing that the Soviets be given an Aide Mémoire from the United States on U.S. POWs having been transported into the Soviet Union. Dulles tells the U.S. Embassy that the Soviets should be told "we have reliable accounts of transfers of POWs at Manchouli." Dulles also refers to a recent report from Hong Kong on POW transfers which "corroborates previous indications that UNC POWs might have been shipped to Siberia during Korean hostilities." (SBS citing declassified cable, April 19, 1954.)

May 5, 1954: The Secretary of State instructs the American Embassy Moscow to deliver the following note: The United States Government has recently received reports which support earlier indications that American prisoners of war who had seen action in Korea have been transported to the Union of Soviet Socialist Republics and that they are now in Soviet custody. The United States desires to receive urgently all information available to the Soviet Government concerning these American personnel and to arrange for their repatriation at the earliest possible time. (SBS citing declassified cable.)

January 1955: The State Department reports information from a German POW who had been imprisoned in the Soviet Union that 9 American fliers from Korea were at Kirov, in the Soviet Union. (SBS citing declassified State Department Berlin Communication 420 12, January 1955, No. 4-32.)

October 1957: The American Consulate in Strasbourg, France, receives information from a Polish National who had been held as a prisoner in the Russian concentration camp of Bulun, in the province of Yakutak. The source reports having been held with three American soldiers who had been captured during the Korean War. (SBS, citing State Department declassified cable, October 21, 1957.)

September 8, 1961: Foreign Service Dispatch #23, U.S. Embassy Brussels, Belgium. A Polish refugee who had served seven and one half years in the GULAG near Bulun in the vicinity of Yakutsk informed Embassy personnel that he had met in the camp two U.S. Army prisoners captured in Korea, one an infantry lieutenant and the other a commando or paratrooper sergeant. (TFR, no citation.)

February 5, 1962: A *Miami News* article refers to POW information from a Russian MVD intelligence officer who defected to the West in Tokyo in 1954. The agent is reported to have stated that officials in the Soviet Embassy in Tokyo had reported to him that U.S. POWs from Korea had been taken to Russia. (SBS with no citation.)

1975: A Romanian POW since 1945, George Risiou, escapes from the Soviet Union with five others. He reports 900 American POWs still held in a secret KGB prison camp. He states that Soviet authorities had assigned Russian names to American, English, French and other POWs there for deniability. (SBS citing John Brown, Sunday *Oregonian*, December 2, 1990.)

July 8, 1990: American Red Cross spokeswoman Donna Schneider in Seattle, Washington, states that her agency knows of 12 reported sightings of American POWs in Siberia, some as recently as the 1970s. In the same article, former director of the Foreign News Service, Zygmunt Nagorski, Jr., states that during the 1950s his foreign reporters had an extensive "source network" of truck drivers and other working-class Soviets employed at or near prisons in Molotov, Khabarovsk, Chita, Omsk, Chermoz, and elsewhere. Nagorski claims his sources informed him that there were still up to 1,000 American POWs in

Siberia from the Korean War when he last had contact with them in the late 1950s. (SBS citing the *Los Angeles Times*, July 8, 1990.)

September 14, 1990: Former DIA Director Lt. General Daniel Graham states on CBN, "They [the Soviets] would come with a list of specialties and find out whether such specialties existed among the UN prisoners in the camps in North Korea and China . . . and then they would ship them off." (SBS, no citation.)

May 7, 1991: An article in *Na Strazhe* by Major Valerii Amirov quotes former Red Army colonel Grigorii Dzhagarov as stating that he was a part of a secret program in Korea, for which he was decorated, tasked with hunting for the wreckage of U.S. aircraft and for downed pilots. The article also outlines how the Soviets took Americans from Korea for military knowledge. Major Amirov has also told one private investigator that he has located witnesses who were at the Soviet-China border "secret window" through which captured Americans in Korea crossed into Soviet control. Amirov also stated that he has located at least one witness who was on the secret train that transported captured U.S. Korean War POWs to secret interrogation sites in the USSR. (TFR, no citation.)

December 1991: Major Valerii Amirov, a military journalist from Sverdlovsk, testified before the Russian Parliament subcommittee on POW/MIAs to the effect that he had interviewed a former KGB official in Kazakhstan who related that he had been involved in the transportation of U.S. Korean War POWs to Kazakhstan. Major Amirov subsequently was informed by his command that they were highly displeased with his interest in the POW/MIA issue and his action in testifying before Parliament. (TFR, no citation.)

January 6, 1992: The Chairman and Vice-Chairman of the Select Committee on POW/MIA Affairs both receive correspondence from retired Colonel Philip Corso, former National Security Staff Assistant to President Dwight Eisenhower. Corso states, "When I was a member of the National Security Council on the White House Staff under President Eisenhower (1953-57), I interrogated Yuri Alexandrovitch Rastvorov, a Russian KGB officer who defected to the U.S. from the USSR embassy in Japan in January, 1954. . . . Rastvorov revealed that Russian diplomats coming to Japan had seen U.S. POWs in the USSR. Rastvorov personally had seen a trainload of U.S. POWs heading into Siberia after changing trains at the Manchurian-Russian border . . . I submitted my report. . . . In a few days, President Eisenhower decided not to make this information public because he was concerned about adverse effects on the families of the missing POWs." (SBS, no citation for this quotation.)

August 4, 1992: A U.S. representative to the Joint Commission on POW/MIAs interviews Vladimir Y. Voronin, a former Russian prisoner at Khabarovsk, Siberia, who reports having observed three Americans who arrived at his camp in October 1952, and left three months later. Voronin thinks they may have been associated with the Vlasov contingent. Joint Commission investigators are following up on leads provided during this interview. (SBS, no citation.) (TFR, no citation.)

August 19, 1992: Select Committee investigator in Moscow interviews Russian Colonel (retired) Gavriil Ivanovich Korotkov, a Far East expert with the Scientific Research Institute, formerly part of the Soviet Ministry of Defense. Colonel Korotkov reports he served from July 1950 to mid-1954 as part of a General Staff analytical group reporting to the Commander in Chief of the Soviet Far East Military District on developments from the ongoing war in Korea. Korotkov outlines in great detail the fact the Soviets interrogated American POWs in Korea. Korotkov states that on several occasions he had visited the Soviet Naval Base at Pos'Yet, located in the USSR/China/North Korea Tri-Border Region, which served as a transit point for the movement of American servicemen north to Khabarovsk, Siberia. Although there was an airfield nearby, he believes that the bulk of the Americans transported from Pos'Yet to Khabarovsk were transported by rail, but most likely at least some of the American POWs were moved from North Korea or China by air. Although Korotkov did not know the exact number, he states that the number of American Korean War POWs processed through Khabarovsk was in the hundreds. Korotkov states that operational directives during the Korean Conflict said that Americans should be captured alive, not killed. Korotkov further states that the North Koreans were quite willing to allow the Russians direct access and eventual control over

American POWs. Finally, Korotkov states that he personally interrogated two American POWs. He could not remember the names of any of the American POWs who were processed through Khabarovsk, except for a Lt. Colonel Black. Korotkov is reported by Select Committee investigator to be "highly credible and forthcoming." (SBS, no citation.)

September 1, 1992: Russian newspaper interview with retired Soviet Air Force officer Vladimir Roshine, who was posted to North Korea during the war. Roshine was assigned the mission of acquiring an intact American aircraft for shipment to the USSR for exploitation. In the interview, Roshine describes hard copy documents that he read that described the capture of an American for shipment to the USSR. (TFR, no citation.)

October 27, 1992: U.S. investigators on the U.S.-Russian Joint Commission interview a Russian citizen, Nikolay D. Kazersky, who served four and a half years in prison in Zimka camp near Knyazhpogost, Russia. He reports that in the fall of 1952 or the spring of 1953, he had an encounter with an American pilot from California who had been shot down in North Korea and forced to land in Soviet territory near Vladivostock. The pilot said he had a plane of three, and that his radioman had been in Zimka as well. The pilot did not know what happened to the third member. The pilot remained at Zimka for three to six months, and was then transferred to an unknown location. (SBS, no citation.)[50]

November 11, 1992: Lt. Colonel Philip Corso stated that he had received firm evidence that could support the assertion that two trainloads of U.S. POWs, 450 per train (900 total), had been transported to the Soviet Union. He had ample evidence on a third train. The esimate of 900 was firm with the number for the third train bringing the total as high as 1,200. (TFR, no citation.)

---

[50]Kazersky was identified by RAND researchers who passed this information along to TFR through Yuri Pankov's newsletter, *Letter from Russia*.

Appendix 9

ADDITIONAL EVIDENCE CONCERNING SIGHTINGS OF AMERICAN POW/MIAs IN THE
PEOPLE'S REPUBLIC OF CHINA

Found in: Chapter Six, Volume 1
Source of this information: Senator Bob Smith (R-NH) and Army Task
Force Russia (TFR).

In July 1973 Representative Richardson Preyer (D-NC) chaired
hearings on the theory and practice of communism. A former member of
the Chinese Communist Party, Wu Shu-jen, testified that in 1960 he had
seen "around 80 Westerners" working in a factory in Tsingtao, a city in
Shantung Province. Wu Shu-jen said that he was told the foreigners were
"former missionaries who served as foreign spies, and some are U.S. POWs
from the Korean War. They are those stubborn elements that refuse to
repent."[1]

Additional reports of Americans in the PRC have been collected by
Senator Bob Smith and released as *Chronology of Policy and Intelligence
Matters Concerning Unaccounted for U.S. Military Personnel at the End of
the Korean Conflict and During the Cold War.*[2] These reports follow.
The page numbers refer to the Senator's report.

March 12, 1951: French intelligence sources inform the U.S. Far
East Command that "according to report valued C-3 and dated December 9,
1950, 3,000 American POWs have been moved to the Korean border with
China by December 1950." The report adds that another 1,200 "lightly
wounded" American POWs had been placed at an Air Defense hospital in
An'Tung, Manchuria. (p. 2. Source: March 12, 1951, declassified State
Department cable, no citation.)

April 9, 1951: The Central Intelligence Agency reports that source
(still classified 11/10/92) has reported that "Officers captured in

---

[1]U.S. Congress, House, Committee on Internal Security, *Annual
Report for the Year 1973* (Washington, D.C.: Government Printing Office,
1974), pp. 88-89. Senator Smith's summary states that Wu "claims that a
factory official told him they were American POWs." *Chronology of
Policy and Intelligence Matters*, p. 39.

[2]Prepared by the Office of Senator Bob Smith, Vice-Chairman, Select
Committee on POW/MIA Affairs, November 10, 1992. Press release.

North Korea by the Chinese Communists are now interned in a former army prison in Mukden, Manchuria. Enlisted men are confined in concentration camps in T'unghua. The daily routine includes physical exercise, political training in Marxism and Leninism, and analysis of the Korean War by Communist political directors." The date of the information is early April 1951, according to CIA. CIA notes that another report, S0-54598, had also referred to U.S. POW camps in Mukden. (p. 2. Source: S0617354, Central Intelligence Agency, no citation.)

May 8, 1951: The CIA reports that, according to a source, 25 American prisoners of war from Korea arrived in Canton by rail from Hankow at 6:00 pm on April 11, 1951, and were being held by 50 armed police and some plainclothesmen at facilities at Tung Hua Road. (p. 2. Declassified report No. S063715, CIA, no citation.)

May 8, 1951: According to a September 6, 1951, CIA report, 30 American prisoners of war depart Mukden, Manchuria, for Hankow by rail. The prisoners are reported in good spirits and tidily dressed. (p. 2. CIA declassified report September 6, 1951, no citation.)

May 29, 1951: The CIA reports that, according to a source, 45 American prisoners of war arrived in Canton at 6:00 pm on April 23, 1951, on two special cars of the Canton-Hankow railroad, and were being held at facilities on Tung Hua Road. It is reported that on April 30, 1951, Chinese Communist authorities in Peiping ordered that American POWs held at Tung Hua be taken to Kwailan. It is further reported that at 3:00 am on May 2, the POWs were moved in two trucks, accompanied by four armored cars, to the Tasht'on Rail Station. (p. 3. Source: Declassified CIA report No. S065066, May 29, 1951, no citation.)

June 27, 1951: The CIA reports that, according to one source, "By April 15, 1951, approximately 500 American prisoners of war from Korea had arrived in Hankow, and on April 18th, some of them were paraded through the streets of Hankow under heavy guard. . . . In mid-April, 60 prisoners of war, most of whom were American, arrived in Canton via the Canton-Hankow railroad, and were being detained at facilities at Tung Hua Road in Canton. . . . In mid-June 1952, 52 American POWs from Korea were still incarcerated in the Baptist church on Tung Hua Road, Canton.

(p. 3.   Source: Declassified CIA Report No. S066740, June 27, 1951, no citation.)

August 11, 1951: The CIA reports information from a subsource that, according to a North Korean staff member of the State Security Bureau in Seoul on 12 February 1951, "all American prisoners of war were sent to camps in Mukden, Tunghua, and Antung Provinces of Manchuria, where they were put to hard labor in mines and factories." (p. 3. Source: Declassified CIA Report No. S065823, no citation.) In another CIA report, a source states that "on August 2, 52 American POWs from Korea, who had been held in the Baptist church on Tung Hua Road, Canton, left Canton by train for Peiping via Hankow under guard of a platoon of Chinese Communist soldiers." (p. 3.   Source: Declassified CIA Report No. S069870, no citation.)

August 22, 1951: The CIA reports that, according to a source, some 40 UN POWs in Canton, including British and American officers and enlisted men, have participated in "propaganda tours and street demonstrations" in Canton in early May 1951. (p. 3.   Source: Declassified CIA Report No. S070338, no citation.)

August 24, 1951: The CIA reports that, according to a source, "78 American prisoners of war are in a camp at No. 35, Lane 1136 Yuyen Road, Shangai. They have no freedom of movement and are not free to talk. They must attend meetings daily to study Communist doctrine. Camp officers are appointees of the East China Bureau and the East China Military Area, and four English speaking Soviets." Ten names of alleged U.S. servicemen, written in Chinese, are provided "from a scrap of paper picked up in the POW camp." (p. 4. Source: Declassified CIA Report No. S070512, no citation.)

September 6, 1951: 60 American prisoners of war are reported being held in Canton as of mid-July, according to a CIA source (Note: According to another source (August 11, 1951), 52 American POWs were moved from Canton on August 2, 1951, by rail to Peiping). (p. 4. Source: Declassified CIA Report, September 6, 1951, no citation.)

September 27, 1951: According to a CIA source, as of late August 1951, "Many American prisoners of war are being used in Peiping for propaganda purposes." (p. 4. No source or citation.)

September 28, 1951: The CIA reports information from a source that as of mid-September, 21 American prisoners of war are confined at Lo Chia Shan in Wuch'ang, Communist China, and that their political instruction is being carried out by a former Chinese student in America and a Soviet major. (p. 4. Source: Declassified CIA Report No. S072900, September 28, 1951, no citation.)

October 4, 1951: The CIA reports that, according to a source, the Chinese Communists held a meeting on August 1, 1951, to celebrate Army Day. "During the meeting, 5 American prisoners of war, captured in Korea, were escorted by Communist soldiers to the rostrum. Two of them addressed the gathering." (p. 4. Source: Declassified CIA Report No. S073337, October 4, 1951, no citation.)

October 23, 1951: 170 UN prisoners of war are reported by a CIA source to have arrived in Canton by train from Hankow on October 3, 1951. (p. 4. Source: Declassified CIA Report No. S074469, no date, no citation.)

October 25, 1951: A CIA source reports the existence of an American and British POW camp at Shamsen, Canton, and lists some of the names, in Chinese, of U.S. 8th Army personnel. The names are not further evaluated by CIA. (p. 4. Source: Declassified CIA Report No. S074807, October 25, 1951, no citation.)

October 27, 1951: A CIA source reports that 125 American prisoners of war were observed walking to Antung, China, on the night of March 25, 1951. (p. 4. Source: Declassified CIA report, no date, no citation.)

January 4, 1952: A CIA source reports that in mid-November 1951, "the UN prisoners of war who arrived in Canton on October 3 were removed and sent elsewhere. Complete secrecy was maintained during the move from Shamsen, Canton to a destination unknown." (p. 6. Source: Declassified CIA Report No. 79124, no date, no citation.)

January 5, 1952: A CIA source reports that 13 American and 8 British prisoners of war were transferred by rail from Canton to Hankow. CIA also reports they have another report of U.S. POWs in the Canton area "performing hard labor on airfields." (p. 6. Source: Declassified CIA Report, January 5, 1952, no citation.)

February 6, 1952: A CIA source reports that around December 27, 1951, "the Chinese Communists moved 300 U.S. POWs . . . into a concentration camp near Tat'ung. The prisoners are under the instruction of Europeans." CIA reports that the report is possibly a fabrication as the information appears doubtful. (p. 6. Source: Declassified CIA Report, February 6, 1952, no citation.)

February 14, 1952: A CIA source reports that about the first week of January, the Chinese Communists were parading U.S. captives (prisoners of war) in Paoshan, Yunnan Province, for propaganda purposes. The source reports the Communists point out the U.S. soldiers to the spectators, saying "these are the people we've been fighting--and have conquered." (p. 6. Source: Declassified CIA Report, February 14, 1951, no citation.)

April 15, 1952: The CIA reports that, according to one source, "in November 1951, about 50 American prisoners of war were brought under guard from Shanghai to Hangchow, and were taken to Maochiafou and placed in the detention center there." The report further states that as of February 10, 1952, 15 of them were taken elsewhere, leaving only 35. Maochiafou is reported as "probably near Hangchow." (pp. 7-8. Source: Declassified CIA Report, April 15, 1952, no citation.)

May 2, 1952: The CIA reports that, according to a source, "in April 1952 there were 35 American prisoners of war at the Maochiafou Camp. The following is a partial list of the Americans." No evaluation of the names is done by CIA. (p. 8. Source: Declassified CIA Report, May 2, 1952, no citation.)

July 17, 1952: The CIA, in a report from a still classified source, states: "On 6 January 1952, four hundred United States prisoners, including three hundred Negroes, were being detained . . . in Mukden, Manchuria. . . . All prisoners held there, with the exception of three second lieutenants, were enlisted personnel. . . . The prisoners, dressed in Communist Chinese Army uniforms, were not required to work. . . . Two hours of indoctrination were conducted daily by staff members of the Northeast Army Command. Prisoners were permitted to play basketball in the courtyard." (p. 8. Source: CIA Report No. S091634, July 17, 1952, no citation.)

July 15, 1953: The CIA reports information from a source that "in late May 1953, approximately 1,500 UN prisoners of war were confined in a camp at Tungchutin, Tientain, in Communist China. The majority of these prisoners of war were American Marine officers and men who were sent to this camp after recovery from wounds."[3] CIA comments that "a POW camp once tentatively accepted in Tientain, was dropped from available listings in January 1953 because of lack of recent reports concerning it." (p. 10. Source: Declassified CIA Report, July 15, 1953, no citation.)

Finally, in December 1992 Senator Bob Smith reported following a visit to Pyongyang that North Korean officials confirmed that U.S. POWs had been transferred to the PRC during the Korean War and never returned. Smith concluded the United States "must press Chinese officials" for POW data. "This is where the answers lie," he said. Smith said the North Koreans would be more forthcoming concerning POWs and remains in the future.[4] In February 1993, UNCMAC officials noted that in subsequent talks with North Korean officials, the North Koreans disavowed Smith's statements. One North Korean was quoted as saying, "Smith is two-faced. We never told him that."[5]

---

[3]DoD casualty data as of December 31, 1953, indicate 306 Marine MIAs "died or presumed dead" and 31 unrepatriated POWs. Even if every man in this category actually lived in captivity as alleged, the total (337) is far below the majority (751) alleged in this report.

[4]Carleton R. Bryant, "N. Korea: POWs sent to China," *Washington Times*, December 23, 1992. "Reports of unreturned U.S. Korean War POWs said to be confirmed," *Military News Wire Service*, December 23, 1992.

[5]Interview with UNCMAC officials, Seoul, South Korea, February 16, 1993.

Appendix 10

STATEMENT BY THE HON. STEPHEN S. JACKSON, DEPUTY ASSISTANT SECRETARY OF DEFENSE (MANPOWER, PERSONNEL, AND RESERVE)

Found in: Chapter Seven, Volume 1
Source of this information: U.S. Congress, House Subcommittee on the Far East and the Pacific, *Return of American Prisoners of War Who Have Not Been Accounted for by the Communists* (Washington, D.C.: U.S. Government Printing Office, 1957), pp. 2-5.

Shortly after the official exchange of POWs had been completed in September 1953, officials of the UN Command handed the Communist side a list of 3,404 names of mission UN Command personnel including the names of 944 United States servicemen of whom we had reason to believe the Communists should have some knowledge. At the outset I should like to make it clear that in placing this demand for an accounting on the Communists, the UN Command did not intend to imply that we were charging the Communists with holding this large group of Americans alive and against their will.

Through unilateral efforts of the United States Government . . . the list of 944 had been reduced to 526 by August 1954. This reduction came about because the efforts we had made produced conclusive evidence of death for 418 of the original list.

Even though the Communist side under the terms of the armistice agreement owed us an accounting for the complete 944, we presented them with a revised list of 526 in the fall of 1954, hoping that the reduced list might result in a more satisfactory accounting by the Communists. Such was not the case.

In the meantime, in June of 1954, at the Geneva Conference on Korea and Indochina, the Department of State initiated certain actions which will be described to you by the Department of State representatives here today. Due to these actions by State, plus further efforts to uncover additional information, the list was further reduced to 450.

For the past several years the Department of Defense and the Department of State have worked jointly and cooperatively in continuing efforts to secure from the Communists a satisfactory accounting. In support of the efforts of the Department of State, the Department of Defense and the military services have concentrated on an intensive effort to collect every scrap of information and intelligence regarding the unaccounted-for 450. The military services, under a quarterly report requirement, have been producing individual dossiers on each case. These dossiers have been made available to Ambassador U. Alexis Johnson for his negotiations with representatives of the Chinese Communist regime at Geneva.

A breakdown of the 450 unaccounted-for personnel is as follows: Army, 244; Navy, 3; Air Force, 190; Marines, 13.

Due to the inevitable confusion at the time the exchange of POWs was completed in Korea in September 1953, and due to a certain amount of inaccurate reporting regarding the subject of missing POWs, the impression is still current among some segments of the American public that the United States Government believes that a large group of American military personnel are alive and still held in Asian countries by Communist captors. While the possibility exists that there may still be some personnel held, alive and against their will, we do not have any further positive information or intelligence from any source that such is the case. Because of the lack of positive information to support the contention that any of our military are still held, as well as a lack of conclusive information to indicate that they are all deceased, I am sure you will realize the difficulty we face in attempting to comfort the next of kin and to satisfy the understandable and patriotic concern which has been expressed by so many Americans on this subject.

Appendix 11

THE UNCMAC 450 LIST

Found in: Chapter Seven, Volume 1
Source of this information: U.S. Congress, House Subcommittee on the Far East and the Pacific of the Committee on Foreign Relations, *Return of American Prisoners of War Who Have Not Been Accounted For By The Communists* (Washington, D.C.: U.S. Government Printing Office, 1957), pp. 27-32.

The May 1957 450 List[1]

Army	244[2]
Navy	3
Marines	13
Air Force	190
Total	450[3]

U. S. Army

Name	Service No.	Grade
Abbott, Charles L.	RA17258068	Pvt
Aki, Clarence H.	RA30115989	Cpl
Alcorn, Phillip F.	RA27020444	Pvt
Amano, Yutaka	RA19302624	Sergeant
Arrendondo, Isidoro	US56095247	Pfc
Balbi, Joseph A	US51142209	Pfc
Bastie, William R., Jr.	RA11202604	Pvt
Bedell, Norman C.	RA16318848	Pvt
Bellar, Bennie E.	RA14326111	Cpl
Beller, James E.	RA18333098	Pvt
Bernard, Elton J	RA18281438	Cpl
Besemer, Robert L.	RA16263944	Cpl
Billigmeier, Milton P	RA37541823	Cpl
Boyd, Harold R.	RA15378325	Cpl
Bradford, Leonard G.	RA19328814	Sergeant
Brock, James B.	RA19312025	Pfc
Broome, Otis L.	US51019384	Pfc
Brown, Bill E.	US53078083	Pfc
Brown, James C.	RA17232851	Pfc
Bull Clifford F.	RA18254336	Pfc
Buster, Johnnie J.	RA19338734	Pfc
Buttrey, William V.	RA19350567	Pfc
Buxman, Roger F.	0987439	1st Lieutenant
Callis, Henry O	RA14296259	Pfc
Carter, Andrew	RA13271442	Cpl
Chaney, James O	RA18132707	Pvt
Chavez, Daniel	RA19329106	Cpl
Clatterbuck, Roland W.	RA13017216	Sergeant
Clifton, William L.	RA13343182	Cpl

---

[1]U.S. Congress, House Subcommittee on the Far East and the Pacific of the Committee on Foreign Relations, *Return of American Prisoners of War Who Have Not Been Accounted For by the Communists* (Washington, D.C.: U.S. Government Printing Office, 1957), pp. 27-32. Misspellings and other errors are corrected on this list wherever they have been noted.

[2]246 in December 1957.

[3]452 in 1958.

Cole, Merle L., Jr.	RA17261360	Pvt
Cornell, Roy G.	RA15263153	Pvt
Cozad, Kenneth L.	RA15275155	Cpl
Crabb, Dean R.	US55171051	Pfc
Craig, Paul E.	ER14326994	Pfc
Crevelling, Alyron G.	RA12116821	Sergeant
Crews, Irvine T.	RA13306423	Sergeant
Cruz-Ramos, Jesus	US50116808	Pfc
Dahms, Donald E.	RA21716812	Pfc
Davis, Esekiel A.	RA16333109	Pvt
Day, Dave H	RA23299105	Pvt
Demoll, Casimire T.	RA38171941	Sergeant
DeSau, Lawrence K.	RA13335669	Pvt
Desautels, Richard G.	RA11188218	Cpl
Dick, William L., Jr.	RA16314645	Pvt
Dill, Paul N.	01322529	1st Lieutenant
Dove, Leroy J.	RA16302584	Pfc
Dulyea, Harold B.	RA16323924	Pvt
Dumas, Roger A.	RA21004481	Pfc
Ellas, Daniel A.	RA13311710	Pvt
Evans, Junior C.	RA18337236	Pvt
Fetzer, Leo E.	RA15281807	Pfc
Figureid, Ronald	RA22815294	Cpl
Fischer, James F.	US56136976	Pfc
Flores, Willie S.	RA18031261	Cpl
Frech, John, Jr.	0060879	2nd Lieutenant
Fulk, Lester E.	US33158005	Pfc
Fuller, Terrell J.	US57300174	Pfc
Gardner, James D.	RA13333358	Pvt
Garver, Charles E.	RA13328481	Pfc
Gilley, Homer B.	RA15410649	Cpl
Glasser, Gerald W.	RA13260232	Cpl
Goetz, George R.	RA35800374	Master Sergeant
Grenier, Donald T.	RA21724933	Pvt
Gresser, Arnold G.	RA19350234	Pfc
Grimsley, Robert L.	RA13321150	Pfc
Hadnot, Charles D.	RA14276776	Pvt
Haag, Douglas H.	02101071	2nd Lieutenant
Harnage, Lawrence A.	RA14337390	Pfc
Harpster, Fred W.	RA 35863803	Pvt
Harry, Edward S., Jr.	RA18283271	Pvt
Haynie, Robert E.	RA19360132	Pvt
Hebert, Sylvio L.	ER11149106	Pvt
Hogan, Kenneth A.	RA19354580	Pvt
Holt, Crenshaw A.	0058927	1st Lieutenant
Hoogacker, Phillip T.	RA16315593	Pvt
Houston, James L.	RA26793789	Pfc
Howell, James	RA15261277	Pfc
Hoysradt, Donald O.	RA11167423	Pfc
Hughes, Wayne G.	RA23410679	Pvt
Hull, Leonard O.	RA12242197	Cpl
Humiston, Donald L.	US51009999	Pfc

Humiston, Donald L.	US51009999	Pfc
Ishida, Mitsuyoshi	RA10103947	Pfc
Jarrett, Carl E.	RA17278829	Cpl
Jennings, John E., Jr.	ER36778696	Cpl
Jerome, Richard	RA13333318	Pvt
Jewett, Richard G.	02003239	2nd Lieutenant
Jinks, Leonard W. E.	RA15057580	Pfc
Johnson, Donald R.	RA11197364	Pvt
Johnson, Leroy	RA18352468	Pvt
Johnson, Myron	RA13344121	Pvt
Johnson, Ray	RA18341449	Cpl
Jones, Kassidy K	ER38605309	Pfc
Kalama, Herbert	RA10101615	Sergeant
Kidd, Elmer O	RA12114881	Pfc
King, Ralph K.	US55220035	Pvt
Klingler, James F.	RA13298760	Pvt
Konze, Anthony	RA12325352	Pfc
Kost, Stanley	ER13287925	Pfc
Krygowski, Francis	RA11189504	Pfc
Lagoni, Ditlei J.	RA16265716	Sergeant 1st class
LaPointe, John N.	RA11192758	Pfc
Lee, Enill	RA18223291	Pfc
Levitski, Walter J.	ER16306844	Pvt
Linebough, Orvill F.	RA19356698	Pvt
Litchfield, Billie	RA17218055	Sergeant
Lopes, Alfred, Jr.	RA15297270	Pfc
Louviere, Ray V.	RA18282808	Cpl
Malanga, Angelo S.	RA12279700	Cpl
Masters, Louis R.	RA13273131	Pvt
Mattingly, Donald L.	RA38569409	Sergeant
McClure, Clarence, Jr.	RA13355549	Pvt
McDaniel, William	024088	Maj
McDowell, William	RA18294333	Pfc
Meagher, Neil W.	RA19340378	Cpl
Meyers, Robert E.	RA13314858	Pfc
Mireles, Marcario	RA18353729	Pfc
Moreland, Harry D.	0555419	Capt
Morris, Russel F.	RA35169826	Cpl
Munoz, Moises	US50117033	Pfc
Nearhood, John W.	RA16315922	Cpl
Nicowski, Anthony J.	RA12348736	Cpl
Nystrom, John W.	0970527	1st Lieutenant
O'Brien, Raymond J.	RA18303460	Pfc
Ottesen, Eugene L.	US57313689	Cpl
Overgard, Elwood E.	ER38127552	Cpl
Peiffer, Alfred G.	02014870	1st Lieutenant
Peters, James	RA30123141	Cpl
Peterson, Lyle E.	RA19351553	Pvt
Pickard, Maxie L.	RA20811182	Sergeant
Pierce, Albert G.	RA37934620	Pfc
Pitts, John W.	RA14318711	Pfc
Preas, Curious M.	RA18337006	Pfc

Quigg, John F.	RA12304824	Cpl
Ragin, Carl W.	RA13353133	Pvt
Rausch, Charles L.	RA16267642	Cpl
Reddick, Frank T.	RA13300101	Sergeant
Reimer, Walter F.	RA12293602	Cpl
Renneberg, Anthony	RA28130719	Pvt
Richey, Aggie L.	RA19325608	Pvt
Ridgeway, Junior V.	RA16267704	Pfc
Riley, John F.	RA18314836	Cpl
Roden, Tracy R.	RA6285109	Pfc
Roop, Donald H.	RA15421785	Pfc
Rose, Nokomis J.	RA33212378	Pvt
Royer, Charles B.	RA38649112	Cpl
Rozear, John M., Jr.	RA12314868	Cpl
Samezyk, Stanley J.	RA16303702	Pfc
Samora, Jose M.	RA17278528	Pfc
Sampson, James W.	RA15378976	Pfc
Sanders, James B.	RA18283828	Pfc
Sanford, Royal W.	RA13349848	Pfc
Schanck, Russel D.	RA16381081	Pfc
Schnepper, Paul W.	US55293260	Pfc
Schonder, William D.	RA19256326	Pvt
Schuring, Gerald G.	RA17228038	Pfc
Seggie, William R.	RA13260817	Pvt
Serwise, Luther D.	ER35096983	Sergeant
Sharp, James W.	RA36081641	Cpl
Shepard, Robert A.	RA13257820	Cpl
Shibao, Hiroshi	US56010180	Pfc
Smith, Lawrence J.	ER38487422	Sergeant
Snider, Carl G., Jr.	ER37154633	Pfc
Snider, Glenn A.	RA39480119	Master Sergeant
Snodgrass, Robert G.	RA19357430	Pfc
Sorrentino, Anthony T.	RA12325141	Pfc
Spiller, William R.	ER18305154	Pfc
Springer, William	RA12333808	Pfc
Stansbury, William H., Jr.	RA17245840	Pfc
Starling, Robert G.	RA14333967	Pfc
Steger, William H.	RA16254756	Pfc
Stone, Neil H.	US55280508	Pfc
Sternad, John T.	ER37505463	Pfc
Stidham, Floyd D.	RA15267441	Pfc
Stiles, George W.	ER19284333	Pfc
Stoeber, Waiter, Jr.	RA13257783	Pfc
Stumpf, Marion F.	RA17059498	Pfc
Sweeney, John R.	RA12329620	Pfc
Switzer, Contee L.	RA17280811	Pfc
Takahara, Sam, O.	02030786	1st Lieutenant
Tatarakis, George C.	RA19306236	Cpl
Thomas, Mitchell C.	02014760	2nd Lieutenant
Thompson, Harwood H.	ER12246136	Pfc
Tish, Clarence A., Jr.	RA14287845	Pfc
Tomlinson, Marvin F.	RA6249933	Sergeant 1st class

Toole, Arnold	RA16280172	Cpl
Torres, Louis P.	RA16273385	Pfc
Tucker, Lloyd L.	RA18337483	Pfc
Van Wyk, Clayton F.	RA27031343	Pfc
Vernon, Raymond A.	US51134261	Pvt
Vickers, Wendell	RA13269020	Cpl
Vranic, Anthony	TS55005643	Pfc
Walgzak, Castnir F.	RA16316451	Pvt
Walker, Archie	RA19304659	Pfc
Wallen, James A.	RA15236536	Pfc
Ware, Raymond O.	RA17281042	Pvt
Watkins, Samuel K.	RA14364811	Pvt
Watson, James D.	RA18344264	Cpl
Weaver, Edward P.	RA13315911	Pfc
Webb, Jerald C.	RA24484357	Pfc
Westphall, Johnnie S.	RA19329233	Cpl
White, Waddell	RA17284623	Pvt
White, William F.	RA16268651	Pfc
Williams, Albert	RA14301914	Pfc
Willis, Charles A.	ER57307012	Pfc
Wilson, Merble E.	RA15242639	Pvt
Wilson, Richard L.	RA16328280	Cpl
Winrader, Howard W.	RA23786250	Pfc
Wood, Lyle E.	RA17247032	Cpl
Woods, Joseph H.	RA12314320	Pfc
Wooster, Audrey H.	RA18224279	Sergeant
Worley, Frank	RA14366839	Pvt
Wright, Edward C.	ER37515113	Cpl
Yoshida, Kanji	US50000110	Pfc
Young, Charles H.	RA13271083	Cpl
Young, Russell V.	RA19328611	Pvt
Zawacki, Frank J.	RA15267535	Cpl

The following names appear in
this order in this position
in the 1984 389 list.

Adams, Joseph J.	RA12305738	Pfc
Bond, Elihue, Jr.	RA15338774	Pfc
Bradford, Edward F., Jr.	RA11167803	Pvt
Brooks, Lloyd K.	RA14315399	Pfc
Brown, Alfred R.	RA18321108	Cpl
Brown, Frank M.	0370561	Maj
Calhoun, Cecil O.	RA16308092	Cpl
Colon-Perez, Jose S.	RA30452103	Pfc
Cox, Joseph D.	02017966	Capt
Cunningham, John F.	RA12305730	Pfc
Dansberry, Earl L.	RA16180861	Sergeant
Davis, Sam H.	RA18358881	Pfc
DeCosta, Salvatore	RA32911260	Sergeant
Denchfield, Raymond O.	0058879	1st Lieutenant
Dixon, Roosevelt, Jr.	RA13264790	Sergeant

Dunlap, Alva F.	RA15274377	Pfc
Earl, James E.	RA18259856	Sergeant
Efland, Donald O.	ER51045004	Pfc
Evans, Edward R.	RA15234142	Cpl
Fennell, Isaac, Jr.	ER42150267	Sergeant
Gregory, Robert S.	RA13313861	Cpl
Hester, Will H.	RA15381580	Pvt
Marshall, Alfred	ER12251545	Pfc
McSwain, Leon	RA14226936	Cpl
Miller, Raymond H.	ER13313722	Pfc
Minor, Donald W.	RA11188081	Pvt
Mrotek, Lawrence M.	ER57500731	Pfc
Mulock, Arthur F.	02200206	2nd Lieutenant

U. S. Navy

Biesterveld, Thomas Clarence	506698	Ensign
Brown, William Edmund	496712	Ensign
Cochran, Billy Edward	475207	Lieutenant jg

U. S. Marine Corps

Baker, Billy W.	624946	Pfc
Bookamire, Gerald R.	1249268	Pfc
Chidester, Arthur A.	05234	Colonel
DeLacy, Arthur D.	051658	2nd Lieutenant
Eagan, James K.	07760	Maj
Gleaves, James A., Jr.	051308	2nd Lieutenant
Green, James L.	1175542	Pfc
Lewis, William T., Jr.	11681313	Pfc
Morrow, Billy J.	1188495	Pfc
Nelson, Forest A.	044100	2st Lieutenant
Taylor, Charles A.	633516	Pfc
Tuttle, Raymond J.	1035628	Pfc
Young, Robert J.	1092372	Pfc

U. S. Air Force

Adler, Ernest M.	A02073084	1st Lieutenant
Akin, Roland M.	A02094960	1st Lieutenant
Allen, Jack V.	16683A	Capt
Anderson, Robert E.	A01911386	1st Lieutenant
Andrews, Robert B.	A0813127	Capt
Arms, John W.	A02225726	2nd Lieutenant
Ashley, Gilbert L., Jr.	A0666215	Capt
Austin, Arthur M.	A01289023	Maj
Beardall, Harold M.	A0769375	Capt
Bell, Donald E.	A0814007	1st Lieutenant
Bell, William J.	22108A	1st Lieutenant
Bergmann, Louis H.	AF17124468	Sergeant
Biggs, Elmer T.	A02092623	1st Lieutenant
Bigham, Donald G.	A0767469	Capt
Black, Wayne F.	A0599631	Capt
Bolt, Donald D.	A0837772	1st Lieutenant
Botter, William J	AF33570888	Staff Sergeant
Brennan, John C.	AF11227081	Airman 3rd class
Burrell, Jackson A.	A02081396	Capt
Burten, Woodrow	A02101608	1st Lieutenant

Bushroe, Sterling J	A01911963	1st Lieutenant
Carlisle, Osborne T.	A0426554	Capt
Cave, James A.	AF13411410	Airman 2nd class
Cherry, Clarence M.	AF19201403	Staff Sergeant
Cogswell, Robert W.	11880A	Maj
Collins, Joseph A	A0807154	Capt
Connors, Archibald H., Jr	A02221996	1st Lieutenant
Cooper, Spencer R.	AF21900368	Airman 1st class
Coulter, John R.	A01909263	1st Lieutenant
Crane, Alvin E., Jr.	A01903066	1st Lieutenant
Crutchfield, James F.	A0736133	Lieutenant Colonel
Culbertson, Gene A.	A0718487	Capt
Davies, Howard J.	A01909468	1st Lieutenant
Davis, Norman G.	AF15209199	Staff Sergeant
Davis, Ramon R.	A0767144	1st Lieutenant
Denn, Willard M.	AF16329167	Airman 2nd class
DeRosier, Albert P.	A01340348	1st Lieutenant
Differ, Patrick M.	AF13021311	Master Sergeant
Dorsey, Joyce T.	AF17167105	Technical Sergeant
Dougherty, Joseph S.	AF13041845	Staff Sergeant
Duer, Victor L.	A0753626	Staff Sergeant
Duncan, James H.	AF14101683	1st Lieutenant
Edens, Malcolm B.	A0789892	Maj
Evans, Emmett O.	A02060489	1st Lieutenant
Ferree, Nolan H.	A02222141	2nd Lieutenant
Festini, Steve J.	13030A	1st Lieutenant
Fleming, James W., Jr.	A0780156	1st Lieutenant
Foster, Robert R.	A0550110	1st Lieutenant
Foulks, James A., Jr.	A02080021	Capt
Fuehrer, Alois A.	AF13233572	Airman 1st class
Gahan, John W.	AF15380313	Sergeant
Gallant, James A.	AF15295553	Airman 2nd class
Garrison, Fred II	A0791811	Capt
George, Winifred R.	AF14140942	Technical Sergeant
Gibb, Robert D.	13053A	Capt
Glessner, Milton F., Jr	3375A	Lt. Colonel
Golden, Newman C.	A0934440	1st Lieutenant
Gross, Robert F.	AF14226221	Master Sergeant
Guilfoyle, Cornellus P.	A0739549	Capt
Guthrie, Edward S., Jr.	22193A	1st Lieutenant
Guthrie, Marvin I.	AF6388833	Staff Sergeant
Hamblin, Robert W.	AF12127986	Technical Sergeant
Hammon, Keith R.	AF152306651	Technical Sergeant
Harker, Charles A., Jr	A02224102	2nd Lieutenant
Harrell, Guy B., Jr.	A0391377	Capt
Haskett, William T., Jr.	A0790664	Capt
Hawkins, Luther B., Jr.	A0812589	Capt
Hays, Melvin B.	AF39192109	Airman 3rd class
Heer, David T.	A02223002	2d Lieutenant
Heise, Arthur	A0750985	Capt
Henry, Dewey R.	A0927982	1st Lieutenant
Hoff, Warren N.	A02084887	1st Lieutenant

Holcom, William L.	A0933359	1st Lieutenant
Holz, Scott A.	A0190608	1st Lieutenant
Horner, John J.	A01911849	1st Lieutenant
Hoult, Arthur W.	AF6953553	Staff Sergeant
Howell, Howard D.	13402A	Capt
Hudson, Lawrence N.	A02092806	1st Lieutenant
Hyatt, Don	A0674199	Capt
Ishida, Nidemero	AF19415365	Airman 2nd class
Jacobs, Harrison C.	A01909723	1st Lieutenant
Jacobson, Paul J.	A04222046	1st Lieutenant
Jamison, Joseph S.	AF12287088	Technical Sergeant
Jensen, Morton H.	AF27358781	Technical Sergeant
Jensen, Wayne F.	AF19405070	Staff Sergeant
Johnson, Gerald E.	AF13337205	Airman 3rd class
Johnson, Johnny M.	AF18012750	Technical Sergeant
Jones, James L.	AF16226038	Airman 3rd class
Jones, Oliver E.	A01911207	1st Lieutenant
Karpowicz, Jerome	AF16395206	Airman 1st class
Keene, Kassel M.	A0420472	Maj
Keister, Harold O.	A0785071	Capt
Kelleher, Robert P.	AF11205730	Airman 1st class
Kepford, Joseph O.	A0818388	Capt
King, Alfred H.	A01912154	1st Lieutenant
Kirk, Charles F.	A02079748	1st Lieutenant
Knapp, Kingdon R.	A0885977	Capt
Knueppel, Raymond J.	A0707938	Capt
Koontz, Frederick R.	A01909920	1st Lieutenant
Krumm, Robert N.	A0804464	Capt
Kuehner, Gordon V., Jr.	A0832161	1st Lieutenant
Laier, Robert H.	18039A	1st Lieutenant
Larkin, Hugh F.	A0437976	Capt
Layton, Laurence C.	A01910250	1st Lieutenant
Lewis, Jack	12658A	Capt
Lewis, Wayne E.	AF17306085	Airman 1st class
Lewis, Wilbur E.	A0772859	2nd Lieutenant
Logan, Samuel P.	11287A	Maj
Long, Joseph S., Jr.	A0724957	Maj
McAdoo, Ernest R.	AF13337425	Airman 1st class
McAllaster, John A., Jr.	A0757831	Capt
McFee, Claude D.	AF19245204	Staff Sergeant
McKee, Robert E.	A02089113	Capt
McLoughlin, Robert J.	AF12335474	Airman 2nd class
Martin, Dominique K.	A01909619	1st Lieutenant
Mast, Clifford N.	AF19417343	Staff Sergeant
Miller, Henry D.	A01852083	1st Lieutenant
Mitchell, Bernard	AF31378023	Airman 1st class
Mooradian, Ara	A0932011	Capt
Moore, John G.	A0886003	Capt
Myers, Thomas E.	13136A	Capt
Nelson, Lawrence A.	A02221692	1st Lieutenant
Nichols, James L.	AF17326268	1st Lieutenant
Nickles, Rudolf	AF12383404	Airman 1st class

Nye, Glenn C.	1768A	Colonel
O'Brien, Warren E.	A0827259	Capt
Olcott, Ray W.	A01909367	1st Lieutenant
Olsen, Arthur R.	A02069417	1st Lieutenant
O'Meara James J., Jr.	AF16354305	Airman 2nd class
O'Neal, Julius E.	4792A	Lieutenant Colonel
Osborne, Jess A., Jr.	AF13351603	Airman 3rd class
O'Toole, Damian F.	AF13462243	Airman 2nd class
Oyler, Ernest R.	A0744348	Capt
Padilla, Alexander B.	A0336092	Capt
Palmer, Alford C.	A02223160	2nd Lieutenant
Palmiotti, Nicholas M.	AF12313035	Airman 1st class
Parham, Charles E., Jr.	AF14103757	Cpl
Peck, James K.	A0741690	1st Lieutenant
Penninger, Roger W.	A0778935	1st Lieutenant
Peterson, Norman W.	AF17312946	Airman 2nd class
Phelps, Ralph L.	AF17291247	Staff Sergeant
Phillips, Duane M.	19732A	2nd Lieutenant
Pincus, Herbert	A0946510	1st Lieutenant
Pope, James D.	AF14404363	Airman 2nd class
Porter, James H.	AF14397423	Airman 1st class
Poynor, Com F.	A0725476	1st Lieutenant
Pratt, Charles W.	16993A	Capt
Raymond, Gerald W.	AF19363298	Staff Sergeant
Rehm, Harry M.	A02089519	1st Lieutenant
Rhinehart, Charles W.	A01911442	1st Lieutenant
Ritter, Herbert E.	A0666440	1st Lieutenant
Rodney, Daryl E.	AF19400458	Airman 1st class
Rountree, Fred D.	17495A	Capt
St. Mary, Robert R.	AF16385446	Airman 1st class
Schauer, Gilbert J.	A02068874	1st Lieutenant
Schmitt, Warren W.	AF17151509	Airman 2nd class
Schneidtt, Norman W.	A0810255	Capt
Schwab, Edward A.	AF12359965	Cpl
Selman, Clifford G.	A01864097	1st Lieutenant
Shaddick, John P. III	A02221920	1st Lieutenant
Sheehan, Robert E.	A0547956	1st Lieutenant
Shields, Thomas L.	A0837209	Capt
Smith, James D., Jr.	A02282046	2nd Lieutenant
Southerland, John E.	A01910800	1st Lieutenant
Spath, Charles R.	A01910283	1st Lieutenant
Spence, Marvin J.	A0732780	Maj
Starck, John S.	A01909876	1st Lieutenant
Steele, Robert C.	A0720030	Capt
Stefas, Frank	AF19363340	Airman 1st class
Stevenson, Frank J.	AF13405299	Airman 3rd class
Sweney, Bruce A.	A01912252	1st Lieutenant
Tahsequah, Meach	10985A	Lieutenant Colonel
Thompson, Charles R.	A02222047	2nd Lieutenant
Thompson, Raymond	AF15432409	Airman 1st class
Tilch, Philip W.	AF13327852	Sergeant
Tiller, Horace N.	AF19052764	Master Sergeant

Trantham, Archie P.	A0725822	Capt
Turner, Harold P.	A01283518	Capt
Van Fleet, James A., Jr.	17852A	Capt
Vanwey, William N.	AF18342248	Airman 2nd class
Wahlgren, Edward C.	A0695337	1st Lieutenant
Webb, Edward A.	AF18350787	Airman 2nd class
Weeks, Grady M.	AF14114882	Staff Sergeant
West, Carl E.	AF13346889	Airman 2nd class
Whitman, William H.	AF13360399	Airman 1st class
Williamson, Kenneth E.	AF125255731	Staff Sergeant
Wood, Melvin C.	11313A	Maj
Wormack, Thelbert B.	A01908612	1st Lieutenant
Worth, George W., Jr.	AF19311283	Staff Sergeant
Zeigler, Joseph P.	A02224628	1st Lieutenant

In December 1957 two missing Army personnel, Pfc Connie M. Conner (RA 19360219) and Pvt Donald Dickinson (RA 19341489) were added to the list, bringing the total to 452.[4]

---

[4]Milton to Assistant to the Secretary of Defense, May 23, 1958.

Appendix 12

CRITERIA FOR REDUCING THE 450 LIST TO 389

Found in: Chapter Seven, Volume 1
Source of this information: Department of Defense

TEXT OF DOD STATEMENT ON REDUCTION OF LIST FROM 452 TO 391
(JUNE 1960)

The Department of Defense announced today that the list of
unaccounted-for prisoners of war from the Korean War was being
reduced from its earlier figure of 452 to 391.

When the United Nations Command placed its first demand on the
Chinese Communists and the North Koreans for an accounting,
immediately after the completion of the prisoner exchange in
the fall of 1953, the figure of unaccounted-for Americans
stood at 944. Through partial accounting by the Chinese
Communists and North Koreans, but mainly through the continued
efforts of the UN Command and other U.S. governmental agencies
to establish the facts in each individual case, the figure was
reduced by June 1955 to 450. It was subsequently increased to
452 based on re-examination of intelligence and information
from repatriates.

A provision of the Armistice Agreement which brought about the
cease-fire in Korea had stipulated that each side would render
to the other side a full accounting on any prisoner of war
whether alive or dead of whom they had any knowledge.

The Department of Defense, in reducing the figure to 392
emphasizes that while all of the original list of 944 except
for these 391 now have been accounted for, this accounting has
been accomplished largely, not by the Chinese Communists and
North Koreans as stipulated in the Armistice Agreement, but
through the efforts of U.S. Graves Registration Units and the
U.S. Intelligence Agencies, working with little or no
cooperation or assistance from the North Koreans or Chinese
Communists.

Repeated demands for an accounting have been made through the
Military Armistice Commission in Korea and by Department of
State officials in discussions at Geneva and Warsaw with
representatives of the Chinese Communist regimes. To date,
the Chinese Communist officials at Geneva and Warsaw have
refused to discuss the matter, stating that it should be taken
up with the Military Armistice Commission in Korea. The
Chinese Communist and North Korean representatives on the
Military Armistice Commission, however, have stated flatly
that they have rendered an accounting and refuse to entertain
any request for further effort. In this stalemated situation
the U.S. Government has proceeded to follow every possible

course of inquiry in an attempt to solve the problem. These
efforts will continue in the future.

In making this public announcement on the reduction, the
Department of Defense also emphasizes that the United States
Government has no reliable information from any source to
indicate that any of the American servicemen remaining on the
list of 391 unaccounted-for since the Korean hostilities are
still alive and held in Chinese Communist prisons. Although
the possibility cannot be completely foreclosed that some few
of them might still be alive, there are no reliable facts to
support a more favorable conclusion.

The reductions in the list, by Service, are as follows:

Army:	From 246 to 190
Navy:	None. Remains 3.
Air Force:	From 190 to 186
Marine Corps:	From 13 to 12.

In all cases the next of kin and other interested parties have
been notified by letter concerning deletions from the list.

Appendix 13

CASUALTY DATA FOR PERSONNEL ON 389 LIST

Found in: Chapter Seven, Volume 1
Source of this information: UNCMAC and CILHI casualty data.

U.S. Army (188)[1]

Bold = Listed as POW in CILHI records

Plain text: Listed as MIA in CILHI records

?? = Cannot locate individual deceased personnel file.
** = Buried April 28, 1969, in Hawaii

Name	Service No.	Grade

Aki, Clarence H.   RA30115989   **Cpl**
Declared POW August 12, 1950. Reported to be alive by repatriates as of October 14, 1950

Alcorn, Phillip F.   RA27020444   **Pvt**
Declared MIA February 18, 1951. Eyewitnesses reported capture. Last known to be alive February 18, 1951.

Arrendondo, Isidoro   US56095247   **Pfc**
Declared POW January 8, 1952. Eyewitnesses reported capture. Captured enemy reported Arrendondo was a POW.

Bastie, William R., Jr.   RA11202604   **Pvt**
Declared MIA on February 4, 1951. Name appeared in *National Guardian*, August 8, 1951. Mentioned by repatriate. Added March 7, 1956: Four repatriated prisoners reported that subject was in a POW camp in the spring of 1951. He was left behind when the bulk of the prisoners were marched north to POW Camp #1 because of his poor physical condition.

Bedell, Norman C.   RA16318848   Pvt
Declared MIA on July 27, 1950. Appeared in undated photograph.

Beller, James E.   RA18333098   Pvt
Declared MIA on July 27, 1950. Appeared in undated photograph.

---

[1]RG219 Army Intelligence--Korean Project. Decimal File 1950-1956, decimal 383.6. Notations following a name derive from information provided under the category, "Nature of evidence on which POW deemed to be alive and in Communist hands" in the Army's "POW Casualty List" compiled for RECAP-K. This file was offered to Lt. Tom Vhay, ISA/MIA-POW Affairs, who said it was of no relevance to the work of the U.S.-Russian Commission on MIA-POW Affairs. The National Archives then offered this file to the author of this study.

Bernard, Elton J   RA18281458   **Cpl**
Declared MIA on December 1, 1950. Repatriate said subject was captured December 2, 1950.

Besemer, Robert L.   RA16263944   **Cpl**
Declared MIA on July 25, 1950. Appeared in undated photograph.

Billigmeier, Milton P.   RA37541823   **Cpl**
Declared MIA on July 27, 1950. Appeared in undated photograph. Added March 7, 1956: One repatriated POW stated that subject was a prisoner and last seen at the Sunchon tunnel October 20, 1950.

Boyd, Harold R.   RA15378325   Cpl
Declared MIA on February 12, 1951. Repatriate said subject was a prisoner of the enemy, date unknown. Added March 7, 1956: Several repatriated POWs reported subject was a prisoner in 1951, one giving the camp as #1.

Bradford, Leonard G.   RA19328814   Sergeant
Declared MIA on July 27, 1950. Appeared in undated photograph.

Brock, James B.   RA19312025   Pfc
Declared MIA on December 12, 1950. Repatriate saw subject in the hands of the enemy, date unknown.

Broome, Otis L.   US51019384   Pfc
Declared MIA on August 8, 1951. Added March 7, 1956. One returnee reported subject was a prisoner in Camp #5 in August 1952.

Brown, James C.   RA17232851   Pfc
Declared MIA on December 1, 1950. Identified by repatriates. Last known alive April 25, 1953.

Bull Clifford F.   **RA18254336**   **Pfc**
Declared MIA on August 10, 1950. Name found on blackboard indicating prisoner.

Buster, Johnnie J.   RA19338734   Pfc
Declared MIA August 1, 1950. Name found on blackboard in area previously occupied by the enemy.

Buttrey, William V.   RA19350567   Pfc
Declared MIA on December 6, 1950. Named in enemy propaganda broadcasts.

Buxman, Roger F.   0987439   1st Lieutenant
Declared MIA on June 5, 1953. Reported captured in command report.

Callis, Henry O   **RA14296259**   **Pfc**
Declared MIA on July 27, 1950. Identified by repatriates. Last known alive July 29, 1950.

Carter, Andrew   RA13271442   Cpl
Declared MIA on November 25, 1950. Named in Radio Moscow broadcast, July 22, 1951.

Chaney, James O   RA18132707   Pvt
Declared MIA on June 2, 1953. Repatriate said subject was captured.
Last known alive June 3, 1953.

Chavez, Daniel   RA19329106   Cpl
Declared MIA on December 1, 1950. Name appeared in an unidentified
Chinese Communist publication, date unknown.

Clatterbuck, Roland W.   **RA13017216**   **Sergeant**
Declared MIA on February 13, 1951. Repatriate identified subject as
prisoner, date unknown.

Clifton, William L.   RA13343182   Cpl
Declared missing on November 2, 1950. Repatriate saw subject in
captivity, date unknown.

Cole, Merle L., Jr.   RA17261360   Pvt
Declared MIA on August 16, 1950. Repatriate identified subject as
prisoner, date unknown.

Conner, Connie M.   **RA19360219**   **Private 1st Class**
Declared MIA on December 6, 1950. Wrote a letter in POW status.
(Conner was added to the 450 list when it became the 452 list.)

Cornell, Roy G.   RA15263153   Pvt
Declared MIA on November 26, 1950. Name mentioned in the *National
Guardian*.

Cozad, Kenneth L.   **RA15275155**   **Cpl**
Declared MIA on July 30, 1950. Name found on blackboard. Appeared in
undated photograph. Added March 7, 1956: Two returnees reported having
seen subject in a POW camp.

Craig, Paul E.   ER14326994   Pvt 1st class
Declared MIA on February 12, 1951. Mentioned in Radio Peking broadcast
June 27, 1951. Signed statement that UN planes killed POWs.

Crevelling, Alyron G.   RA12116821   Sergeant
Declared MIA on February 12, 1951. Last known alive March 1951.

Crews, Irvine T.   RA13306423   Sergeant
Declared MIA December 12, 1950. Named in propaganda broadcast.

Cruz-Ramos, Jesus   US50116808   Pfc
Declared MIA June 9, 1953. Was on OP duty. Did not return. No body
found. Search made same day. Last known alive June 9, 1953.

Dahms, Donald E.   RA21716812   Pfc
Declared MIA on July 25, 1950. On Far East Command POW list. Last
known alive approximately October 1950.

Davis, Esekiel A.   RA16333109   Pvt
Declared MIA on February 11, 1951. Named in *National Guardian* August 8, 1951.

Day, Dave H   RA23299105   Pvt
Declared MIA on December 2, 1950. Identified by repatriates. Last known alive July 1952.

Demoll, Casimire T. **RA38171941**   **Sergeant**
Declared MIA on February 4, 1951. Named in Radio Peking broadcast June 22, 1951 and in *National Guardian* August 8, 1951. Last known alive April 1951.

DeSau, Lawrence K.   RA13335669   Pvt
Declared MIA on July 25, 1950. Reported captured in command reports. Last known alive approximately October 1950.

Desautels, Richard G. **RA11188218**   **Cpl**
Declared captured on December 1, 1950. Repatriates were POWs at the same time as subject. Added March 7, 1956: Many returnees reported on subject. He was captured by the Chinese and apparently worked closely with them for several months. He drove their trucks, attended to firing boilers and learned to speak the Chinese language fairly well. Several witnesses reported having seen him shortly before the last repatriation.

Dick, William L., Jr.   RA16314645   Pvt
Declared MIA on August 15, 1950. Name found on blackboard in an area previously occupied by the enemy. Last known alive approximately October 1950.

Dickinson, Donald R.   RA19341489   Pvt
No information. (Dickinson was added when the 450 list became the 452 list.)

Dill, Paul N.   01322529   1st Lieutenant
Declared MIA on December 3, 1950. Repatriate said subject was in Camp #1 when he was released. Last known alive April 1953.

Dove, Leroy J.   **RA16302584**   **Pfc**
Declared MIA on July 27, 1950. Name appeared on blackboard and on list of POWs received by UNC.

Dulyea, Harold B.   RA16323924   Pvt
Declared MIA on July 25, 1950. Repatriate said subject was POW same time as he was.

Dumas, Roger A.   RA21004481   Pfc
Declared MIA on November 4, 1950. Repatriate said subject was in Camp #5 with him at the time of his release. Last known alive July 1953.

Ellas, Daniel A.   RA13311710   Pvt
Declared MIA on July 27, 1950. Name found on blackboard located in area previously occupied by the enemy.

Evans, Junior C.   RA18337236   Pvt
Declared MIA on December 13, 1950. Sent a letter while in POW status.

Fetzer, Leo E.   **RA15281807**   **Pfc**
Declared MIA on July 31, 1950. Identified by repatriates. Last known
alive October 1950.

Figureid, Ronald   **RA22815294**   **Cpl**
Declared MIA on February 15, 1951. Dog tag found in North Korea.

Fischer, James F.   US56136976   Pfc
Declared MIA on June 11, 1953. Was in combat area as letter bearer.
Area searched immediately but no body found. Evidently captured. Last
known alive June 11, 1953.

?? Flores, Willie S.   RA18031261   Cpl
Declared MIA on September 1, 1951. Added March 7, 1956: Two returnees
reported that they saw subject after he was captured.

?? Frech, John, Jr.   0060879   2nd Lieutenant
Declared MIA on July 25, 1950. Named in propaganda broadcasts.

Fulk, Lester E.   US33158005   Pfc
Declared captured on August 3, 1952. Last known alive August 3, 1952.

Fuller, Terrell J.   US57300174   Pfc
Declared MIA on February 12, 1951. Seen by repatriate in Hoeng Song.
Last known alive February 13, 1951.

Garver, Charles E.   **RA13328481**   **Pfc**
Declared MIA on February 12, 1951. Repatriate saw subject taken north
by enemy forces.

Gilley, Homer B.   **RA15410649**   **Cpl**
Declared MIA on December 2, 1950. Reported to be a prisoner by
repatriates. Last known alive December 2, 1950.

Glasser, Gerald W.   **RA13260232**   **Cpl**
Declared captured May 18, 1951. Seen alive at camp #1. Last known
alive June 1953. Added March 7, 1956: Sixty-six returnees reported
that subject was a prisoner. The statements indicated that he was in
Camp #1, Chang-Song, North Korea. In the spring of 1953 he was taken
away in a jeep by Chinese officers. He was in good health at the time
and there was nothing to indicate that his removal from camp was in the
nature of an arrest as he was and his camp companions were given candy
and cigarettes before leaving.

Goetz, George R.   **RA35800374**   **Master Sergeant**
Declared MIA on November 8, 1950. Surrounded and captured November 8,
1950.

Grenier, Donald T.   **RA21724933**   **Pvt**
Declared MIA on July 27, 1950. Name appeared on blackboard. Last known
alive approximately October 1950.

Gresser, Arnold G.   RA19350234   Pfc
Declared MIA on July 25, 1950. Name found on blackboard found in area
previously occupied by the enemy. Last known alive approximately
October 1950.

Grimsley, Robert L.   RA13321150   Pfc
Declared MIA on February 12, 1951. Named in propaganda broadcasts and
other press reports. Last known alive April 22, 1951.

Haag, Douglas H.   02101071   2nd Lieutenant
Declared MIA on July 12, 1950. Name included on a list of POWs compiled
by the Far East Command. Area in which Lieutenant was in was overrun.
He was obviously captured.

Hadnot, Charles D.   RA14276776   Pvt
Declared MIA on July 27, 1950. Identified in photograph of prisoners.
Name seen on blackboard.

Harnage, Lawrence A.   RA14337390   Pfc
Declared MIA on July 29, 1950. Subject identified in photograph of
prisoners. Name seen on blackboard.

?? Harpster, Fred W.   RA 35863803   Pvt
No information.

Harry, Edward S., Jr.   RA18283271   Pvt
Declared MIA on July 27, 1950. Name seen on a blackboard located in
area previously occupied by the enemy.

Haynie, Robert E.   RA19360132   Pvt
Declared MIA on August 2, 1950. Subject's mother received a letter from
a repatriate who said he was a prisoner at the same time as subject.
Last known alive October 14, 1950.

Hebert, Sylvio L.   ER11149106   Pvt
Declared MIA on February 2, 1951. Named in enemy propaganda broadcasts.

Hogan, Kenneth A.   RA19354580   Pvt
Declared MIA on July 27, 1950. Name appeared on UNC list of unconfirmed
POWs. Name also appeared on blackboard and face in picture.

Holt, Crenshaw A.   0058927   1st Lieutenant
Declared MIA on August 16, 1950. Appeared in press pictures.

Hoogacker, Phillip T.   RA16315593   Pvt
Declared MIA on July 27, 1950. Repatriate said he saw subject on a
march between Seoul and Pyongyang. last known alive September 1950.

Houston, James L.   RA26793789   Pfc
Declared MIA on February 14, 1951. Repatriate said he was a prisoner at
the same time as subject.

Howell, James   RA15261277   Pfc
Declared MIA on February 14, 1951. Name mentioned in International Red
Cross reports, Chinese press and other press.

Hoysradt, Donald O.   RA11167423   Pfc
Declared captured on November 21, 1950. Name included on UNC list of
POWs.

Hughes, Wayne G.   RA23410679   Pvt
Declared MIA on February 13, 1951. Repatriate said he was POW same time
as subject. Last known alive prior to April 4, 1951.

Hull, Leonard O.   **RA12242197**   **Cpl**
Declared MIA on July 20, 1950. Repatriate said he was POW same time as
subject. Last known alive September 1950.

Humiston, Donald L.   US51009999   Pfc
Declared MIA on July 22, 1952. Repatriate said subject was taken away
by a Chinese litter team.

Ishida, Mitsuyoshi   RA10103947   Pfc
Declared MIA on December 7, 1950. Repatriate said he was prisoner at
same time as subject. Last known alive December 1950.

Jarrett, Carl E.   RA17278829   Cpl
Declared MIA on May 18, 1951. Repatriate said he was a prisoner. Last
known alive May 22, 1951. Added March 7, 1956: Returnees stated that
subject was wounded and captured. He fell out of the march and was not
seen subsequently.

Jennings, John E., Jr. **ER36778696**   **Cpl**
Declared MIA on February 12, 1951. Name appeared in *China Monthly
Review* newspaper. Repatriate saw subject date unknown. Added March 7,
1956: Returnee reported subject was in POW camp at Pyoktong in Spring
1951.

Jerome, Richard   RA13333318   Pvt
Declared MIA on July 30, 1950. Name found on a blackboard. Repatriate
said he had been a prisoner with subject.

Jinks, Leonard W. E.   RA15057580   Pfc
Declared MIA on July 16, 1950. Named in an enemy propaganda broadcast.
Repatriate said he had been a prisoner with subject. Last known alive
October 14, 1950.

Johnson, Donald R.   RA11197364   Pvt
Declared MIA on February 12, 1951. Name appeared in *National Guardian*
August 4, 1951. Reported POW by International Red Cross.

Johnson, Leroy   RA18352468   Pvt
Declared MIA on February 14, 1951. Repatriate said subject was a
prisoner at the same time he was. Last known alive February 14, 1951.

Johnson, Myron   RA13344121   Pvt
Declared MIA on February 12, 1951. Peking broadcast June 29, 1951
stated subject had been captured. Last known alive June 29, 1951.

Johnson, Ray   **RA18341449**   **Cpl**
Declared MIA on September 1, 1950. Repatriate said subject was the
victim of an atrocity.

Jones, Kassidy K   ER38605309   Pfc
Declared MIA on February 12, 1951. Repatriate said subject was prisoner
with him.

Kalama, Herbert   RA10101615   Sergeant
Declared MIA on July 20, 1950. Repatriate saw subject alive in
Pyongyang. Last known alive October 14, 1950.

Kidd, Elmer O   RA12114881   Pfc
Declared MIA on November 30, 1950. Was in a convoy which was surrounded
by the enemy. Last known alive December 1950.

King, Ralph K.   US55220035   Pvt
Declared MIA date illegible. Was on patrol. Could not be located.
Ground was searched by two patrols. Searched entire area and could find
no trace of subject.

Klingler, James F.   RA13298760   Pvt
Declared MIA on February 1, 1951. Repatriate was a prisoner at same
time as subject. Last known alive February 16, 1951.

?? Konze, Anthony   RA12325352   Pfc
Declared MIA on September 1, 1950. Repatriate indicates subject was an
atrocity victim while in the hands of the enemy.

Kost, Stanley   ER13287925   Pfc
Declared MIA on February 12, 1951. Repatriate saw subject as POW. Last
known alive November 1951.

Krygowski, Francis   **RA11189504**   **Pfc**
Declared MIA July 27, 1950. Name on a blackboard in an area previously
occupied by the enemy.

Lagoni, Ditlef J.   **RA16265716**   **Sergeant 1st class**
Declared MIA on August 10, 1950. Identified by repatriates as captured.
Last known alive September 1950.

LaPointe, John N.   RA11192758   Pfc
Declared MIA on November 2, 1950. Named in propaganda broadcasts.

Lee, Enill   RA18223291   Pfc
Declared MIA on November 27, 1950. Two repatriates saw subject as POW,
date unknown. On list of POWs received from UNC Far East.

Levitski, Walter J.   **ER16306844**   **Pvt**
Declared MIA on February 12, 1951. Repatriate saw subject on a march to
Pyongyang. Name appeared in foreign press. Last known alive April 30,
1951.

Linebough, Orvill F.   RA19356698   Pvt
Declared MIA on July 27, 1950. Name found on blackboard in an area
previously occupied by the enemy.

Litchfield, Billie   RA17218055   Sergeant
Declared MIA on December 2, 1950. Repatriate said he saw subject as POW
on an unknown date.

Lopes, Alfred, Jr.   RA15297270   Pfc
Declared MIA February 13, 1951. Repatriate said he saw subject in hands
of enemy forces being marched north.

Louviere, Ray V.   RA18282808   Cpl
Declared MIA on February 13, 1951. Repatriate said he saw subject in
hands of enemy forces being marched north. Last known alive March 18,
1951.

Malanga, Angelo S.   **RA12279700**   **Cpl**
Declared MIA on August 16, 1950. Name found on blackboard. Last known
alive approximately October 1950.

Masters, Louis R.   RA13273131   Pvt
Declared MIA on July 27, 1950. Name found on blackboard. Named as POW
on a list provided by UNC Far East. Last known alive approximately
October 1950.

Mattingly, Donald L.   RA38569409   Sergeant
Declared MIA on July 29, 1950. Name found on blackboard. Named as POW
on a list provided by UNC Far East. Last known alive approximately
October 1950.

McClure, Clarence, jr.   RA13355549   Pvt
Declared MIA on February 14, 1951. Participated in propaganda
broadcasts.

McDowell, William   RA18294333   Pfc
Declared MIA on December 2, 1950. Named in enemy propaganda broadcasts.

Meagher, Neil W.   RA19340378   Cpl
Declared MIA on November 2, 1950. Identified as POW by North Koreans.

Meyers, Robert E.   RA13314858   Pfc
Declared MIA on December 1, 1950. Plane was found but no body was
found. Must have been captured.

Mireles, Marcario   RA18353729   Pfc
Declared MIA on July 27, 1950. Name seen on blackboard in area
previously occupied by the enemy. Last known alive approximately
October 1950.

Moreland, Harry D.   0555419   Capt
Declared captured on October 27, 1952. Repatriate saw subject in enemy
hands on November 9, 1952. Added March 7, 1956: The information in
this is conclusive as to capture. Subject survived the crash of his
plane but suffered the loss of his left leg near the knee. He was moved
in a truck to a hospital in a mountain camp approximately 100 miles
distant. On or about November 2, 1952 his right leg was amputated.
Sometime during November 1952 Captain Moreland was taken from his room
and was not seen subsequently.

Morris, Russel F.   RA35169826   Cpl
Declared MIA on February 13, 1951. Named in enemy press several times.
Last know alive August 1951.

Munoz, Moises   US50117033   Pfc
Declared MIA on November 24, 1952. Repatriates said he had been
captured. Last known alive November 24, 1952.

Nearhood, John W.   RA16315922   Cpl
Declared MIA on August 8, 1950. Name appeared on a blackboard. Last
known alive October 1950.

Nicowski, Anthony J.   **RA12348736**   **Cpl**
Declared MIA on February 13, 1951. Repatriates said he had been
captured. Named in enemy propaganda broadcasts.

Nystrom, John W.   **0970527**   **1st Lieutenant**
Declared MIA on May 18, 1951. Repatriates said he had been captured.

Ottesen, Eugene L.   **US57313689**   **Cpl**
Declared MIA on February 15, 1951. Repatriates said he had been
captured. Last known alive February 15, 1951.

Overgard, Elwood E.   **ER38127552**   **Cpl**
Declared MIA on February 13, 1951. Peking radio on March 22, 1951
quoted subject's letter to his wife and son. Shown as POW in the
National Guardian. Escapee reported subject a prisoner on approximately
March 15, 1951 near Chunchon, South Korea.

Peiffer, Alfred G.   **02014870**   **1st Lieutenant**
Declared MIA on September 17, 1950. Subject was in an airplane crash.
No remains were found in the aircraft or in the vicinity. Accounted as
captured September 17, 1950.

Peterson, Lyle E.   **RA19351553**   **Pvt**
Declared MIA on July 27, 1950. Repatriate said he saw subject in the
hands of the enemy on July 27, 1950.

<u>?R?</u> Pickard, Maxie L.   RA20811182   Sergeant
No information.

Pierce, Albert G.   RA37934620   **Pfc**
Declared MIA on February 13, 1951. Repatriate said subject was a POW on November 17, 1951.

Pitts, John W.   **RA14318711**   **Pfc**
Declared MIA on November 13, 1950. Repatriate was a prisoner with subject. Last known alive December 20, 1950.

Preas, Curious M.   RA18337006   Pfc
Declared MIA on August 8, 1950. Name found on a blackboard in an area previously occupied by the enemy.

Quigg, John F.   RA12304824   Cpl
Declared MIA on November 2, 1950. Named in propaganda broadcasts.

Ragin, Carl W.   RA13353133   Pvt
Declared MIA on February 12, 1951. Repatriate says subject was marched north. Last known alive February 23, 1951.

Rausch, Charles L.   RA16267642   Cpl
Declared MIA on December 2, 1950. Source says subject was POW when he was repatriated. Last known alive April 1953.

Reddick, Frank T.   RA13300101   Sergeant
Declared MIA on February 13, 1951. Repatriate saw subject in captivity. Last known alive March 13, 1951.

?? Reimer, Walter F.   RA12293602   Cpl
Declared MIA on September 1, 1950. Repatriate says subject was captured at same time.

Richey, Aggie L.   **RA19325608**   **Pvt**
Declared MIA on July 27, 1950. Name found on a blackboard in an area previously occupied by the enemy. Last known alive approximately October 1950.

Roden, Tracy R.   RA6285109   Pfc
Declared MIA on August 11, 1950. Name found on a blackboard in an area previously occupied by the enemy.

Rose, Nokomis J.   **RA33212378**   **Pvt**
Declared MIA on February 12, 1951. Identified by repatriate as prisoner.

Royer, Charles B.   **RA38649112**   **Cpl**
Declared MIA on August 11, 1950. Appeared in photographs. Last known alive approximately October 1950.

Rozear, John M., Jr.   **RA12314868**   **Cpl**
Declared MIA on July 29, 1950. Name found inside a North Korean prison. Last known alive September 1950.

Samora, Jose M.   **RA17278528**   **Pfc**
Declared MIA on February 12, 1951. Repatriate says he saw subject captured. Last known alive April 3, 1951.

Sampson, James W.   **RA15378976**   **Pfc**
Declared MIA on February 12, 1951. Repatriate said he saw subject as POW. Last known alive February 15, 1951.

Sanford, Royal W.   **RA13349848**   **Pfc**
Declared MIA on November 11, 1950. Possible atrocity case.

Schanck, Russel D.   **RA16381081**   **Pfc**
Declared captured on October 26, 1952. Captured same time as a repatriate.

Schnepper, Paul W.   US55293260   Pfc
Declared MIA on May 29, 1953. Command report indicated capture. Last known alive May 29, 1953.

Schonder, William D.   RA19256326   Pvt
Declared MIA on February 13, 1951. Named by Peking radio on June 27, 1951. Reported to have signed a statement that UN planes killed POWs.

Schuring, Gerald G.   RA17228038   Pfc
Declared MIA on November 39, 1950. Named in enemy propaganda broadcast May 5, 1951.

Seggie, William R.   RA13260817   Pvt
Declared MIA on February 12, 1951. Named in enemy propaganda broadcasts. Last known alive February 18, 1951.

Serwise, Luther D.   ER35096983   Sergeant
Declared MIA on February 12, 1951. Source indicated subject was the victim of an atrocity. Named in enemy propaganda broadcast June 22, 1951.

Sharp, James W.   **RA36081641**   **Cpl**
Declared MIA on ? December 1950. Name included in *National Guardian* as POW.

Shepard, Robert A.   RA13257820   Cpl
Declared MIA on November 28, 1950. Sources indicated subject was possibly alive.

Smith, Lawrence J.   ER38487422   Sergeant
Declared MIA February 12, 1951. Last known alive February 22, 1951. Added on March 7, 1956: Returnee reported subject was in POW camp #1.

Snider, Carl G., Jr.   ER37154633   Pfc
Declared MIA February 12, 1951. Repatriates stated he had been a POW. Peking broadcast of June 23, 1951 reported subject as one of the signatories on a statement re: bombing.

Snodgrass, Robert G.   RA19357430   Pfc
Reported MIA on February 12, 1951. Named in propaganda broadcasts and in intelligence reports.

Spiller, William R.   ER18305154   Pfc
Declared MIA on February 12, 1951. On March 7, 1956 a note was added that on March 7, 1956 two returnees reported that subject was a prisoner about March 1951.

Springer, William   RA12333808   Pfc
Declared MIA on July 27, 1950. Name and face seen in undated photograph.

Steger, William H.   RA16254756   Pfc
Declared MIA on July 27, 1950. Name seen on blackboard in area previously occupied by the enemy.

Stone, Neil H.   US55280508   Pfc
Declared MIA on June 30, 1953. Subject's helmet and backpack were found at site of disappearance. Believed that he was taken prisoner.

Sternad, John T.   ER37505463   Pfc
Declared MIA on February 14, 1951. Source states he saw him while captive of the Chinese.

Stoeber, Walter, Jr.   RA13257783   Pfc
Declared MIA on January 1, 1951. Grounds for POW status are illegible.

Stumpf, Marion F.   RA17059498   Pfc
Declared MIA on December 12, 1950. Identified as POW by repatriates.

Sweeney, John R.   RA12329620   Pfc
Declared MIA on February 13, 1951. Identified by name in enemy press and by repatriates as POW.

Switzer, Contee L.   RA17280811   Pfc
Declared captured on February 14, 1951. Identified as POW by repatriates.

Tatarakis, George G.   RA19306236   Cpl
Declared MIA on February 19, 1952. Repatriates identified him as POW.

Takahara, Sam, O.   02030786   1st Lieutenant
Declared MIA in ?? 1950. Identified in enemy propaganda broadcasts.

?? Thomas, Mitchell C.   02014760   2nd Lieutenant
Declared MIA on July 27, 1950. Identified as POW by repatriates.

Tish, Clarence A., Jr.   RA14287845   Pfc
Declared MIA on July 25, 1950. Last known alive in enemy hands on day of capture.

Tomlinson, Marvin F.   **RA6249933**   **Sergeant 1st class**
Declared MIA on February 14, 1951. Identified by name in Chinese press three times.

Toole, Arnold   **RA16280172**   **Cpl**
Declared MIA on August 11, 1950. Name was seen on a blackboard in an area previously occupied by the enemy.

Torres, Louis P.   RA16273385   Pfc
Declared MIA on September 1, 1950. Identified as POW by repatriates.

Tucker, Lloyd L.   **RA18337483**   **Pfc**
Declared MIA on August 11, 1950. Was identified by repatriates and in a group photograph of POWs on August 18, 1950.

Van Wyk, Clayton F.   **RA27031343**   **Pfc**
Last known alive March 18, 1951 by repatriates.

Vernon, Raymond A.   US51134261   Pvt
Declared MIA July 5, 1952.

Vranic, Anthony   **TS55005643**   **Pfc**
Declared MIA August 11, 1950. Identified as POW by repatriates.

Walczak, Castnir F.   **RA16316451**   **Pvt**
Declared MIA on August 17, 1950. Identified as POW in enemy propaganda broadcasts.

Walker, Archie   **RA19304659**   **Pfc**
Captured [illegible], 1950. Identified as POW in propaganda broadcast of March 23, 1951 and in press.

Wallen, James A.   **RA15236536**   **Pfc**
Declared captured on July 25, 1950. Name seen on a blackboard.

Ware, Raymond O.   **RA17281042**   **Pvt**
Name appeared in *National Guardian* as POW.

Watkins, Samuel K.   **RA14364811**   **Pvt**
No information.

Watson, James D.   RA18344264   Cpl
Declared MIA on December 2, 1950. Named appeared in *National Guardian* as POW.

Webb, Jerald C.   **RA24484357**   **Pfc**
Declared MIA on December 2, 1950. Repatriate identified him as POW.

White, Waddell   **RA17284623**   **Pvt**
Declared MIA on January 4, 1951. Reported to be POW in Command reports and by repatriates.

Williams, Albert   RA14301914   **Pfc**
Declared MIA on November 27, 1950. Last seen alive by repatriates
November 28, 1950.

Wilson, Merble   RA15242639   **Pfc**
Declared captured on February 15, 1951. Identified in an enemy
propaganda photograph. Last known alive on February 23, 1951.

Wilson, Richard L.   RA16328280   **Cpl**
Declared MIA on July 27, 1950. Reported to be alive in POW status by
repatriates on 19-20 September 1950.

Winrader, Howard W.   RA23786250   **Pfc**
Declared MIA on January 28, 1951. Named in Peking news release June 29,
1951, mentioned in *China Monthly Review* August 1951, *Shanghai News*, July
3, 1951, and *National Guardian,* August 29, 1951.

Woods, Joseph H.   RA12314320   **Pfc**
Declared MIA on February 6, 1951. Referred to by name in the *China
Monthly Review* in July and August, 1951 and the *National Guardian* on
August 29, 1951.

Wooster, Audrey H.   RA18224279   **Sergeant**
Declared MIA on February 13, 1951. Repatriate saw him in enemy hands.
Last known alive February 15, 1951.

Worley, Frank   RA14366839   **Pvt**
Declared MIA on February 12, 1951. Named in a Peking radio broadcast on
June 28, 1951.

Wright, Edward C.   ER37515113   **Cpl**
Declared MIA on February 12, 1951. Repatriated POWs identified him as a
POW being moved north on March 29, 1951.

** Yoshida, Kanji   US50000110   Pfc
Declared MIA on May 25, 1951. Interrogation of other UN prisoners and
interrogation of enemy POW are the source of this information.

Young, Charles H.   RA13271083   **Cpl**
Declared MIA on February 1, 1951. Command report notes that sources saw
him as POW.

Young, Russell V.   RA19328611   **Pvt**
Declared MIA on July 27, 1950. Command reports suggested he was POW.
Name was found on a blackboard in an area previously occupied by the
enemy.

Zawacki, Frank J.   RA15267535   **Cpl**
Declared MIA on August 16, 1950. Zawacki's name had been seen on a
blackboard in an area previously occupied by the enemy.

U.S. Navy (3)		
Biesterveld, Thomas Clarence	506698	Ensign
Brown, William Edmund	496712	Ensign
Cochran, Billy Edward	475207	Lt (junior grade)
U.S. Marine Corps (12)		
Bookamire, Gerald R.	1249268	Pfc
Chidester, Arthur A.	05234	Colonel
DeLacy, Arthur D.	051658	2nd Lieutenant
Eagan, James K.	07760	Maj
Gleaves, James A., Jr.	051308	2nd Lieutenant
Green, James L.	1175542	Pfc
Lewis, William T., Jr.	11681313	Pfc
Morrow, Billy J.	1188495	Pfc
Nelson, Forest A.	044100	2st Lieutenant
Taylor, Charles A.	633516	Pfc
Tuttle, Raymond J.	1035628	Pfc
Young, Robert J.	1092372	Pfc
U. S. Air Force (186)[2]		
Name	Serial Number	Grade or Rank

Adler, Ernest M.   A02073084   **1st Lieutenant**
Reported MIA October 15, 1951. The altitude of the aircraft reported would seriously limit the chances of successful bailout and landing. Enemy personnel may have located the crew members other than the one who evaded capture.

Akin, Roland M.   A02094960   **1st Lieutenant**
Reported MIA September 12, 1951. The validity of a letter referring to Akin received by the Department of State on April 11, 1955 is very questionable and is not considered to provide substantial information. Nevertheless, it is possible that Akin did survive and was subsequently captured by enemy forces.

Allen, Jack V.   16683A   Capt
Reported MIA July 1, 1953. Allen ordered his crew to bail out near Chodo Island. Subsequently, the wreckage of a burning B-26 was observed. Subsequent search revealed no trace of Allen.

Anderson, Robert E.   A01911386   1st Lieutenant
Reported MIA May 21, 1952. The report that Anderson was seen in Camp #2 appears to be of very doubtful validity.

Andrews, Robert B.   A0813127   **Capt**
Same as for Ernest M. Adler.

---

[2]Comments following each name are taken from Air Force Manual No. 200-25, Department of the Air Force, January 16, 1961. The Air Force *does not* refer to these individuals as *unrepatriated POWs*. "Purpose: This manual contains data on each of the 187 Air Force officers and airmen who were 'missing in action' as a result of the Korean conflict. It is provided for use by intelligence personnel of the United States and its allies in acquiring additional information regarding their fate."

Arms, John W.   A02225726   2nd Lieutenant
Reported MIA June 5, 1953. One of the two crew members, possibly both,
survived the crash and were captured.

Ashley, Gilbert L., Jr.   **A0666215**   **Capt**
Reported MIA January 29, 1953. Ashley's B-29 was shot down on January
29, 1953. It caught fire, crashed and exploded. Three crewmen were
repatriated. They reported four other members of the crew of 14 had
bailed out. Ashley was not reported to be among them.

Austin, Arthur M.   A01289023   Maj
Reported MIA April 27, 1951. Austin's plane contacted ground control at
Taegu at 1920, April 26, 1951. This was the last known contact.

Beardall, Harold M.   **A0769375**   **Capt**
Reported MIA May 21, 1951. Beardall was alive and in enemy hands in
late October or early November 1951. He may have died while a POW but
there is no confirmation.

Bell, Donald E.   A0814007   1st Lieutenant
Reported MIA January 26, 1952. At 0105, January 26 1952, Bell's plane
radioed that it was about to strike a target. The plane was not heard
from again.

Bell, William J.   22108A   1st Lieutenant
Reported MIA October 7, 1952. Bell's aircraft was hit during a bombing
run. No parachutes were sighted in the air or on the ground, though the
plane was out of sight for 45 seconds in a cloud on its way down. Bell
could have bailed out while the plane was out of sight or survived the
crash, but neither seem likely.

Bergmann, Louis H.   **AF17124468**   **Sergeant**
Reported MIA April 12, 1951. Reported to be a prisoner by several
repatriates. Reported to have died in Pak's Palace.

Biggs, Elmer T.   **A02092623**   **1st Lieutenant**
Reported MIA January 3, 1952. Biggs was captured by the enemy. He may
have been injured, burned or wounded.

Bigham, Donald G.   **A0767469**   **Capt**
Reported MIA November 9, 1951. It is probable Bigham landed in the
water some distance from an island. He may have survived and was
possibly picked up by the enemy.

Black, Wayne F.   **A0599631**   **Capt**
Reported MIA October 23, 1951. All of the crew of the B-29 had time to
clear the aircraft. The fact that five other crewmen were captured
indicates a strong possibility that others were, too.

Bolt, Donald D.   **A0837772**   **1st Lieutenant**
Reported MIA October 2, 1950. Bolt made a forced landing in a rice
field, got out of his aircraft and waved to circling planes. Bolt was
last seen just before darkness. There have been no further reports.

Botter, William J.   **AF33570888**   **Technical Sergeant**
Same as for Wayne F. Black.

Brennan, John C.   AF11227081   Airman 3rd class
Reported MIA November 14, 1952. The repatriated aircraft commander
reported that there was a good possibility Brennan was in enemy hands.
The evidence cannot be taken as conclusive proof, however, since it is
possible the enemy could have obtained their information by other means.

Burrell, Jackson A.   A02081396   Capt
Reported MIA June 5, 1952. Burrell probably bailed out successfully and
landed in the water. This being the case, he could have been either
picked up by enemy forces at sea or drowned.

Burten, Woodrow   A02101608   1st Lieutenant
Reported MIA October 2, 1950. Burten was bailed out, landed and waved
to circling aircraft. He was subsequently captured by enemy forces.

Bushroe, Sterling J   **A01911963**   **1st Lieutenant**
Reported MIA September 11, 1951. Bushroe successfully bailed out of his
plane and was captured by enemy forces.

Carlisle, Osborne T.   **A0426554**   **Capt**
Reported MIA February 28, 1952. All crew members seem to have had time
to bail out before the crash. It is conceivable, however, that Carlisle
may not have successfully cleared the aircraft, since he was the
aircraft commander and therefore the last to bail out.

Cave, James A.   AF13411410   Airman 2nd class
Same as for J. A. Burrell.

Cherry, Clarence M.   AF19201403   Staff Sergeant
Reported MIA September 9, 1950. There is a good chance Cherry was
removed from a hospital and taken to an unknown destination by North
Koreans.

Cogswell, Robert W.   11880A   Maj
Same as for Wayne F. Black.

Collins, Joseph A   A0807154   Capt
Reported MIA September 2, 1951. Since one member of the crew survived
the accident, it is possible Collins did too.

Cooper, Spencer R.   AF21900368   Airman 1st class
Reported MIA April 7, 1952. Information pertaining to Cooper being a
POW is probably true.

Coulter, John R.   A01909263   1st Lieutenant
Reported MIA December 1, 1950. At about 0100, December 1, 1950, while
in the vicinity of Seoul, he contacted control and was not heard from
again.

Crane, Alvin E., Jr.   A01903066   1st Lieutenant
Reported MIA September 12, 1951. It is very probable Crane was captured by enemy forces.

Crutchfield, James F.   A0736133   Lieutenant Colonel
Reported MIA July 23, 1952. Crutchfield successfully bailed out of his aircraft and was captured by the enemy.

Culbertson, Gene A.   A0718487   Capt
Reported MIA February 23, 1953. It is possible the plane ditched or that the crew bailed out over water near the coast. The report that Culbertson was at Kaesong awaiting repatriation is of questionable validity.

Davies, Howard J.   A01909468   1st Lieutenant
Reported MIA March 6, 1952. Davies's aircraft disappeared without a trace.

Davis, Norman G.   AF15209199   Staff Sergeant
Reported MIA September 12, 1951. It is possible that Davis was the sole survivor on his aircraft, but a Chinese POW's testimony to this effect has no substantiating evidence.

Davis, Ramon R.   A0767144   1st Lieutenant
Reported MIA October 5, 1950. Davis was seen climbing out of his aircraft, apparently uninjured, and walking off into the nearby hills. There have been no further reports.

Denn, Willard M.   AF16329167   Airman 2nd class
Same as for Osborne T. Carlisle.

DeRosier, Albert P.   A01340348   1st Lieutenant
Same as for Rolan M. Akin.

Differ, Patrick M.   AF13021311   Master Sergeant
Reported MIA December 30, 1952. Differ may have decided to stay with the aircraft until it was too late for successful bailout. The facts at hand do not, however, rule out the possibility that he jumped successfully and was later captured.

Dorsey, Joyce T.   AF17167105   Technical Sergeant
Reported MIA October 3, 1950. It is possible the report of execution of three American crewmen may be associated with the crew of Dorsey's aircraft. It is possible information obtained in Little Switch pertained to Marvin E. Dorsey and not SSgt Joyce M. Dorsey.

Dougherty, Joseph S.   AF13041845   Staff Sergeant
Reported MIA October 23, 1951. Dougherty was seen to bail out of a stricken B-29 over the water but was not seen thereafter.

Duer, Victor L.   **A0753626**   **Staff Sergeant**
Reported MIA April 30, 1952. After Duer reported a fire in the cockpit he said he was bailing out. Wreckage of the aircraft was located but there was no sign of Duer.

Duncan, James H.   AF14101683   **1st Lieutenant**
Reported MIA September 9, 1950. Duncan may have successfully bailed out and been captured.

Edens, Malcolm B.   A0789892   **Maj**
Reported MIA November 28, 1950. Edens probably died while in captivity before reaching a POW camp. Repatriates reported seeing Edens in severe pain with frostbite, infection and exposure.

Evans, Emmett O.   A02060489   1st Lieutenant
Reported MIA November 8, 1952. The fact that the B-29 was subjected to explosive decompression and went into a spin may have prevented successful bailout by crewmen other than Hill, Hall and Schluter, who were thrown clear. The Reconnaissance Activities report indicates a slight possibility that one other crew member survived and was captured.

Festini, Steve J.   **13030A**   **1st Lieutenant**
Reported MIA May 21, 1951. It is possible Festini cleared the aircraft and landed safely.

Fleming, James W., Jr.   A0780156   1st Lieutenant
Same as for Emmett O. Evans.

Foster, Robert R.   A0550110   1st Lieutenant
Reported MIA December 30, 1952. Foster may have decided to stay with the aircraft and attempt to land in friendly territory due to injured on board. It is also possible that he bailed out and was captured.

Foulks, James A., Jr.   **A02080021**   **Capt**
Same as for Wayne F. Black.

Fuehrer, Alois A.   AF13233572   Airman 1st class
Same as for Wayne F. Black.

Gahan, John W.   AF15380313   Sergeant
Reported MIA November 30, 1950. The name that appeared on the unofficial POW list may have actually referred to Gahan. It is also possible that Gahan was among the four Air Force personnel reportedly shot by the enemy after the enemy overran Gahan's tactical air control party.

Gallant, James A.   AF15295553   Airman 2nd class
Reported MIA October 23, 1951. There was sufficient time between the emergency and the crash for the crew members to abandon the B-29. Therefore, it is possible that the Communists have knowledge of Gallant's fate.

Garrison, Fred II   A0791811   Capt
Same as for Emmett O. Evans.

George, Winifred R.   **AF14140942**   **Technical Sergeant**
Reported MIA December 28, 1950. Plane disappeared after a bombing run. No further mention of George.

Gibb, Robert D.   **13053A**   **Capt**
Reported MIA December 16, 1951. Gibb's aircraft did not return after a bombing run. Aerial search of area could not be made.

Glessner, Milton F., Jr.   3375A   Lt. Colonel
Reported MIA February 2, 1951. It is very probable that Glessner was badly injured or did not survive the crash.

Golden, Newman C.   A0934440   1st Lieutenant
Reported MIA October 17, 1951. Plane on fire, Golden radioed he was about to bail out. Flaming wreckage but no sign of Golden found.

Gross, Robert F.   AF14226221   Master Sergeant
Reported MIA April 30, 1951. Gross's C-47 made a distress call then vanished. Aerial search was unavailing.

Guilfoyle, Cornelius P.   A0739549   Capt
Reported MIA April 7, 1951. The information pertinent to reports of Guilfoyle being a POW is probably true.

Guthrie, Edward S., Jr.   22193A   1st Lieutenant
Reported MIA November 14, 1952. There is a good possibility that Guthrie bailed out successfully and was captured by the enemy.

Guthrie, Marvin I.   AF6388833   Staff Sergeant
Same as for Winifred R. George.

Hamblin, Robert W.   **AF12127986**   **Technical Sergeant**
Reported MIA October 23, 1951. Although four members of the B-29 were rescued from the water, Hamblin was not seen by those rescued. It is possible he survived.

Hammon, Keith E.   AF15230651   Technical Sergeant
Same as for Emmett O. Evans.

Harker, Charles A., Jr.   A02224102   2nd Lieutenant
Reported MIA May 3, 1953. At 2115 hours on May 3, Harker's plane disappeared from the radar scope. There was no indication that Harker was experiencing difficulty. No further word from or sightings of his aircraft.

Harrell, Guy B., Jr.   A0391377   Capt
Reported MIA November 25, 1951. On December 5, 1951 the 9th ROK Division reported that crew members, believed to be personnel of the Harrell crew, had bailed out inside enemy lines, about 5 miles northeast of Ch'Orwong. Search of the area revealed no sign of the missing aircraft or crew.

Haskett, William T., Jr.   **A0790664**   **Capt**
Reported MIA April 14, 1951. Haskett bailed out successfully and attempted to evade.

Hawkins, Luther R., Jr.   A0812589   **Capt**
Reported MIA May 24, 1952. In all probability Hawkins accomplished
successful bailout and landed alive in enemy territory. It is quite
possible that he was shot while attempting to evade captors.

Hays, Melvin B.   AF39192109   Airman 3rd class
Same as for James A. Gallant.

Heer, David T.   A02223002   2d Lieutenant
Reported MIA December 30, 1952. Heer may have decided to stay with the
aircraft until it was too late for successful bailout. The facts at
hand do not, however, rule out the possibility that he jumped
successfully and was later captured.

Heise, Arthur   **A0750985**   **Capt**
Reported MIA January 10, 1953. It is possible Heise may have stayed
with the aircraft too long and that the information reported by the
Chinese, that Heise was dead, is correct. The rest of the crew was
repatriated.

Henry, Dewey R.   A0927982   1st Lieutenant
Reported MIA January 29, 1953. There is a possibility that subject
survived the aircraft incident in enemy territory. This is
substantiated by statements of repatriated crew members which indicate
that there was sufficient time to evacuate the aircraft subsequent to
the emergency and that at least seven of the 14 crew members are known
to have parachuted.

Hoff, Warren N.   A02084887   1st Lieutenant
Reported MIA March 6, 1952. Aircraft disappeared with no trace.

Holcom, William L.   A0933359   1st Lieutenant
Reported MIA August 8, 1952. The aircraft was hit and apparently
severely damaged, thus necessitating an immediate bailout at low
altitude. The bailout was transmitted on VHF since it was heard by
other aircraft. The crew probably didn't receive the bailout order.

Holz, Scott A.   A0190608   1st Lieutenant
Reported MIA April 7, 1952. The information pertaining to reports of
Holz being a POW is probably true. He was probably captured about April
7, 1952.

Horner, John J.   A01911849   1st Lieutenant
Reported MIA October 23, 1951. It appears there was sufficient time
between the emergency and the crash of the aircraft in Communist
territory for the crew members to abandon the B-29. Therefore, it is
possible that the Communists have knowledge of Horner's fate.

Hoult, Arthur W.   **AF6953553**   **Staff Sergeant**
Reported MIA September 9, 1950. The possibility exists Hoult
successfully bailed out and was subsequently captured.

Howell, Howard D.   **13402A**   **Capt**
Reported MIA July 12, 1951. The information obtained from the enemy POW about two American pilots appears to be hearsay and is not conclusive. If the report is correct, it is possible Howell was captured by enemy forces.

Hudson, Lawrence N.   A02092806   1st Lieutenant
Same as for Lt. Horner.

Hyatt, Don   A0674199   Capt
Reported MIA September 9, 1950. One repatriate said Hyatt had been in Camp #2 briefly before being taken to an unknown location. Two other repatriates said they did not see Hyatt there.

Ishida, Nidemero   AF19415365   Airman 2nd class
Same as for Lt. Henry.

Jacobs, Harrison C.   **A01909723**   **1st Lieutenant**
Reported MIA December 27, 1950. Jacobs was probably lost temporarily over water. It is possible Jacobs never gained sufficient altitude for bailout since the aircraft received damage on both his left control surfaces. The remainder of his flight failed to locate any trace of aircraft or pilot.

Jacobson, Paul J.   A04222046   1st Lieutenant
Reported MIA February 12, 1953. Jacobson had sufficient altitude to make a successful bailout. He may have landed north of the Yalu. Aircraft in formation with him were searching for missing aircraft from too high an altitude (20,000-38,000 feet) to observe any bailout or aircraft crash.

Jensen, Morton H.   AF27358781   Technical Sergeant
Reported MIA November 19, 1952. It is possible Jensen landed safely in enemy territory and was subsequently captured. It is also possible that he may have hit the water and failed to survive.

Jensen, Wayne F.   AF19405070   Staff Sergeant
Same as for Lt. Evans.

Johnson, Gerald E.   **AF13337205**   **Airman 3rd class**
Same as for Lt. Horner.

Johnson, Johnny M.   **AF18012750**   **Technical Sergeant**
Same as for Lt. Horner.

Jones, James L.   **AF16226038**   **Airman 3rd class**
Reported MIA April 7, 1951. The fact that rescue was in the area and picked up another crew member but could find no other survivors is evidence that a search of the area had been made. The fact that the aircraft exploded within seconds after the bailout order was given indicated that possibly the crewmembers did not bail out or survive.

Jones, Oliver E.   **A01911207**   **1st Lieutenant**
Reported MIA October 22, 1951. Jones, though bailing out, did not clear the aircraft. The altitude of the aircraft (nose down) during bailout in all probability resulted in Jones being hit by the aircraft. This resulted in injury and consequently his failure to pull the ripcord.

Karpowicz, Jerome   AF16395206   Airman 1st class
Reported MIA May 17, 1953. Evidence indicates Karpowicz bailed out of the aircraft. There is nothing to indicate whether bailout was successful or not. The garbled radio transmission may have originated with Karpowicz.

Keene, Kassel M.   **A0420472**   **Maj**
Same as for Morton H. Jensen.

Keister, Harold O.   A0785071   Capt
Reported MIA August 30, 1951. Evidence indicates that there is a possibility that Keister and other crew members bailed out.

Kelleher, Robert P.   AF11205730   Airman 1st class
Same as for Lt. Evans.

Kepford, Joseph O.   **A0818388**   **Capt**
Reported MIA October 7, 1950. Kepford successfully bailed out of his aircraft and was alive when he landed.

King, Alfred H.   A01912154   1st Lieutenant
Reported MIA February 23, 1953. It is possible that the aircraft ditched or the crew bailed out over water near the coast.

Kirk, Charles F.   A02079748   1st Lieutenant
Same as for Lt. Evans.

Knapp, Kingdon R.   A0885977   Capt
Reported MIA June 7, 1951. Aircraft disappeared with no trace.

Knueppel, Raymond J.   **A0707938**   **Capt**
Reported MIA April 22, 1951. Knueppel was last seen in a parachute by his pilot. Crew members had ample time to bail out since aircraft was observed to be under control to at least 1,500 feet.

Koontz, Frederick R.   **A01909920**   **1st Lieutenant**
Reported MIA September 2, 1951. One member of the crew bailed out successfully and was subsequently captured. This indicates a possibility that Koontz may also have been captured.

Krumm, Robert N.   **A0804464**   **Capt**
Same as for Lt. Horner.

Kuehner, Gordon V., Jr.   **A0832161**   **1st Lieutenant**
The summary in the Air Force report mentions Lt. Robert A. Gehman, but says nothing about Gordon V. Kuehner.

Laier, Robert H.   18039A   **1st Lieutenant**
Reported MIA June 19, 1951. Laier was probably successful in surviving the crash of his aircraft and was subsequently captured. The unofficial broadcast from Radio Peking was probably true.

Larkin, Hugh F.   A0437976   **Capt**
Reported MIA December 5, 1951. Larkin bailed out successfully; however, he probably landed in the water. This being the case, he may have been picked up by an enemy vessel or may not have survived the water landing.

Layton, Laurence C.   A01910250   **1st Lieutenant**
Reported MIA September 2, 1951. It is apparent that Layton successfully bailed and landed in the water off enemy controlled territory. It is also possible that he may have been captured by the Communists.

Lewis, Jack   12658A   Capt
Reported MIA May 21, 1951. It is possible that the report that only one crew member cleared the aircraft before it exploded at low altitude is true. It is also possible, to a lesser degree, that Lewis could have cleared the aircraft and landed safely.

Lewis, Wayne E.   AF17306085   **Airman 1st class**
Reported MIA March 22, 1952. No definite conclusion can be reached because of the absence of authentic information. Basis for the report that subject crashed into a mountain is unknown. The report by the Korean farmer may be true though he gave an incorrect date of the sighting. The possibility also exists that the British report was in error since an Airman David Lewis was repatriated in Big Switch.

Lewis, Wilbur E.   A0772859   **2nd Lieutenant**
Reported MIA June 11, 1952. Aircraft disappeared without a trace.

Logan, Samuel P.   11287A   **Maj**
Reported MIA September 9, 1950. It appears conclusive Logan successfully bailed out and was captured by enemy forces probably near the scene of the crash.

Long, Joseph S., Jr.   A0724957   Maj
Reported MIA April 7, 1952. The information pertaining to reports of Long being a POW is probably true.

McAdoo, Ernest R.   AF13337425   **Airman 1st class**
Same as for Lt. Horner.

McAllaster, John A., Jr.   A0757831   Capt
Reported MIA April 4, 1952. There is no evidence to confirm or deny the possibility that McAllaster may have survived and been captured.

McFee, Claude D.   AF19245204   Staff Sergeant
Reported MIA December 6, 1950. McFee had ample time to bail out since the altitude (4,000 feet) was sufficient and the emergency was such that the aircraft could be controlled. The boats which were sighted could have been enemy fishing boats, and he may have been picked up and turned over to the enemy.

McKee, Robert E.   A02089113   **Capt**

Reported MIA October 18, 1950. 8th Army JAG reported that a source saw two Americans parachute to the ground. North Korean soldiers killed them. Report referenced above may be true, and the individuals mentioned may possibly be identified with McKee and crew.

McLoughlin, Robert J.   AF12335474   **Airman 2nd class**

Same as for Morton H. Jensen.

Martin, Dominique K.   A01909619   **1st Lieutenant**

Reported MIA May 5, 1952. Martin landed intact and attempted to evade.

Mast, Clifford N.   AF19417343   **Staff Sergeant**

Reported MIA July 4, 1952. The aircraft was under control and there was sufficient time for Mast to bail out. (This is evidenced by the fact that 11 members of this crew of 13 were repatriated. One member was dead prior to bailout.) Mast, in all probability, was panicky. However, it is doubtful that Mast would remain aboard a burning aircraft after observing the crew bail out. Assuming Mast bailed out last and consequently landed a considerable distance from the other members of his crew, which in all probability resulted in his not being associated with the crew after capture. Mast was not seen or heard from subsequent to bailout. Some crew members believe Mast was captured and either killed or taken to Manchuria, though they could give no evidence to support their belief.

Miller, Henry D.   A01852083   **1st Lieutenant**

Reported MIA December 8, 1951. The circumstances of loss indicate that there is a possibility that Miller may not have cleared the aircraft before it crashed.

Mitchell, Bernard   AF31378023   **Airman 1st class**

Reported MIA January 14, 1951. Since Mitchell reported the fire it appears he had sufficient time to abandon the aircraft and in all likelihood did so immediately following his report.

Mooradian, Ara   A0932011   **Capt**

Same as for Lt. Black.

Moore, John G.   A0886003   **Capt**

Reported MIA August 30, 1951. Search missions reported three parachutes. Evidence suggests there is a possibility Moore and other crew members bailed out.

Myers, Thomas E.   13136A   **Capt**

Reported MIA October 2, 1950. The initial observations of other members of the flight indicate Myers may have been injured during bailout or landing. The fact that later observations revealed no trace of Myers is not conclusive evidence that he was alive since enemy forces could have removed the body and the chute. It is also possible that he was alive and managed to free himself from the tree and arrive safely on the ground. The report of a Maj. Myers coming through a POW camp during Big Switch is possibly true but not of conclusive nature. At the time of loss, Myers was a captain not a major.

Nelson, Lawrence A.   A02221692   1st Lieutenant
Same as for Capt. Carlisle.

Nichols, James L.   AF17326268   1st Lieutenant
Same as for Morton H. Jensen.

Nikles, Rudolf   AF12383404   Airman 1st class
Reported MIA December 30, 1952. Nikles may have decided to stay with
the aircraft until it was too late for successful bailout. The facts at
hand do not, however, rule out the possibility that he jumped
successfully and was later captured.

Nye, Glenn C.   1768A   Colonel
Same as for William J. Bell.

O'Brien, Warren E.   A0827259   Capt
Reported MIA September 9, 1952. In all probability O'Brien bailed out
successfully and landed intact in enemy territory.

Olcott, Ray W.   A01909367   1st Lieutenant
Same as for Lt. Adler.

Olsen, Arthur R.   A02069417   1st Lieutenant
Same as for Lt. Henry.

O'Meara, James J., Jr.   AF16354305   Airman 2nd class
Same as for Lt. Henry.

O'Neal, Julius E.   4792A   Lieutenant Colonel
Reported MIA October 23, 1951. Since crew members were definite in
identifying O'Neal's parachute as being in the air, it is possible he
may have survived and later been captured.

Osborne, Jess A., Jr.   AF13351603   Airman 3rd class
Same as for Lt. Horner.

O'Toole, Damian F.   AF13462243   Airman 2nd class
Reported MIA December 30, 1952. There appears to be little doubt that
the enemy had either captured O'Toole or had found his body. The latter
is considered the most probable.

Oyler, Ernest R.   A0744348   Capt
Reported MIA September 9, 1950. There is insufficient evidence on which
to base any firm conclusions. The possibility exists that Oyler may
have successfully bailed out and was subsequently captured.

Padilla, Alexander B.   A0336092   Capt
Reported MIA October 9, 1950. Conclusion: Padilla survived the
airplane crash.

Palmer, Alford C.   A02223160   **2nd Lieutenant**
Reported MIA September 5, 1952. There is a reasonable possibility that subject aircraft was hit by other friendly aircraft and that Palmer was unable to bail out prior to crash. The FEAF report concerning Palmer's possible presence in a POW camp appears to be of very doubtful validity.

Palmiotti, Nicholas M.   AF12313035   **Airman 1st class**
Reported MIA August 30, 1951. There is a possibility Palmiotti and other crew members bailed out.

Parham, Charles E., Jr.   AF14103757   **Cpl**
Reported MIA November 25, 1951.   Although subject was never heard from again and statement by one who reported seeing parachutes and flares never verified, it indicates a possibility that subject was one of the seven who escaped the aircraft and survived.

Peck, James K.   A0741690   **1st Lieutenant**
Same as for Morton H. Jensen.

Penninger, Roger W.   A0778935   **1st Lieutenant**
Reported MIA October 23, 1951. There is some question as to exactly how many crewmen actually got out of the aircraft. Subject therefore may have successfully bailed out and was not identified or observed.

Peterson, Norman W.   AF17312946   Airman 2nd class
Reported MIA March 6, 1952. Aircraft disappeared without a trace. Subsequent air search for missing plane made with negative results.

Phelps, Ralph L.   AF17291247   **Staff Sergeant**
Same as for Lt. McAllaster.

Phillips, Duane M.   19732A   **2nd Lieutenant**
Reported MIA April 7, 1951. There appear to be inconsistencies in the information in various statements. A search of the area where Phillips was lost was made. The fact that the aircraft exploded within seconds after the bailout order was given indicates that possibly all the crew members did not bail out or survive.

Pincus, Herbert   A0946510   **1st Lieutenant**
Same as for William J. Bell.

Pope, James D.   AF14404363   **Airman 2nd class**
Reported MIA January 29, 1953. Although subject was never heard from again and statement by one who reported seeing parachutes and flares never verified, it indicates a possibility that subject was one of the seven who escaped the aircraft and survived.

Porter, James H.   AF14397423   **Airman 1st class**
Same as for Morton H. Jensen.

Poynor, Com. F.   A0725476   **1st Lieutenant**
Same as for Lt. Horner.

Pratt, Charles W.   16993A   **Capt**
Reported MIA November 8, 1951. Seconds after Pratt radioed he was hit he immediately called he was bailing out. No parachutes were observed in the area by the wingman.

Raymond, Gerald W.   AF19363298   **Staff Sergeant**
Reported MIA May 7, 1951. The other two members of Raymond's crew were subsequently returned to military control. One evaded capture and the other was repatriated during Big Switch. Information from the surviving crew members reveals that Raymond was not seen to bail out. Immediately after the B-26 was hit Raymond was called but gave no answer.

Rehm, Harry M.   A02089519   **1st Lieutenant**
Reported MIA December 30, 1952. Rehm may have decided to stay with the aircraft until it was too late for successful bailout. The facts at hand do not, however, rule out the possibility that he may have jumped successfully and was later captured.

Rhinehart, Charles W.   A01911442   **1st Lieutenant**
Reported MIA January 29, 1952. It is possible Rhinehart may have slipped his harness too soon and may have suffered injury on landing in the water.

Ritter, Herbert E.   A0666440   **1st Lieutenant**
Reported MIA October 1, 1951. Ritter may possibly have been wounded as a result of the MiG attack or may have been injured on bailout.

Rodney, Daryl E.   AF19400458   **Airman 1st class**
Reported MIA December 30, 1952. It appears Rodney was wounded and unable to attempt bailout. There is more indication that one other crew member was attempting to help him. As a result both may have failed to clear the aircraft in time.

Roundtree, Fred D.   17495A   **Capt**
Reported MIA January 14, 1951. Rountree bailed out successfully. Other crew member who also bailed out heard one report of an American in the vicinity guarded by two Chinese. The crewman was of the opinion, however, that Roundtree was dead.

Schauer, Gilbert J.   A02068874   **1st Lieutenant**
Reported MIA April 7, 1952. The fact that allegedly no mention was made of Schauer in a propaganda broadcast that included the other members of his crew is not conclusive in any way. It is possible that if Schauer landed intact he may have been captured subsequent to the broadcast.

Schmitt, Warren W.   AF17151509   **Airman 2nd class**
Same as for Lt. Evans.

Schneidt, Norman W.   A0810255   **Capt**
Same as for Lt. Evans.

Schwab, Edward A.   AF12359965   Cpl
Reported MIA January 29, 1953.

Selman, Clifford G.   A01864097   1st Lieutenant
Reported MIA May 17, 1953. Evidence indicates Selman bailed out of the aircraft. There is nothing to indicate whether bailout was successful or not.

Shaddick, John P. III   **A02221920**   **1st Lieutenant**
Same as for Lt. Henry.

Sheehan, Robert E.   **A0547956**   **1st Lieutenant**
Reported MIA January 23, 1952. There is no doubt Lt. Sheehan was alive after landing. Although there is nothing to substantiate it, there is a good possibility that he would have paddled to the island where he may have been subsequently captured.

Shields, Thomas L.   A0837209   Capt
Reported MIA October 23, 1951. There is some question as to exactly how many crewmen actually got out of the aircraft. Subject therefore may have successfully bailed out and was not identified or observed.

Smith, James D., Jr.   **A02282046**   **2nd Lieutenant**
Reported MIA November 25, 1951. A report was received on December 5, 1951 from 9th ROK Division that crew members, believed to be personnel of this crew, had bailed out inside enemy lines, about five miles northwest of Ch'Orwong. Search of area was negative.

Southerland, John E.   A01910800   1st Lieutenant
Reported MIA June 6, 1953. Lt. Southerland bailed out successfully and attempted to evade.

Spath, Charles R.   A01910283   1st Lieutenant
Reported MIA February 3, 1952. FEAF report indicates that Lt. Spath survived the loss of his plane and was later captured by the enemy.

Spence, Marvin J.   **A0732780**   **Maj**
Reported MIA September 9, 1950. The only available evidence points to the possibility that Maj. Spence successfully bailed out and was subsequently captured by enemy forces.

Starck, John S.   **A01909876**   **1st Lieutenant**
Reported MIA July 18, 1951. The circumstances of loss indicate very strongly that Lt. Starck was probably killed on landing. The contradictory statement of one repatriate is not considered to be firm enough evidence to assume that Lt. Starck survived the landing.

Steele, Robert C.   **A0720030**   **Capt**
Reported MIA March 6, 1952. A repatriate in Little Switch reported Lt. Steele was seen January 1952 at POW Camp #2 along with two other officers who were repatriated and subsequently denied any knowledge of Lt. Steele.

Stefas, Frank   AF19363340   **Airman 1st class**
Reported MIA September 17, 1951. It appears the determination of Capt. Wright's death is based on a very limited inspection of a badly burned body. There is no firm evidence to prove that this body could not have been that of Capt Hearn or Sgt Stefas.

Stevenson, Frank J.   AF13405299   **Airman 3rd class**
Reported MIA January 29, 1953. Although subject was never heard from again and statement by one who reported seeing parachutes and flares never verified, it indicates a possibility that subject was one of the seven who escaped the aircraft and survived.

St. Mary, Robert   AF16385446   **Airman 1st Class**
Reported MIA September 4, 1953. It is possible the aircraft ditched or the crew bailed out over water.

Sweney, Bruce A.   A01912252   1st Lieutenant
Reported MIA October 2, 1951. Circumstances of loss indicate that Lt. Sweney may have been blown out of his aircraft as a result of the explosion. The fact that he did not move after landing may indicate that he was probably injured or wounded.

Tahsequah, Meech   **10985A**   **Lieutenant Colonel**
Reported MIA December 6, 1950. Maj. Tahsequah had ample time to bail out since the altitude (4,000 feet) was sufficient and the emergency was such that the aircraft could be controlled. The boats which were sighted could have been enemy fishing boats, and he may have been picked up and turned over to the enemy.

Thompson, Charles R.   A02222047   **2nd Lieutenant**
Reported MIA on November 25, 1951. A report was received on December 5, 1951 from 9th ROK Division that crew members, believed to be personnel of this crew, had bailed out inside enemy lines, about five miles northwest of Ch'Orwong. Search of area was negative.

Thompson, Raymond   AF15432409   **Airman 1st class**
Same as for Morton H. Jensen.

Tilch, Philip W.   AF13327852   **Sergeant**
Declared MIA on November 26, 1950. Evidence available indicates that in all probability Sgt. Tilch was in very bad condition and unlikely to survive. There is, however, no conclusive evidence to prove that he subsequently died.

Tiller, Horace N.   AF19052764   **Master Sergeant**
Same as for Morton H. Jensen.

Trantham, Archie P.   A0725822   **Capt**
Capt. Trantham probably bailed out successfully; however, position of bailout indicates that he landed in the water. This being the case, Capt. Trantham could have been picked up by enemy forces at sea or may not have survived the parachute landing.

Turner, Harold P.   A01283518   Capt
Same as for Lt. Henry.

Van Fleet, James A., Jr.   17852A   Capt
Reported MIA April 4, 1952. There is no evidence to confirm or deny the
possibility that Lt. Van Fleet may have survived and been captured.
[Van Fleet's father, General James A. Van Fleet, was once Commander of
the U.S. Eighth Army in Korea.]

Vanwey, William N.   AF18342248   Airman 2nd class
Same as for Lt. William John Bell.

Wahlgren, Edward C.   A0695337   1st Lieutenant
Same as for Thomas L. Shields.

Webb, Edward A.   AF18350787   Airman 2nd class
Same as for Thomas L. Shields.

Weeks, Grady M.   AF14114882   Staff Sergeant
Reported MIA August 8, 1952. The aircraft was hit and apparently
severely damaged, thus necessitating an immediate bailout at low
altitude. The bailout was transmitted on VHF since it was heard by
other aircraft. The crew probably did not receive the bailout order.

West, Carl E.   AF13346889   Airman 2nd class
Same as for Thomas L. Shields.

Whitman, William H.   AF13360399   Airman 1st class
Same as for Morton Henry Jensen.

Williamson, Kenneth E.   AF125255731   Staff Sergeant
Reported MIA September 9, 1950. The possibility exists SSgt. Williamson
successfully bailed out and was subsequently captured.

Wormack, Thelbert B.   A01908612   1st Lieutenant
Declared MIA August 14, 1950. Lt. Wormack successfully bailed out of
his aircraft and was seen freeing himself from his chute and walking.

Worth, George W., Jr.   AF19311283   Staff Sergeant
Reported MIA January 1951. Statements from repatriates indicate Sgt.
Worth was captured, held at Pyongyang and was last seen alive in the
spring of 1951. Information received indicated St. Worth was in very
poor physical condition (malnutrition) when last seen. Repatriate
assumed he was dead.

Zeigler, Joseph P.   **A02224628**   **1st Lieutenant**
Reported MIA April 23, 1953. Lt. Zeigler landed alive on enemy
territory by parachute. Was not seen afterwards.

Appendix 14

PERSONNEL REMOVED FROM THE 450 LIST

Found in: Chapter Seven, Volume 1
Source of this information: UNCMAC and CILHI casualty data.

Bold = Appears on Battle Monuments 8,182 list as of 1993.

U.S. Army

Remains recovered and identified[1]

Abbott, Charles L.	RA17258068	Pvt
Amano, Yutaka	RA19302624	Sergeant
Balbi, Joseph A.	US51142209	Pfc
Bellar, Bennie E	RA14326111	Cpl
Calhoon, Cecil O.	RA16308092	Cpl
Colon-Perez, Jose S.	RA30452103	Pfc
Cunningham, John F.	RA12305730	Pfc
Crabb, Dean R.	US55171051	Pfc
Denchfield, Raymond O.	0058879	1st Lieutenant
Gardner, James D.	RA13333358	Pvt
Jewett, Richard	0-02003239	2nd Lieutenant
McDaniel, William[2]	024088	Maj
Peters, James	RA30123141	Cpl
Ridgeway, Junior V.	RA16267704	Pfc
Roop, Donald H.	RA15421785	Pfc
Samezyk, Stanley J.	RA16303702	Pfc
Stiles, George W.	ER19284333	Pfc

Army resolved cases including grounds for removal from 450 List

---

[1]Memorandum from Assistant Secretary of the Army Hugh M. Milton II to the Assistant to the Secretary of Defense (Special Operations), Subject: Korean War Prisoner Documentation, May 23, 1958, "Names being removed from list of men for whom an accounting is demanded." The remains of Balbi and Jewett were discovered and recovered in 1960 in the DMZ where they disappeared September 19, 1952. The remains were identified and the next of kin were notified of the identifications on September 19, 1960.

[2]Murdered at the Sunchon tunnel by North Koreans on October 22, 1950. Remains returned during Operation Glory (N-17076, Passenger list #19) as unknown. Sunchon is 100 miles northwest of recovery site reported by Communists. Remains identified 14 Oct 55.

Adamo, Joseph J. Eyewitnesses reported seeing remains after Adamo died of combat wounds near Tokchon, North Korea, Dec 1950 - Jan 1951	Service number: RA12305738 Date of incident: MIA 30 Nov 50	**Rank:** Pfc **CILHI status:** MIA **Final status:** KIA(BNR)
Bond, Elihue, Jr. Name appeared on two unconfirmed POW lists (Dec 51 and July 52). Confirmed POW by Adjutant General. Eyewitnesses reported Bond died from malnutrition and Beri Beri in January 1951 near Chunggan, North Korea. No identification media buried with the remains.	RA15338774 1 Aug 50	Pfc POW(BNR) POW(BNR)
Bradford, Edward F., Jr. Unconfirmed POW. No other indication in records.	RA11167803 27 Jul 50	Pvt MIA Unknown
Brooks, Lloyd K. Eyewitnesses reported Brooks was killed in action on 2 Nov 50.	RA14315399 2 Nov 50	Pfc MIA KIA(BNR)
Brown, Alfred R. Two returnees said they saw Brown after he died in 1951 of malnutrition at Chunggung.	RA18321108 2 Nov 50	Cpl POW(BNR) POW(BNR)
Brown, Frank M. Three returnees said they were eyewitnesses to the fact Brown was killed in action. Wounded 1 Dec 50 and died 1 Dec 50 near Kunuri, North Korea.	0370561 30 Nov 50	Maj MIA KIA(BNR)
Cox, Joseph D. Conclusive evidence Cox was killed in action by enemy fire at Kunu-ri, North Korea on 30 Nov 50.	02017966 30 Nov 50	Capt MIA KIA(BNR)

Dansberry, Earl L. Wounded by UNC planes strafing. Eyewitnesses reported Dansberry died of malnutrition and dysentery in a POW camp ca. July 1951.	RA16180861 19 May 51	Sergeant MIA POW(BNR)
Davis, Sam H. Chinese said he had been "captured and escaped." Never confirmed. Mentioned by name in two Radio Peking broadcasts (1 Oct 52, 26 Dec 51). No indication in records why Davis was included in the original UNCMAC list.	RA18358881 13 Feb 51	Pfc MIA No indication
DeCosta, Salvatore Presumed dead in a plane crash (YD 4620 3900' 125 52'). No organized search of crash site since it was in enemy territory. No indication why DeCosta was on original UNCMAC list.	RA32911260 18 Oct 50	Sergeant MIA No indication
Dixon, Roosevelt, Jr. Two eyewitnesses reported Dixon's death in Camp #5 of malnutrition and dysentery. Burial detai56him.	RA13264790 11 Nov 50	Sergeant POW(BNR) POW(BNR)
Dunlap, Alva F. Determined to have died "in the hands of enemy forces" at Camp #5, Pyoktong. Wounded at Kunuri. Captured and died of malnutrition on 15 Feb 51.	RA15274377 1 Dec 50	Pfc POW(BNR) POW(BNR)
Earl, James E. Reported in propaganda broadcasts (26 Dec 51 and 1 Oct 52) as "escaped." Died of malnutrition and dysentery en route from Mining Camp to Chon Son on 13 May 51.	RA18259856 1 Jan 51	Sergeant POW(BNR) POW(BNR)
Efland, Donald O. Conclusive evidence KIA near Unsan 2 Nov 50.	ER51045004 No date	Pfc MIA POW(BNR)

Evans, Edward R. Conclusive evidence died of malnutrition at Camp #5, Pyoktong, 15 Apr 51.	RA15234142 No date	Cpl MIA POW(BNR)
Fennell, Isaac, Jr. Conclusive evidence died of malnutrition at Camp #1, May- June 1951.	ER42150267 12 Feb 51	Sergeant POW(BNR) POW(BNR)
Gregory, Robert S. Conclusive evidence Gregory died of malnutrition at Camp #5, Pyoktong on 31 Dec 50.	RA13313861 2 Nov 50	Cpl POW(BNR) POW(BNR)
Hester, Will H. Conclusive evidence Hester died of malnutrition at a POW camp ten miles northeast of Chungun in November 1950.	RA15381580 20 Jul 50	Pvt MIA POW(BNR)
Marshall, Alfred Unconfirmed POW. Mentioned in Peking propaganda broadcast 28 Jun 51. Eyewitnesses report Marshall died of malnutrition, dysentery, Beri Beri and high fever in March 1951.	ER12251545 14 Feb 51	Pfc POW(BNR) POW(BNR)
McSwain, Leon Conclusive evidence McSwain died of pneumonia on 28 Dec 50 at a mining camp in North Korea.	RA14226936 1 Dec 50	Cpl POW(BNR) POW(BNR)
Miller, Raymond H. Change in status from MIA to KIA(BNR) occurred 28 Nov 50.	ER13313722 28 Nov 50	Pfc POW(BNR) KIA(BNR)
Miner, Donald W. Conclusive evidence Miner died of dysentery at Camp #5, Pyoktong, January 1951.	RA11188081 12 Jul 50	Pvt POW(BNR) POW(BNR)
Mrotek, Lawrence M. Died "while in the hands of the opposing forces" of food poisoning and malnutrition at Camp #5, Pyoktong.	ER57500731 12 Feb 51	Pfc MIA POW(BNR)

Mulock, Arthur F. Died of malnutrition at Chungha-dong, Camp #3, July- August 1951.	02200206 20 Jul 50	2nd Lieutenant MIA POW(BNR)
O'Brien, Raymond J. Died of malnutrition somewhere near Chunggong, North Korea, Sept-Oct 1950.	RA18303460 20 Jul 50	Pfc MIA Died in enemy custody
Renneberg, Anthony Died 11 Oct 50 near Pyongyang in enemy hands. Cause unknown.	RA28130719 27 Jul 50	Pvt MIA POW(BNR)
Riley, John F. Communists reported Riley was "captured and escaped." Two eyewitnesses reported he died in March 1951 at Camp #5, Pyoktong, of dysentery.	RA18314836 13 Feb 51	Cpl POW(BNR) POW(BNR)
Sanders, James B. No records at CILHI.	RA18283828	Pfc Resolved
Shibao, Hiroshi Conclusive evidence Shibao was killed in action 20 Jul 50.	US56010182 20 Jul 50	Pfc MIA KIA(BNR)
Snider, Glenn A. Wounded then captured. Died 31 Mar 51 of malnutrition at Death Valley Camp.	RA39480119 28 Nov 50	Master Sergeant MIA POW(BNR)
Sorrentino, Anthony T. U.S. P-51 aircraft strafed U.S. positions and killed Sorrentino on 16 Jul 50 during combat operations one mile south of Kum River, near Taejon.	RA12325141 16 Jul 50	Pfc MIA KIA(BNR)
Stansbury, William H., Jr.[3] Status changed from POW to "captured by hostile force" on 9 Jan 53. Died of malnutrition in vicinity of Mampo, North Korea.	RA17245840 3 Mar 54	Pfc POW(BNR) "Died in hands of hostile force"

---

[3]See the integrated blackboard search below.

Starling, Robert C.
Returnees reported Starling
died 12 Feb 51 of wounds
received 30 Nov 50. Died at
Camp #5, Pyoktong, North
Korea.

RA14333967
1 Dec 51

Pfc
MIA
POW(BNR)

Stidham, Floyd D.
Four returnees reported
Stidham was killed in action
on 27 Nov 50 near Unsan,
North Korea.

RA15267441
28 Nov 50

Pfc
MIA
KIA(BNR)

Thompson, Harwood H.
Returnee saw Thompson dead on
19 May 51 after being
"strafed by plane" near
Chipyong Ni.

ER12246136
15 Feb 51

Pfc
POW(BNR)
KIA(BNR)

Vickers, Wendell
Unconfirmed POW. Died 31 May
51 of malnutrition en route
to Camp #1.

RA13269020
12 Feb 51

Cpl
MIA
"Died in hands of
hostile force"

Weaver, Edward P.
Reported to have died of
malnutrition and pneumonia in
March 1951 at Camp #5,
Pyoktong.

RA13315911
1 Dec 50

Pfc
POW(BNR)
POW(BNR)

Westphall, Johnnie S.
Two repatriates reported
Westphall's death. One
witnessed death, the other
witnessed burial. Died of
malnutrition at Camp #5,
Pyoktong on 10 Jun 51.

RA19329233
1 Dec 50

Cpl
MIA
POW(BNR)

White, William F.
Reported to have died of
malnutrition at Camp #1 on 12
Oct 51.

RA16268651
2 Dec 50

Pfc
MIA
POW(BNR)

Willis, Charles A.
Unconfirmed POW. Reported by
Communists to be "captured
and escaped." Returnees
reported Willis died of
pneumonia 31 Mar 51 en route
to a POW camp in North Korea.

ER57307012
13 Feb 51

Pfc
POW(BNR)
"Died in hands of
hostile force"

Wood, Lyle E.   RA17247032   Cpl
Reported to have died of   16 Aug 50   MIA
dysentery on 20 Oct 50 at   "Died in hands of
Pyongyang, North Korea.   hostile force"

Navy

No change.

U.S. Marine Corps

Baker, Billy W.   624946   Pfc
No records at CILHI.   Resolved

Air Force

Connors, Archibald H., Jr.   A02221996   1st Lieutenant
No records at CILHI.   Resolved

Ferree, Nolan H.   A02222141   2nd Lieutenant
Killed in action 13 Feb 52.   13 Feb 52   MIA
F-84E pilot. No parachute   Resolved
seen after ejection. Remains
returned during Operation
Glory (N-15996). Remains
identified, "There appears to
be excellent agreement with the
known records for Nolan Ferree."
Buried at Ft. Rosecrans National
Cemetery, 18 May 56.

Jamieson, Joseph S.   AF12287088   Technical Sergeant
No records at CILHI.   Resolved

Wood, Melvin C.   11313A   Maj
No records at CILHI   Resolved

Appendix 15

ROSTER OF AMERICANS BURIED IN NORTH KOREAN CEMETERIES, JUNE 1953[1]

Found in: Chapter Eight, Volume 1
Source of this information: RG92 Entry 1894 Box 649 Office of the Quartermaster General, Misc File 1953-54, Army Far East (Current Death), 333.1 Army Far East.

Note: The names in **bold** that appear in Appendix 15 appear on both the roster of burials in North Korea and the roster of military personnel received through Operation Glory as reported by the Communist side. These claims were subsequently verified by the U.S. CIU. Thus the plain text names appear to be missing from the Glory manifests, were never exhumed and delivered, or were not buried in the first place.

Koto-Ri #1

NAME	RANK	SERIAL NUMBER	PLOT	ROW	GRAVE
Taylor, James F.	Pvt	647109		1	1
Obersman, Edward J.	Pfc	664531		1	2
Chase, Lester T.	Capt	015428		1	3
Hopkins, Earl G.	TSgt	235799		1	4
Sowell, Lester I.	Pfc	1055923		2	5
Reynolds, Philip A.	Cpl	1078521		2	6
Kitchens, William M., Jr.	Pfc	658413		2	7
Mathewson, Bruce Jr.	SSgt	254123		2	8
Duffin, James R.		3028923		3	9
Trynoski, Emil	Cpl	1111914		3	10
Mark, Hubert D.	Pfc	655454		3	11
, Bernard E.	Sgt	RA 16216331		3	12
Campbell, Joseph F.	Pfc	RA 34948269		4	13
Allen, Joseph N.	Pvt	RA 11177308		4	14
Baley, Morris E.	Sgt	RA 15232819		4	15
Andrews, Leon E.	Cpt	RA 31402624		4	16

---

[1]RG92 Entry 1894 Box 649 Office of the Quartermaster General, Misc File 1953-54, Army Far East (Current Death), 333.1 Army Far East.

Koto-Ri #2

NAME	RANK	SERIAL NUMBER	PLOT	ROW	GRAVE
Bean, Harry R.	Sgt	581917	None	None	None
Bell, Floyd K.	Cpl	RA 19306274	None	None	None
Berry, Robert M.	HM	3446?70	None	None	None
Beyer, Harold A.	Pfc	1112739	None	None	None
Briscoe, Albert A.	1st Lt	047265	None	None	None
Bruce, Thomas C.	Pfc	1100294	None	None	None
Burns, Buford L.	SSgt	302510	None	None	None
Burroughs, Kenneth C.	Pfc	1093058	None	None	None
Caillouet, James B.	Pfc	1072152	None	None	None
Unknown X-1000			None	None	None
Caron, Clayton W.	Pfc	1072405	None	None	None
Carr, James T.	Pvt	RA 19367251	None	None	None
Carroll, Daniel J.	TSgt	294343	None	None	None
Caruso, Mathew	Sgt	661958	None	None	None
Casagrand, Robert E.	Pfc	565077	None	None	None
Chandler, Bobby J.	Pfc	1056791	None	None	None
Clark, Thomas L.	Cpl	1049440	None	None	None
Colin, Raymond F.	Pfc	1113443	None	None	None
Corman, Conrad L.	Pfc	1108073	None	None	None
Cottier, Darrell R.	Pfc	567118	None	None	None
Crews, Elwood S., Jr.	Sgt	1088344	None	None	None
Dallas, Jack E.	Pfc	RA 15283309	None	None	None
Daniel, Roy T.	Pfc	1083342	None	None	None
Davis, Gerald O., Jr.	Sgt	652456	None	None	None
Davis, James L.	Cpl	613025	None	None	None
Davis, Ralph A.	MSgt	248035	None	None	None
Didier, Donald J.	Pfc	1072011	None	None	None
Dillon, Edward V.	Pfc	801945	None	None	None
Dugan, Francis X.	Cpl	565385	None	None	None
Dunne, John M.	1st Lt	041182	None	None	None
Ehrlich, Leland E.	Sgt	576704	None	None	None
Ervin, Burt	Cpl	504740	None	None	None
Figg, Dennard M.	Cpl	654162	None	None	None
Fisher, James R.	Cpl	RA 16326977	None	None	None
Flook, Arnold R.	1st Lt	0-1798919	None	None	None
Foust, Frank A.	Pfc	1093877	None	None	None
France, Donald R.	Capt	013596	None	None	None
Giddings, Joseph A. Jr.	1st Lt	059183	None	None	None
Gillean, Durston D.	Pfc	1115744	None	None	None
Gowman, David W.	Sgt	1082822	None	None	None
Graske, Lawrence E.	Cpl	1049313	None	None	None
Hancock, Richard E.	Pfc	1112656	None	None	None
Hanks, Woodrow I.	Pfc	649107	None	None	None
Hannuksela, Arnold G.	SSgt	575592	None	None	None
Harriman, Sheldon L.	Sgt	RA 36468411	None	None	None

Harris, Richard G.	Pfc	293562	None	None	None
Haynes, Otis S., Jr.	Sgt	866731	None	None	None
Hellem, James W. L.	Pfc	643512	None	None	None
Holland, Francis E.	Pfc	1078993	None	None	None
Janowsky, Paul J.	Pfc	1088929	None	None	None
Jensen, John R.	Cpl	1075311	None	None	None
Keith, James W.	Sgt	14298068	None	None	None
Kerekes, Joseph	Sgt	RA 12257309	None	None	None
King, James A.	SSgt	285417	None	None	None
Kotara, Fabian T.	Pfc	1083694	None	None	None
Larsen, Charles H.	SSgt	326691	None	None	None
Laukaitis, Joseph	Pfc	1097232	None	None	None
Lawson, Frank, J.	TSgt	275630	None	None	None
Lawton, John D.	Pfc	1036651	None	None	None
Lesko, John F.	Sgt	487359	None	None	None
Locke, Roscoe H.	Cpl	1079686	None	None	None
Love, Rudolph	Cpl	635736	None	None	None
Lundberg, David L.	Pfc	1091992	None	None	None
Marchese, John	HM 3	317754	None	None	None
Mark, Oscar H., Jr.	HM 3	5581968	None	None	None
Mathews, Kenneth, J.F.	Pfc	1113097	None	None	None
Mayo, Joseph H.	Cpl	1070254	None	None	None
McAndrews, Charles A.	Pfc	1071991	None	None	None
McClung, William J.	MSgt	245635	None	None	None
McGregor, Dale A.	Sgt	659346	None	None	None
McGuiness, Clarence	1st Lt	037612	None	None	None
Meany, Shannon L., Jr.	TSgt	319776	None	None	None
Melton, Roy G.	Pfc	1067559	None	None	None
Montez, Horacio N.	Pfc	1075116	None	None	None
Olsen, Eugene P.	Pfc	1058313	None	None	None
Overton, Donald R.	Cpl	280562	None	None	None
Pence, George A.	Pfc	812997	None	None	None
Pope, Ray	Sgt	1096406	None	None	None
Reid, Alva L.	Pfc	655259	None	None	None
Rider, Alexander D.	SSgt	443270	None	None	None
Rucker, John D.	Cpl	300504	None	None	None
Sage, Samuel S.	Pfc	659375	None	None	None
Schultz, Robert W.	Sgt	899682	None	None	None
Severson, Robert N.	Sgt	561099	None	None	None
Shelquist, Harry Jr.	SSgt	8160312	None	None	None
Shenk, Henry H.	SSgt	404030	None	None	None
Smith, Ben T., Jr.	Pvt	US 44189175	None	None	None
Smith, Gerald J.	Pfc	354042	None	None	None
Snyder, Walter A.	Pvt	RA 15295388	None	None	None
Sorensen, Mainerd A.	Capt	010109	None	None	None
Stanley, Vernon I.	MSgt	259022	None	None	None
Stebner, Arthur R.	Sgt	666935	None	None	None
Stenz, John J.	SSgt	610109	None	None	None

Sturtevant, Roger V.	Pfc	663193	None	None	None
Svisarovich, George A.	Sgt	897067	None	None	None
Tant, Leonard E.	SSgt	292182	None	None	None
Thompson, Richard H.	Pfc	666762	None	None	None
Unknown X-1			None	None	None
Unknown X-2			None	None	None
Vaydich, John M.	Cpl	571753	None	None	None
Ward, William A., Jr.	Cpl	1027650	None	None	None
Webb, John B.	Pfc	1080567	None	None	None
Wiedau, Jame L.	Pfc	1105584	None	None	None
Williams, Jack W.	Cpl	562557	None	None	None
Williams, Richard G.	Pfc	1113201	None	None	None
Winnington, William P., Jr.	Pfc	1071168	None	None	None
Wolf, William C.	Sgt	584449	None	None	None
Wood, William A.	SSgt	413984	None	None	None

Sukchon

NAME	RANK	SERIAL NUMBER	PLOT	ROW	GRAVE
Hagan, Cladius F.	Pfc	RA 34623430	1	1	.1
Ta???, Raymond W.	Sfc	RA 36967465	1	1	.2
Taylor, Claude R.	1st Lt	AO 708348	1	1	.3
Crowe, Marshall, Jr.	Cpl	RA 151?9523	1	1	4
Ralihan, George E.	M/Sgt	RA 42079568	1	1	5
?urnighan, Harry E.	Pfc	RA 14276839	1	1	6
Da??, Edward L.	Sgt	RA 35320087	1	1	7
Powers, John K.	Pfc	RA 15423864	1	1	8
Hammond, Emmett T.	Cpl	RA 34350051	1	1	9
Thomson, Donald J.	Pfc	RA 13288295	1	1	10
Ascencio, Henry R.	Pfc	RA 19341169	1	2	11
Hartman, Guy G.	Sgt	RA 44191491	1	2	12
Miller, Charles L.	Cpl	RA 15422419	1	2	13
Wently, David C.	Pfc	RA 43006538	1	2	14
Smith, Joe W.	Rct	RA 25528113	1	2	15
Smith, Robert J.	Cpl	RA 15063654	1	2	16
Hughey, Harry R.	Cpl	RA 13272483	1	2	17
Hansel, Morgan B.	1st Lt	O-1825120	1	2	18
Watkins, Jack G.	M/Sgt	RA 18243313	1	2	19
White, Dale, I.	Pfc	RA 18293143	1	2	20
Bogenschild, Howard J.	Pvt	RA 16321641	1	3	21
Duarte, William R.	Cpl	RA 18263588	1	3	22
Gosv??r, Aubrey P.	Pfc	RA 19300182	1	3	23
Cottrell, Raymond A.	Sgt	RA 37295735	1	3	24
Bennett, Richard W.	Pvt	RA 1929?502	1	3	25
Pinakton, Virgil F.	Pfc	RA 16310513	1	3	26
Helnarski, Wiadyslaw L.	Pfc	RA 12348440	1	3	27
Norman, James W.	Pvt	RA 28099060	1	3	28
Haworth, Perry R.	Sgt	RA 38589268	1	3	29
Williamson, Herbert	Pfc	RA 18281319	1	3	30
Moore, Thomas O., Jr.	Pfc	RA 18281319	2	1	1
Earl, Robert J., Jr.	Pvt	RA 18361237	2	1	2
Robinson, Max E.	Sgt	RA 15271419	2	1	3
McKenna, Edward J.	Pfc	RA 12265929	2	1	4
Dwight, Ernest, F.	Sgt	RA 791?798?	2	1	5
Allied			2	1	6
Allied			2	1	7
Allied			2	1	.8
Allied			2	1	.9
Allied			2	1	10
Allied			2	1	11
Dorrion, Neil K.	SFC	RA 33679894	2	1	12
UNK X-3 BTB: Hellen, R.D.	Pfc	RA 10107067	2	2	13
Lindsey, John Richard	Pfc	RA 17266102	2	2	14
Rasmussen, Ray L.	Pfc	RA 17273?66	2	2	15

Unknown X-4	Unk	Unk	2	2	16	
Allen, James Edward	Pfc	RA 122676984	2	2	17	
Tamaru, Charles Y.	Sgt	RA 10102109	2	2	18	
Koyle, Grant W.	Cpl	RA 39915930	2	2	19	
Salecyi, Chester J.	Cpl	RA 36791783	2	2	20	
Unknown X-7	?	RA 14151585	2	2	21	
Finn, Clifford C.	Pfc	RA 21904275	2	2	22	
Mertes, Allen Clarence	Pfc	RA 16301561	2	2	23	
Parsons, Earl J.	Pfc	RA 15379833	2	2	24	
Hoff, Stanford I.	Pfc	RA 19335649	2	2	24	
Maury, Edward O.	Cpl	RA 14328921	2	3	26	
Bounds, Norman L.	Cpl	RA 17233633	2	3	27	
Robson, Raymond C.	Pfc	ER 13204015	2	3	28	
Hammer, Carl P.	Cpl	RA 16299597	2	3	29	
Allied			2	3	30	
Allied			2	3	31	
Allied			2	3	32	
Allied			2	3	32	
Allied			2	3	33	
Allied			2	3	34	
Allied			2	3	35	
Allied			2	3	36	
Jones, Mack D.	Sgt	RA 74999125	2	4	37	
Koontz, Eugene	Pfc	RA 13269454	2	4	38	
Harsy, Leonard G.	SFC	RA 16072283	2	4	39	
Mills, Daroll E.	Sgt	RA 14287028	2	4	40	
Huggins, Horace W.	?	RA 1425?421	2	4	41	
Unk X-11 BTB: Arias, Milton, Jr.	Cpl	RA 18223144	2	4	42	
Dees, Roy A.	SFC	RA 14210095	2	4	43	
Enos, Ormell L.	Cpl	RA 36177656	2	4	44	
Albright, Harry E.	Maj	047947	2	4	46	
Woodward, Ernest A.	SFC	RA 38068443	2	4	47	
Lopez, Ray W.	Cpl	RA 39003664	2	4	48	
Allied			2	4	49	
Allied			2	5	50	
Allied			2	5	51	
Allied			2	5	52	
Allied			2	5	53	
Allied			2	5	54	
Magana, Edwardo	Pfc	RA 19338268	2	5	55	
Whalen, Richard D.	Pvt	RA 15297498	2	5	56	
Fairchild, Leslie	Sgt	RA 34212002	2	5	57	
Lasuer, Will C.	Cpl	RA 37680058	2	5	58	
Handy, Kenneth N.	Pvt	RA 11190547	2	5	59	
Currie, Norman R.	Cpl	RA 16315515	2	5	60	
White, Sherman Howard	Sgt	RA 6668711	2	6	61	
Matton, Henry E., Jr.	Pvt-2	RA 16329216	2	6	62	

Fores, Andres	Pfc	RA 13317588	2	6	63
Shifflet, William F.	Pfc	RA 15296452	2	6	64
Finley, Jerry L.	Pfc	RA 192850088	2	6	65
Sloat, John A.	Pfc	RA 19341107	2	6	66
Kincaid, James E.	Pfc	RA 13337899	2	6	67
Lawson, John E.	Pfc	RA 7001260	2	6	68
Bryce, Oscar H.	Cpl	RA 19314208	2	6	69
Croft, James A.	?	RA 18330907	2	6	70
DeCapot, Francis R.	Pvt-2	RA 11145269	2	6	71
Kibler, Linn E.	Pfc	RA 19315?04	2	6	72
Redcloud, Mitchell, Jr.	Cpl	RA 162299515	2	7	73
Harper, Joseph T.	Pvt	RA 14341869	2	7	74
Gentry, Willie G.	Sfc	RA 34148935	2	7	75
Stafford, Richard	Pfc	RA 16277747	2	7	76
Goodwin, Martin H.	Pfc	RA 35059145	2	7	77
Brown, Eugene D.	Cpl	RA 12242447	2	7	78
Fairrow, Clarence	Pfc	RA 18346855	2	7	79
Black, Robert H.	Pfc	RA 12291810	2	7	80
Kirkpatrick, Leslie W.	2nd Lt	0-59140	2	7	81
Martinez, Joseph A.	Pfc	RA 19316763	2	7	82
Harrington, Eldridge	Sfc	RA 17010292	2	7	83
Larrabee, David A.	Pfc	RA 11199328	2	7	84
Anderson, Heriger A.	Capt	AO 777974	2	8	85
Moore, Louis A.	Pfc	RA 13341007	2	8	86
Hardwick, Kenneth L.	Pvt	RA 21930472	2	8	87
Dickerson, Norman E.	Cpl	RA 35902974	2	8	88
Grace, Edward	Sfc	RA 15012?00	2	8	89
Goss, George C.	Cpl	RA 13314043	2	8	90
McKinney, Arnold E.	Sfc	RA 6152618	2	8	91
Unk X-13 BTB Point, Ray	M/Sgt	RA 6859159	2	8	92
Wallace, Willard D.	Cpl	RA 18282758	2	8	93
Trent, Ira V.	Pvt	RA 15379941	2	8	94
Stewart, Graham	M/Sgt	RA 34014346	2	8	95
Satterfield, Glenn Ray	Pvt	RA 15281668	2	8	96
Coca, Valentin	Sfc	RA 6866104	2	9	97
Clark, Clifford E.	Pfc	RA 15274382	2	9	98
Black, Winfield M.	M/Sgt	RA 19016211	2	9	99
Corley, Johnny M.	Pfc	RA 14337849	2	9	100
Richardson, Clark Bright	Pfc	RA 18271214	2	9	101
Balboni, Joseph W.	Pfc	RA 11194795	2	9	102
Moore, John W.	Pfc	RA 14237213	2	9	103
Burns, William T.	Sfc	RA 34150801	2	9	104
Caron, James N., Jr.	Pfc	RA 14300219	2	9	105
Trent, James O.	Sfc	RA 34582162	2	9	106
Peavey, Billy R.	Pfc	RA 18281062	2	9	107
Bates, Elmore C.	Sgt	RA 6289434	2	9	108
McWherter, Vance B.	2nd Lt	0-973796	2	10	109
Bunten, Hasel, Jr.	Pvt-2	RA 14334838	2	10	110

Turnbull, Robert	Pfc	RA 16315485	2	10	111
EMPTY GRAVE			2	10	112
Wallace, James M.	Cpl	RA 16293508	2	10	113
Clevenger, James N.	Sfc	RA 35783898	2	10	114
Davis, Herbert H.	Pvt-2	RA 13328419	2	10	115
Panotaki, Peter J.	Pfc	RA 13265429	2	10	116
Cooke, Leney D.	Pfc	RA 21012540	2	10	117
Zappetti, Anthony J.	Pfc	RA 12301533	2	10	118
Allied			2	10	119
Unk			2	10	120
Nichols, Joe H.	Pvt	RA 16294504	2	11	121
Tyner, John T.	Pfc	RA 19315991	2	11	122
Dawson, James G.	Pfc	RA 13309717	2	11	123
Horony, John A.	2nd Lt	0-2212010	2	11	124
Allied			2	11	125
Allied			2	11	126
Allied			2	11	127
Allied			2	11	128
Evans, William V.	Cpl	RA 12313141	2	11	129
Rogers, Gerald E.	Cpl	RA 14214919	2	11	130
Masin, Nathan	Capt	0-977023	2	11	131
Monroe, Billy J.	Cpl	RA 17252011	2	11	132

Pukchong

NAME	RANK	SERIAL NUMBER	PLOT	ROW	GRAVE
Sargent, Karl	Pfc	RA 15408658	A	1	1
Carpenter, Wesley B.	Sgt	RA 46037371	A	1	2
Johnston, George E.	Pfc	RA 14262461	A	1	3
Biselis, Frank	Pfc	RA 20256413	A	1	4
Farnesi, Robert E.	Cpl	RA 13303863	A	1	5
Klenz, Richard	Pfc	RA 19346445	A	1	6
O'Neill, Edward	Pfc	RA 12293385	A	1	7
Dewitt, Robert C.	Cpl	RA 15272954	A	1	8
Calveige, Thomas J.	Pfc	RA 38571170	A	1	9
Ashley, Alfred B.	Cpl	RA 12287040	A	1	10
Baker, Leonard A.	Pvt	RA 6264309	A	1	11
Greaner, Howard J.	Cpl	RA 15273717	A	1	12
McLaughlin, Jack E.	Pfc	RA 46021396	A	2	13
Gilland, J. W.	Pvt	RA 14347023	A	2	14
Davis, Troy C.	Pfc	RA 18334063	A	2	15
Brownwell, Donald L.	Pfc	RA 13301490	A	2	16
Reade, Donald L.	Pfc	RA 11161306	A	2	17
Banger, Calvin K.	Pvt-2	RA 13293404	A	2	18
Hammontree, Fred F.	Pvt	RA 13285848	A	2	19
Ware, Harry W., Jr.	2nd Lt	0-59343	A	2	20
Honixfelt, Jack	Pfc	RA 1230280	A	2	21
Van Workman, Jeremiah F.	LtCol	0-256108	A	2	22
Baker, Lee D.	Pvt	RA 15293317	A	2	23
Farmer, Paul C.	Cpl	RA 15422172	A	2	24
Nichols, David H.	Cpl	RA 18260969	A	3	25
Halverson, Donald E.	1st Lt	0-1333069	A	3	26
King, Jack E.	Pfc	RA 14323859	A	3	27
Verret, Howard P.	Pvt	RA 16283864	A	3	28
Porter, Rogers	2nd Lt	01013293	A	3	29
Scott, Robert L.	Pfc	RA 13332630	A	3	30
Freeman, Harry W.	Cpl	RA 16276628	A	3	31
Lawrence, Emory T.	Pfc	RA 15275840	A	3	32
Fornica, Andrew H.	2nd Lt	0-986355	A	3	33
Tipton, Wiley J.	Sfc	RA 35915572	A	3	34
Beardslee, Daniel E.	Pfc	RA 16262079	A	3	35
Taft, Pual B.	Pvt	RA 19360008	A	3	36
Davidovic, John	Pfc	RA 13299790	A	4	37
Landmesser, Robert A.	Pfc	RA 13149292	A	4	38
Watkins, Roy R., Jr.	2nd Lt	0-2206410	A	4	39
Wood, Marvin R.	Cpl	RA 19322364	A	4	40
Ripley, Julian Raymond	Sgt	RA 17245029	A	4	41
Conover, Adelbert	Pfc	RA 19341944	A	4	42
Morford, Raymond E.	Pfc	RA 16314996	A	4	43
Henry, Wilbert R.	Pfc	RA 13298973	A	4	44
Wright, John L.	Cpl	RA 25306636	A	4	45

Morales, Tony	Pfc	RA 39108897	A	4	46
Colao, Salvadore	Pvt	RA 13299920	A	4	47
Chandler, John	Pfc	RA 19336127	A	4	48
McCollum, Leon B.	Pfc	RA 46064829	A	5	49
Flowers, Odis D.	Pfc	RA 34163450	A	5	50

Wonsan

NAME	RANK	SERIAL NUMBER	PLOT	ROW	GRAVE
Unk X-1 (Group Burial)			A	1	1
Brown, George Clayton, Jr.	Sgt	536658	A	1	2
Hoolahan, Patrick W.	Cpl	578082	A	1	3
Deiss, Henry, Jr.	Pfc	630559	A	1	4
Lorah, Roy L.	Pfc	529071	A	1	5
Unk X-2			A	1	6
Carpenter, Charles F.	Pfc	1073096	A	1	7
Atwell, Victor W.	Pfc	650862	A	1	8
Reinhold, John C.	HN	3352982	A	1	9
Crannell, Lyman T.	Sgt	985259	A	1	10
Nuckel, Donald G.	Pfc	1078517	A	1	11
Evans, Kenneth O.	Pfc	1092846	A	1	12
Pluta, Justyn C.	Pfc	1123839	A	2	13
Marker, Wayne A.	Pfc	1095421	A	2	14
Goss, Fredrick C.	Cpl	629075	A	2	15
Williams, Fredrick R.	Pfc	1102683	A	2	16
Schaffer, Bruce A.	Pfc	1113849	A	2	17
Engelhart, Donald	Pfc	600572	A	2	18
Powell, Marian J.	Pfc	638941	A	2	19
Nacci, Julius C.	Pfc	1074317	A	2	20
Bauerfeind, George C.	Pfc	668244	A	2	21
Roberts, Clayton L.	Sgt	402518	A	2	22
Corin, Ernest J.	Pfc	652252	A	2	23
Hall, Stephen C.	Pfc	1100030(?)	A	2	24
Mollnon, Chester E.	Sgt	347060	A	3	25
Toto, Edward J.	Pfc	111?952	A	3	26
McCarty, Claude J., Jr.	Cpl	659675	A	3	27
Porter, Bill J.	Pfc	111?952	A	3	28
Gargan, John F.	Cpl	RA 11190210	A	3	29
Aliff, Thomas R.	Pfc	1116262	A	3	30
Gall, Francis C.	Pfc	801477	A	3	31
Beeler, James D.	2nd Lt	050153	A	3	32
Hammond, Hugo	Pfc	623926	A	3	33
Rogers, Vincent	Pfc	810714	A	3	34
Shirey, Roy E.	Pfc	662198	A	3	35
Dugo, Thomas Anthony, Jr.	HN	3651945	A	3	36
Smith, Donald R., Jr.	Pfc	10?4745	A	4	37
Redmon, Hugh I.	Pfc	1087732	A	4	38
Biedka, Matthew J.	TSgt	376152	A	4	39
Bailey, William C.	Pfc	RA 19350559	A	4	40
Smith, Richard Yorke	1st Lt	0-311?3	A	4	41
Humphrey, Veloy G.	Cpl	293616	A	4	42
Landers, Lloyd Wayne	Sgt	306611	A	4	43
Miller, Sam Q.	Sgt	668919	A	4	44
Busch, George W.	Pfc	1082385	A	4	45

Thompson, Leonard F.	Pfc	662298	A	4	46
Bucherich, Edward J.	Cpl	458888	A	4	47
Forsgren, Eugene R.	Pfc	622330	A	4	48
Happer, Harry James	HN	2547089	A	5	49
Stacy, C.C.B.	HM 3	9984549	A	5	50
Menard, Nelson J.	Pfc	1122427	A	5	51
Walker, Leonard I.	Pfc	658022	A	5	52
Welsh, J.D.	Pfc	639050	A	5	53
Klinger, Edwin J.	Pfc	1055191	A	5	54
McGregor, Robert Carson	1st Lt	0-27781	A	5	55
Reese, Leon	Sgt	939481	A	5	56
Lee, Doyle Lionel	Sgt	1055191	A	5	57
Beard, Beverly R.	Sgt	500967	A	5	58
Keller, Harold W.	Pfc	650797	A	5	59
Anderson, Gerald P.	1st Lt	0-41115	A	5	60
Christensen, Thomas A., Jr.	DN	416?756	A	6	61
Short, Raymond U.	Pfc	1099922	A	6	62
Wells, Nils L.	SSgt	264791	A	6	63
Morgan, Jack W.	Pfc	RA 18282072	A	6	64
Taylor, Olin J.	Pfc	1113257	A	6	65
Woods, Isaac T.	M/Sgt	RA 38039982	A	6	66
Wood, Gene A.	Pvt	RA 15259866	A	6	67
Schmidt, Robert C.	Pfc	RA 17358394	A	6	68
Edwards, Charles Phillips	Cpl	RA335?0624	A	6	69
Grider, Kenneth G.	Cpl	RA 35823420	A	6	70
Wolfe, Lowell T.	Cpl	1072???	A	6	71
Vanraay, B.E.F.	S/Sgt	303947	A	6	72
Navarro, Adolfo	Sgt	RA 10403300	A	7	73
Medina, Luis	Sgt	RA 10400224	A	7	74
Santos-Cruz, Domingo	Pvt	RA 30451747	A	7	74
Myers, Donald Eugene	Capt	0-27516	A	7	76
Rutler, Charles C.	M/Sgt	RA 34673463	A	7	77
Evans, Edwin L.	Pfc	RA 14288165	A	7	78
Schultze, Paul R.	1st Lt	0-947563	A	7	79
Nevarez-Diaz, Candido	Pfc	RA 30400254	A	77	80
Brim, Zephry	Cpl	RA 14277533	A	7	81
Torres, Desiderio	Pfc	RA 39422253	A	7	82
Young, Leslie, Jr.	Sgt	RA 38739273	A	7	83
Perez, Juan A.	Sfc	RA 10401386	A	7	84
Chappell, Gene A.	Pfc	RA 18335821	A	8	85
Cintron, Miguel	Cpl	RA 30403799	A	8	86
Piercy, Roderick A.	Pvt	RA 20468525	A	8	87
Thomas, Jack Allen	Sgt	330579	A	8	88
Pinella, Andrew V.	Cpl	55732	A	8	89
Corson, Bruce H.	S/Sgt	279326	A	8	90
Golden, Richard M.	Pfc	593681	A	8	91
Trent, John C.	2nd Lt	0-62710	A	9	92
Knox, Alexander S.	M/Sgt	Ra 6267409	A	8	93

Martin, James	Cpl	RA 35736460	A	8	94
Dickens, John N., Jr.	Cpl	RA 13064242	A	8	95
Kerr, Lee Clin	Cpl	RA 34726055	A	8	96
Martin, Boyd M.	Pfc	RA 26331986	A	9	97
Woods, William E.	Pvt	RA 17279417	A	8	98
Timmins, John W.	2nd Lt	O-58634	A	9	99
Van Ellsberg, Charles C.	Pvt	RA 19313745	A	9	100
Burnett, Avery E.	Cpl	RA 14297243	A	9	101
McGonigle, Harry T.	Cpl	RA 13382567	A	9	102
Becker, James M.	1st Lt	O-28616	A	9	103
Schlitz, Carl J.	1st Lt	O-1120039	A	9	104
Hillburger, Harry S.	Pvt	RA 16310183	A	9	105
Gilbert, Russell J.	Pfc	RA 13166749	A	9	106
Smith, Lawrence	Cpl	RA 13271311	A	9	107
Fukumoto, Ralph T.	Pvt	RA 10104482	A	9	108
Pace, Horace	Cpl	RA 18297526	A	10	109
Crim, Arthur E.	Pfc	RA 154244?5	A	10	110
Bates, Lonzo	Sgt	RA 38436724	A	10	111
Ramada, Mitsuo	Pvt	RA 10104244	A	10	112
Tredway, Thomas E., Jr.	Pvt	RA 13349737	A	10	113
Amigh, Harry L.	Sgt	RA 13287067	A	10	114
Carr, Harold Jr.	Pvt	RA 14324107	A	10	115
Fuller, Kemper	Pvt	RA 15421767	A	10	116
Vortherms, Harold B.	Pfc	RA 17261239	A	10	117
Love, Roosevelt	Pvt	RA 15299791	A	10	118
Walker, James	Pfc	RA 16179238	A	10	119
Reed, Nathaniel	Pvt	RA 18259970	A	10	120
Sullivan, John L.	Pvt	RA 14346701	A	11	121
Villafane-Vasquez, Gregorio	Sgt	RA 10200515	A	11	122
Robinson, James	Sfc	RA 34103343	A	11	123

Hungnam

NAME	RANK	SERIAL NUMBER	PLOT	ROW	GRAVE
Hardin, William G.	Cpl	1084495	A	1	1
Albing, John E.	T/Sgt	314442	A	1	2
Pointer, Max Owens, Jr.	Cpl	456508	A	1	3
Bradshaw, Billie F.	Pfc	1079489	A	1	4
Green, Homer	Cpl	668320	A	1	5
Betthauser, Michale D.	Pfc	606451	A	1	6
Barajas, Robert F.	Sgt	296175	A	1	7
Alfaro, Eddie C.	Pfc	1059722	A	1	8
Marchant, David T.	Pfc	1112972	A	1	9
Gertzen, Norman	Sgt	1058015	A	1	10
Morris, Jesse E.	T/Sgt	268556	A	1	11
Marzec, John Francis	Pfc	1116736	A	1	12
Koehler, Buddy N.	Pfc	1041199	A	2	13
Hayes, John C.	Cpl	854728	A	2	14
Castaing, Claude C.	Cpl	1053360	A	2	15
Donkers, Harry Winfield	Pfc	1?2702?	A	2	16
Sharp, J. D.	1st Lt	?43645	A	2	17
Peach, Earl F.	Sgt	537449	A	2	18
Connolly, Gerald J.	Cpl	1065764	A	2	19
Keeth, Paul O.	Pfc	1116221	A	2	20
Groh, Edmund Phillips, Jr.	Pfc	1047281	A	2	21
Appleby, Billy R.	Pfc	1117924	A	2	22
Madvig, John Lloyd	Cpl	1047274	A	2	23
Bigden, Jack Beverly	Sgt	283012	A	2	24
Lutz, William H.	Pfc	1058270	A	3	25
Ashbaker, Orville E.	Pfc	AF 19334053	A	3	26
Dana, Lewis J.	Pfc	1072423	A	3	27
Pele, Maika	Pfc	10559781	A	3	28
McDaniel, Claude C.	Pfc	1100623	A	3	29
Frederick, Willard N.	Pfc	641006A	A	3	30
Nickles, Richard L.	Pfc	1054??6	A	3	31
Poynter, James I.	Sgt	309715	A	3	32
McKay, James M.	Sgt	514251	A	3	33
Bickley, David R.	Pfc	1095733	A	3	34
Totten, Douglas E.	Cpl	272940	A	3	35
Kosel, Donald R.	Pfc	1063950	A	3	36
Loney, Ropbert P.	Cpl	511978	A	4	37
Chapman, Theodore W.	Pfc	1016871	A	4	38
Sparks, Huil D.	Pfc	665556	A	4	39
Ford, Paul L.	Pfc	1116186	A	4	40
Bailey, Robert F.	Cpl	1057198	A	4	41
Boles, Louis C.	Sgt	603099	A	4	42
Fife, Walter M.	Pfc	549489	A	4	43
Vaughn, William C	Pfc	666908	A	4	44
Jagiello, Joseph A.	S/Sgt	870275	A	4	45

Reynolds, Promus F.	Pfc	928584	A	4	46
Long, Hansford D.	Sgt	613490	A	4	47
Custer, William K., Jr.	Pfc	841630	A	4	48
Hays, Robert C.	Lt(jg)	174413	A	5	49
Ward, John L.	Pfc	1074538	A	5	51
Barnes, Kenneth L.	Col	559767	A	5	50
Mooney, Gordon W.	Cpl	641998	A	5	52
Mosciski, Eugene M.	Pfc	1092201	A	5	53
Tucker, Drexel E.	Pfc	659434	A	5	54
Reem, Robert D.	2nd Lt	049636	A	5	55
Rowland, Eugene E.	Cpl	605440	A	5	56
Pardue, Billy J.	Pfc	655275	A	5	57
Jack, Nick S.	Pfc	854397	A	5	58
Bard, Ward O.	S/Sgt	17?753	A	5	59
Allen, Hubert O.	Cpl	927640	A	5	60
Foster, Charlie	Sgt	881584	A	6	61
Carrozo, Peter M.	Sgt	1074505	A	6	62
Feeney, Donald G.	Pfc	656744	A	6	63
Snider, John K.	Pfc	1079503	A	6	64
Milander, Samuel H.	Pfc	664051	A	6	65
Turner, Roy F.	Pfc	1072473	A	6	66
Van Frayen, Donald L.	Pfc	1026937	A	6	67
Biles, Dwayne L.	Pfc	1063352	A	6	68
Williamson, Falvius J.	Sgt	1005642	A	6	69
McCoskey, Charles A., Jr.	Pfc	1101515	A	6	70
Williams, John D.	Cpl	62988863	A	6	71
Krider, Robert O.	Pfc	664538	A	6	72
Miller, Gordon A.	Pfc	1063321	A	7	73
Penney, Chester O., Jr.	1st Lt	044929	A	7	74
Carter, Horace J.	Pfc	1082265	A	7	75
Drust, Donald J.	Cpl	1071298	A	7	76
McDowell, John F.	Pfc	1088567	A	7	77
Hudson, George M.	Cpl	638993	A	7	78
Highley, Maynard L.	Cpl	626140	A	7	79
Clivares, Secundino V.	Pfc	1083801	A	7	80
Bowden, Eugene W.	Pfc	1079638	A	7	81
Garner, Gordon	S/Sgt	282367	A	7	82
Holcomb, Lester A.	1st Lt	0-821019	A	7	83
Warren, Leonard E.	M/Sgt	RA 14302323	A	7	84
Woods, Robert E.	Cpl	1098346	A	8	85
Elliott, Bill	Sgt	RA 35473494	A	8	86
McGovern, James V.	Pfc	1078346	A	8	87
Davidson, Douglas E.	Pfc	564044	A	8	88
Mock, Bobbie F.	Pfc	1100179	A	8	89
Blazewicz, Stanley A.	Pfc	622857	A	8	90
Eppley, Franklin H.	Pfc	1113219	A	8	91
Bre??krueutz, John J.	2nd Lt	AO 19?9107	A	8	92
Bolyard, Richard L.	Cpl	655580	A	8	93

Olivigni, Francis J.	Sgt	344627	A	8	94
Fant, Albert H.	Sgt	578435	A	8	95
Knudson, Lamar A.	1st Lt	037237	A	8	96
Zelazo, Alfred	Cpl	651787	A	9	97
Wilson, Robert V.	1st Lt	15784A	A	9	98
Gish, William H.	S/Sgt	AF 13020404	A	9	99
Currin, Willie L.	Cpl	US 520060801	A	9	100
Dazey, Charle E.	Pfc	1079677	A	9	101
Flynn, Walter M.	Cpl	953570	A	9	102
Grass, Garland A.	Cpl	504974	A	9	103
Gorena, Dionicio J., Jr.	Pfc	659657A	A	9	104
Owens, Andrew H.	Sgt	RA 78480?95	A	9	105
Ashby, Billie J.	Pfc	669137	A	9	106
Kueny, Robert A.	Pfc	667179	A	9	107
Miles, Gerald D.	Pfc	667316	A	9	108
Snodgrass, James F.	M/Sgt	RA 32068273	A	10	109
Erola, Wesley E.	Pvt	ER 55011111	A	10	110
Faris, Robert W.	Pfc	RA 36066454	A	10	111
Cook, John E.	Pfc	RA 1235163	A	10	112
Nedley, George R., Jr.	Pfc	RA 13344155	A	10	113
Coates, Williard H.	2nd Lt	062465	A	10	114
Arendale, Hugh R.	Pvt	RA I4352111	A	10	115
Farley, Louis G.	Pfc	1045319	A	10	116
Cuevas, Alfredo	Pfc	RA 19342026	A	10	117
Nash, Joseph D.	Pvt	RA 33747345	A	10	118
Willis, Fleming O.	Pfc	RA 57300127	A	10	119
Ragland, Robert W.	Pfc	1096060	A	10	120
Cabral, David E.	Cpl	1031199	A	11	121
Paine, George H.	Cpl	RA 11163980	A	11	122
Foor, Howard O.	2nd Lt	049837	A	11	123
Tillman, Gerald D.	S/Sgt	575719	A	11	124
Moreno, Manuel H.	Pfc	611422	A	11	125
Meszaros, Joseph B.	Pfc	1104210	A	11	126
Watson, Leonard	Cpl	RA 14270821	A	11	127
Finnegan, Robert J.	Pfc	632281	A	11	128
Woodward, Francis	Pfc	630200	A	11	129
MacRockwell, Corwin	M/Sgt	378827	A	11	130
Salena, Anthony R.	Cpl	601393	A	11	131
Rice, Joseph J.	Pfc	601690	A	11	132
Casey, William A.	Cpl	1090312	A	12	133
Storey, Leroy G.	Pfc	1098186	A	12	134
McRoberts, James H.	Capt	026995	A	12	135
Driskill, William C.	Pfc	1094018	A	12	136
Trainer, Atlee B.	Pfc	649132	A	12	137
Endsley, Wendall C.	2nd Lt	050019	A	12	138
Belville, James E.	Pfc	1056906	A	12	139
Mitchell, Grady B., Jr.	1st Lt	049074	A	12	140
Pickett, James T.	Pfc	1065774	A	12	141

Hoagland, Allan B.	Cpl	633665	A	12	142
Ogden, James W.	Pfc	586381	A	12	143
Craig, Joseph L., Jr.	Sgt	638774	A	12	144
Hutchins, Fletcher M.	Pfc	1042394	B	1	145
Zeltman, William F.	Pfc	1069793	B	1	146
McDonald, Alton G.	Sgt	82229517	B	1	147
Haussler, Ernest E.	Sgt	325170	B	1	148
Jones, William E.	Pfc	1091330	B	1	149
Handler, Irwin	Pfc	1075820	B	1	150
Bowling, Warren	Pvt	662878	B	1	151
Storansly, Paul N.	Capt	022955	B	1	152
Gullage, James E.	Cpl	661411	B	1	153
Taylor Paul K.	Pfc	616713	B	1	154
Manning, William R.	Pfc	653552	B	1	155
Martin, Paul E.	Cpl	1029114	B	1	156
Cummings, Chester E.	Sgt	1048359	B	2	157
Ogden, Frank S.	Pfc	660466	B	2	158
Reinke, Lawrence L.	Pfc	1063296	B	2	159
Holbrook, Robert J.	Pfc	1112973	B	2	160
Baker, John E.	2nd Lt	049814	B	2	161
Cannizzaro, Thomas	Sgt	560582	B	2	162
Hanrahan, Edward J.	S/Sgt	255755	B	2	163
Jarrett, Charles E.	Pfc	1125879	B	2	164
Blankenberg, John A.	Sgt	326093	B	2	165
Sullivan, James J.	Sgt	1073668	B	2	166
Metzger, William C.	Pfc	1101615	B	2	167
Williams, Tommie J.	Sgt	1070806	B	2	168
Mathis, Lawrence E.	Sgt	666222	B	3	169
Derby, Robert K.	Pfc	659483	B	3	170
Shelnut, John C.	Capt	016535	B	3	171
Frazier, Vance N.	Cpl	414482	B	3	172
Williams, Donald	Pfc	670098	B	2	173
Baxter, William F.	M/Sgt	284221	B	3	174
McGinnis, Thomas L.	Pfc	1076709(?)	B	3	175
Hagenah, Edward R.	Lt Col	05046	B	3	176
Lund, Daryl D.	Pfc	1084904	B	3	177
Baugh, William B.	Pfc	655899	B	3	178
Flores, Fidel G.	Pfc	1075449	B	3	179
Goss, Harvey A.	2nd Lt	049771	B	3	180
Fulton, William Jr.	Cpl	492718	B	4	181
Climino, Larry R.	Pfc	1093449	B	4	182
Dolan, Raymond E.	Cpl	65820?	B	4	183
Fay, Preston S., Jr.	Pfc	1112955	B	4	184
Dalier, Daniel J.	Pfc	1107504	B	4	185
Levasseur, Ronald N.	Pfc	1094587	B	4	186
Bradley, Donald J.	Sgt	659463	B	4	187
Schnader, William A., Jr.	Sgt	1024463	B	4	188
Collier, Donald R.	Pfc	611759	B	4	189

Thrash, James E.	Cpl	587706	B	4	190
Owen, Herbert R.	Pfc	RA 14319201	B	4	191
Vollo, Andrew E.	Cpl	658342	B	4	192
May, Delmar E.	Sgt	596412	B	5	193
Mattox, Charles H.	2nd Lt	049977	B	5	194
Maid, Louis C.	Cpl	627375	B	5	195
Woolcocks, Thomas	Pfc	670670	B	5	196
Cluff, Anthony D.	Pvt	1059245	B	5	197
Puckett, James D.	Pfc	1124066	B	5	198
McNulty, Russell F.	Cpl	1088640	B	5	199
Radcliffe, Derrance S.	Maj	05792	B	5	200
McElwee, Stanley D.	1st Lt	028473	B	5	201
Garcia, Frank D.	Sgt	629133	B	5	202
Carter, Leonard P.	Pfc	661677	B	5	203
Earles, James S.	Pfc	544597	B	5	204
Watkins, Willie J.	Sfc	RA 34572267	B	6	205
Nunnery, Henry C.	Sfc	RA 34093667	B	6	206
Herbert, Robert J.	Sgt	RA 18278513	B	6	207
Mahone, Eddie R.	Pvt	RA 16324116	B	6	208
Hemphill, Charles J	M/Sgt	RA 33083342	B	6	209
Cabiness, Joseph B.	Cpl	RA 13241537	B	6	210
Foreman, Doyle	Pvt-2	RA 18291454	B	6	211
Shires, Edgar T., Jr.	1st Lt	0-1327675	B	6	212
French, Elvin E.	Pfc	RA 18293539	B	6	213
Evans, James L.	Pfc	RA 15415929	B	6	214
Renner, James E.	Cpl	1028733	B	6	215
Powell, Arthur E.	Pfc	1063118	B	6	216
Yearwood, Lemaster B.	Cpl	276893	B	7	217
Barnes, Howard J.	Pfc	1064208	B	7	218
Schafenacker, Edward F.	S/Sgt	468414	B	7	219
Dougherty, William J.	Pfc	360400	B	7	220
Weems, Henry M.	Sgt	337978	B	7	221
Kraus, Louis C.	Sgt	633868	B	7	222
Ward, Calvin B.	Pfc	1110936	B	7	223
Walsh, David C.	Pfc	1091355	B	7	224
Warlie, Will N.	Cpl	669700	B	7	225
Wentworth, Jerome D.	Cpl	1079808	B	7	226
Rosenthal, Joerome C.	Pfc	669394	B	7	227
Fellis, Theodore	Pfc	1053532	B	7	228
Reis, George F.	Pfc	1091448	B	8	229
Black, Paul E.	Pfc	662182	B	8	230
Kelly, Warren A.	Cpl	665393	B	8	231
Plumb, Reed E.	Pfc	1102418	B	8	232
Taylor, Lawrence I.	1st Lt	044861	B	8	233
Pacelle, Louis M.	Pfc	1095080	B	8	234
Cowles, Ray W.	Pfc	1053159	B	8	235
Carter, Doyle	Pfc	1094158	B	8	236
Bowers, Raymond T.	Cpl	583800	B	8	237

Parrish, P. O.	Cpl	658878	B	8	238
Oliver, Jack G.	Pfc	823253	B	8	239
Monroe, Tracy W., Jr.	Pfc	6354268	B	8	240
Hrabcsak, Michael	Sgt	250056	B	9	241
Grigelis, Charles	Sgt	665492	B	9	242
Jesko, Raymond E.	Pfc	1064779	B	9	243
Godfrey, Leland C.	Pvt	1059061	B	9	244
Grant, Frederick E.	Pfc	654216	B	9	245
Greene, William J.	Pfc	1030424	B	9	246
Christopherson, Donald G.	Sgt	637365	B	9	247
Rice, Howard	Pfc	RA 16164?59	B	9	248
Wagner, Carl R.	Pvt	RA 15424509	B	9	249
Palmer, Thomas F.	Cpl	RA 15378161	B	9	250
Hartley, James E.	Pfc	RA 18064126	B	9	251
Smith, Bernard L.	Pvt	RA 19368855	B	9	252
Brooks, Lawrence C.	Pvt-2	RA 18043146	B	10	253
Maret, Paul F.	Pfc	RA 2357?876	B	10	254
Lewis, Robert N.	Pvt	RA 19257478	B	10	255
Purdy, Donald E.	Cpl	RA 1630840	B	10	256
Williams, Reynolds	Pfc	RA 14327618	B	10	257
Gros, Eno J., Jr.	Pfc	ER 18275877	B	10	258
Moore, Howard E.	Pvt	RA 13349643	B	10	259
Wakefield, Franklin G.	Cpl	RA 13164313	B	10	260
Roby, Donnie F.	Pfc	RA 15275433	B	10	261
Simmons, Clarence, A.	Sfc	RA 38179706	B	10	262
Mulik, George	Pfc	RA 13315206	B	10	263
Willis, Albert E., Jr.	1st Lt	0-2014608	B	10	264
Ferris, Edward R.	Cpl	AF 1179666	B	11	265
Brennie, Daniel A.	Pvt	RA 12306830	B	11	266
Binkley, James F.	Pvt	RA 15381249	B	11	267
Pederson, Leroy O.	Pfc	RA 15253632	B	11	268
Lysaght, Joseph W.	Cpl	RA 11168213	B	11	269
Burks, Joseph H.	HN	9413309	B	11	270
Mattson, John A.	Cpl	1064180	B	11	271
Matasorsky, Francis J.	Pfc	665091	B	11	272
Booker, Dorsie	1st Lt	047794	B	11	273
Napier, Golden	Pfc	1102249	B	11	274
Compton, John T.	Pfc	670884	B	11	275
Joseph, Johnnie Jr.	Cpl	RA 15256651	B	11	276
Ferguson, Vincent A.	Pfc	ER 17251384	B	12	277
Concannon, Joseph F.	Capt	0-1290035	B	12	278
Williams, Jim E.	Pfc	RA 6312801	B	12	279
Hurd, Charles W., Jr.	Sfc	RA 37742869	B	12	280
Minkler, Donald T.	Cpl	RA 32657191	B	12	281
Cinplay, Mitchell J.	Pfc	1051889	B	12	282
Vaughan, Jack E.	HN	5690429	B	12	293
Strainic, Lawrence N.	Cpl	1079355	B	12	284
Albert, Dewillis L.	Pfc	1095392	B	12	285

Luke, John E.	Pfc	667249	B	12	286
Terrio, Donald	Pfc	1084626	B	12	287
Anderson, Richard N.	Pfc	1103211	B	12	288
McKay, Murdock	Pfc	567905	C	1	289
Whitney, Ralph Henry	Pfc	1056988	C	1	290
Stewart, Charles F.	HM3	3155197	C	1	291
Lee, William T.	Cpl	RA 14316058	C	1	292
Hallwell, Robert H.	Pfc	1065525	C	1	293
Long, Donald G.	Cpl	RA 19308252	C	1	294
Vella, Joseph P.	Pfc	1112561	C	1	295
Sheperd, Robert	Pvt	608246	C	1	296
Jageacks, John Thomas	Pfc	1071546	C	1	297
Castiglione, Paul	Pvt	1046677	C	1	298
Moore, William David	Pfc	1097458	C	1	299
Gordon, John R.	?	529323	C	1	300
Swoape, Jessee Clark	Pfc	1074780	C	2	301
Weil, Richard M.	Cpl	1037486	C	2	302
Pierce, Desmond	M/Sgt	RA 6249224	C	2	303
Kilduff, John Edward	Cpl	548595	C	2	304
Umbauch, Ernest J.	S/Sgt	333872	C	2	305
Coleman, D. L.	Pfc	627179	C	2	306
Coleman, Glyn A.	Pfc	RA 24789861	C	2	307
Faulconer, Paul D.	Pfc	1098332	C	2	308
Walker, Donald M.	Pfc	1125896	C	2	309
Hess, Irvin Woodrow	Pfc	649168	C	2	310
Morency, Adelorde G.	1st Lt	0-39321	C	2	311
McClelland, Herbert H.	Pfc	1043051	C	2	312
Lucas, Bobby D.	Pfc	1064462	C	3	313
Keery, William P.	Pfc	640084	C	3	314
Ramirez, Alvaro, Jr.	Cpl	1084040	C	3	315
Zawlocki, Richard C.	Pfc	670545	C	3	316
Blacklidge, Jack W.	Cpl	1108941	C	3	317
Slotabec, Robert C.	Pfc	1071979	C	3	318
Rodden, David L.	Pfc	1050888	C	3	319
Anderson, Fred L.	Pfc	1087437	C	3	320
Mullins, Charlie Jr.	Pfc	1118931	C	3	321
Allen, Jack	Pfc	1063275	C	3	322
Weidemann, Maurice H.	Pfc	1070882	C	3	323
Foster, Henry M.	T/Sgt	357743	C	3	324
Williams, Leslie C.	2nd Lt	049933	C	4	325
Downs, William J.	Sgt	307977	C	4	326
Schmidt, Robert H.	Pfc	1094272	C	4	327
Marston, Bobby R.	Pfc	RA 14346111	C	4	328
Puhr, George S., Jr.	Cpl	1071625	C	4	329
Smith, Marcus H.	Pvt	RA 39495385	C	4	330
Snyder, Walter Henry, Jr.	Pfc	1038235	C	4	331
Kurcaba, Joseph R.	1st Lt	0-39091	C	4	332
Mussatto, Michael E.	Pfc	1082859	C	4	333

Peveto, Malcolm B.	S/Sgt	316556	C	4	334
Ingraham, Gerald E.	Pfc	601844	C	4	335
Nash, W. E. III	Pfc	666632	C	4	336
Leeds, Joseph R.	Cpl	649831	C	5	337
Cartalino, Thomas	Pfc	RA 36642838	C	5	338
Page, John U.D.	Lt Col	0-29085	C	5	339
Nelson, Ernest Edward	Pfc	RA 19351663	C	5	340
Henry, Roper	M/Sgt	267613	C	5	341
West, Carl A.	Pfc	1013081	C	5	342
Hughes, Harold D.	S/Sgt	244019	C	5	343
Ludes, William J.	Cpl	1066187	C	5	344
Kimmins, John D.	S/Sgt	370138	C	5	345
Copitzky, Arnold L.	Pfc	1117193	C	5	346
Baccari, Hugo V.	Pfc	1061714	C	5	347
Foley, Arthur A., Jr.	Cpl	552121	C	5	348
Minser, Robert A.	Cpl	660680	C	6	349
Wilson, Charles R.	Sfc	RA 18365703	C	6	350
Dale, Harold E.	Pvt	RA 16328654	C	6	351
Morris, Arvell H.	Cpl	RA 37106967	C	6	352
Sabo, James Jr.	Pfc	667222	C	6	353
Skiles, Phillip C.	Pfc	RA 13?31034	C	6	354
Wise, Earl E.	Sgt	RA 33861159	C	6	355
Priddy, Lawrence Parker, Jr	Pfc	1102492	C	6	356
Kipp, K. R.	Sgt	513734	C	6	357
Szwajkos, John Joseph	HN	235446	C	6	358
Rivera-Ildefonso, Antonio	Pfc	ER 304226?6	C	6	359
Reyes-Ruiz, Beniono	Cpl	ER 30431807	C	6	360
Romero, Antonio	Sgt	RA 10404997	C	7	361
Apanto, Juan B.(?)	Pfc	ER 30433573	C	7	362
Heu, Herbert F.Y.	S/Sgt	970851	C	7	363
Kleber, Clifford J.	Pfc	1088906	C	7	364
Cowden, Bruce P.	Cpl	RA 12300306	C	7	365
Wojtowicz, Matthew (N)	Pfc	1118859	C	7	366
Brooks, Charles H.	Cpl	RA 14197936	C	7	367
Jenkins, Vernon D.	Sgt	RA 37685556	C	7	368
Duvernay, Alfred E.	Cpl	RA 14300386	C	7	369
Alcazar-Lugo, Antonio A.	Pfc	RA 30427883	C	7	370
Del Toro, Raymond	Pfc	RA 2193 7063	C	7	371
Gallart, Guadalupe	Pvt	RA 29151951	C	7	372
Lawson, Venson	Cpl	RA 13320000	C	8	373
Vega, Victor M.	Pfc	ER 57011034	C	8	374

Hungnam #2

NAME	RANK	SERIAL NUMBER	PLOT	ROW	GRAVE
Cron, Eugene	Pfc	RA 15380385	A	1	1
Wadsworth, John Wilson	Cpl	RA 13278907	A	1	2
Penland, Raymond D.	Sfc	RA 7081897	A	1	3
Hockaday, Lonnie	Pvt	RA 13213606	A	1	4
Dilver, James A.	Pfc	RA 43047539	A	1	5
Johnson, Jefferson	Cpl	RA 38386754	A	1	6
Vickers, Ivey E.	Cpl	ER 53009035	A	1	7
Salter, Alfred L.	Pfc	RA 13269588	A	1	8
Harris, Manual	Cpl	US 54010046	A	1	9
Wilson, Douglas C.	1st Lt	0-2019683	A	1	10
Roberson, Eugene	Sfc	RA 34065369	A	1	11
Martin, Robert V.	Pvt	RA 17274243	A	1	12
Rhyner, Eugene A.	Pfc	RA 16284566	A	1	13
Spears, Woodroe W.	Cpl	38731329	A	1	14
Mize, Augrey W.	Sgt	RA 38062118	A	1	15
Gonzalez-Osorio, Eusebio	Pfc	RA 29188056	a	1	16
Hunter, Robert ?	Cpl	RA 15293498	A	1	17
Luhrs, Paul Vincent	Pfc	1091538	A	1	18
Traylor, James M.	M/Sgt	RA 6389487	A	1	19
Dowling, Henry E.	Cpl	300014?1	A	1	20
Murphy, John D.	Pfc	ER 37787080	A	1	21
Davis, Bobby	Pvt	RA 15381895	A	1	22
Bonner Robert L.	Pvt	RA 15424891	A	1	23
Thompson, William A.	Pfc	RA 14270052	A	1	24
Stuckey, Frederick	Pvt	RA 13344901	A	1	25
Bynum, Jackie B.	Pvt	RA 14330435	A	1	26
Velazquez, Pedro	Cpl	RA 30417793	A	1	27
Worley, Forest Edward	Pfc	RA 15259234	A	1	28
West, Charles Edgar	Cpl	RA 35780945	A	1	29
Decker, Hobart	Cpl	35098620	A	1	30
Tyler, Maxine	Cpl	RA 38649846	A	2	31
Bogart, Clayton L.	Pfc	RA 16281555	A	2	32
Tennent, Joseph T.	2d cook	Merchant Marine	A	2	33
Godwin, Aubrey	Pfc	RA 14264862	A	2	34
Mullen, Roland B.	Pvt	RA 13344804	A	2	35
McLean, Artis	Pfc	14339968	A	2	36
Lemons, Bennie Z.	M/Sgt	RA 6924523	A	2	37
Jerz, Thaddeus J.	Cpl	12324492	A	2	38
Williams, Charles J.	Cpl	12306533	A	2	39
Ring, Conyard L.	Pfc	RA 18351728	A	2	40

Pyongyang

NAME	RANK	SERIAL NUMBER	PLOT	ROW	GRAVE
Romero, Martin Z.	Sfc	RA 39693141	1	1	1
Brown, Herbert W.	Pfc	RA 12300268	1	1	2
Pogue, James F.	Pfc	RA 6928725	1	1	3
Fillion, Phillip J.	Pfc	RA 16284886	1	1	4
Unknown X-1			1	1	5
Hephner, Clayton F.	Pvt	RA 16264666	1	1	6
Prince, Marvin E.	Pfc	RA 15199336	1	1	7
Unk X-2			1	1	8
Unk X-3			1	1	9
Unk X-4			1	1	10
Unk X-5			1	1	11
Unk X-6			1	1	12
Unk X-7			1	1	13
Unk X-8			1	1	14
Unk X-9			1	1	15
Dease, George B.	Pfc	RA 14340690	1	2	16
Gutierrez, Fidencio	Pfc	RA 28104461	1	2	17
McElroy, Forest E., Jr.	Cpl	RA 14144900	1	2	18
Chaffin, Roy O.	Pfc	RA 15251796	1	2	19
Olsen, Hugh A.	Pfc	RA 11198681	1	3	20
Bailey, Henry M.	Pfc	RA 37895991	1	2	21
Boggs, Virgil	Cpl	RA 15379142	1	2	22
Glenn, Charles F.	Pvt	RA 16289384	1	2	23
Ronan, Harold J.	Pvt-2	RA 46068313	1	2	24
Nemec, Stephen P.	Cpl	RA 15266221	1	2	25
Henderson, Delbert E.	Cpl	RA 15418372	1	2	26
Lemay, George	Sgt	RA 11166909	1	2	27
Hoag, Arnold A.	Cpl	RA 16251468	1	2	28
Kirk, Harold E.	Pfc	RA 18174733	1	2	29
Attwood, Walter	Sgt	RA 33804908	1	2	30
Lawrence, Irvin G.	Pfc	RA 16299222	1	3	31
Hrab, Jurij B.	Cpl	RA 13267425	1	3	32
Hopkins, Robert J.	2nd Lt	0-2014452	1	3	33
Greene, Claud Jr.	Pfc	RA 14292908	1	3	34
?rull, Welton P., Jr.	Cpl	RA 44129378	1	3	35
Pigott, Marlin L.	Pvt	RA 13346056	1	3	36
Marshall, George G.	Pfc	RA 14244924	1	3	37
Richetta, John	Cpl	RA 13264590	1	3	38
Gilbert, Dennis A.	Cpl	RA 16279854	1	3	39
Maldonado, Luciano	Pfc	RA 19313585	1	3	40
Dulin, Daniel	Cpl	RA 14322985	1	3	41
Tonche, Paul A., Sr.	Cpl	RA 18311270	1	3	42
Coale, William E.	Sfc	RA 18259984	1	3	43
Romero, Nelson R.	Pfc	RA 18197403	1	3	44
Fagg, Cecil W.	Sfc	RA 39711223	1	3	45

Fallanca, Fortunato C.	Pfc	RA 21912146	1	4	46
Pospyhalla, Dale A.	Pfc	RA 16323243	1	4	47
Durham, Charles Harvey	Pfc	RA 19323651	1	4	48
Stavos, Lester Carlton	Cpl	RA 17263848	1	4	49
Abreu, Manuel Jr.	Pfc	RA 12294304	1	4	50
Rowlette, Louis	Sgt	RA 35467082	1	4	51
Walk, Arnold E.	Cpl	RA 16018362	1	4	52
Bailey, Paul R.	Pfc	RA 13285855	1	4	53
Unknown X-114			1	4	54
Ackerman, Jack M.	Pvt	RA 16266426	1	4	55
Garcia, Ernesto, Jr.	Pfc	RA 16255745	1	4	56
Segura, George P.	Pvt-2	RA 19358076	1	4	57
Hendricks, Charles H.	Pvt-2	RA 16294533	1	4	58
Granberry, Carl J.	Pfc	RA 14289888	1	4	59
Wooldridge, Claude C.	Pvt-2	RA 19329883	1	4	60
Lewandowski, Frank J.	Sfc	RA 13177449	1	5	61
Wilson, Richard G.	Pfc	RA 17252005	1	5	62
Nawricki, Stanley	Cpl	RA 13282966	1	5	63
Littlehawk, John	Pfc	RA 18273543	1	5	64
Renfrow, Norman E.	Pvt	RA 17276852	1	5	65
Lopez, Peter R.	Sgt	RA 19294633	1	5	66
Shreves, Jim C.	Pfc	RA 18248895	1	5	67
Eason, Theon Oliff	1st Lt	AO 1909973	1	5	68
Unknown X-11			1	5	69
Menges, Robert R.	Cpl	RA 19316738	1	5	70
Brown, Donald C.	Cpl	RA 42195545	1	5	71
Mealor, Richard H.	1st Lt	0-28264	1	5	72
Unknown X-12			1	5	73
Unknown X-13			1	5	74
Unknown X-14			1	5	75
Hunsickee, Kenneth P.	Cpl	RA 15357945	1	6	76
Franco, Julio E.	Pfc	US 56000485	1	6	77
Mikesoll, Harold E.	Pfc	RA 36442859	1	6	78
Dorsey, Harold R.	Pfc	RA 15281637	1	6	79
Counts, Woodrow W.	Cpl	RA 15215302	1	6	80
Phillips, Howard	Cpl	RA 14313161	1	6	81
Hodges, William E.	Pvt	RA 19357873	1	6	82
Garcia, Leonard P., Jr.	Cpl	RA 18134427	1	6	83
Justice, Alvis	Pvt	RA 35999290	1	6	84
Ambrose, Thomas	Cpl	RA 14281064	1	6	85
Bass, William T., Jr.	Pfc	RA 14313568	1	6	86
Stone, Oliver Jr.	Pvt	RA 14283603	1	6	87
Shinde, Robert M.	Sgt	RA 39084228	1	6	88
Ruthstrom, Carroll O.	Pvt-2	RA 18358805	1	6	89
Bell, Joseph T.	Cpl	RA 13265544	1	6	90
Unknown X-15			1	7	91
Unknown X-16			1	7	92
Unknown X-17			1	7	93

Unknown X-18			1	7	94
Unknown X-19			1	7	95
Stidham, Henry	Cpl	RA 35659422	1	7	96
Poole, Jack E.	Pfc	RA 16286184	1	7	97
Unknown X-20			1	7	98
Unknown X-21			1	7	99
Ray, Harold	Sfc	RA 35411588	1	7	100
Bernal, Joe M.	Pfc	RA 39597793	1	7	101
Samolinski, Stanley	Pfc	RA 16303975	1	7	102
Newman, George R.	Pfc	RA 15411542	1	7	103
Unknown X-23			1	7	104
McKittrick, Paul E.L.	Pvt	RA 16321907	1	7	105
Hall, Raymond Earl	Pfc	RA 16358843	1	8	106
Ceanda, Marcelo C.	Pfc	RA 18254161	1	8	107
?origian, Frank W.	Sgt	RA 37580885	1	8	108
Moore, James R.	Pfc	RA 17259199	1	8	109
Cas?ana, Pete	Pvt	RA 19357353	1	8	110
Seaffron, Paul	Pvt	RA 23764736	1	8	111
Parenti, Glendon	Sfc	RA 38662770	1	8	112
Kamoku, Benjamin S.	Pvt	RA 29030855	1	8	113
Rivera, Floyd	Pvt	RA 37720948	1	8	114
Filler, Clemond W.	Pfc	RA 19326496	1	8	115
Hall, Hedrey D.	Pfc	RA 14314942	1	8	116
Blanton(?), Emory M.	Pfc	RA 14252969	1	8	117
Starkey, Clyde M.	M/Sgt	RA 6236312	1	8	118
S?smeros, Rudolph	Pvt	RA 38701092	1	8	119
Salvie, Robert J.	Cpl	RA 13300?64	1	8	120
Wirtz, Harold D.	Pvt-2	RA 17270373	1	9	121
Brown, Edward L.	Pfc	RA 16310573	1	9	122
Johnson, Arnold	Cpl	RA 36965148	1	9	123
Corley, Freddie O.	Pfc	RA 18295935	1	9	124
Chadwick, Richard	Cpl	RA 18326430	1	9	125
Lacey, Robert L.	M/Sgt	RA 6388942	1	9	126
Pierce, Robert D.	Pfc	RA 19313592	1	9	127
Lewis, Daniel H.	Pfc	RA 19341718	1	9	128
Phipps, Je?hl B.	Pfc	RA 18221601	1	9	129
Misuraco, Jerome A.	Pfc	RA 17270905	1	9	130
Lee, Elvin M.	2nd Lt	0-2262281	1	9	131
Hewett, Francis L.	Cpl	RA 17251808	1	9	132
Inghram, Samuel D.	Sfc	RA 19308149	1	9	133
Quirez, John A.	Cpl	RA 18279561	1	9	134
Gilson, William A.	Cpl	RA 17218881	1	9	135
Van H(?)arn, Henry W.	Pvt	RA 19354218	1	9	136
Taylor, Oscar Leo	Pvt	RA 19341654	1	9	137
King, Ralph	Pfc	RA 35685568	1	9	138
Spence, Grover C.	Cpl	RA 7002463	1	10	139
Williams, Johnny Jr.	Pfc	RA 18280239	1	10	140
Farmer, Joseph	Cpl	RA 14346374	1	10	141

Lord, Ira F., Jr.	Sgt	AF 18145309	1	10	142
Bolling, Lawrence	Cpl	RA 13234678	1	10	143
Hayes, Dover D.	Pvt	RA 18351789	1	10	144
Cheers, James L.	Pvt	RA 16310124	1	10	145
Helms, Euriah	Pvt	RA 18351794	1	10	146
Ross, Emanuel	Sfc	RA 34028527	1	10	147
Davenport, Curtis Jr.	Pvt	RA 15299678	1	10	148
Cowger, Donald C.	Pfc	RA 19328467	1	10	149
Nestor, David L.	Pfc	RA 13312994	1	10	150
Friel, John P., Jr.	Sgt	430?7911	1	11	151
Riley, Francis A.	Sgt	RA 6245792	1	11	152
Thibault, Arthur J.	Sgt	RA 11179188	1	11	153
Johnson, Joseph	Pvt-2	RA 11191531	1	11	154
Armstrong, Billy J.	Sfc	RA 17230694	1	11	155
Tye, Leonard E.	Pfc	RA 19318817	1	11	156
Worden, Arthur J.	Pfc	RA 21918140	1	11	157
Frisz, Charles D.	Pfc	RA 14329329	1	11	158
Church, Freddie E.	?	RA 24439075	1	11	159
Knopp, Roy E.	?	RA 27851417	1	11	160
Thornton, Bobby O.	Sfc	RA 14197196	1	11	161
Mauro, Robert S.	Cpl	RA 11178855	1	11	162
Gruser, Laverne A.	?	RA 16284086	1	11	163
Sid?ti, Anthony R.	Pvt	RA 21006748	1	11	164
Hendrickson, Jack K.	Cpl	RA 18254396	1	11	165
Jacobs, Norval E.	M/Sgt	RA 35843737	1	12	166
Flynn, Jerry P.	2nd Lt	0-191?342	1	12	167
Ramos, Carmen, M.	1st Lt	0-60981	1	12	168
Brinksmeyer, Alfonso S.	Cpl	RA 16296791	1	12	169
Wright, Robert	Sgt	RA 6973187	1	12	170
Dune(?), Roy E.	Pvt	RA 44005358	1	12	171
Simpson, Robert L.	1st Lt	AO 7637?7	1	12	172
Cooke, Glen L.	Cpl	RA 19063036	1	12	173
Jones, William P.	Sgt	RA 12285533	1	12	174
Krawcion(?), Nick	2bd Lt	0-2262262	1	12	175
Sutp??, Harold A.	Pfc	RA 13271008	1	12	176
Sheldon, Donald F.	Cpl	RA 12284819	1	12	177
Butynsky, Raymond W.	Pvt-2	RA 12285886	1	12	178
Warnke, Walter W.	Cpl	RA 17246218	1	12	179
Potratz, Donald B.	Pfc	RA 12348757	1	12	180
Adams, John Q.	Pvt	RA 19357843	1	13	181
Tremblay, Aurel N.	Sfc	RA 31480157	1	13	182
Feyereisen, Robert F.	Cpl	RA 37705995	1	13	183
Reese, Jodie S., Jr.	Pvt	RA 18139391	1	13	184
Davis, Henry Lee	Pfc	RA 14281714	1	13	185
Naylor, Clifford M.	Pfc	RA 16307293	1	13	186
Kerns(?), John A., Jr.	Cpl	RA 14244936	1	13	187
Sha?ver, James A.	Cpl	RA 15410598	1	13	188
Bevilock, Ersel	Sfc	RA 6883691	1	13	189

Lynch, Harold M.	Pvt	RA 37582980	1	13	190
Loving, Charles R.	Cpl	RA 13290631	1	13	191
Hill, Wayne W.	Pfc	RA 16304101	1	13	192
Voyles, Eugene R.	Pfc	RA 15418780	1	13	193
Finn, Harold W.	Pvt	RA 45045498	1	13	194
Blair, Elzie L.	Pvt	RA 14338197	1	13	195
Hodge, Floyd L.	Cpl	RA 14268564	1	14	196
Pareso, John H.	Cpl	RA 16316524	1	14	197
Sullivan, Edward T.	Pfc	RA 111?2197	1	14	198
Gariati, Louis J., Sr.	M/Sgt	RA 6573894	1	14	199
Scheliber, Robert C.	Sfc	RA 14293232	1	14	200
Ellison, J. ?.	Sgt	RA 16293521	1	14	201
Greer, John A.	Pfc	RA 13240931	1	14	202
Oaks, Paul N.	Pfc	RA 19?43957	1	14	203
Rickman, Evans	?	RA 21697773	1	14	204
Thompson, H .R.	2nd lt	AO-1909419	1	14	205
Heryla, Andrew	T/Sgt	AF 16247303	1	14	206
Harrison, Lewis T., Jr.	1st Lt	0-948576	1	14	207
Barrow, Henry G.	Sfc	RA 349?9741	1	14	208
Unknown X-112			1	14	209
Gilardi, Robert D.	Cpl	RA 19292298	1	14	210
Willis, Doyle D.	Pfc	RA 19294267	1	15	211
Mesa, Rudy V.	Pvt	RA 18310994	1	15	212
Moore, Claude F., Jr.	Pvt	RA 14279874	1	15	213
Morris, Milton Jr.	Cpl	RA 14293576	1	15	214
Patterson, Ithal T.	Pvt	RA 25638377	1	15	215
Witherell, Francis K.	Cpl	RA 3293?577	1	15	216
Aitkens, Virgil F.	Pvt	RA 16315705	1	15	217
Knapp, Donald W.	Pvt	RA 1632-716	1	15	218
Shepard, Harold R.	Pvt	RA 14339752	1	15	219
Ellison, John Y.	Sfc	RA 20951322	1	15	220
Latanation, Mike	Sfc	RA 13012045	1	15	221
Musser, Alvin D.	Cpl	RA 16307192	1	15	222
Winkler, Marvin I.	Pvt	RA 13304302	1	15	223
Hines, Leonard	Sgt	RA 33180282	1	15	224
Pattison, Orlando R.	Pvt	RA 16293916	1	15	225
Counts, Charles M.	Cpl	RA 13292673	1	16	226
Zenter, Frederick	1st Lt	AO 3101405	1	16	227
Dow, Earl G.	Pfc	US 57504099	1	16	228
Frazier, William H., Jr.	Maj	0-39094	1	16	229
Abbey, Augustus	Cpl	RA 17235581	1	16	230
Nathan, Napoleon	Cpl	RA 33920287	1	16	231
Pearson, James R.	Cpl	RA 11176989	1	16	232
Schramm, Frederick O.	Cpl	RA 42171334	1	16	233
Wiskoski, John L.	Sfc	RA 11016465	1	16	234
Galloway, David L.	Cpl	RA 14313995	1	16	235
Meade, Freeman R.	Pfc	RA 15410016	1	16	236
Pritchett, Donald D.	Pfc	RA 13329834	1	16	237

Worth, Phillip L.	Pfc	RA 16261551	1	16	238
Bass, Charlie O.	Pfc	RA 14312246	1	16	239
Jacobs, James Edward	Sgt	RA 13147435	1	16	240
Tohill, Howard Midler	Pvt	RA 18367046	2	1	241
McInnis, Norman	Pfc	RA 38056213	2	1	242
Muse, Earl L.	Cpl	RA 23742???	2	1	243
Evans, Everette R.	Cpl	RA 19343042	2	1	244
Sharp, Franklin D.	Pvt	RA 17290650	2	1	245
Davis, Frederick F.	Sgt	RA 12145601	2	1	246
Unknown X-77			2	1	247
Unknown X-79			2	1	248
Unknown X-80			2	1	249
Holdway, Donald F.	Cpl	RA 16259751	2	1	250
Miller, Russell R.	Cpl	RA 19195997	2	1	251
Hall, Robert B.	Sgt	RA 1628?987	2	1	252
??enstra, Robert W.	Sfc	RA 31262902	2	1	253
???es, ???? B.	Sgt	RA 44137377	2	1	254
?eiele, Andre J.	Cpl	US 51093076	2	1	255
Shoemaker, John Wilson	1st Lt	0-60367	2	2	256
Vich, Steve	Pfc	RA 35890170	2	2	257
Sciommano, Daniel F.	Sgt	RA 12291577	2	2	258
Mendez, Baron III	Cpl	RA 12280063	2	2	259
Unknown X-88			2	2	260
Seeberg, Irving L.	Capt	0-1643322	2	2	261
Walker, Noah	Pfc	RA 34087727	2	2	262
Justice, Wallace	Pfc	RA 15041968	2	2	263
Hanlin, Robert J.	Sgt	RA 11178882	2	2	264
Corson, Harold G.	Pfc	RA 13311449	2	2	265
Beaty, Benjamin L.	Sgt	RA 34659380	2	2	266
Wooten, Franklin D.	Pfc	RA 14340688	2	2	267
Lee, Raymond Earl	Pvt	RA 14145912	2	2	268
Howard, Cordeli	Sgt	RA 34189689	2	2	269
Orr, Clyde (Claude?)	Sfc	RA 14000851	2	2	270
Ellerington, William G.	Pfc	RA 12287113	2	2	271
Sanchez, Robert M.	Cpl	RA 19302908	2	3	272
Strickland, Terrell	Pfc	RA 14241423	2	3	273
Rector, John W.	Pfc	RA 15293930	2	3	274
Jamison, Hugh D.	Cpl	RA 3?883299	2	3	275
Linphigum(?), William B.	Pvt	RA 13?395?0	2	3	276
Shea, James W., Jr.	Pfc	RA 12?5181?	2	3	277
McMahon, James D.	Pfc	RA 13??4012	2	3	278
Walters, Dallas J.	Cpl	RA 16307181	2	3	279
Bland, Bennie	Sgt	RA 44058025	2	3	280
Adams, Wilbur J.	Cpl	RA 13309469	2	3	281
Boardman, Stuart A.	Cpl	RA 11192019	2	3	282
Johnson, Donald R.	Cpl	RA 11164750	2	3	283
Unknown X-83			2	3	284
Cory, Matthew R.	M/Sgt	RA 33986695	2	3	285

Collins, Louis E.	Sgt	RA 16286248	2	4	286
McJankers, James M.	Cpl	RA 14330578	2	4	287
Murphy, William J.	Pfc	RA 15280633	2	4	288
Unknown X-97			2	4	289
McKinnon, Mackey D.	Sgt	RA 19324120	2	4	290
Romero, Joe C.	Pfc	RA 17240401	2	4	291
Bartholow, Gerald	Cpl	RA 15280301	2	4	292
Unknown X-98			2	4	293
Unknown X-99			2	4	294
Smith, William Stewart	Sgt	RA 16303749	2	4	295
Wehinger, John J.	Pfc	RA 12340719	2	4	296
Gibson, Royce C.	Pfc	RA 15423666	2	4	297
Mitcheltree, Kermit	Sfc	RA 20313955	2	4	298
Johnson, John E.	Sfc	RA 20820482	2	4	299
Voyles, Ray F.	Sgt	RA 37616676	2	4	300
Jackson, Harold	Pvt	RA 15296440	2	5	301
Harris, James	Sgt	RA 38032019	2	5	302
Henson, Robert E.	Pvt	RA 13344?78	2	5	303
Wise, Gordon L.	Pfc	RA 19375527	2	5	304
Unknown X-84			2	5	305
Unknown X-85			2	5	306
Bynum, Kenneth G.	Cpl	RA 19305295	2	5	307
Cardwell, Hugh T.	Pfc	RA 14237212	2	5	308
Bly, Richard Lee	Cpl	RA 43002571	2	5	309
Unknown X-86			2	5	310
Dauphiney, Elton	Sgt	RA 18301?66	2	5	311
Mosley, W. M.	Cpl	RA 18333368	2	5	312
Clements, Terrell C.	Pfc	RA 14347181	2	5	313
?emura, ???suo	Sgt	RA 3?107805	2	5	314
Nicholas, Morris	Sfc	RA 6533491	2	5	315
Charnetski, Peter Frank	1st Lt	0-202693?	2	6	316
Naylor, Lewis J.	M/Sgt	RA 13205048	2	6	317
Shelton, Lyle Roland	Pfc	RA 17250416	2	6	318
Joy, William G.	Pfc	RA 16310763	2	6	319
Grossman, Benjamin N.	Sgt	RA 35454866	2	6	320
Hunt, William Clifton	Pvt	RA 15424030	2	6	321
Whelan(?), Francis E.	Pfc	RA 19106069	2	6	322
Hall, Raymond F.	Cpl	RA 16278086	2	6	323
Gandy, John E.	2nd Lt	0-22623?9	2	6	324
Croom, Archie T., Jr.	?	ER 20408151	2	6	325
Suter, Paul J.	Pfc	RA 1327312?	2	6	326
?arcom(?), Jimmie E.	?	RA 17234027	2	6	327
Griffith, George H.	Cpl	RA 19333075	2	6	328
Estes, Richard L.	Pfc	RA 16319434	2	6	329
Brown, Emory L.	Pvt	RA 39197586	2	6	330
Unknown X-90			2	7	331
Unknown X-89			2	7	332
Valliere, Carlton Charles	Pfc	RA 16304779	2	7	333

Welch, Gene Joseph	Pfc	RA 16304986	2	7	334
Graham, Robert L.	Pvt	RA 13336385	2	7	335
We?zel, Frank John	Pfc	RA 16283465	2	7	336
Ferguson, Raymond A.	Sgt	RA 14290457	2	7	337
Baldonado, Joe R.	Cpl	RA 19324868	2	7	338
Unknonw X-91			2	7	339
Unknown X-92			2	7	340
Riley, James H.	Pvt-2	RA 18275?33	2	7	341
Unknown X-93			2	7	342
Unknown X-94			2	7	343
Unknown X-95			2	7	344
Unknown X-96			2	7	345
Brewster, Billy B.	1st Lt	0-1824678	2	8	346
Delaney, James G.	Pfc	RA 13298?94	2	8	347
Elleison, Junior E.	Sgt	RA 16292458	2	8	348
Hawes, Charles Raymond	Cpl	RA 15379198	2	8	349
Sample, Harold N.	Pfc	RA 17171592	2	8	350
Bishop, James E.	Pvt-2	ER 25528469	2	8	351
Exline, Billie J.	Pvt	ER 18320546	2	8	352
Campbell, Alton R.	Pfc	RA 16302708	2	8	353
Espinoza, Richard D.	Pvt	RA 16309946	2	8	354
Dziura, Edward M.	Pvt	RA 20821870	2	8	355
Peterson, Earl Woodrow	Sfc	RA 39128003	2	8	356
Thomas, William B.	Pfc	RA 13293947	2	8	357
Ribbs, Rollo D.	Pfc	AF 16310347	2	8	358
Werkman, James W.	Cpl	RA 13148064	2	8	359
Musone, Angelo Anthony	Cpl	RA 12027210	2	8	360
Sims, Shelby T.	Pvt	RA 16324061	2	9	361
Kelly, George A.	Pfc	RA 15278376	2	9	362
Keane, Richard E.	Sfc	RA 32922336	2	9	363
Miller, Raymond L.	Pfc	RA 17234986	2	9	364
Gillet, Richard	Cpl	ER 11145521	2	9	365
Estell, Carl K.	Pfc	RA 17261387	2	9	366
Jasperson, Charles	Pfc	RA 45038677	2	9	367
Pena, Urbano	Pfc	RA 18224579	2	9	368
Woods, George Harry	Pfc	RA 11195427	2	9	369
Ozias, Walter Eugene	Pvt	RA 16291887	2	9	370
Porter, Carter S.	Pvt	RA 24755436	2	9	371
Sasser, L?oris	Pvt	RA 18258480	2	9	372
Brooks, Marvin R.	Cpl	RA 14298690	2	9	373
Smith, Arthur B.	Sgt	RA 16308452	2	9	374
Bryant, Harold F.	Cpl	RA 1434-664	2	9	375
Merrill, John Nelson	1st Lt	0-2014595	2	10	376
Thompson, George M.	1st Lt	0-1686827	2	10	377
Marek, Thomas D.	Sgt	RA 16309558	2	10	378
Beisswanger, Charles	Cpl	RA 36336391	2	10	379
Green, Joseph Thomas	Cpl	RA 13273846	2	10	380
Amthor, Ferdinand V.	Pfc	RA 13273624	2	10	381

Wilkerson, Desmond R.	Pfc	AF 39946254	2	10	382
Wagner, William G.	Ensign	USN 301502	2	10	383
Parker, Robert Blaine	1st Lt	18003A	2	10	384
Houston, Bernard	Pfc	RA 18351213	2	10	385
Urbanski, Darold D.	Pfc	RA 17276843	2	10	386
Connaughton, George W.	Lt Col	0-312051	2	10	387
Ball, Cecil R.	Pfc	RA 13165335	2	10	388
Werber, James F.	Pvt	RA 19338375	2	10	389
Lewis, Albert E.	Pfc	RA 11192458	2	10	390
Andrew, Joseph J.	Pfc	RA 162254222	3	1	391
Duke, Joseph J.	Cpl	RA 13032839	3	1	392
Hutchison, Jack W.	Pvt-2	RA 16330746	3	1	393
Ellis, Richard D.	Pfc	RA 15252599	3	1	394
Wilson, Wallace	Cpl	RA 18278592	3	1	395
Spann, Joseph F.	Pfc	RA 16293216	3	1	396
Morrie, Flowers Jr.	M/Sgt	RA 14006120	3	1	397
Grooms, Arthur	Pvt	RA 14297839	3	1	398
Hamm, Robert A.	Pvt	RA 16290175	3	1	399
Parrish, Watson	Sgt	RA 15045796	3	1	400
Ke, Robert W.	Cpl	RA 10735547	3	1	401
McLean, Gerald W.	Pvt	RA 15423673	3	1	402
Dean, Tulon V.	Sgt	RA 34611640	3	1	403
Rooksberry, Robert E.	1st Lt	0-1317244	3	1	404
Hare, Clement J.	Cpl	RA 6885751	3	1	405
Coker, Martin A.	Capt	0-1310069	3	2	406
Price, William P.	Cpl	RA 14314803	3	2	407
Miller, John A.	M/Sgt	RA 6384327	3	2	408
Osborne, Harold H.	1st Lt	0-2262263	3	2	409
Booth, Guy R.	Sgt	RA 14342441	3	2	410
Grause, Joseph W., Jr.	Pfc	RA 15227999	3	2	411
Smith, Bernard	Pvt	RA 23557630	3	2	412
Godfrey, Earl J.	Pfc	RA 32640463	3	2	413
Bond, Malcolm D.	Pfc	RA 18320829	3	2	414
Voyles, William E.	Pfc	US 55001542	3	2	415
Gunnell, Rex C.	Capt	RA 0-39434	3	2	416
Clark, Alvin L.	S/Sgt	AF 36797631	3	2	417
Fisher, Levin F.	Cpl	RA 13319017	3	2	418
Rodriguez, Bonifacio	Pfc	RA 18224276	3	2	419
Unknown X-101			3	2	420
Matthews, Jack H.	Cpl	RA 13261008	3	3	421
Keenan, James F.	Cpl	ER 32615988	3	3	422
Riley, Alfred	Pvt	RA 21018580	3	3	423
McDowell, Charles W.	Pfc	RA 14313030	3	3	424
Smith, Anthony M.	Pfc	RA 13351635	3	3	425
Brinson, Gilbert D.	Cpl	RA 15274021	3	3	426
Thomson, Joseph A.	Cpl	RA 36272803	3	3	427
Daniels, Asher	Cpl	RA 13320449	3	3	428
Modos, Emery L.	Pvt	RA 15277141	3	3	429

			3	3	430
Unknown X-115			3	3	430
Bramhill, Ray G.	Pfc	RA 17101756	3	3	431
Unknown X-113			3	3	432
Villarreal, Christobol T.	Sgt	RA 18198444	3	3	433
Abele, Robert P.	Cpl	RA 11195479	3	3	434
McCann, John L.	Cpl	RA 13289721	3	3	435
Gill, Samuel F., Jr.	Pfc	RA 14322606	3	4	436
Petersen, Maun T.	1st Lt	0-1185761	3	4	437
Dye, Doyle J.	Pvt	RA 25299035	3	4	438
Talley, James W.	Pfc	RA 14352186	3	4	439
Juneau, Wilson L.	Pvt	RA 18304288	3	4	440
Braswell, Vernon L.	Pfc	RA 14282413	3	4	441
Faulkner, Robert A.	Pfc	RA 15424031	3	4	442
Darrell, Roy E.	Pfc	RA 25186675	3	4	443
Cahow, Samuel G.	Pfc	RA 17229663	3	4	444
McCammack, Robert V.	Sgt	RA 16311788	3	4	445
Cady, Roy J.	Pfc	RA 13272491	3	4	446
Gurecky, Edwin M.	Pfc	RA 18297016	3	4	447
Owens, Charles H.	Sgt	RA 13161284	3	4	448
Fashone, Raymond A.	Pfc	RA 12116475	3	4	449
Kniznick, Bernard	1st Lt	0-1048048	3	4	450
Jenkins, Jesie R.	Cpl	RA 6928134	3	5	451
Flynn, John A.	Cpl	RA 16288243	3	5	452
Hartley, Clarence G.	Pfc	RA 19367655	3	5	453
Plumb, Albert W.	Pvt	RA 11194318	3	5	454
White, Donald R.	Sgt	RA 15416504	3	5	455
Moats, Melvin	Pfc	RA 13289734	3	5	456
Griese, Robert R.	Pf	RA 37044031	3	5	457
Heinlein, Frederick	Pfc	RA 13272228	3	5	458
Greenwood, Ivan J.	Pfc	RA 12286093	3	5	459
Briscoe, Kenneth J.	Pfc	RA 19345392	3	5	460
Pettit, John W.	Sgt	RA 16279729	3	5	461
Melton, Leamon S.	?	ER 44033141	3	5	462
Beard, Richard R.	M/Sgt	RA 6894102	3	5	463
Leaks, William M.	Pfc	RA 13274793	3	5	464
Hartong, John J.	1st Lt	0-1314628	3	5	465
Stephens, Cleo	Sgt	RA 6285736	3	6	466
Tansil, Issiah	Cpl	RA 34152903	3	6	467
Lasua, Lawrence	Sgt	RA 10734629	3	6	468
Sheehan, John G.	1st Lt	0-59822	3	6	469
Jurkowski, Robert	Sgt	RA 16311211	3	6	470
McCaine, Douglas	Cpl	RA 13270939	3	6	471
Leftwick, Albert	Pfc	RA 15266892	3	6	473
Lathan, Climon N., Jr.	Pfc	RA 14363373	3	6	474
White, Elvin J.	Pfc	RA 18293397	3	6	475
Hoerner, Gabriel R.	Pfc	RA 13299817	3	6	476
Patterson, Joseph A.	Cpl	US 53020064	3	6	477
DeCorrevont, Floyd	Sfc	RA 35965876	3	6	478

Name	Rank	Serial No.			
Richards, Louis J.	Pfc	RA 14312930	3	6	479
Esguer, Libarado E.	Cpl	RA 19322841	3	6	480
Stuckey, Donald L.	Pfc	RA 13330422	3	7	481
Empty			3	7	482
Empty			3	7	483
Empty			3	7	484
Empty			3	7	485
Empty			3	7	486
Empty			3	7	487
Empty			3	7	488
Empty			3	7	489
Empty			3	7	490
Empty			3	7	491
Empty			3	7	492
Empty			3	7	493
Empty			3	7	494
Empty			3	7	495
Wallace, Zeachriah H., Jr.	Cpl	RA 16286395	3	8	496
Wilson, Aubrey	Cpl	RA 15420509	3	8	497
Crosby, Harry H.	Sgt	RA 34607564	3	8	498
England, David E.	Pfc	RA 15269470	3	8	499
Lowery, James E.	Pfc	RA 15299642	3	8	500
Truxes, Arthur H., Jr.	Capt	0-27834	3	8	501
La Quatra, Santo J.	Cpl	RA 13299476	3	8	502
Striegel, Joseph W.	Pfc	RA 26336691	3	8	503
Newbauer, James L.	Pfc	RA 15271111	3	8	504
Desiderio, Reginald B.	Capt	0-1301272	3	8	505
Lelatora, Loreto	Sgt	RA 19237213	3	8	506
Lopez, Carlos	M/Sgt	RA 18197334	3	8	507
Williams, Herbert H.	Pfc	RA 13304844	3	8	508
Garrett, Harry A.	Pvt	RA 133335277	3	8	509
Henry, William F.	Cpl	RA 43047577	3	8	510
Empty			3	9	511
Empty			3	9	512
Empty			3	9	513
Empty			3	9	514
Empty			3	9	515
Empty			3	9	516
Empty			3	9	517
Empty			3	9	518
Empty			3	9	519
Empty			3	9	520
Empty			3	9	521
Empty			3	9	522
Empty			3	9	523
Empty			3	9	524
Empty			3	9	525
Hone, William R.	Capt	0-2018694	3	10	526

Farabee, William L.	Pvt-2	RA 17274603	3	10	527
Swenson, Kenneth	Capt	0-1308394	3	10	528
Moriarty, Henry I.	Pfc	RA 17245055	3	10	529
Charette, Robert J.	Pvt	RA 11195461	3	10	530
Castle, William B.	Sgt	RA 39211472	10	10	531
Rose, Glenn A.	Pfc	RA 11195856	3	10	532
Wade, John G.	Pfc	RA 24776926	2	10	533
Tibbits, Marvin W.	Pfc	RA 17219325	3	10	534
Harwood, Chester L.	Sgt	RA 6575336	3	10	535
Fields, Oliver M.	Sfc	RA 19315193	3	10	536
?othman, Louis P.	Cpl	RA 16280707	3	10	537
Dancik, John	Pfc	RA 33085009	3	10	538
Graham, John H.	Pfc	RA 39548022	3	10	539
Hosler, Robert E.	Pfc	RA 16311138	3	10	540
Nixon, Richard A.	Sgt	RA 19325931	4	1	541
Regnier, Robert D.	WOJG	W-903725	4	1	542
Firnges, Eugene H.	Sfc	RA 32722386	4	1	543
Miles, Claude M.	Pfc	RA 57307085	4	1	544
Rivas, John S.	Pfc	RA 19331437	4	1	545
Sullivan, Joseph W.	Cpl	RA 1007091	4	1	546
Allen, Robert F.	PFc	RA 13315185	4	1	547
Fitzpatrick, William E.	1st Lt	0-2019156	4	1	548
Cotter, Gerard F.	Cpl	RA 21908777	4	1	549
Thompson, Floyd	Pfc	RA 18347541	4	1	550
Coss, Donald C.	Pfc	RA 19243316	4	1	551
Stroud, Arthur H.	Cpl	RA 162761?4	4	1	552
Ibay, Joe W.	Pvt	RA 39107134	4	1	53
Lane, Brink E.	Pfc	RA 16311257	4	1	554
Sundquist, Larry	Pfc	RA 19361800	4	1	555
Empty			4	2	556
Empty			4	2	557
Empty			4	2	558
Empty			4	2	559
Empty			4	2	560
Empty			4	2	561
Empty			4	2	462
Empty			4	2	563
Empty			4	2	564
Empty			4	2	565
Empty			4	2	566
Empty			4	2	567
Empty			4	2	568
Empty			4	2	569
Emtpy			4	2	570
Harless, Walter R.	Cpl	RA 36439897	4	3	571
Kobage, Andrew J.	Cpl	RA 6896543	4	3	572
Graves, William E.	Capt	0-682696	4	3	573
Ellis, James H.	M/Sgt	RA 6245643	4	3	574

Thomas, Kenneth D.	Cpl	RA 13272455	4	3	575
Rix, James C.	Cpl	RA 14338085	4	3	576
Owens, Richard K.	Sgt	RA 19253111	4	3	577
Sipes, Robert J., Jr.	Pvt	RA 15381781	4	3	578
Rarick, Robert Taylor	Pvt-2	RA 16297012	4	3	579
Holliday, Delbert J.	Pvt-2	RA 17207410	4	3	580
Deason, Charles Leo	Pfc	RA 14294696	4	3	581
Monday, Jessie	?fc?	RA 17234350	4	3	582
August, Chester Robert	Pvt-2	RA 13311738	4	3	583
Unknown X-107			4	3	584
Parreau, Lionel Robert	Sgt	RA 11202199	4	3	585
Empty			4	4	586
Empty			4	4	587
Empty			4	4	588
Empty			4	4	589
Empty			4	4	590
Empty			4	4	591
Empty			4	4	592
Empty			4	4	593
Empty			4	4	594
Empty			4	4	595
Empty			4	4	596
Empty			4	4	597
Empty			4	4	598
Empty			4	4	599
Empty			4	4	600
Hulsey, Ray Dean	Cpl	RA 14342990	4	5	601
Stuart, James Franklin	Cpl	RA 38303248	4	5	602
Pennington, James H.	Pfc	RA 34886055	4	5	603
Larsen, James M.T.	Pfc	RA 17269128	4	5	604
Anderson, Stanley A.	2nd Lt	0-1686733	4	5	605
Wagner, Burton A.	Sfc	RA 16242452	4	5	606

Appendix 16

ROSTER OF ISOLATED BURIALS IN NORTH KOREA AS OF JUNE 1953

Found in: Chapter Eight, Volume 1
Source of this information: U.S. Graves Registration Service records located at CILHI.

Name	Rank	Serial Number	Map Coordination
MARSHALL, Richard L.	Unk.	19319540	1168-1524 Vicinity of Andong
THOMPSON Albert	Unk.	RA13283204	1109.9-1465.8 Kumch'on Korea Plot No. 1, Row No. 1, Grave No. 2
HOEFLER, George M.	Sgt.	RA37866756	BV 6848. 6 Kilometers South of Huichon, North Korea
SANCHEZ-MENDEZ, Juan	Pvt.	ER30416362	Hungnam, Korea
HALL, Charles H.	Pvt.	RA16253964	70.15-49.30 Plot No. 1, Row No. 1, Grave No. 1
CUNNINGHAM, James L.	Pvt.	RA1322272039	70.15-49.30 Plot No. 1, Row. No. 1 Grave No. 4
KING, Eddie	Pfc.	32294076	Kunsan, Korea 70.15-49.30 Plot No. 1, Row No. 1 Grave No. 5
ALVARADO, Richard L.	Pfc.	1107668	1:50,000-TA 4273B1 Map of Korea
CLARK, Bob E.	Pfc.	1084751	1:50,000-TA 4170V Map of Korea
CUBRANICH, Donald J.	Pfc.	579461	TA 4273B1- 1:50,000 Map of Korea
DALE, Buford, L.	S/Sgt.	248080	TA 4177V1- 1:50,000 Map of Korea
FISHER George L.	HM3	752-55-48	TA 4177V1- 1:50,000 Map of Korea
FLORES, Froelan	Pfc.	1083846	TA 4179V- 1:50,000 Map of Korea

GAUTREAU, Norman	Pfc.	661425	TA 4177V1-1:50,000 Map of Korea
GEORGE, Walter W.	Pfc.	1090672	TA 4179V-1:50,000 Map of Korea
GIESEXING, John	Pfc.	669680	TA4177V1-1:50,000 Map of Korea
GZIK, Richard S.	Pfc.	1114026	TA 4177M-1:50,000 Map of Korea
HORNING, James W., Jr.	Pfc.	1042294	TA 4179-1:50,000 Map of Korea
HUFF, Clarence H., Jr.	Cpl.	1047753	TA 4177V1-1:50,000 Map of Korea
HUNT, Frekerick S.	Pfc.	1074411	TA 4173Z-1:50,000 Map of Korea
MILLINGTON, James B.	Cpl.	1054230	TA 417F4-1:50,000 Map of Korea
PHILLIPS, Lee H.	Cpl.	654797	TA 4272E-1:50,000 Map of Korea
SIMMONS, Bryan E.	Cpl.	624513	TA 4179V-1:50,000 Map of Korea
SMICKLEY, Arthur L.	Pfc.	1082473	TA 418H1-1:50,000 Map of Korea
SOUTH, Bobby G.	Pfc.	1106236	TA 4177V1-1:50,000 Map of Korea
STATES, Douglas	Pfc.	661129	TA 4180H1-1:50,000 Map of Korea
UNKNOWN	Unk.	Unk.	TA 4177V1-1:50,000 Map of Korea
UNKNOWN	Unk.	Unk.	TA 4176F4-1:50,000 Map of Korea
UNKNOWN	Unk.	Unk.	TA 4177M-1:50,000 Map of Korea
VIRGADUNO, Anthony P.	Cpl.	1078608	TA 4177v1-1:50,000 Map of Korea
LAWRENCE, George W., Jr.	Pfc.	1099399	TA 4179V-1:50,000 Map of Korea
ROMANCHIK, Richard	Pfc.	1094323	TA 4177G5-1:50,000 Map of Korea

STROPES, **Dale L.**	T/Sgt.	338703	TA 4177V1- 1:50,000 Map of Korea
TIBBITT, Gerald K.	Sgt.	575792	TA 4177V- 1:50,000 Map of Korea
ZALEK, Anthony M., Jr.	Cpl.	658697	TA 4177V1- 1:50,000 Map of Korea
JOHNSEN, Norman D.	Pfc.	667105	TA 41720- 1:50,000 Map of Korea

Appendix 17

ISOLATED BURIALS ON NORTH KOREAN TERRITORY GROUPED BY SERVICE

Found in: Chapter Eight, Volume 1
Source of this information: U.S. Graves Registration Service records located at CILHI.

U.S. Army

I.B. No.	Reported Remains	Rec'd Glory	Un-recovered	Map Sheet	Grid Coordinate	Geographic Coordinate	Remarks
3	3	-	3	6635-III	CV 433 735	40°24'06" 127°09'15"	None
4	1	-	1	6635-III	CV 433 745	40 24 37 127 09 15	None
6	27	-	27	6635-III	CV 437 735	40 24 06 127 09 30	None
7	1	-	1	6635-III	CV 406 782	40 27 28 127 07 15	None
9	1	-	1	6635-III	CV 369 805	40 27 50 127 04 37	None
10	1	-	1	6635-III	CV 389 779	40 26 27 127 06 00	None
11	1	-	1	6635-III	CV 405 753	40 25 05 127 07 14	None
13	4	-	4	6635-III	CV 390 797	40 27 22 127 06 01	None
14	1	-	1	6635-III	CV 417 765	40 25 43 127 07 00	None
16	2	-	2	6635-III	CV 403 773	40 26 07 127 07 06	None
17	6	-	6	6635-III	CV 395 765	40 25 42 127 06 29	None
18	1	-	1	6635-III	CV 419 743	40 24 32 127 08 14	None
21	1	-	1	6635-III	CV 377 765	40 25 40 127 05 13	None
25	1	-	1	6635-III	CV 405 835	40 29 27 127 07 05	None
26	13	-	13	6635-III	CV 405 795	40 27 16 127 07 10	None
27	4	-	4	6635-III	CV 423 753	40 25 05 127 08 30	None
28	2	-	2	6635-III	CV 397 771	40 26 01 127 06 35	None
29	2	-	2	6635-III	CV 423 757	40 25 17 127 08 30	None

30	1	-	1	6635-III	CV 399 819	40 28 33	127 06 40	None
31	7	-	7	6635-III	CV 379 831	40 29 12	127 05 15	None
32	2	-	2	6635-III	CV 423 753	40 25 05	127 08 30	None
33	1	-	1	6635-III	CV 409 725	40 23 30	127 07 32	None
34	2	-	2	6635-III	CV 419 805	40 27 57	127 08 07	None
35	1	-	1	6635-III	CV 42 73	40 23 50	127 08 17	None
36	1	-	1	6635-II	CV 547 659	40 20 07	127 17 19	None
37	1	-	1	6634-I	CV 541 557	40 13 57	127 18 40	None
40	1	-	1	6635-II	CV 549 807	40 28 06	127 17 17	None
43	1	-	1	6634-I	CV 563-545	40 13 57	127 18 40	None
44	2	1	2	6634-1	CV 541 557	40 14 35	127 17 00	None
45	1	-	1	6635-III	CV 392 759	40 25 22	127 06 17	None
46	1	-	1	6635-III	CV 403 803	40 27 48	127 07 01	None
47	1	-	1	6635-III	CV 439 735	40 24 06	127 08 55	None
48	1	-	1	6635-III	CV 405 759	40 25 23	127 07 14	None
49	1	-	1	6635-III	CV 521 687	40 21 31	127 15 25	None
50	1	-	1	6635-III	CV 373 805	40 27 47	127 04 52	None
51	1	-	1	6635-III	CV 397 769	40 25 50	127 06 35	None
52	1	-	1	6635-III	CV 381 805	40 28 21	127 05 22	None
53	1	-	1	6635-III	CV 377 765	40 25 40	127 05 10	None

54	4	-	4	6634-I	CV 707 537	40 13 40 127 28 50	None
55	4	-	4	6635-III	CV 419 761	40 25 30 127 08 12	None
56	1	-	1	6634-I	CV 541 489	40 10 54 127 17 03	None
58	5	3	2	6635-III	CV 413 827	40 29 00 127 07 38	None
59	9	-	9	6635-III	CV 423 743	40 24 21 127 08 29	None
60	1	-	1	6635-III	CV 395 775	40 26 14 127 06 26	None
61	1	-	1	6635-III	CV 419 763	40 25 38 127 08 10	None
63	12	2	10	6635-III	CV 405 829	40 29 08 127 07 07	None
68	1	-	1	6634-I	CV 549 629	40 18 32 127 17 30	None
69	1	-	1	6635-III	CV 411 769	40 25 56 127 07 35	None
70	1	-	1	6635-III	CV 369 825	40 28 52 127 04 35	None
71	1	-	1	6635-III	CV 415 795	40 27 17 127 07 52	None
72	1	-	1	6635-III	CV 409 823	40 28 51 127 07 23	None
74	1	-	1	6635-III	CV 379 835	40 29 26 127 05 15	None
75	1	-	1	6635-III	CV 419 809	40 28 05 127 08 07	None
76	1	-	1	6634-II	CV 591 433	40 07 55 127 20 44	None
78	1	-	1	6635-III	CV 405 745	40 25 10 127 07 15	None
80	1	-	1	6635-III	CV 433 733	40 24 00 127 09 15	None
81	4	-	4	6635-III	CV 415 821	40 28 42 127 07 47	None
83	3	-	3	6635-III	CV 405 793	40 27 10 127 07 10	None

84	1	-	1		6635-III	CV 433 723	40 23 27 127 09 15	None
85	1	-	1		6635-III	CV 377 823	40 28 47 127 05 03	None
86	1	-	1		6634-I	CV 555 547	40 14 01 127 18 01	None
87	1	-	s		6635-III	CV 507 709	40 22 45 127 14 26	None
89	1	-	1		6635-III	CV 439 733	40 24 00 127 09 37	None
92	1	-	1		6635-III	CV 403 787	40 26 54 127 07 04	None
94	1	-	1		6635-III	CV 412 771	40 26 04 127 07 48	None
95	1	-	1		6635-III	CV 371 805	40 27 48 127 04 42	None
96	1	-	1		6635-III	CV 417 765	40 25 42 127 07 59	None
99	1	-	1		6635-III	CV 44 72	40 23 16 127 09 44	None
100	1	-	1		6634-I	CV 397 831	40 29 13 127 06 30	None
102	1	-	1		6634-I	CV 554 649	40 19 36 127 17 12	None
103	1	-	1		6634-I	CV 557 543	40 13 51 127 18 11	None
105	8	-	8		6635-III	CV 412 771	40 26 04 127 07 37	None
106	8	5	3		6635-III	CV 413 791	40 27 05 127 07 46	None
107	2	-	2		6635-III	CV 415 775	40 26 14 127 07 52	None
108	1	-	1		6635-III	CV 419 725	40 23 31 127 08 13	None
109	3	-	3		6635-III	CV 411 665	40 20 16 127 07 46	None
110	1	-	1		6635-III	CV 429 729	40 23 45 127 08 55	None
111	1	-	1		6635-III	CV 413 777	40 26 17 127 07 25	None

112	2	–	2	6635-III	CV 414 807	40 27 56 127 07 45	None
113	1	–	1	6635-III	CV 143 771	40 26 05 127 06 45	None
117	1	–	1	6430-II	BT 708 808	38 42 14 126 21 53	8 POWs app. 200 yds. North of Suan from Schoolhouse
121	2	–	2	6331-III	YD 371 303	39 05 35 125 44 28	28 POW's buried in a Korean cemetery which is located 1/2 mile due north of the village of Tongf-ri in the northern outskirts of Pyongyang. All Americans were buried on the highest hill in the cemetery. Each remains was buried with ID tags or bottle with personal data.
127	1	–	1	6428-I	BT 764 331	38 13 20 126 26 44	Buried app. 1/2 mi SW of Hanpori
129	6	–	6	6332-I	YD 46 86	39 35 32 125 51 55	Buried in vicinity of Yongwonni-ni

No.		Qty	Sheet	Grid	Latitude	Longitude	
132	-	1	6434-I	BV 676 506	40 10 42	126 16 14	
			1 mile NW of Huichon				
133	-	1	6836-III	DA 298 186	40 49 10	128 10 05	
			Buried in Pungsan NK, located on hillside 50° behind a house which is behind a schoolhouse which faces a highway. A grain elevator is across from the schoolhouse.				
135	-	1	6628-IV	CT 292 368	38 15 58	127 02 50	None
138	-	11	6430-IV	BV 607 078	38 53 22	126 14 25	
			10 miles N of Sinjang-dong.				
141	-	1	6430-II	BU 607 970	38 47 43	126 19 00	
			Near Sinjong-dong.				
143	-	1	6333-II	YE 462 116	39 49 23	125 52 37	
			Buried just off the trail.				

U.S. Air Force

I.B. No.	Reported Remains	Rec'd Glory	Un- recovered	Map Sheet	Grid Coordinate	Geographic Coordinate	Remarks
1	1	-	1	6129 I	XC 7173	38 35 34 124 56 50	
	Body washed ashore, buried by natives.						
2	1	-	1	6332 I	YD 464 763	38 30 17 125 52 01	
	Buried near crashed plane, N of Sunchon on the Sunchon-Kunchon-Kunu-ri road. Just off to the right of the road.						
4	1	-	1	6227 III	XB 7987	37 49 02 125 02 05	
	Wounded and bailed out over island. Helicopter arrived and found him dead. Remains buried on island. A donkey leader knows location of grave.						
5	1	-	1	6337 IV	CV 725 158	39 53 05 127 30 30	
	Near Tongsibil-li near Hamhung, buried on riverside.						

Branch of Service and Nationality Unknown

I.B. No.	Reported Remains	Rec'd Glory	Un-recovered	Map Sheet	Grid Coordinatinate	Geographic Coordinate	Remarks
				Unknown			
116	1	0	1	6430-II	BT 764 836	43°40'35" 126°25'46"	Buried beside the road
118	1	-	1	6430-II	BT 660 999	38°49'14" 126°18'50"	App. 150 yds. prior to reaching a 90' turn enroute to Yul-li.
119	17	-	17	6430-IV	BT 404 102	38°50'00" 126°00'30"	App. 300 yds. NW of Pisokkol.
120	1	-	1	6330-I	YD 498 187	38°59'10" 125°53'00"	App. 50 yds. E of road sign marked "12 K".
124	10	-	10	6331-I	YD 501 503	39°16'12" 125°53'58"	Buried app. 450 yds. E of the railroad on the saddle of hill 220. Between the central & southern peaks. Each remains buried with ID tags or burial bottle.
125	18	-	18	6332-II	YD 506 618	39°22'21" 125°54'35"	Buried app. 375 yds E of railroad on the crest of nearest (middle) finger of hill 95. Each remains was buried with ID tags or burial bottle, containing personal data.

No.			Map Sheet	Grid Coordinates	Latitude	Longitude	Remarks
126	5	-	5	6331-III	YD 373 242	39°02'15"	125°44'31"	Buried W. of the railroad station across the tracks in a westerly direction in the draw running N & S. The graves are marked with crosses and are in the shape of mounds. ID tags or bottles were buries with the remains.
128	4	-	4	6729-I	CT 918 708	37°35'00"	127°45'35"	4 personnel from Co L, 187 ABN Rct, buried by Unit CO.
131	45	-	45	6234-I	YE 07 62	40°17'25"	125°26'30"	45 U.N. POWs buried in a big trench near "Anpung-Ni. Died while POW.
136	5 or 8	-	5 or 8	6331-III	YD 367 238	39°02'06"	125°44'32"	5 or 8 POWs buried on a wooded hill west of the railroad station in northern part and across a small draw. Some of the graves have two bodies. All have ID tags or burial bottles.
137	4	-	4	6430-II	BT 670-0970	38°47'37"	126°19'00"	4 POWs buried in a school yard at Sinjung-Dong
139	2	-	2	6430-IV	BU 612 085	38°53'44"	126°14'45"	2 POW's buried in village.
140	1	-	1	6529-IV	BT 838 672	38°31'50"	126°31'07"	1 POW buried south of villlage of Wongye-Ri.

| 142 | 1 | - | 1 | 6430-II | BT 743 835 | 38°40'29" 126°24'17" | 1 POW died & was left for Koreans to bury. |
| 144 | Unk | - | Unk | 6634-II | CV 68 30 | 40°00'50" 127°27'14" | Unk number of Americans (Probably Marines) near Orori. |

Unrecovered Isolated Burials Source of Information: Memorial Division, QM, AFFE

I.B. No.	Reported Glory	Rec'd Glory	Unrecovered	Map Sheet	Grid Coordinates	Latitude	Longtitude	Remarks
145	8		8	6428-II	BT687129	38°02'15"	126°21'52"	
146	20		20	6331-II	YD385237	39 02 25	125 45 20	
147	6		6	6331-II	YD409335	39 07 20	125 47 10	
148	10		10	6331-I	YD505484	39 15 10	125 54 20	
149	4		4	6729-I	CT919708	38 35 00	127 45 30	
150	45		45	6235-II	YE059710	40 22 35	125 25 45	
151	2		2	6430-II	BT738985	38 48 33	126 23 45	
152	1		1	6333-II	YE472122	39 49 40	125 52 30	
153	1		1	6129-I	XC712719	38 35 30	124 58 00	
154	1		1	6332-I	YD513763	39 30 15	125 55 15	
155	1		1	6227-IV	XB786910	37 51 07	125 01 45	
156	1		1	6733-I	CV724157	39 53 08	127 30 22	
157	1		1	6635-IV	CV379848	40 30 07	127 05 15	
158	3		3	6635-III	CV444733	40 24 00	127 10 00	
159	1		1	6635-III	CV430744	40 24 30	127 09 00	
160	27		27	6635-III	CV430660	40 20 00	127 09 15	
161	1		1	6635-III	CV406777	40 26 22	127 07 15	

162	1	1		6635-III	CV434818	40 28 30	127 09 15
163	1	1		6635-III	CV335803	40 27 29	127 02 15
164	1	1		6635-IV	CV398869	40 31 15	127 06 30
165	1	1		6635-III	CV405845	40 29 56	127 07 00
166	3	3		6635-IV	CV424854	40 30 28	127 04 22
167	4	4		6635-III	CV395757	40 25 13	127 06 30
168	1	1		6635-III	CV406855	40 30 30	127 12 30
169	1	1		6635-III	CV482822	40 28 45	127 12 30
170	6	6		6635-III	CV388764	40 25 30	127 06 00
171	14	14		6635-III	CV406817	40 28 22	127 07 08
172	5	5		6635-III	CV419752	40 25 00	127 08 15
173	2	2		6635-III	CV391768	40 25 45	127 06 15
174	2	2		6635-II	CV417752	40 25 03	127 08 14
175	2	2		6635-III	CV418801	40 27 37	127 08 00
176	1	1		6634-I	CV546556	40 14 35	127 17 15
177	1	1		6634-II	CV546434	40 07 55	127 17 05
178	1	1		6635-III	CV385664	40 20 10	127 06 00
179	1	1		6635-III	CV365711	40 22 40	127 04 30
180	1	1		6635-III	CV385768	40 25 45	127 05 45
181	1	1		6635-III	CV378801	40 27 38	127 05 15

182	4			4		6635-III	CV408760	40 25 25	127 07 25
183	1			1		66634-IV	CV436589	40 16 08	127 09 35
184	9	3		6		6635-III	CV421835	40 29 25	127 08 15
185	1			1		6635-III	CV388681	40 21 05	127 06 09
186	1			1		6635-III	CV408768	40 25 45	127 07 22
187	1					6635-III	CV405803	40 27 08	127 07 45
188	1					6635-III	CV502722	40 23 00	127 14 25
189	1					6635-III	CV376834	40 29 20	127 05 00
190	1					6634-III	CV395374	40 04 30	127 07 00
191	6	4		2		6635-III	CV407822	40 28 45	127 07 30
192	3	2		1		6635-III	CV403790	40 27 00	127 07 00
193	1					6635-III	CV404790	40 26 40	127 06 45
194	1					6634-I	CV572472	40 10 00	127 19 20
195	1					6734-III	CV870305	40 01 15	127 40 30
196	1					6635-II	CV702763	40 25 35	127 28 08
197	1					6634-I	CV544562	40 19 50	127 17 15
198	2	1		1		6635-III	CV392831	40 29 10	127 06 12
199	1					6634-I	CV651547	40 14 08	127 24 48
200	8					6635-III	CV410780	40 26 25	127 07 30
201	8	7		1		6635-III	CV410700	40 27 00	127 07 25

No.	Qty	Map Sheet	Code	Latitude	Longitude
202	2	6635-III	CV406689	40 21 30	127 07 30
203	1	6635-III	CV416722	40 23 20	127 08 10
204	3	6635-III	CV408781	40 26 30	127 07 30
205	1	6635-III	CV83724	40 23 27	127 09 15
206	1	6635-III	CV409782	40 26 33	127 07 28
207	2	6635-III	CV410804	40 27 45	127 07 30
208	1	6635-III	CV409775	40 26 15	127 07 30
209	1	6528-III	BT997201	38 06 38	126 42 58.5
210	1	6429-II	BT685484	38 21 22	126 21 00
211	1	6528-I	CT142322	38 14 35.2	126 52 41.3
212	3	6528-I	CT215292	38 11 45.3	126 57 43
213	1	6528-I	CT214291	38 11 42.2	126 57 38.7
214	1	6528-I	CT211274	38 10 45.7	126 57 25 5
215	2	6528-I	CT209265	38 10 13.7	126 57 17.3
216	1	6635-I	CA712005	40 38 07.5	126 28 41.5
217	4	6527-IV	BS905906	37 50 35.5	126 37 10.1
218	1	6527-IV	BS947948	37 52 59.3	126 39 51.5
219	1	6527-IV	BS948957	37 53 22.5	126 40 00
220	1	6527-IV	BS961950	37 53 00	126 40 48.3
221	1	6527-I	CT038036	37 57 43.3	126 46 00

222	1	6527-I	CT048052	37 58 33.2	126 46 40
223	1	6527-I	CT061057	37 58 57.5	126 47 29.8
224	1	6527-I	CT038062	37 59 07.2	126 46 27.2
225	1	6527-I	CT046073	37 59 47 2	126 46 27.2
226	1	6527-I	CT087068	37 59 32.7	126 49 19.2
227	1	6527-I	CT087062	37 59 16.8	126 49 19.2
228	1	6433-IV	BV492175	39 52 25	126 04 00.5
229	1	6331-III	YD370260	39 03 15.0	125 44 35
230	2	6431-IV	BU612492	39 15 42	126 13 53
231	2	6531-IV	BU982450	39 14 05	126 39 42
232	1	6536-II	CA176187	40 48 10	126 50 20
233	1	6536-II	CA268105	40 53 00	126 57 48
234	2	6331-III	YD350289	39 04 55.3	125 43 00
235	1	6333-II	YE402095	39 48 15	125 48 18.2
236	4	6333-II	YE437044	39 45 23	125 50 38.5
237	1	6532-III	BU886724	39 28 40.5	126 32 30.3
238	8	6728-I	CT976418	38 19 26.5	127 49 43.5
239	1	6728-I	DT093408	38 18 58.9	127 57 44.3
240	1	6730-III	CT880880	38 44 16.3	127 42 38.9
241	1	6630-II	CT499914	38 45 45.2	127 16 12.5

242	2	6730-III	CT886880	38 44 16.3	127 43 08.2
243	15	6730-III	CT896880	38 44 16.3	127 43 43.5
244	1	6829-I	DT391658	38 32 30	128 18 05.5
245	1	6829-I	DT384642	38 31 42	128 17 40.5
246	2	6829-I	DT388643	38 31 44	128 17 56.7
247	1	7036-III	EA131023	40 40 30	129 09 20
248	5	6629-II	CT570574	38 27 27	127 21 40
249	2	6631-I	CU502520	39 18 00	127 15 40
250	13	6729-II	CT975468	38 22 00	127 49 35
251	2	6729-II	CT975468	38 22 00	127 49 36
252	2	6729-II	CT978468	38 22 00	127 49 52
253	20	6729-II	CT972460	38 21 32	127 49 25
254	1	6729-II	DT013450	38 21 03	127 52 18
255	1	6629-III	CT468578	38 27 30	127 14 33.5
256	1	6630-III	CT468976	38 49 07	127 134 05
257	1	6630-III	CT474956	38 47 55	127 14 32
258	1	6630-III	CT474956	38 47 50	127 14 35
259	1	6630-III	CT4769532	38 47 45	127 14 40
260	1	6630-II	CT496925	38 46 17	127 16 06.2
261	1	6630-II	CT497925	38 46 17	127 16 09.7

No.	Count		Map	Catalog	Latitude	Longitude
262	1		6630-III	CT488928	38 46 27	127 15 32.5
263	1		6630-III	CT491928	38 46 29	127 15 42.5
264	1		6630-III	CT490947	38 47 47	127 15 40.5
265	1		6630-III	CT488980	38 49 17	127 15 30.7
266	2		6834-I	DV472581	40 16 15	128 22 47.1
267	1		6836-IV	DA300216	40 50 47	128 10 10.1
268	1		6729-III	CT863561	38 27 00	127 41 52
269	1		6729-III	CT860512	38 24 20	127 41 40
270	1		6729-III	CT858511	38 24 15	127 41 32
271	4		6729-II	CT942480	38 22 35	127 47 23
272	1		6729-II	CT941477	38 22 25	127 47 20
273	26		6729-II	CT942478	38 22 30	127 47 123
274	1		6729-II	CT949475	38 22 20	127 47 52
275	43		6729-II	CT942475	38 22 25	127 47 26
276	1		6729-II	CT942474	38 22 20	127 47 26
277	2		6729-II	CT947474	38 22 09	127 47 10
278	5		6729-II	CT942472	38 22 12	127 47 22
279	1		6729-II	CT960464	38 21 45	127 48 38
280	8		6729-II	CT968469	38 22 02	127 49 10
281	1		6729-II	CT971484	38 22 50	127 49 18

282	3	6729-II	CT979479	38 22 30	127 49 48
283	11	6729-II	CT979479	38 22 31	127 49 53
284	2	6729-II	CT985477	38 22 30	127 50 10
285	4	6729-II	CT973469	38 22 03	127 49 28
286	6	6729-II	CT973468	38 22 00	127 49 28
287	12	6729-II	CT973467	38 21 55	127 49 28
288	1	6729-III	CT865512	38 24 20	127 42 03
289	1	6729-III	CT858505	38 24 00	127 41 32
290	1	6729-III	CT866507	38 24 05	127 42 05
291	1	6729-III	CT867507	38 24 03	127 42 10
292	2	6729-III	CT871499	38 23 37	127 42 24
293	1	6729-III	CT880500	38 23 42	127 43 02
294	2	6729-III	CT879499	38 23 39	127 42 57
295	1	6729-III	CT884500	38 23 48	127 43 22
296	1	6729-III	CT851517	38 24 00	127 41 35
297	2	6829-I	DT405708	38 35 25	128 19 05
298	3	6829-I	DT400708	38 35 15	128 18 40
299	1	6829-I	DT399696	38 34 36	128 18 35
300	1	6829-I	DT398691	38 34 20	128 18 35
301	1 1	6934-IV	DV665641	40 19 52	128 36 18.8

302	1		7139-II	EB658255	41 46 58	129 47 30	
303	2		7140-III	EB613554	42 03 05	129 44 23	
304	1		7138-IV	EB510044	41 35 40	129 36 42.4	
305	2		7138-IV	EA446962	41 31 16	129 32 08.4	
306	25		6331-II	YD427222	39 01 06	125 48 16	

LIST OF BURIAL SITES OF U.N. PERSONNEL INTERRED BY UNC IN NORTH KOREA

Number of Remains	Latitude	Longitude
1	38° 40' 33"	126° 25' 46"
8	38° 02' 15"	126° 21' 52"
1	38° 49' 15"	126° 18' 15"
17	38° 54' 25"	126° 00' 35"
1	38° 59' 05"	125° 53' 05"
28	39° 05' 35"	125° 44' 30"
20	39° 02' 00"	125° 45' 25"
6	39° 07' 20"	125° 47' 10"
10	39° 15' 10"	125° 54' 20"
18	39° 22' 20"	125° 54' 34"
5	39° 02' 20"	125° 44' 35"
1	38° 13' 18"	126° 26' 45"
4	38° 35' 00"	127° 45' 30"
6	39° 36' 05"	125° 51' 50"
1	39° 19' 40"	125° 37' 20"
45	40° 22' 35"	125° 25' 45"
1	40° 10' 35"	126° 16' 15"
1	40° 49' 10"	128° 10' 10"

1	39° 01' 50"	125° 42' 25"
1	38° 16' 00"	127° 02' 50"
7	39° 02' 05"	125° 44' 05"
4	38° 47' 40"	126° 18' 50"
11	38° 53' 25"	126° 14' 25"
2	38° 53' 45"	126° 14' 45"
1	38° 31' 50"	126° 31' 10"
2	38° 48' 33"	126° 23' 45"
1	38° 40' 30"	126° 24' 20"
1	39° 49' 40"	125° 52' 30"
1	40° 00' 45"	127° 27' 15"
1	38° 35' 30"	124° 58' 00"
1	39° 30' 15"	125° 55' 15"
3	38° 52' 00"	127° 59' 02"
1	37° 51' 07"	125° 01' 45"
1	39° 53' 08"	127° 30' 22"
1	40° 30' 07"	127° 05' 15"
1	40° 24' 00"	127° 09' 15"
3	40° 24' 00"	127° 10' 00"
1	40° 24' 30"	127° 09' 00"

17	40° 25' 00"	127° 07' 30"
27	40° 20' 00"	127° 09' 15"
1	40° 26' 22"	127° 07' 15"
1	40° 28' 30"	127° 09' 15"
1	40° 27' 39"	127° 02' 15"
1	40° 31' 15"	127° 06' 30"
1	40° 29' 56"	127° 07' 00"
3	40° 30' 28"	127° 04' 22"
4	40° 25' 13"	127° 06' 30"
1	40° 30' 30"	127° 07' 08"
1	40° 28' 45'	127° 12' 30"
2	40° 26' 00"	127° 06' 45"
6	40° 25' 30"	127° 06' 00"
1	40° 24' 00"	127° 08' 00"
1	40° 24' 00"	127° 09' 15"
2	40° 25' 15"	127° 06' 00"
1	40° 25' 30"	127° 05' 08"
4	40° 25' 00"	127° 07' 15"
1	40° 25' 27"	127° 04' 00"
1	40° 25' 32"	127° 04' 12"

1	40° 29' 23"	127° 07' 00"
14	40° 28' 22"	127° 17' 08"
5	40° 25' 00"	127° 08' 15"
2	40° 25' 45"	127° 06' 15"
2	40° 25' 03"	127° 08' 14"
1	40° 28' 30"	127° 06' 22"
7	40° 29' 09"	127° 05' 00"
2	40° 24' 58"	127° 07' 27"
1	40° 27' 28"	127° 07' 15"
2	40° 27' 37"	127° 08' 00"
1	40° 28' 43"	127° 08' 00"
1	40° 20' 05"	127° 17' 05"
1	40° 14' 35"	127° 17' 15"
1	40° 16' 18"	127° 17' 15"
1	40° 20' 50"	127° 16' 00"
1	40° 07' 55"	127° 17' 05"
1	40° 21' 34"	127° 16' 50"
1	40° 21' 47"	127° 16' 10"
1	40° 14' 00"	127° 18' 35"
2	40° 14' 30"	127° 17' 00"

1	40° 20' 10"	127° 06' 00"
1	40° 27' 45"	127° 06' 50"
1	40° 23' 55"	127° 09' 25"
1	40° 25' 13"	127° 07' 00"
1	40° 21' 30"	127° 14' 30"
1	40° 22' 40"	127° 04' 30"
1	40° 25' 45"	127° 05' 45"
1	40° 27' 38"	127° 05' 15"
1	40° 25' 30"	127° 05' 00"
4	40° 13' 41"	127° 28' 38"
4	40° 25' 25"	127° 07' 25"
1	40° 16' 08"	127° 09' 35"
1	40° 20' 20"	127° 17' 10"
5	40° 29' 00"	127° 07' 30"
9	40° 29' 25"	127° 08' 15"
1	40° 21' 05"	127° 06' 09"
1	40° 25' 40"	127° 07' 15"
2	40° 24' 00"	127° 09' 23"
13	40° 29' 00"	127° 06' 55"
1	40° 23' 55"	127° 08' 25"

1	40° 14' 25"	127° 17' 15"
1	40° 26' 30"	127° 15' 25"
1	40° 18' 40"	127° 16' 00"
1	40° 25' 45"	127° 07' 22"
1	40° 28' 48"	127° 04' 15"
1	40° 27' 08"	127° 07' 45"
1	40° 28' 40"	127° 07' 10"
1	40° 23' 00"	127° 14' 25"
1	40° 29' 20"	127° 05' 00"
1	40° 27' 50"	127° 08' 00"
1	40° 18' 20"	127° 17' 15"
4	40° 08' 05"	127° 20' 45"
3	40° 17' 40"	127° 17' 45"
1	40° 04' 30"	127° 07' 00"
1	40° 16' 30"	127° 17' 30"
5	40° 24' 00"	127° 09' 00"
6	40° 28' 45"	127° 07' 30"
4	40° 24' 00"	127° 12' 40"
3	40° 27' 00"	127° 07' 00"
1	40° 23' 15"	127° 08' 40"

1	40° 28' 45"	127° 04' 50"
2	40° 14' 00"	127° 18' 00"
1	40° 22' 45"	127° 14' 45"
3	40° 23' 05"	127° 16' 08"
1	40° 23' 45"	127° 09' 23"
4	40° 10' 08"	127° 19' 45"
1	40° 26' 40"	127° 06' 45"
1	40° 10' 00"	127° 19' 20"
1	40° 26' 00"	127° 07' 27"
1	40° 01' 15"	127° 40' 30"
2	40° 25' 35"	127° 28' 08"
1	40° 22' 15"	127° 15' 45"
1	40° 19' 50"	127° 17' 15"
2	40° 23' 10"	127° 09' 20"
1	40° 29' 10"	127° 06' 12"
1	40° 14' 25"	127° 16' 45"
1	40° 14' 08"	127° 24' 48"
2	40° 13' 50"	127° 18' 05"
	40° 24' 05"	127° 08' 15"
8	40° 26' 25"	127° 07' 30"

8	40° 27' 00"	127° 07' 25"
2	40° 21' 30"	127° 07' 30"
1	40° 23' 20"	127° 08' 10"
3	40° 26' 30"	127° 07' 30"
1	40° 23' 27"	127° 09' 15"
1	40° 26' 33"	127° 07' 28"
2	40° 27' 45"	127° 07' 30"
1	40° 26' 15"	127° 07' 30"
1	38° 06' 38"	126° 42' 58.5"
1	38° 21' 22"	126° 21' 00"
1	38° 14' 35.2"	126° 52' 41.3"
3	38° 11' 45.3"	126° 57' 43"
1	38° 11' 42.2"	126° 57' 38.7"
1	38° 10' 45.7"	126° 57' 25.5"
2	38° 10' 13.7"	126° 57' 17.3"
1	40° 38' 07.5"	126° 28' 41.5"
4	37° 50' 35.5"	126° 37' 10.1"
1	37° 52' 69.3"	126° 39' 51.5"
1	37° 53' 22.5"	126° 40' 51.5"
1	37° 53' 00"	126° 40' 48.3"

1	37° 57' 43.3"	126° 46' 00"
1	37° 58' 33.2"	126° 46' 40"
1	37° 58' 57.5"	126° 47' 29.8"
1	37° 59' 07.2"	126° 45' 54.7"
1	37° 59' 47.2"	126° 46' 27.2"
1	37° 59' 32.7"	126° 49' 19.2"
1	37° 59' 16.8"	126° 49' 19.2"
1	39° 52' 25"	126° 04' 00.5"
1	39° 03' 15.0"	125° 44' 35"
2	39° 15' 42"	126° 13' 53"
2	39° 14' 05"	126° 39' 42"
1	40° 48' 10"	126° 50' 20"
1	40° 43' 00"	126° 57' 48"
2	39° 04' 55.3"	125° 43' 00"
1	39° 48' 15"	125° 48' 18.2"
4	39° 45' 23"	125° 50' 38.5"
1	39° 28' 40.5"	126° 32' 30.3"
8	38° 19' 26.5"	127° 49' 43.5"
1	38° 18' 58.9"	127° 57' 44.3"
1	38° 44' 16.3"	127° 42' 38.9"

1	38° 45' 45.2"	127° 16' 12.5"
2	38° 44' 16.3"	127° 43' 08.2"
15	38° 44' 16.3"	127° 43' 43.5"
1	38° 32' 30"	128° 18' 05.5"
1	38° 31' 42"	128° 17' 40.5"
2	38° 31' 44"	128° 17' 56.7"
1	40° 40' 30"	129° 09' 20"
5	38° 27' 27"	127° 21' 40"
2	39° 18' 00"	127° 15' 40"
13	38° 22' 00"	127° 49' 35"
2	38° 22' 00"	127° 49' 36"
2	38° 22' 00"	127° 49' 52"
20	38° 21' 32"	127° 49' 25"
1	38° 21' 03"	127° 52' 18"
1	38° 27' 30"	127° 14' 33.5"
1	38° 49' 07"	127° 14' 05"
1	38° 47' 55"	127° 14' 32"
1	38° 47' 50"	127° 14' 35"
1	38° 47' 45"	127° 14' 40"
1	38° 46' 17"	127° 16' 06.2"

	Latitude	Longitude
1	38° 46' 17"	127° 16' 09.7"
1	38° 46' 27"	127° 15' 32.5"
1	38° 46' 29"	127° 15' 42.5"
1	38° 47' 47"	127° 15' 40.5"
1	38° 49' 17"	127° 15' 30.7"
2	40° 16' 15"	128° 22' 47.1"
1	40° 50' 47"	128° 10' 10.1"
1	38° 27' 00"	127° 41' 52"
1	38° 24' 20"	127° 41' 40"
1	38° 24' 15"	127° 41' 32"
4	38° 22' 35"	127° 47' 23"
1	38° 22' 25"	127° 47' 20"
26	38° 22' 30"	127° 47' 23"
1	38° 22' 20"	127° 47' 52"
43	38° 22' 25"	127° 47' 26"
1	38° 22' 20"	127° 47' 26"
2	38° 22' 09"	127° 47' 10"
5	38° 22' 12"	127° 47' 22"
1	38° 21' 45"	127° 48' 38"
8	38° 22' 02"	127° 49' 10"

1	38° 22' 50"	127° 49' 18"
3	38° 22' 30"	127° 49' 48"
11	38° 22' 31"	127° 49' 53"
2	38° 22' 30"	127° 50' 10"
4	38° 22' 03"	127° 49' 28"
6	38° 22' 00"	127° 49' 28"
12	38° 21' 55"	127° 49' 28"
1	38° 24' 20"	127° 42' 03"
1	38° 24' 00"	127° 41' 32"
1	38° 24' 05"	127° 42' 05"
1	38° 24' 03"	127° 42' 10"
2	38° 23' 37"	127° 42' 24"
1	38° 23' 42"	127° 43' 02"
2	38° 23' 39"	127° 42' 57"
1	38° 23' 38"	127° 43' 22"
1	38° 24' 00"	127° 41' 35"
2	38° 35' 15"	128° 19' 05"
3	38° 35' 15"	128° 18' 40"
1	38° 34' 36"	128° 18' 43"
1	38° 34' 20"	128° 18' 35"

1	40° 19' 52"	128° 36' 18.8"	
1	41° 46' 58"	129° 47' 30"	
2	42° 03' 05"		
1	41° 35' 40"		
2	41° 31' 16"	129° 32' 08.4'	
25 Public Cemetary in Pyongyang	39° 01' 06"	125° 48' 16"	
805 Total			

Appendix 18

ROSTER OF UNC AIR CRASHES ON NORTH KOREAN TERRITORY WITH ESTIMATE OF DECEASED CREWMEN

Found in: Chapter Eight, Volume 1
Source of this information: U.S. Graves Registration Service records located at CILHI.

1. The attached roster, was presented to the senior member of the United Nations Command Military Armistice Commission, by Headquarters Korean Communications Zone (KCOMZ).

2. The original roster gave location of crash in longitude and latitude only, which was converted to transverse mercator grid system, and added, for the convenience of this Headquarters.

3. There were three hundred seventeen (317) crash sites involving four hundred five (405) casualties, on the roster presented by KCOMZ.

4. Original records this Headquarters recorded, five (5) crash sites, involving seven (7) casualties.

5. For all general purposes these two were consolidated which resulted in three hundred twenty two (322) crash sites and four hundred twelve (412) casualties, recorded by this Headquarters.

Burial No.	Number Remains	Crash Site		Grid Coordination	MS	Plane Type
		Latitude	Longitude			
1	1	38 35 30	124 58 00	XC 712 719	6129-I	B-29
2	1	39 30 15	125 55 15	XD 513 763	6332-I	B-29
3	3	38 52 00	127 59 02	DU 119 020	6730-I	B-26
4	1	37 49 05	125 02 50	XB 7987	6229-III	F-4U
5	1	39 53 08	127 30 22	CU 724 157	6733-IV	F-80
6	3	39 22 00	125 47 00	YD 395 606	6332-II	B-26
7	3	38 44 30	128 30 00	DT 565 877	6830-II	B-26
8	3	39 23 00	125 56 00	YD 527 631	6332-II	B-26B
9	3	39 45 00	125 40 00	YE 284 029	6333-III	B-26
10	4	39 08 00	127 07 00	CU 374 328	6631-III	B-26
11	3	38 48 00	125 46 00	YC 400 978	6330-II	B-26
12	1	39 18 00	126 17 00	BU 657 531	6431-I	F-80
13	1	39 01 00	125 45 00	YD 381 217	6331-III	F-80
14	1	39 39 00	125 45 00	YC 393 811	6329-IV	F-80
15	1	39 01 00	124 45 00	No map of area	---	F-80
16	1	39 54 00	125 48 00	YE 392 199	6333-I	F-80
17	1	39 54 00	125 28 00	YE 107 192	6233-I	F-86
18	1	38 50 00	127 28 00	CT 668 989	6630-II	F-80
19	1	39 42 00	125 06 00	XD 801 961	6233-III	F-80
20	1	39 55 00	124 40 00	XE 424 194	6133-IV	F-80
21	1	40 10 00	126 17 00	BV 687 493	6434-II	F-80
22	1	38 12 00	126 35 00	BT 883 303	6528-IV	F-51
23	1	38 22 00	125 45 00	YC 402 496	6329-III	F-51
24	1	39 04 00	125 50 00	YD 451 276	6331-II	F-51
25	1	39 01 00	125 45 00	YD 381 218	6331-III	F-51
26	1	39 02 00	125 41 00	YD 322 235	6331-III	F-51
27	1	39 30 00	125 40 00	YD 293 752	6332-III	F-51
28	1	39 28 00	125 58 00	YC 588 614	6329-II	F9-F
29	1	40 36 00	127 06 00	CV 393 956	6635-IV	F404
30	1	39 28 00	124 37 00	XD 391 695	6132-III	F-80
31	1	40 36 00	127 06 00	XD 391 695	6132-III	F404
32	1	39 28 00	124 37 00	XD 391 695	6132-III	F-80
33	1	38 10 00	126 28 00	BT 782 269	6428-II	F9F3
34	1	40 22 00	127 17 00	CV 540 694	6635-II	F4U
35	1	39 20 00	127 35 00	CU 779 543	6731-IV	F-51
36	1	41 02 00	126 19 00	BA 744 455	6437-II	AD-3
37	1	39 10 00	126 04 00	BU 465 389	6431-III	F-51
38	1	38 28 00	125 43 00	YC 371 606	6329-III	F4U
39	8	39 23 00	125 45 00	YD 368 625	6332-III	B-29
40	4	39 01 00	127 15 00	CU 485 197	6631-III	B-26
41	1	39 35 00	124 45 00	XD 503 826	6132-IV	F-51
42	1	39 20 00	127 28 00	CU 671 545	6631-I	F-51
43	1	39 11 00	125 58 00	YD 563 408	6331-I	F-51
44	1	39 08 00	125 38 00	YD 275 345	6331-III	F-51
45	1	39 27 00	127 15 00	CU 494 676	6632-III	F-51
46	1	39 12 00	127 22 00	CU 590 398	6631-I	F-51
47	1	38 52 00	125 48 00	YD 428 052	6330-I	F-80
48	1	38 04 00	125 30 00	YC 193 158	6228-II	AD-4
49	1	38 39 00	126 32 00	BT 952 672	6529-IV	F-51
50	1	39 03 00	125 50 00	YD 452 258	6331-II	F-51

Burial No.	Number Remains	Crash Site		Grid Coordination	MS	Plane Type
		Latitude	Longitude			
51	1	40 06 00	124 48 00	XE 533 399	6134-II	F-80
52	1	39 58 00	128 10 00	DV 288 241	6833-IV	F4U
53	1	40 28 00	128 50 00	DV 859 792	6935-II	F4U
54	1	39 02 00	125 38 00	YD 278 234	6331-III	F-51
55	1	38 06 00	126 28 00	BT 779 195	6428-II	F4U
56	3	39 12 00	125 43 00	YD 345 421	6331-IV	B-26
57	1	38 20 00	126 48 00	CT 077 446	6528-I	F-51
58	1	38 14 00	125 45 00	YC 406 349	6328-IV	F-80
59	1	40 11 00	128 34 00	DV 631 477	6934-IV	F4U
60	1	39 25 00	125 45 00	YD 367 662	6332-III	F-80
61	1	37 55 00	126 42 00	BS 979 986	6527-IV	F-51
62	1	39 47 00	124 35 00	XE 355 044	6133-III	F-80
63	6	39 57 00	125 00 00	XE 708 236	6133-I	B-29
64	1	39 00 00	125 45 00	YD 382 199	6330-IV	F-51
65	1	40 18 00	125 08 00	XE 811 628	6234-IV	F-51
66	1	38 29 00	126 50 00	CT 111 613	6529-II	F-80
67	1	39 07 00	125 42 00	YD 335 328	6331-III	B-26
68	1	40 10 00	125 51 00	YE 428 497	6334-II	F-51
69	1	39 29 00	126 05 00	BU 492 740	6432-III	F-80
70	1	38 25 00	126 07 00	BT 484 555	6429-III	F-84
71	1	39 15 00	127 45 00	CU 922 448	6731-IV	F-80
72	1	38 57 00	125 48 00	YD 425 145	6330-I	F-51
73	1	39 19 00	125 30 00	YD 155 545	6231-I	F-80
74	1	38 23 00	126 02 00	BT 409 519	6429-III	F-51
75	1	39 11 00	127 17 00	CU 516 381	6631-I	Mark 11
76	1	38 04 00	126 33 00	BT 851 157	6528-III	F-51
77	1	38 06 00	127 23 00	DT 452 167	6828-II	F4U
78	1	38 33 00	126 47 00	CT 068 688	6529-I	F-84
79	1	38 35 00	126 13 00	BT 577 738	6429-IV	F-51
80	1	38 13 00	126 52 00	CT 133 317	6528-I	F-51
81	3	39 26 00	126 17 00	BU 661 679	6432-II	B-26
82	1	38 27 00	125 47 00	YC 427 590	6329-II	F-4U
83	1	39 13 00	125 37 00	YD 259 436	6331-IV	F-80
84	10	39 05 00	125 05 00	XD 802 277	6231-III	B-29
85	1	40 26 00	129 00 00	EV 001 754	6935-II	F4U
86	1	38 53 00	128 03 00	DU 175 039	6830-IV	F4U
87	1	38 23 00	126 27 00	BT 773 510	6429-II	F-80
88	1	38 28 00	126 32 00	BT 847 601	6529-III	F-51
89	1	39 28 00	126 32 00	BU 876 711	6532-III	F-51
90	9	39 54 00	124 33 00	XE 323 174	6133-IV	B-29
91	1	38 18 00	126 29 00	BT 800 416	6428-I	F-51
92	1	39 12 00	125 40 00	YD 302 419	6331-IV	F-80
93	1	39 57 00	127 27 00	CV 678 229	6633-I	F4U
94	1	39 13 00	126 34 00	BU 899 433	6531-IV	AD2
95	2	38 25 00	126 14 00	BT 584 552	6429-III	B-26
96	1	39 00 00	125 45 00	YD 381 199	6330-IV	F-80
97	1	38 17 00	126 36 00	BT 902 394	6528-IV	F-84
98	1	38 08 00	126 27 00	BT 766 233	6428-II	F-80
99	1	39 11 00	125 38 00	YD 275 399	6331-IV	F-80
100	1	39 25 00	126 35 00	BU 919 654	6532-III	F-80

Burial No.	Number Remains	Crash Site		Grid Coordi- nation	MS	Plane Type
		Latitude	Longitude			
101	1	39 50 00	126 05 00	BV 504 129	6433-III	F-80
102	10	38 51 00	125 20 00	YD 025 023	6230-I	B-29
103	2	38 26 00	126 08 00	BT 499 573	6429-III	F7F
104	1	38 53 00	126 04 00	BU 455 076	6430-IV	F-51
105	1	40 33 00	127 08 00	CV 418 901	6635-IV	Unk
106	1	38 31 00	125 30 00	YC 180 657	6229-I	F4U
107	1	39 25 00	124 40 00	XD 434 639	6132-III	F-51
108	1	38 20 00	126 47 00	CT 063 446	6528-I	F-80
109	1	38 20 00	126 21 00	BT 684 457	6428-I	F-51
110	1	38 53 00	128 04 00	DU 190 038	6830-IV	F-51
111	1	38 06 00	126 24 00	BT 720 196	6428-II	F-51
112	9	39 11 00	125 25 00	YD 087 395	6231-I	B-29
113	1	38 45 00	127 44 00	CT 899 894	6730-III	F-80
114	1	38 40 00	127 46 00	CT 931 801	6729-I	F4U
115	1	38 25 00	127 45 00	CT 909 524	6729-III	F4U
116	1	38 25 00	126 15 00	BT 599 552	6429-III	F-84
117	1	38 17 00	125 44 00	YC 391 403	6328-IV	F-51
118	1	38 19 00	126 39 00	BT 945 432	6528-IV	F-51
119	1	39 24 00	126 04 00	BU 474 649	6432-III	F-80
120	1	38 27 00	127 07 00	CT 356 571	6629-III	F4U
121	1	39 26 00	126 21 00	BU 720 678	6432-II	F-80
122	Not Used	---	---	---	---	---
123	1	38 28 00	127 35 00	CT 764 582	6729-III	AD-4
124	1	38 17 00	126 51 00	CT 120 389	6528-I	F-51
125	1	39 26 00	125 57 00	YD 540 685	6332-II	F-80
126	1	39 07 00	127 40 00	CU 847 301	6731-III	B-26
127	1	38 53 00	125 37 00	YD 270 068	6330-IV	F4U
128	1	38 18 00	126 35 00	BT 887 415	6528-IV	F-51
129	1	40 42 00	129 12 00	EA 170 049	7036-III	F4U
130	1	38 52 00	126 43 00	CU 017 039	6530-IV	F4U
131	1	38 44 00	125 47 00	YC 417 905	6330-II	F-51
132	1	39 08 00	126 55 00	CU 200 333	6531-II	AD-2
133	1	39 15 00	125 40 00	YD 301 475	6331-IV	F-80
134	3	39 14 00	126 47 00	CU 086 446	6531-I	B-26
135	1	38 50 00	127 25 00	CT 626 991	6630-II	F4U
136	1	38 04 00	126 50 00	CT 099 151	6528-II	F-51
137	1	38 51 00	126 35 00	BU 903 025	6530-IV	F-51D
138	1	38 34 00	127 05 00	CT 331 701	6629-IV	F-51
139	1	39 39 00	124 54 00	XD 632 809	6132-I	F-51
140	1	38 57 00	125 38 00	YD 282 141	6330-IV	F-80
141	1	39 36 00	125 34 00	YD 203 861	6332-IV	F-84
142	1	39 27 00	127 37 00	CU 811 672	6732-III	AD-4
143	1	38 17 00	125 37 00	YC 274 401	6328-IV	F-80
144	1	39 34 00	125 52 00	YD 462 832	6332-I	F-80
145	3	39 35 00	125 53 00	YD 476 851	6332-I	B-26
146	1	39 35 00	125 57 00	YD 533 852	6332-I	F9F
147	1	38 24 00	127 33 00	CT 734 507	6729-III	F-51D
148	1	39 13 00	126 54 00	CU 187 425	6531-I	F2H
149	1	39 41 00	125 13 00	XD 901 945	6233-III	F-80
150	1	39 19 00	126 19 00	BU 687 549	6431-I	F4U4

Burial No.	Number Remains	Crash Site		Grid Coordi- nation	MS	Plane Type
		Latitude	Longitude			
151	1	38 13 00	126 18 00	BT 636 329	6428-I	F-80
152	1	39 00 00	126 05 00	BU 474 204	6430-IV	F-51
153	1	39 38 00	127 24 00	CU 627 879	6632-I	AD-4L
154	1	38 09 00	126 55 00	CT 175 241	6528-II	F-80C
155	1	38 03 00	126 23 00	BT 703 143	6428-II	Sea Fury
156	1	39 37 00	125 30 00	YD 145 878	6232-I	F-84
157	1	38 28 00	126 54 00	CT 168 592	6529-II	F-51
158	1	38 47 00	125 15 00	XC 954 947	6230-III	F-84
159	1	39 08 00	126 03 00	BU 449 353	6431-III	F-80
160	2	39 06 00	127 34 00	CU 760 284	6731-III	F7F
161	1	39 37 00	125 34 00	YD 203 880	6332-IV	F-80
162	1	39 40 00	125 55 00	YD 501 944	6332-I	F-80
163	1	38 17 00	128 04 00	DT 183 372	6828-IV	TNDY
164	1	39 07 00	125 44 00	YD 363 328	6331-III	F-80
165	1	39 06 00	126 30 00	BU 838 305	6431-II	F-80
166	1	38 13 00	126 27 00	BT 768 326	6428-I	F-4U
167	1	39 18 00	125 33 00	YD 198 528	6331-IV	F-51
168	1	38 36 00	125 42 00	YC 352 754	6329-IV	F-51
169	1	38 21 00	127 33 00	CT 733 452	6729-III	F4U
170	1	38 40 00	125 07 00	XC 842 815	6229-IV	F4U
171	1	38 27 00	125 52 00	YC 502 593	6329-II	F4U
172	1	38 40 00	125 44 00	YC 378 829	6329-IV	F-84
173	1	38 49 00	126 43 00	CT 016 984	6330-III	F-51
174	1	39 07 00	127 07 00	CU 372 310	6631-III	F9F
175	1	39 07 00	126 30 00	BU 839 323	6431-II	AD-4
176	1	38 57 00	127 54 00	DU 047 114	6730-I	F4U
177	1	38 55 00	126 27 00	BU 789 102	6430-I	F-80
178	1	39 02 00	125 48 00	YD 424 328	6331-II	F4U
179	1	39 13 00	127 18 00	CU 532 417	6631-I	F4U
180	1	38 21 00	126 53 00	CT 151 463	6329-II	F4U
181	1	38 47 00	127 47 00	CT 942 931	6730-II	F4U
182	1	38 38 00	125 13 00	XC 929 779	6229-IV	F-80
183	1	38 51 00	125 45 00	YD 388 033	6330-IV	F-80
184	1	37 39 00	125 46 00	---	No map	F-80
185	1	38 33 00	126 53 00	YC 514 704	6329-I	F-51
186	3	38 27 00	126 52 00	CT 139 574	6329-II	B-26
187	1	39 22 00	126 44 00	CU 047 595	6332-III	F-84
188	1	38 27 00	125 55 00	YC 545 594	6329-II	F-80C
189	1	38 29 00	125 44 00	YC 384 626	6329-III	F-84
190	3	37 55 00	126 00 00	YC 637 004	6327-I	B-26
191	1	39 31 00	127 09 00	CU 390 753	6632-IV	AD-4D
192	1	38 40 00	127 42 00	CT 869 802	6729-IV	F-9F
193	1	39 30 00	126 32 00	BU 878 747	6332-III	F-9F
194	1	38 23 00	128 10 00	DT 272 483	6829-III	Helicopter
195	1	38 37 00	125 38 00	YC 293 771	6329-IV	Meteor MK
196	1	38 37 00	125 53 00	YC 511 799	6329-I	Meteor MK
197	1	38 29 00	125 43 00	YC 431 624	6329-II	F4U
198	1	38 10 00	126 55 00	CT 175 259	6528-II	F-51
199	1	39 21 00	126 02 00	BU 444 594	6432-III	F-80
200	1	39 32 00	125 52 00	YD 463 794	6332-I	F-80

Burial No.	Number Remains	Crash Site		Grid Coordi- nation	MS	Plane Type
		Latitude	Longitude			
201	1	39 33 00	127 14 00	CU 482 796	6632-IV	F4U
202	1	38 20 00	127 59 00	DT 111 429	6728-I	F-51
203	1	39 07 00	125 40 00	YD 305 326	6331-III	F-84
204	1	39 43 00	125 05 00	XD 785 981	6233-III	F-80
205	1	39 56 00	126 03 00	BV 479 241	6433-IV	F-80
206	1	38 27 00	126 48 00	CT 080 575	6529-II	F-51
207	1	38 26 00	127 43 00	CT 881 542	6729-III	F-51
208	1	39 27 00	127 12 00	CU 452 679	6632-III	F-9F
209	1	39 01 00	127 27 00	CU 639 194	6631-II	AD-3
210	1	38 17 00	126 40 00	BT 959 394	6528-IV	F4U
211	1	38 32 00	126 58 00	CT 228 665	6529-I	F-94
212	1	40 07 00	126 19 00	BV 714 438	6434-II	F-80
213	1	38 27 00	126 41 00	BT 979 579	6529-III	F-51
214	1	38 22 00	128 03 00	DT 169 465	6829-III	AD-2
215	1	39 53 00	125 08 00	XE 824 166	6233-IV	F-86
216	1	39 24 00	126 48 00	CU 105 630	6532-II	AD-4
217	1	39 49 00	125 53 00	YE 468 109	6333-II	F-84
218	1	39 36 00	125 21 00	YD 018 856	6232-I	F-84
219	1	39 06 00	125 54 00	YD 507 316	6331-II	F-84
220	1	39 16 00	126 34 00	BU 901 488	6531-IV	F-9F
221	1	39 19 00	127 17 00	CU 518 529	6631-I	F9F
222	1	40 04 00	126 09 00	BV 569 386	6434-III	F-84
223	1	38 03 00	125 18 00	YC 017 135	6228-II	F4U
224	1	38 24 00	126 38 00	BT 934 524	6529-III	Mark 8
225	1	39 14 00	125 52 00	YD 462 461	6331-I	F4U
226	1	38 41 00	126 32 00	BT 854 841	6530-III	F4U
227	1	39 38 00	125 17 00	XD 958 892	6232-I	F-51
228	1	39 20 00	127 15 00	CU 492 548	6631-IV	AD-4
229	1	38 23 00	127 23 00	CT 589 491	6629-II	F-51
230	1	39 23 00	125 38 00	YD 267 623	6332-III	F-51
231	1	39 23 00	125 38 00	YD 267 623	6332-III	F-84
232	1	40 30 00	126 58 00	CV 277 847	6535-II	F9F
233	1	38 48 00	126 25 00	BT 757 974	6430-II	F-84
234	1	38 47 00	126 14 00	BT 596 959	6430-III	F-80
235	1	38 44 00	125 23 00	YC 071 895	6230-II	Meteor MK 8
236	1	39 58 00	126 07 00	BV 537 276	6433-IV	F-80
237	1	39 20 00	127 20 00	CU 564 547	6631-I	F4U
238	1	39 48 00	124 49 00	XE 554 067	6133-II	F-84
239	1	38 23 00	127 46 00	CT 922 486	6729-II	F9F
240	1	39 45 00	124 49 00	XE 555 011	6133-II	F-84
241	1	38 22 00	127 59 00	DT 112 466	6729-II	F9F
242	1	38 25 00	128 05 00	DT 199 521	6829-III	F-51
243	1	38 27 00	125 53 00	YC 516 593	6329-II	Meteor MK 8
244	1	38 22 00	127 29 00	CT 676 472	6629-II	T-6
245	1	38 17 00	127 04 00	CT 309 386	6628-IV	F-80
246	1	39 18 00	126 39 00	BT 944 413	6528-IV	AD-4
247	1	38 54 00	125 47 00	YD 413 089	6330-I	F-51
248	1	39 19 00	127 19 00	CU 548 528	6631-I	AD-4
249	1	39 50 00	127 29 00	CV 702 099	6633-II	F4U
250	1	38 57 00	125 57 00	YD 559 149	6330-I	F4U

Burial No.	Number Remains	Crash Site		Grid Coordi- nation	MS	Plane Type
		Latitude	Longitude			
251	1	38 08 00	126 56 00	CT 189 222	6528-II	F-84
252	1	38 40 00	125 54 00	YC 523 835	6329-I	Meteor MK 8
253	2	38 25 00	126 09 00	BT 513 534	6429-III	F7F
254	1	38 33 00	125 02 00	XC 769 684	6229-IV	F4U
255	1	38 34 00	127 45 00	CT 911 690	6729-IV	F-51
256	1	38 56 00	127 42 00	CU 873 099	6730-IV	F4U
257	1	38 45 00	127 49 00	CT 971 893	6730-II	F9F
258	2	39 00 00	125 47 00	YD 409 200	6330-I	AD
259	1	38 34 00	125 07 00	XC 844 704	6229-IV	F-86
260	1	38 14 00	126 57 00	CT 206 334	6528-I	F-80
261	1	38 07 00	126 52 00	CT 103 205	6528-II	F-51
262	2	37 56 00	125 26 00	YC 138 008	6227-I	F7F
263	1	38 57 00	127 24 00	CU 614 120	6630-I	F-84
264	1	39 00 00	127 27 00	CU 639 175	6630-I	F-51
265	1	38 55 00	127 09 00	CU 396 087	6630-IV	Meteor MK 8
266	1	39 04 00	127 29 00	CU 688 249	6631-II	AU-1
267	1	38 51 00	125 30 00	YD 169 027	6230-I	Sea Fury
268	1	38 03 00	126 13 00	BT 558 146	6428-III	F-80
269	1	39 52 00	127 50 00	DV 002 132	6733-I	AD-4
270	1	40 28 00	129 00 00	---	No map	F4U
271	1	39 25 00	125 37 00	YD 254 659	6332-III	F-80
272	1	38 25 00	126 56 00	CT 196 536	6539-II	RF-51D
273	1	39 25 00	126 57 00	CU 236 646	6532-II	F-84
274	1	40 10 00	128 05 00	DV 219 463	6834-III	F4U
275	2	39 08 00	126 47 00	CU 083 336	6331-II	Cessna
276	1	39 00 00	125 45 00	YD 382 199	6330-IV	F-84
277	1	39 04 00	125 42 00	YD 338 236	6331-III	F-84
278	1	39 07 00	125 48 00	YD 422 331	6331-II	AD-2
279	1	38 34 00	125 49 00	YC 454 721	6329-I	F-80
280	1	40 00 00	125 14 00	XE 906 297	6233-IV	F-84
281	1	38 21 00	125 51 00	YC 490 481	6329-II	Meteor MK 8
282	2	38 00 00	126 42 00	BT 981 078	6527-IV	Cessna
283	1	38 27 00	127 10 00	CT 401 569	6629-III	F-84
284	1	40 20 00	127 33 00	CV 766 653	6734-IV	F-80
285	1	38 19 00	127 04 00	CT 309 424	6628-IV	F4U0
286	4	38 34 00	126 49 00	CT 097 705	6529-I	B-26
287	1	38 31 00	125 48 00	YC 442 664	6329-I	F-84
288	1	38 33 00	127 47 00	CT 939 672	6729-I	AD-2
289	2	38 20 00	126 50 00	CT 106 446	6528-I	L-19
290	1	38 17 00	127 08 00	CT 367 336	6628-IV	AD-3
291	1	38 28 00	127 27 00	CT 648 543	6629-II	F4U
292	1	38 33 00	128 13 00	DT 318 667	6829-IV	F-84
293	1	38 47 00	127 57 00	CT 941 931	6730-II	AD-2
294	1	37 46 00	125 37 00	YB 305 827	6327-III	AU-1
295	1	38 47 00	125 47 00	YC 416 959	6330-II	AU-1
296	1	39 26 00	127 10 00	CU 422 660	6632-III	F-51
297	1	38 42 00	125 07 00	XC 841 853	6230-III	F4U
298	1	38 24 00	127 27 00	CT 646 509	6629-II	F-80
299	1	38 23 00	127 27 00	CT 646 491	6629-II	F-80

Burial No.	Number Remains	Crash Site		Grid Coordination	MS	Plane Type
		Latitude	Longitude			
300	1	38 31 00	126 53 00	CT 154 648	6529-I	Meteor MK 8
301	1	39 26 00	125 14 00	XD 921 668	6232-III	F-84
302	1	40 13 00	124 33 00	XE 317 525	6134-IV	F-86
303	1	38 45 00	126 30 00	BT 828 916	6430-II	F-80
304	1	39 18 00	125 54 00	YD 500 536	6331-I	F-80
305	1	40 10 00	126 17 00	BV 686 493	6434-II	F-84
306	1	39 40 01	126 50 10	CU 144 926	6532-II	F-84
307	1	38 43 00	127 37 00	CT 798 859	6730-III	AU-1
308	1	38 26 00	125 53 00	YC 516 574	6329-II	Sea Fury
309	1	38 09 00	124 53 00	XE 649 237	6128-II	Sea Fury
310	1	40 04 00	128 00 00	DV 147 353	6734-II	F9F
311	1	39 02 00	126 09 00	BU 532 329	6431-III	F-84
312	1	38 27 00	127 52 00	DT 009 559	6729-II	F-84
313	1	38 23 00	127 47 00	CT 937 486	6729-II	AU-1
314	1	38 57 00	127 24 00	CT 613 121	6630-I	F-86
315	1	39 25 00	126 35 00	BU 920 653	6532-III	F-84
316	1	38 47 00	127 23 00	CT 596 936	6630-II	F-84
317	1	38 35 00	127 50 00	CT 984 707	6729-I	F-84
318	1	38 45 00	126 14 00	BT 596 923	6430-III	F-80
319	1	39 30 00	125 59 00	YD 563 761	6332-II	F-84
320	1	38 29 00	125 03 00	XC 786 610	6229-III	F4U
321	1	40 27 00	127 10 00	CV 445 788	6635-III	F9F
322	1	39 48 00	125 36 00	YE 226 084	6333-III	F-80
323	1	40 13 00	128 22 00	DV 462 516	6834-I	F4U

Appendix 19

ROSTER OF BURIALS ON NORTH KOREAN TERRITORY SUBMITTED TO THE COMMUNIST SIDE BY UNCMAC

Found in: Chapter Eight, Volume 1
Source of this information: U.S. Graves Registration Service records located at CILHI.

No. of Remains	Latitude	Longitude	Grid Coordinate	MS	Burial No.	Burial No.	Latitude	Longitude	Grid Coordinate	MS	Remains Recovered within 1000 Meters	Table Note No.	Variation
1	38 40 33	126 25 46	BT 764835	6430-II	306	116	43 40 35	126 25 46	BT 764836	6430-II	0	1	
8	38 02 15	126 21 52	BT 687129	6428-II	145	117	38 42 14	126 21 53	BT 708868	6430-II	0	2	74KM
1	38 49 15	126 18 15	BT 660998	6430-II	307	118	38 49 14	126 18 50	BT 660999	6430-II	0	3	100M
17	38 54 25	126 00 35	BU 407103	6430-IV	308	119	38 50 00	126 00 30	BT 404102	6430-IV	0	4	350M
1	38 59 05	125 53 05	YD 501187	6330-I	309	120	38 59 10	125 53 00	YD 498187	6330-I	0	5	300M
28	39 05 35	125 44 30	YD 373361	6331-III	310	121	39 05 35	125 44 28	YD 371303	6331-III	0	6	580M
20	39 02 00	125 45 25	YD 385237	6331-II	146	122	39 01 58	125 45 18	YD 386236	6331-II	1	7	150M
6	39 07 20	125 47 10	YD 409335	6331-II	147	123	39 07 15	125 47 27	YD 409335	6331-II	0	8	
10	39 15 10	125 54 20	YD 505484	6331-I	148	124	39 16 12	125 53 58	YD 501503	6331-I	0	9	1KM 925M
18	39 22 20	125 54 45	YD 509618	6332-II	311	125	39 22 21	125 54 35	YD 506618	6332-II	0	10	300M
5	39 02 20	125 44 35	YD 376241	6331-III	312	126	39 02 15	125 44 31	YD 373242	6331-III	0	11	310M
1	38 13 18	126 26 45	BT 76633	6428-I	313	127	38 13 20	126 26 44	BT 764331	6428-I	1	12	290M
4	38 35 00	127 45 30	CT 919708	6729-I	149	128	37 35 00	127 45 35	CT 918708	6729-I	0	13	100M
6	39 36 05	125 51 50	YD 460871	6332-I	314	129	39 35 32	125 51 55	YD 4686	6332-I	0	14	1KM 100M
1	39 19 40	125 37 20	YD 260559	6331-IV	315	130	39 19 40	125 37 18	YD 261559	6331-IV	1	15	100M
45	40 22 35	125 25 45	YD 059710	6235-II	150	131	40 17 25	125 26 30	YE 0762	6234-I	0	16	14KM 250M
1	40 10 35	126 16 15	BV 675506	6434-I	316	132	40-10-42	126 16 14	BV 676506	6434-I	1	17	100M
1	40 49 10	128 10 10	DA 302185	6836-III	317	133	40 49-10	128 10 05	DA 298186	6836-III	0	18	415M

1	39 01 50	125 42 25	YD 342232	6331-III	318	134	39 01 55	125 42 17	YD 342234	6331-III	1	19	200M	
1	38 01 50	127 02 50	CT 292368	6628-IV	319	135	38 15 58	127 02 50	CT 292368	6628-IV	0	20		
7	39 02 05	125 44 05	YD 367238	6331-III	320	136	39 02 06	125 44 32	YD 367278	6331-III	0	21		4KM
4	38 47 40	126 18 50	BT 668070	6430-II	321	137	38 47 37	126 19 00	BT 670970	6430-II	0	22	200M	
11	38 53 25	126 14 25	BU 607077	6430-IV	322	138	38 53 22	126 14 25	BV 607078	6430-IV	0	23	100M	
2	38 53 45	126 14 45	BU 613085	6430-IV	323	139	38 53 44	126 14 45	BU 612085	6430-IV	0	24	100M	
1	38 31 50	126 31 10	BT 837672	6529-IV	324	140	38 31 50	126 31 07	BT 838672	6529-IV	1	25	100M	
2	38 48 33	126 23 45	BT 738985	6430-II	151	141	38 47 43	126 19 00	BT 6795	6430-II	0	26	570M	7KM
1	38 40 30	126 24 20	BT 742835	6430-II	325	142	38 40 29	126 24 17	BT 743835	6430-II	0	27	100M	
1	39 49 40	125 52 30	VE 472122	6333-II	152	143	39 49 23	125 52 37	YE 462116	6333-II	0	28	200M	1KM
1	40 00 45	127 27 15	CU 682298	6634-II	326	144	40 00 50	127 27 14	CV 6830	6634-II	0	29	300M	
1	38 35 30	124 58 00	XC 712719	6129-I	153	AF1	38 35 34	124 56 50	XC 7173	6129-I	0		110M	1KM
1	39 30 15	125 55 15	XD 513763	6332-I	154	AF2	38 30 17	125 52 01	YD 464763	6332-I	0		900M	4KM
3	38 52 00	127 59 02	DU 119020	6730-I	327	AF3	38 50 55	127 59 17	DU 122002	6730-I	0		810M	1KM
1	39 53 08	127 30 22	CV 724157	6733-IV	156	AF5	39 53 05	127 30 30	CV 725158	6733-IV	0		140M	
1	40 30 07	127 05 15	CV 379848	6635-IV	157	1	40 27 50	127 04 55	CV 373805	6635-III	0		400M	4KM
1	40 24 00	127 09 15	CV 433735	6635-III	328	2	40 24 00	127 09 30	CV 437735	6635-III	11*		400M	
	Illegible													
1	40 24 30	127 09 00	CV 430744	6635-III	159	4	40 24 37	127 09 15	CV 433745	6635-III	0		300M	
17	40 25 00	127 07 30	CV 409753	6635-III	329	5	40 25 05	127 07 44	CV 413755	6635-III	34*		575M	

No.	Lat	Long	CV	Map	ID	No.	Lat	Long	CV	Map	Val	Dist
27	40 20 00	127 09 15	CV 430660	6635-III	160	6	40 24 06	127 09 30	CV 437735	6635-III	11	7KM 575M
1	40 26 22	127 07 15	CV 406777	6635-II	161	7	40 27 28	127 07 15	CV 406782	6635-III	9	500M
1	40 28 30	127 09 15	CV 434818	6635-III	162	8	40 23 30	127 09 25	CV 437725	6635-III	4	9KM 380M
1	40 27 39	127 22 15	CV 335803	6635-III	163	9	40 27 50	127 04 37	CV 369205	6635-III	0	420M
1	40 31 15	127 06 30	CV 398869	6635-IV	164	10	40 26 27	127 06 00	CV 389779	6635-III	0	9KM 75M
1	40 29 56	127 07 00	CV 405845	6635-II	165	11	40 25 05	127 07 14	CV 405733	6635-III	34M	9KM 200M
3	40 30 28	127 40 22	CV 424854	6635-IV	166	12	40 25 42	127 04 30	CV 367765	6635-III	3	???
4	40 25 13	127 06 30	CV 395757	6635-III	167	13	40 27 22	127 06 01	CV 390797	6635-III	0	4KM 35M
1	40 30 30	127 07 08	CV 406855	6635-IV	168	14	40 25 43	127 07 00	CV 417765	6635-III	0	14M 250M
1	40 ????	127 12 30	CV 482822	6635-III	169	15	40 23 55	127 12 55	CV 481731	6635-III	14	????
2	40 26 00	127 06 45	CV 399772	6635-III	330	16	40 25 07	127 07 06	CV 403773	6635-III	7	????
6	40 25 30	127 06 00	CV 388764	6635-III	170	17	40 25 42	127 06 29	CV 395765	6635-III	3	715M
1	40 24 00	127 08 00	CV 416734	6635-III	331	18	40 24 32	127 08 14	CV 419743	6635-III	5	910M
1	40 24 00	127 09 15	CV 433732	6635-III	332	19	40 25 40	127 05 13	CV 377765	6635-III	0	????
2	40 25 15	127 06 00	CV 388758	6635-III	333	20	40 25 23	127 25 25	CV 3976	6635-III	6	275M1
1	40 25 30	127 05 08	CV 376763	6635-III	334	21	20 25 40	127 05 13	CV 377765	6635-III	0	210M
4	40 25 00	127 07 15	CV 406754	6635-III	335	22	40 25 25	127 07 15	CV 406754	6635-III	34	
1	40 25 27	127 04 00	CV 360762	6635-III	336	23	40 25 28	127 04 17	CV ????	6635-III	3	415M
1	40 25 32	127 04 12	CV 362765	6635-III	337	24	40 25 45	127 04 30	CV 36767	6635-III	3	550M
1	40 29 23	127 07 00	CV 405837	6635-III	338	25	40 29 27	127 07 05	CV 405835	6635-III	2	200M

4	40 28 22	127 07 08	CV 406817	6635-III	171	26	40 27 16	127 07 10	CV 405795	6635-III	2		???	230M
5	40 25 00	127 08 15	CV 419752	6635-III	172	27	40 25 05	127 08 30	CV 423753	6635-III	0		2KM	230M
2	40 25 45	127 06 15	CV 391768	6635-III	173	28	40 26 01	127 06 35	CV 397771	6635-III	3			650M
2	40 25 03	127 08 14	CV 417752	6635-III	174	29	40 25 17	127 08 30	CV 423757	6635-III	0			800M
1	40 28 30	127 06 22	CV 384818	6635-III	339	30	40 28 33	127 06 40	CV 399819	6635-III	0		1KM	500M
7	40 29 09	127 05 00	CV 376832	6635-III	340	31	40 29 12	127 05 15	CV 379831	6635-III	0			310
2	40 24 58	127 07 27	CV 408751	6635-III	341	32	40 25 05	127 08 30	CV 423753	6635-III	0		1KM	520M
1	40 27 28	127 07 15	CV 406782	6635-III	342	33	40 23 30	127 07 32	CV 409725	6635-III	0		5KM	680M
2	40 27 37	127 08 00	CV 418801	6635-III	175	34	40 27 57	127 08 07	CV 419805	6635-III	1			410M
1	40 28 43	127 08 00	CV 419823	6635-III	343	35	40 23 50	127 08 17	CV 4273	6635-III	1		9KM	310M
1	40 20 05	127 17 05	CV 547659	6635-II	344	36	40 20 07	127 17 19	CV 547659	6635-II	1			
1	40 14 35	127 17 15	CV 546556	6634-I	176	37	40 13 57	127 18 40	CV 541557	6634-I	0			510M
1	40 16 18	127 17 15	CV 546589	6634-I	345	38	40 16 20	127 17 20	CV 549589	6634-I	0			300M
1	40 20 50	127 16 00	CV 532674	6635-II	346	39	40 20 45	127 15 45	CV 531671	6635-II	1			310M
1	40 07 55	127 17 05	CV 546434	6634-II	177	40	40 28 06	127 17 17	CV 549807	6635-II	0		37KM	415M
1	40 21 34	127 16 50	CV 543688	6635-II	347	41	40 21 35	127 16 35	CV 541687	6635-II	1			210M
1	40 21 47	127 16 10	CV 534693	6635-II	348	42	40 21 45	127 16 08	CV 534691	6635-II	1			200M
1	40 14 00	127 18 35	CV 562546	6634-I	349	43	40 13 57	127 18 40	CV 563545	6634-I	1			140M
2	40 14 30	127 17 00	CV 543687	6635-II	350	44	40 14 35	127 17 00	CV 541557	6634-I	0		13KM	230M
1	40 20 10	127 06 00	CV 385664	6635-III	178	45	40 25 22	127 06 17	CV 392759	6635-III	6			640M

1	40 27 45	127 06 50	CV 402804	6635-III	351	46	40 27 48	127 07 01	CV 403803	6635-III	0		140M
1	40 23 55	127 09 25	CV 436732	6635-III	352	47	40 24 06	127 08 55	CV 439735	6635-III	11*		420M
1	40 25 13	127 07 00	CV 403757	6635-III	353	48	40 25 23	127 07 14	CV 405759	6635-III	10		280M
1	40 21 30	127 14 30	CV 508687	6635-III	354	49	40 21 31	127 15 25	CV 521687	6635-II	0	1KM	300M
1	40 22 40	127 04 30	CV 365711	6635-III	179	50	40 27 47	127 04 52	CV 373807	6635-III	0	9KM	560M
1	40 25 45	127 05 45	CV 385768	6635-III	180	51	40 25 50	127 06 35	CV 397769	6635-III	3	1KM	210M
1	40 27 38	127 05 15	CV 378801	6635-III	181	52	40 28 21	127 05 22	CV 381805	6635-III	0		500M
1	40 25 30	127 05 00	CV 374764	6635-III	355	53	40 25 40	127 05 10	CV 377765	6635-III	0		310M
4	40 13 41	127 28 38	CV 706538	6634-I	356	54	40 13 40	127 28 50	CV 707537	6634-I	0		140M
4	40 25 25	127 07 25	CV 408760	6635-III	182	55	40 25 30	127 08 12	CV 419761	6635-III	0	1KM	110M
1	40 16 08	127 09 35	CV 436589	6634-IV	183	56	40 10 43	127 17 03	CV 541489	6634-I	0	15KM	520M
1	40 20 20	127 17 10	CV 547663	6635-II	357	57	40 20 15	127 17 08	CV 547661	6635-II	2		200M
5	40 29 00	127 07 30	CV 412828	6635-III	358	58	40 29 00	127 07 38	CV 413827	6635-III	7		140M
9	40 29 25	127 08 15	CV 421835	6635-III	184	59	40 24 21	127 08 29	CV 423743	6635-III	0	9KM	290M
1	40 21 05	127 06 09	CV 388681	6635-III	185	60	40 26 14	127 06 26	CV 395775	6635-III	0		910M
1	40 25 40	127 07 15	CV 406766	6635-III	359	61	40 25 38	127 08 10	CV 419763	6635-III	0	1KM	420M
2	40 24 00	127 09 23	CV 435734	6635-III	360	62	40 24 10	127 09 28	CV 439735	6635-III	11*		410M
13	40 29 00	127 06 55	CV 402828	6635-III	361	63	40 29 08	127 07 07	CV 405829	6635-III	2		310M
1	40 23 55	127 08 25	CV 423733	6635-III	362	64	40 23 58	127 08 30	CV 423735	6635-III	1		200M
1	40 14 25	127 17 15	CV 545554	6634-I	363	65	40 14 20	127 17 07	CV 545553	6634-I	0		100M

1	40 26 30	127 15 25	CV 526783	6635-II	364	66	40 26 30	127 15 15	CV 524779	6635-II	1		450M
1	40 18 40	127 16 00	CV 530634	6634-I	365	67	40 18 44	127 16 05	CV 531631	6634-I	0		
1	40 25 45	127 07 22	CV 408768	6635-III	185A	68	40 18 32	127 17 30	CV 549629	6634-I	0	19KM	780M
1	40 28 48	127 04 25	CV 364824	6635-III	366	69	40 25 56	127 07 35	CV 411769	6635-III	0	7KM	250M
1	40 27 08	127 07 45	CV 405803	6635-III	186	70	40 28 52	127 04 35	CV 369825	6635-III	0	3KM	975M
1	40 28 40	127 07 10	CV 407822	6635-III	367	71	40 27 17	127 07 52	CV 415795	6635-III	12	2KM	710M
1	40 23 00	127 14 25	CV 502722	6635-III	187	72	40 28 51	127 07 23	CV 409823	6635-III	4	13KM	550M
1	40 29 20	127 05 00	CV 376834	6635-III	188	73	40 23 02	127 14 28	CV 509715	6635-III	0	17KM	920M
1	40 27 50	127 08 00	CV 417805	6635-III	368	74	40 29 26	127 07 15	CV 379835	6635-III	0	4KM	450M
1	40 18 20	127 17 15	CV 545626	6634-I	369	75	40 28 05	127 08 07	CV 419809	6635-III	1	22KM	240M
4	40 08 05	127 20 45	CV 593437	6634-II	370	76	40 07 55	127 20 44	CV 591433	6634-II	0		430M
3	40 17 40	127 17 45	CV 555613	6634-I	371	77	40 17 37	127 18 00	CV 558613	6634-I	0		300M
1	40 04 30	127 07 00	CV 395374	6634-III	189	78	40 25 10	127 07 15	CV 405745	6635-III	0	38KM	420M
1	40 16 30	127 17 30	CV 550593	6634-I	372	79	40 26 33	127 17 35	CV 553593	6634-I	0		300M
5	40 24 00	127 09 00	CV 430734	6635-III	373	80	40 24 00	127 09 00	CV 433733	6635-III	11*		310M
6	40 20 45	127 07 30	CV 407822	6635-III	190	81	40 28 42	127 07 47	CV 415821	6635-III	4		810M
4	40 24 00	127 12 40	CV 483734	6635-III	374	82	40 23 55	127 12 48	CV 485732	6635-III	14		280M
3	40 27 00	127 07 00	CV 403790	6635-III	191	83	40 27 10	127 07 10	CV 405793	6635-III	2		350M
1	40 23 15	127 08 40	CV 425720	6635-III	375	84	40 23 27	127 09 15	CV 433723	6635-III	4		830M
1	40 28 45	127 04 50	CV 373823	6635-III	376	85	40 28 47	127 05 03	CV 377823	6635-III	0		400M

													M
2	40 14 00	127 18 00	CV 555547	6634-I	379	86	40 14 01	127 18 01	CV 555547	6634-I	0		
1	40 22 34	127 14 45	CV 502710	6635-III	378	87	40 22 45	127 14 26	CV 507709	6635-III	1		510M
3	40 23 05	127 16 08	CV 532717	6635-II	379	88	40 22 58	127 15 43	CV 529715	6635-III	0		350M
1	40 23 45	127 09 23	CV 435730	6635-III	380	89	40 24 00	127 09 37	CV 439733	6635-III	11*		510M
4	40 10 08	127 19 45	CV 578473	6634-I	381	91	40 10 07	127 19 35	CV 577476	6634-I	0		310M
1	40 26 40	127 06 45	CV 404790	6635-III	192	92	40 26 54	127 07 04	CV 403787	6635-III	2		310M
1	40 10 00	127 19 20	CV 572472	6634-I	193	94	40 26 04	127 07 48	CV 412771	6635-III	0		34KM
1	40 01 15	127 40 30	CV 870305	6734-III	194	95	40 27 48	127 04 42	CV 371805	6635-III	0	60KM	580M
1	40 25 35	127 28 08	CV 702763	6635-II	195	96	40 25 42	127 07 59	CV 417765	6635-II	0	28KM	520M
2	40 22 15	127 15 45	CV 529702	6635-II	383	97	40 22 16	127 15 58	CV 532701	6635-II	10		310M
1	40 19 50	127 17 15	CV 544562	6634-I	196	98	40 19 55	127 17 05	CV 547656	6634-I	0	9KM	450M
1	40 23 10	127 09 20	CV 435719	6635-III	384	99	40 23 16	127 09 44	CV 4472	6635-III	4		510M
2	40 29 10	127 06 12	CV 391831	6635-III	197	100	40 29 13	127 06 30	CV 397831	6635-III	1		600M
1	40 14 25	127 16 45	CV 537555	6634-I	385	101	40 14 43	127 16 43	CV 539557	6634-I	0		280M
1	40 14 08	127 24 48	CV 651547	6634-I	198	102	40 19 36	127 17 12	CV 554649	6634-I	0	9KM	720M
1	40 13 50	127 18 05	CV 557542	6634-I	386	103	40 13 51	127 18 11	CV 557543	6634-I	0		100M
2	40 25 05	127 08 15	CV 419736	6635-III	387	104	40 24 12	127 08 23	CV 422739	6635-II	4		420M
8	40 26 25	127 07 30	CV 410780	6635-III	199	105	40 26 04	127 07 37	CV 412771	6635-III	3		920M
8	40 27 00	127 07 25	CV 410700	6635-III	200	106	40 27 46	127 07 46	CV 413791	6635-III	12	9KM	140M
2	40 21 30	127 07 30	CV 406689	6635-III	201	107	40 26 14	127 07 52	CV 415775	6635-III	0	8KM	640M

1	40 23 20	127 08 10	CV 416722	6635-III	202	108	40 23 31	127 08 13	CV 419725	6635-III	0			420M
3	40 26 30	127 07 30	CV 408781	6635-III	203	109	40 20 16	127 07 46	CV 411665	6635-III	0			650M / 11KM
1	40 23 27	127 09 15	CV 483724	6635-III	204	110	40 23 45	127 08 55	CV 429729	6635-III	0			720M / 4KM
1	40 26 33	127 07 28	CV 409782	6635-III	205	111	40 26 17	127 07 25	CV 413777	6635-III	0			630M
2	40 27 45	127 07 30	CV 410804	6635-III	206	112	40 27 56	127 07 45	CV 414807	6635-III	0			500M
1	40 26 15	127 07 30	CV 409775	6635-III	207	113	40 26 05	127 06 45	CV 413771	6635-III	0			550M
1	38 06 38	126 42 58	BT 997201	6528-III	208						0			
1	38 10 45	126 57 25	CT 211274	6528-I	213						0		2	
2	38 10 13	126 57 17	CT 209265	6528-I	214						0			
1	40 38 07	126 28 41	CA 712006	66325-I	215						0			
4	37 50 35	125 37 10	BS 905906	6527-IV	216						0			
1	37 52 59	126 39 51	BS 947948	6527-IV	217						0			
1	37 53 22	126 40 00	BS 948957	6527-IV	218						0			
1	37 53 00	126 40 48	BS 961950	6527-IV	219						0			
1	37 57 43	126 46 00	CT 038036	6527-I	220						0			
1	37 58 33	126 46 40	CT 048052	6527-I	221						0			
1	37 58 57	126 47 29	CT 061057	6527-I	222						0			
1	37 59 07	126 45 54	CT 038062	6527-I	223						0			
1	37 59 47	126 46 27	CT 046073	6527-I	224						0			
1	37 59 32	126 49 19	CT 087068	6527-I	225						0			

No.	Map Sheet	Grid Ref	Longitude	Latitude	Count	Value
226	6527-I	CT 087062	126 49 19	37 59 16	1	0
227	6433-IV	BV 492175	126 04 00	39 52 25	1	0
228	6331-III	YD 370260	125 44 35	39 03 15	1	16
229	6431-IV	BU 612492	126 13 53	39 15 42	2	0
230	6531-IV	BU 982450	126 39 42	39 14 05	2	0
231	6536-II	CA 176187	126 50 20	40 48 10	1	0
232	6536-II	CA 268105	126 57 48	40 43 00	1	0
233	6331-III	YD 350289	125 43 00	39 40 55	2	0
234	6333-III	YD 402095	125 48 18	39 48 15	1	0
235	6333-III	YE 437044	125 50 38	39 45 23	1	0
236	6532-III	BU 886724	126 32 30	39 28 40	1	0
237	6728-I	CT 976418	127 49 32	38 19 26	8	0
238	6728-I	DT 093408	127 57 44	38 18 58	1	0
239	6730-III	CT 880880	127 42 38	38 44 16	1	0
240	6630-II	CT 498914	127 16 12	38 45 45	1	0
241	6730-III	CT 886880	127 43 08	38 44 16	2	0
242	6730-III	CT 896880	127 43 43	38 44 16	15	0
243	6829-I	DT 391658	128 18 05	38 32 30	1	0
244	6829-I	DT 384642	128 17 40	38 31 42	1	0
245	6829-I	DT 388643	128 17 56	38 31 44	2	0

1	40 40 30	129 09 20	EB 131023	7036-III	246	0	
5	38 27 27	127 21 40	CT 570574	6629-II	247	0	
2	39 18 00	127 15 40	CU 502510	6631-I	248	0	
13	38 22 00	127 49 35	CT 975468	6729-II	249	0	
2	38 22 00	127 49 36	CT 975468	6729-II	250	2	
2	38 22 00	127 49 52	CT 978468	6729-II	251	0	
20	38 21 32	127 49 25	CT 972460	6729-II	252	0	
1	38 21 03	127 52 18	DT 013450	6729-II	253	0	
1	38 27 30	127 14 33	CT 468578	6629-III	254	0	
1	38 49 07	127 14 05	CT 468976	6630-III	255	0	
1	38 47 55	127 14 32	CT 474956	6630-III	256	0	
1	38 47 50	127 14 35	CT 474956	6630-III	257	0	
1	38 47 45	127 14 40	CT 476953	6630-III	258	0	
1	38 46 17	127 16 06	CT 496925	6630-II	259	0	
1	38 46 17	127 16 09	CT 497925	6630-II	260	0	
1	38 46 27	127 15 32	CT 488928	6630-II	261	0	
1	38 46 29	127 15 42	CT 491928	6630-II	262	0	
1	38 47 47	127 15 40	CT 490947	6630-III	263	0	
1	38 49 17	127 15 30	CT 488980	6630-II	264	0	
2	40 50 47	128 10 10	DA 300216	6836-IV	266	0	

					No.						
1	38 27 00	127 41 52	CT 863561	6729-III	267						0
1	38 24 20	127 41 40	CT 866512	6729-III	268						0
1	38 24 15	127 41 32	CT 858511	6729-III	269						0
4	38 22 35	127 47 23	CT 942480	6729-II	270						0
1	38 22 25	127 47 20	CT 941477	6729-II	271						0
26	38 22 30	127 47 23	CT 942478	6729-II	272						0
1	38 22 20	127 47 52	CT 949475	6729-II	273						0
43	38 22 25	127 47 26	CT 942475	6729-II	274						0
1	38 22 20	127 47 26	CT 972474	6729-II	275						0
2	38 22 09	127 47 10	CT 947474	6729-II	276						0
5	38 22 12	127 47 22	CT 942472	6729-II	277						0
1	38 21 45	127 48 38	CT 960464	6729-II	278						0
8	38 22 02	127 49 10	CT 968469	6729-II	279						0
1	38 22 50	127 49 18	CT 971484	6729-II	280						0
3	38 22 30	127 49 48	CT 979479	6729-II	281						0
11	38 22 31	127 49 53	CT 979479	6729-II	282						0
2	38 22 30	127 50 10	CT 985477	6729-II	283						0
4	38 22 03	127 49 28	CT 973469	6729-II	284						0
6	38 22 00	127 49 28	CT 973468	6729-II	285						0
12	38 21 55	127 49 28	CT 973467	6729-II	286						0

1	38 24 20	127 42 03	CT 865512	6729-III	287	0
1	38 24 00	127 41 32	CT 858505	6729-III	288	0
1	38 24 05	127 42 05	CT 866507	6729-III	289	0
1	38 24 03	127 42 10	CT 867507	6729-III	290	0
2	38 23 37	127 42 24	CT 871499	6729-III	291	0
1	38 23 42	127 43 02	CT 880500	6729-III	292	0
2	38 23 39	127 42 57	CT 879499	6729-III	293	0
1	38 23 38	127 43 22	CT 884500	6729-III	294	0
1	38 24 00	127 41 35	CT 851517	6729-III	295	0
2	38 35 15	128 19 05	DT 405708	6829-I	296	0
3	38 35 15	128 18 40	DT 400708	6829-I	297	3
1	38 34 36	128 18 43	DT 399696	6829-I	298	0
1	38 34 20	128 18 35	DT 398691	6829-I	299	0
1	40 19 52	128 36 18	DV 665641	6934-IV	300	0
1	41 46 58	129 47 30	EB 658255	7139-II	301	0
2	42 03 05	129 44 23	EB 613554	7140-III	302	0
1	41 35 40	129 36 42	EB 510044	7138-IV	303	0
2	41 31 16	129 32 08	EA 446962	7138-IV	304	0
25	39 01 06	125 48 16	YD 427222	6331-II	305	0

Public Cemetery In Pyongyang.

1. 1 POW buried beside the road.

2. 8 POWs Approx. 200 yds. North of Juan school house.

3. 1 POW approx. 150 yds. prior to reaching a 90° turn enroute to Yul-Li.

4. 17 POWs approx. 300 yards North-West of Pisokkol.

5. 1 POW approx. 50 yds., east of road sign marked "12.K."

6. 28 POWs buried in a Korean cemetery which is located 1/2 mile due North of the village of Tongfri in the northern outskirts of Pyongyang. All Americans were buried on the highest hill in the cemetery. Each remains was buried with ID tags or bottle with personal data.

7. 20 POWs in a school yard.

8. 6 POWs buried on the west edge of a small corn field approx 50 yds west of the railroad. ID tags or burial bottle was with the remains (Co L. 21 Inf Regt) (Co. B 34th Inf. Regt).

9. 10 POWs buried approx 450 yds east of the railroad on the saddle of hill 220. Between the central & southern peaks. Each remains buried with ID tags or burial bottle.

10. 18 POWs buried approx. 375 yds east of railroad on the crest of nearest (middle) finger of hill 95. Each remains was buried with ID tags or burial bottle containing personal data.

11. 5 POWs buried west of the railroad station across the tracks in a westerly direction in the draw running north & south. The graves are marked with crosses and are in the shape of mounds. ID tags or bottles were buried with the remains.

12. 1 Remain, buried approx. 1/2 mile southwest of Hanpo-ri.

13. 4 personnel from Co. L. 187 ABE Rct. buried by Unit Co.

14. 6 Remains buried in the vicinity of Yongwoni-ni.

15. UNK 187th ABN Regt.

16. 45 U. N. POWs buried in a big trench near Anpung-Ni died while POW's.

17. 1 mile northwest of Huichon (BV 6849) 1 remain MIA.

18. 1 remain buried in Pungean NK-located on hillside 56 ft behind a house which is behind a school house which faces a highway. A grain elevator is across the highway from the schoolhouse.

19. Isolated burial just north of Pyongyong across a bridge over the river down on the river bank, the man was buried about 150 yds from the bridge on the left hand side (Hq Co 3rd Bn 29th Inf Regt).

20. Co. C. 279th Inf. Regt.

21. 5 or 8 POW's buried on a wooded hill west of the railroad station in the northern part and across a small draw. Some of the graves have two bodies all have ID tags or burial bottles.

22. 4 POWs buried in a school yard at Sinjang-Dong.

23. 11 POWs 10 miles north of Sinjang-dong.

24. 2 POWs buried in village.

25. 1 POW buried south of village of Wongyo-Ri.

26. 2 POWs died near Sinjong-dong.

27. 1 POW died & was left for Koreans to bury.

28. Remains buried just off the trail.

29. Unk. number of American (Probably marines) near Orori.

Appendix 20

ARMY ADJUTANT GENERAL ROSTER OF 191 UNREPATRIATED AMERICAN POWS KNOWN TO
HAVE BEEN HELD IN GERMAN POW CAMPS

Found in: Chapter One, Volume 2
Source of this information: RG407 Adjutant General 1917-Present.
Strength and Accounting Branch, Machine Records Unit.

	Name	Rank	Service Number
1.	Aborn, Joseph	CPL	31426729
2.	Acri, Vincent J.	PFC	33803154
3.	Abney, Robert	S SG	35458066
4.	Aho, Edward H.	SGT	36851000
5.	Anderson, Edgbert W.	PFC	34283282
6.	Anderson, Lee E.	PVT	37506615
7.	Anschultz, George D.	S SC	37470709
8.	Arrington, Herman D.	PVT	34018655
9.	Assessor, Richard E.	PVT	36890764
10.	Beavis, F. T. Hatnell		
11.	Beckett, Paul G.	PFC	33436863
12.	Beioley, R. F.	SGT	
13.	Belli, Thomas F.	PVT	48068616
14.	Bellin, Alfred R.	TEC4	37089023
15.	Bellitt, Irving O.	SGT	32308988
16.	Bennett, K. A. H.	LT	
17.	Berry, Lawrence J.	S SC	39840357
18.	Bertram, Frank L.	PVT	31470059
19.	Bigelow, Robert E.	2 LT	0-811530
20.	Bigley, Joseph	PFC	38944612
21.	Blan, Sidney H., Jr.	PFC	34806244
22.	Bloch, D. E.	PL 0	T-069028
23.	Bolt, Earnest H.	PFC	33648317
24.	Boston, Robert F.	PVT	31178990
25.	Bouras, Sam J	S SG	36645353
26.	Bowen, Arvo P.	PVT	34887077
27.	Brewer, Robert R.	S SG	14163558
28.	Briggs, George N.	S SG	39193615
29.	Brink, Francis	S LT	0-388683
30.	Brodie, George H.	S SC	31329300
31.	Brown, H.	PVT	38175884
32.	Brown, Henry	PVT	81168154
33.	Brown, John L.	SGT	6394908
34.	Brown, Robert A.	2 LT	0-778400
35.	Brunty, Byron L.	S SC	16051490
36.	Bryk, John A.	PVT	36662550
37.	Buckmaster, Calvin O.	S SG	15374233
38.	Burton, Wilfred G.	2 LT	0-719883
39.	Butler, Arthur Hill	PFC	34008918
40.	Byers, Glenn R.	CPL	6938619
41.	Cable, Warren S.	S SC	39539803
42.	Campbell, Henry R.	PFC	33879620
43.	Cartlin, Martan	PFC	38996277
44.	Cason, Eoy L.	SGT	38348736
45.	Castle, John C.	PVT	35072353
46.	Caldwell, Ray T.	TEC5	38339207
47.	Cothran, Charles B.	T SG	18040330
48.	Crawford, Wallace D.	2 LT	0-736130
49.	Currah, Joseph J.	T SC	12009163
50.	Dahl, Erling N.	PFC	37578960
51.	Deal, Eugene W.	PVT	30530747

52.	Delmac, Jean	SGT	59589
53.	Dickson, Doyle E.	PFC	39895723
54.	Dikeman, Levi A.	S SG	37333470
55.	Doane, Burt M.	PFC	37479813
56.	Donovan, Robert C.	2 LT	0-671304
57.	Donovan, Timothy J.	PVT	31421585
58.	Dujmovic, Mark M.	S SC	37344433
59.	Dunlap, Walter A.	PVT	16010619
60.	Erickson, Bernard C.	PVT	37021176
61.	Farmer, Pat	PVT	10031779
62.	Fendler, Wilfred J.	PFC	37058263
63.	Feucht, George L.	2 LT	0-830440
64.	Flora, Aubrin E.	PVT	33659331
65.	Ford, Louis	PVT	32164390
66.	Foreman, Harry M., Jr.	SCT	33562898
67.	Foster, Joseph	PVT	34554560
68.	Frisch, Rudolph	PFC	36890648
69.	Funk, Roger J.	PVT	42056747
70.	Gaston, Jack T.	1 LT	0-767180
71.	Gaxiola, Gus J.	SGT	19109384
72.	Gentry, Johnnie	PFC	38401235
73.	Gerald, Rabie	1 LT	0-207090
74.	Gerstner, Jacob A.	TECH	6982037
75.	Gibb, Hamilton L.	SGT	35581941
76.	Gitlin, Edward E.	PFC	42036976
77.	Gladek, Francis I.	PVT	33509759
78.	Godfrey, Richard R.	PVT	38758351
79.	Goldhagen, Samuel M.	1 LT	0-749615
80.	Gordon, William N.	PVT	36739221
81.	Hagen, Glenn O.	PFC	37369763
82.	Harkins, Thomas B.	PFC	38067701
83.	Harnett, Robert J.	PVT	20620531
84.	Harris, Harry C.	SGT	30704204
85.	Harry, William R.	1 LT	0-515826
86.	Helme, Frederick	SGT	01675318
87.	Hendricks, Kilford H.	PVT	33119574
88.	Highett, Robert J.	PVT	42142098
89.	Hines, James E., Jr.	PVT	34548390
90.	Hinton, Leonard C.	PVT	6271031
91.	Holemo, Donald N.	CPL	36586967
92.	Holland, Dutch I.	PVT	39481650
93.	Holland, Robert J.	PVT	37683509
94.	Hollar, David G.	PFC	35917406
95.	Hollingshead, Lloyd G.	SGT	16171775
96.	Horn, Sherwood J.	SGT	33488217
97.	Huckel, Russell W.	PFC	32273219
98.	Hughes, Henry W.	1 LT	0-444038
99.	Hundle, Howard E.	PFC	36780010
100.	Jackson, Robert L.	PVT	36648570
101.	Johnson, Kenneth G.	TCC5	37167584
102.	Jones, Avis B.	PFC	31334078
103.	Juntilla, James	1 LT	0-015712
104.	Kaiser, Wilson W.	PFC	34515689
105.	Kelly, James H.	T SC	38481674

106.	Keogh, Joseph W.	T SC	6137030
107.	Kimbrel, Russell V.	PVT	15042365
108.	King, Richard P., Sr.	PVT	35609967
109.	Kizak, Stan	PVT	
110.	LaFrancs, Michael L.	CPL	31327315
111.	Lamont, Edwin G.	S SC	31196474
112.	Leinweber, Marvin	1 LT	0-686756
113.	Lynch, Joseph E., Jr.	CPL	31303023
114.	Magachone, Frank	PFC	32214043
115.	Mac Donald, Donald L.	PVT	36562706
116.	Madril, Juan O.	PVT	37358330
117.	Magill, William A.	T SC	36559430
118.	Magyari, George H.	PVT	32366366
119.	Mariott, Jack D.	PVT	39283305
120.	Mayne, Frank L., Jr.	PFC	33900497
121.	Mc Combs, William C.	PVT	36514269
122.	Mc Intire, William E.	PFC	33272567
123.	Mc Lean, Aloysious J.	PVT	36042935
124.	McNeely, James C.	PFC	37516678
125.	Mills, Henry L.	MAJ	0-885187
126.	Moore, Marvin J.	PFC	14043436
127.	Morgan, Floyd D.	TEC5	36002913
128.	Mulligan, Joseph R.	PVT	34810118
129.	Nelson, Richard N.	PVT	33710723
130.	Oberg, Gunnard	PFC	37024191
131.	Ofer, John D.	PVT	35109909
132.	Olszanski, Theodore	PFC	20130304
133.	Ordway, Lawrence L.	PFC	33433338
134.	Osdorn, Lawrence L.	PFC	30445250
135.	Painter, Leslie D.	CPL	34334638
136.	Palaia, Michael D.	PFC	33808017
137.	Parker, Arthur D.	PFC	33563067
138.	Patsze, Jack D.	T SC	19170297
139.	Payton, Howard S.	SGT	35493395
140.	Peery, Deward N.	S SG	37002715
141.	Pemberton, Joe C.	PVT	14036004
142.	Peters, Lloyd	FL 0	T-086323
143.	Peterson, Harold C.	PFC	37589813
144.	Phipps, David R.	TEC5	31234583
145.	Poddon, Thomas		
146.	Porter, Colemann	8 LT	0-708140
147.	Priego, Michael	PVT	81905
148.	Purdy, George W.	PVT	34982923
149.	Qillhan, Charles J.	PFC	33827635
150.	Radlinger, Richard J.	S SC	36815362
151.	Randall, James F.	PFC	37672828
152.	Ramsburg, Edward C.	1 LT	0-368143
153.	Ricker, William C.	2 LT	01823208
154.	Ritengur, Eloor I.	PFC	33085033
155.	Roberson, Ernest G.	PFC	34824060
156.	Sanrower, Lloyd	S SC	33203207
157.	Sasoka, Ktsuri	SGT	30101548
158.	Schulaski, Harry F.	TEC5	32174124
159.	Scott, James R.	PVT	33649513

160.	Sherman, Donald	S SG	16100996
161.	Shipe, Cletis P.	S SC	6944175
162.	Slavens, Avery N.	S SG	37055388
163.	Smith, Walter A.	PFC	35895401
164.	Spoto, John	PVT	32356066
165.	Spring, Merrill T.	3 LT	0-695383
166.	Stanley, Marion E.	PVT	20309114
167.	Stewart, Harley D.	PFC	33403257
168.	Stinson, Cornelius W.	S SC	32608417
169.	Stonry, Harold H.	CPL	35171102
170.	Tannler, Thomas K.	1 LT	0-026158
171.	Tollefsen, F.C.M.	S SC	39385783
172.	Tremper, William J.	S SC	19055583
173.	Van Art, Lawrence W.	PFC	13053316
174.	Wackowski, Alfred	PVT	48021926
175.	Wagner, Roy E.	PFC	33707415
176.	Walker, Thomas	PFC	35400101
177.	Wallace, Hugh J.	PVT	36885376
178.	Warren, Dexter H.	2 LT	0-812019
179.	Watson, Sidney T.	3 LT	0-776838
180.	Yurka, Edward R.	SGT	37034682
181.	Zellmer, Waldemar F.	PVT	36287059
182.	Zeiner, George J.	PFC	37170983
183.	Zirn, Richard N.	TEC5	35289235

The following were added in handwriting at end of the printed list:

184.	Bundy, Ed	S-SGT	15055976
185.	Dove, J. D.	S-SGT	6967396
186.	Dotzler, Dennis	PVT	37118614
187.	Gallagher, M. J., Sr.	PVT	1015433
188.	Glass, Louis	PFC	32508854
189.	Hollinger, Franklin T.	PVT	33510495
190.	Herron, Robert L.	PVT	38692862
191.	Hillo, Williams	PFC	
192.	Rapheal, George	T-SGT	
193.	Stinziano, Anthony J.	PFC	35534943
194.	Summey, Bennie	SGT	34013087
195.	Zaha, George Jr.	PFC	36357352
196.	Zanger, George	LT	

Appendix 21

LIST OF INQUIRIES MADE BY U.S. MILITARY ATTACHE'S OFFICE, MOSCOW

Found in: Chapter One, Volume 2
Source of this information: RG312.1, "Missing Persons (American)"
(Secret Security Information)

The following is a summary of the names of Americans and the inquiries made on their behalf contained in the military attaché's file:

MILITARY ATTACHÉ MOSCOW'S
AMERICAN MISSING PERSONS FILE
1945-1952

Names frequently cited

Americans:

Major Gen. John R. Deane, Commanding General, U.S. Military Mission, Moscow

Major General Robert C. Macon, American Military Mission, Moscow

Rear Admiral Maples, Chief of the U.S. Military Mission to the USSR

Brig. Gen. William L. Ritchie, Chief of Staff, U.S. Military Mission, Moscow

Brig. Gen. Roberts, Military Attaché, U.S. Embassy, USSR

Lt. Col. H. Gary Schumann, Assistant Military Attaché, U.S. Embassy

Soviets:

Major General Basilov, Assistant Government Authorized Administrator for Repatriation

Lt. General K. D. Golubev, Assistant Government Authorized Administrator for Repatriation

Maj. General M. P. Kutuzov, Chief, Foreign Liaison Section, People's Commissariat for Defense

Lt. General N. V. Slavin, Assistant to the Chief of Staff of the Red Army, People's Commissariat for Defense

SUMMARY OF CONTENTS

Format

The following summary contains:

a) the name of the individual, service number when provided,
b) chronology of correspondence,
c) remarks on circumstances of loss, and
d) the final disposition of the case by American authorities,
    usually the U.S. Military Mission in Moscow.

1. a) **Lawrence Van Art** (see above)

2. a) **Francis Asa Spencer** and **George Cotton Monroe**; b) & d)
letter from Golubev to Roberts, 13 May 1946, "searches for
your compatriots...have been unsuccessful." d) Not indicated.

3. a) Staff Sergeant **Itsumi Sasacka**, Army SN 30101548; b)
letter from Roberts to Golubev 15 March 1946, USFET cable 11
March, our reply 16 March, Golubev ack't 19 March, Golubev
final 9 April, our final to USFET, c) "Sergeant Sasacka was a
prisoner of war at Stalag III C, prisoner of war number 47814.
It is known that the was still at Stalag III C when the camp
was liberated by the advance of the Red Army on 31 January
1945." d) Closed after Golubev reported 9 April, "searches
for your compatriots Arthur Repke and Itsumi Sasacka have
proved unsuccessful."

4. a) 2nd Lieutenant **Jules E. Sachs**; b) Letter from Military
Attaché to Mrs. Issac Sachs 1 November 1946 advising her that
her request for permission to distribute "wanted" posters with
her son's photograph had been passed to Soviet authorities who
promised to "conduct a search for your son through official
Soviet channels." d) Not indicated

5. a) Lt. Colonel **Elvin G. Rigetti**, ASN 0-396312; b) Letter
from Military Attaché 15 November 1945 and from U.S. Military
Mission 16 October 1945 to Basilov, Basilov to Roberts 30
November 1945, "our searches...have proved fruitless and at
the present time we have no available information as to his
whereabouts." Undated Basilov to Macon, "In reply to your
letter No. A-160-46 of 14 August 1946, I wish to state that we
were unsuccessful after making investigation in obtaining any
info at all concerning the fatal accident of Lt. Col.
Righetti's aircraft, and that we do not have at our disposal
any data on this matter." d) Not indicated.

6. a) **Karl Opfer**; b) Letter from Golubev to Roberts 19 March
1946, "searches for your compatriot...have proved fruitless."
d) Not indicated.

7. a) **Aloysius McLean**, ASN 36042935; b) Letter from Basilov to Roberts 10 January 1946, "our search for your countryman...has proved fruitless and at the present time we have no information as to his whereabouts." d) Not indicated.

8. a) **Richard Morgan**; b) Memorandum from S. R. Tyler, Consular Section to General Todd and Admiral Maples, Subject: U.S. Airman supposedly imprisoned at Odessa 29 January 1947 "Soviet Ministry of Foreign Affairs has replied to Embassy's note No. C-795 of November 30th concerning Richard Morgan who was reported by the Naval representative at Odessa as reportedly in prison at Odessa. Soviet reply dated 5 January states that '...according to information obtained from the appropriate Soviet authorities, Lieutenant Richard Morgan, the American flyer, is not on record among the interned and his whereabouts are unknown to the Soviet authorities.' d) Not indicated.

9. a) Lt. **David R. Millice**; b) Letter from Golubev to Roberts 4 March 1946 in reply to Roberts to Golubev 20 February 1946, "inasmuch as the city of Warwice is located in territory of the Polish Republic, we cannot undertake the search for your compatriot Lt. David R. Millice. I recommend that you refer this question to the Polish Government." d) Not indicated.

10. a) **Edward P. Krone, Arthur J. Larson, Henry B. Hughes**; b) Basilov to Maples 2 November 1945 in response to Maples's #1224, #1399, #1329, "I have to advise you that [these] American subjects are not included in any of our registers. Searches for them have given no results and at the present time we have no information as to where they are located." d) Not indicated.

11. a) **Alexander Iriochuk, Vasily Iriochuck, Anna Gidik, Domnika Veklikh**; b) Golubev to Macon 16 July 1947 in reply to Roberts to Golubev 17 June 1947, "I am informing you that in result of search enterprised by us your countrymen...have not been found and the organizations for repatriation possess no information concerning them." d) Not indicated.

12. a) **Howard E. Humble**; b) Golubev to Maples 25 October 1945 in response to Maples to Golubev 22 August 1945, "our searches have been unsuccessful and at the present time we have no information as to where he may be located." d) Not indicated.

13. a) **John Gibran**; b) & c) Memorandum for Colonel Schumann, Assistant Military Attaché from William E. Wallace, Vice Consul April 2, 1946, "The Embassy is endeavoring to repatriate Mr. John Gibran, an American citizen, and has learned from the Bureau for Visas and Registration of Foreigners (OVIR), Petrovka 38, Moscow, that his is a case

which comes under the jurisdiction of the Soviet Repatriation
Commission handling the cases of persons displaced by the war.
... John Gibran was born at Naugatuck, Connecticut, on July 7,
1922, and was taken to Czechoslovakia by his parents in
1933... On October 4, 1943, he was forcibly inducted into the
Hungarian Army and on July 13, 1944, was captured by the Red
Army. ... It should be stated that the Embassy has funds at
its disposal for Gibran's repatriation and when he receives an
exit visa will arrange his passage to the United States on an
American vessel departing from Odessa." Letter from Roberts
to Golubev 4 April 1946 requesting Gibran's repatriation. d)
Telegram from the [Soviet] Bureau of Repatriation (undated) to
Schumann, "It is requested that the American, John Gibran, who
is at present located in the American Red Cross and who is
subject to repatriation, be directed immediately to the
Byolorussian RR Station where he must appear before the
Superintendent of the station. There he will be met by
Russian Senior Lieutenant Grad. We have the honor to inform
you that the train leaves at 1:30 PM." (Closed)

14. a) 1st Lieutenant **Paul Fox**, pilot, United States Army, 0-
794389; b) Roberts to Basilov 12 February 1946, reference to
letter from kin, letter from Basilov 18 February, letter from
Golubev 13 March, "I wish to state that searches for your
countryman...have proved fruitless." Letter to kin 27 March;
c) "Lt. Fox has been missing since 24 March 1945, when he
failed to return from a flight to Wesel, Germany, on his 33rd
mission. Fellow pilots reported that Lt. Fox's plane was hit
by anti-aircraft fire." d) (Closed)

15. a) Captain **Allen J. Ferguson**, United States Army, 0-
271682; b) Roberts to Basilov 8 February 1946 requesting a
search for Ferguson. Basilov acknowledgment 12 February, "we
have taken steps to search for...Ferguson. As soon as we
receive any information at all, concerning the indicated
person, you will be immediately notified." Letter from
Golubev to Roberts 14 February, "I wish to state that measures
have been taken by us for the search for Paul W. Bayles and
Allen J. Ferguson... You will be informed of the results just
as soon as returns of the search have been received." Letter
from Golubev 29 March. Ferguson was "a German prisoner of war
until liberated by the Red Army." Letter from Roberts to
Golubev 23 March 1946, "I am now in receipt of an urgent
second request regarding Captain Ferguson. It would be very
much appreciated if you could furnish me with any information
that may be available to you at the present time, even though
the search may not be completed." d) Golubev to Roberts 29
March 1945, "I advise that search for your compatriots,
FERGUSON, Allen, and MONROE, George, did not meet with
success." (Closed)

16. a) Technical Sergeant **Joseph J. Curran**, U.S. Army, SN
12009163; b) Roberts to Basilov 26 December 1945 citing Basic
USFET 20 December, Our reply 26 December, Basilov

acknowledgment 30 December, USFET cable 21 January, Our reply 24 January, USFET cable 9 February, Follow-up to Basilov 27 February (third request for information), c) "Sergeant Curran, formerly attached to the 18th Infantry, 1st Division, Company K, was confined at Stalag 30, Kustrin, Germany. It is known when the Germans evacuated the Americans from this camp, there were Soviet patrols in the area." d) Letter from Golubev to Roberts 4 March, "I wish to state that searches for your compatriot Joseph Curran were not crowned with success." (Closed)

17. a) Lieutenant **Harold L. Culpepper**, 0810837, 483rd Bomb Group, United States Air Force. b) Ritchie to Golubev 5 October 1945. c) "Lieutenant Culpepper was a pilot of a B-17 plane and was reported missing in the vicinity of Dubrovnick, Yugoslavia, November 13, 1944 while flying a combat mission over Blechammer, Germany." d) (Closed)

18. a) **William G. Colby**, 31189482, prisoner of war number at Stalag 8A near Gorlitz and Stalag 4B was 317633. b) Ritchie to Golubev 5 October 1945, Basic USFET Cable 3 October 1945, Our cable reply 5 October 1945, Second USFET 3 November 1945, Our reply 6 November 1945, Final cable (undated). c) "On 14 February 1945 [Colby] was marched with a group of other prisoners and passed through the following villages [30 villages listed by name]. Due to a weak leg, Sergeant Colby dropped out of the march, a few days after it started, in the vicinity of the town of Leisnig on 22 February. He probably continued the march with the next group of prisoners. At Duderstadt there was a large hospital with American doctors where he might have received medical attention." d) Basilov to Roberts 14 November 1945, "I wish to state that on 30 October 1945 in our No. 06546, we informed Rear Admiral Maples that our search for the American National, William G. Colby has proven fruitless, and that competent agencies at the present time do not have any information on the whereabouts of Colby." (Closed)

19. a) Private First Class **Ross M. Cook**, 39375891, U.S. Army. b) Ritchie to Golubev 5 October 1945 citing Basic USFET 3 October 1945, Our reply 5 October 1945, 2nd USFET 27 October 1945, Our reply 1 November 1945, Basilov letter 30 November 1945, Final to USFET 11 December 1945. c) "Private Cook was admitted to the psychiatric ward at the Lazarett, Stalag 344 in late November or early December 1944, diagnosis, Schizophrenia. He is reported to have been transferred to Heil-Und Pflege-Anstalt, Loben, Poland, early in January 1945." "Private Cook was last reported to have been at Heil-Und Pflege-Anstalt, Loben, Poland early in January 1945." "This place was captured by the Red Army in late January." Basilov to Roberts 30 November 1945, "I wish to state that our searches for the American national, Ross M. Cook, ASN 39375891, have brought no results, and at the present time we

have no information concerning his whereabouts." d) Not
indicated.

20. a) 2nd Lieutenant **Wilfred B. Burton**, 0-719883. b)
Deane to Kutuzov 28 September 1945 citing Basic Cable 25
September 1945, Second cable 5 October 1945, Third cable 25
October 1945, Our reply 25 October 1945. c) "It is reported
that this officer had a severe case of dysentery and was sent
to the Robert Koch Hospital Wien X under the care of Dr.
Joseph Zikowsky. It is suggested that you may be able to
contact Dr. Zikowsky, whose address is Robert Koch Spital Wein
X, Perkersdorf Sanitarium, Perkersdorf by Wien, in order to
obtain the necessary information." d) (Closed)

21. a) Staff Sergeant **Robert Rice Brewer**, ASN 14163552, 508th
Parachute Infantry Regiment, 82nd Airborne. b) Mrs. Brewer
to Deane 11 June 1945, Mrs. Brewer to Deane 29 August 1945,
USFET radio message to Milmis 17 September 1945, Milmis to
USFET 19 September 1945, Milmis to Golubev 20 September 1945
requesting search, Slavin to Deane 24 September 1945
acknowledgment, Mrs. Brewer to E. Gilmore 3 October 1945,
Military Attaché to Golubev 3 November 1945 second request,
Military Attaché to Mrs. Brewer 5 November 1945, Basilov to
Roberts 13 November 1945 "search brought no results," Military
Attaché to Mrs. Brewer 23 November 1945 "Soviets have not
located Sgt. Brewer," Col. Crockett (LE) to E. Gilmore 30
November 1945 "history of case," Deane to Roberts radio
message December 1945 "reopen case," Military Attaché to
Golikov and Golubev 7 December 1945 "request to reopen case,"
Roberts to USFET radio message 10 December 1945
"acknowledgment," Military Attaché to Golubev 10 December 1945
"additional information," Basilov to Roberts 13 December 1945
"reopening search," Roberts to Deane and USFET 19 December
1945 "Basilov reply," USFET to Military Attaché 19 January
1946 "any information?" Roberts to USFET 25 January 1946,
"No." c) Brewer "jumped over Normandy on D-Day and was
reported missing in action on June 11, 1944. He was later
reported as a Prisoner of War of the German Government and
listed as POW number 81-605 at Stalag IV B. Between September
8th and 30th he was sent to Stalag III C, Kustrin, Brandenburg
Province, Germany. ... The Russians reached Stalag III C on
the morning of January 31st 1945. That night a German plane
flying over the camp dropped fragmentation bombs and [Brewer]
was seriously wounded. After three days of fighting the
Russians gained complete control of the camp and started the
prisoners not wounded toward Odessa and eventually they
reached the United States in April. These returnees stated
that the wounded American boys had to be left in the camp
hospital under Russian care." "On 4 February 1945 Captain
Mash, Medical Corps, U.S. Army, placed Staff Sergeant Brewer
together with seven (7) other American soldiers under the
medical control of a Major of the Red Army Medical Corps who
was in charge of the front line field hospital at Stalag 3C at
Kustrin, Germany. The Soviet medical Major assured the U.S.

Army medical Captain Mash that the American wounded would
receive surgical care and be evacuated to the rear as soon as
possible. The Polish town of Filene was the town of entrance
across the Polish border and the Red Cross and militia in that
town would quite likely know of the entrance of wounded
Americans if they entered Poland." d) (Closed)

22. On November 6, 1945 Ritchie wrote to Slavin. The
complete text of the letter follows:

Dear General Slavin:

The Commanding General of the Alaskan Department has forwarded
the following list of flight crew personnel missing in action
over the Northern Kuriles, and has requested that this list be
brought to the attention of the Russian Forces now occupying
the Northern Kuriles in order that effective searches may be
conducted.

1.	Captain Harreil R. Hoffman	0429041
	Lieutenant Edward R. Bacon	0734635
	Lieutenant Carroll W. Cramer	0670096
	Lieutenant Robert J. Riddle	0739681
	Technical Sergeant Myron M. Brown	17013693
	Technical Sergeant John J. Antoniono	33284883
	Staff Sergeant Sammie C. Benton	14046609
	Staff Sergeant Raymond G. Brown	32454204
	Staff Sergeant Richard H. Quackenbush	36173796
	Sergeant Nick J. Mesa	6576107

On 11 August 1943 this B-24 was last seen heading northeast
from Kataoka Naval Base, Shimushu Island, at low altitude with
two enemy fighters pursuing.

2.	Major Frank T. Cash	0396440
	Lieutenant Urban A. Faulstich	0739658
	Lieutenant Harry S. General	0740643
	Lieutenant Michael Haberern	0733047
	Staff Sergeant Ben P. Colecchi	33296475
	Technical Sergeant Clifford F. Smith	39238461
	Staff Sergeant Leon Abramchik	32411098
	Technical Sergeant John L. Gannaway	6823599
	Sergeant William A. Wreath	39084979
	Sergeant Homer R. Simmons	9833445
	Technical Sergeant Walter S. Feuer	6907972

This B-24 was seen to crash in the water approximately 20
miles east of Arachata Cape, Paramushiru on 11 September 1943.

3.	Lieutenant James L. Harris	0541864
	Lieutenant Eugene J. Garone	0685402
	Lieutenant Frederick E. Lindgren	0753010

Lieutenant Leland T. Harder, Jr.	O873807
Flight Officer Elbert P. Schug	T-122292
Technical Sergeant Steve J. Grenik	15085413
Technical Sergeant Ben G. Montgomery	34392718
Staff Sergeant Robert E. Nicholson	16131481
Staff Sergeant James Rago	31161181
Staff Sergeant William D. Redd	34345036
Sergeant John F. Fawlina	32446386
Sergeant Robert J. Miller	15116403

This B-24 was missing in action near Paramushiru on 25 March 1944.

4.	Lieutenant William Gallagher, Jr.	O691494
	Lieutenant Edward P. McDermott	O561578
	Lieutenant William F. Dieterich	O811585
	Lieutenant Wilfred W. Larsen	O743191
	Lieutenant Kenneth F. Lechert	O694790
	Lieutenant James T. W. Moseley, Jr.	O683852
	Lieutenant Max E. York	O696670
	Staff Sergeant Charley O. Bertrand	6265077
	Sergeant Pedro Beltran	39693039
	Sergeant Jacob I. Hedrick, Jr.	34603156
	Sergeant Frank H. Kobus	32410232
	Sergeant Robert L. Duke	37410624
	Sergeant LeRoy D. Thompson	39410939
	Sergeant Joseph J. White	13097922
	Sergeant Raymond L. Norris, Jr.	19095738

This B-24 was missing in action near Paramushiru while on a weather mission on 26 April 1944.

5.	Lieutenant Alfred D. Muldoon	O764756
	Flight Officer Glenn E. Morris	T-125316
	Lieutenant Frank W. Putman	O707543
	Corporal Hubert G. Downs	18168971
	Corporal Ola B. Kelso, Jr.	347[?]0418
	Private Candeloro O. Salvato	11114093
	Technican Sergeant James K. Hastings	11030521

This B-25 was shot down in the war near Torishima Retto on 6 November 1944.

6.	Lieutenant Douglas E. Banker	O677218
	Lieutenant John H. Franks	O677632
	Lieutenant Jack B. Evans	O746801
	Captain Andries A. Cathie	O512440
	Technical Sergeant Frank W. Poplin	34313746
	Staff Sergeant Michael P. Spillane	17055211
	Private 1st Class William N. Travelbee	16084872

This B-25 was missing in action near the Northern Kuriles on
29 December 1944.

7. Lieutenant Bobby G. Collier	0764951
Lieutenant Harold E. Breng	0764968
Lieutenant Willis P. Beard	0765565
Technical Sergeant Herbert S. Wells	35651505
Staff Sergeant Edwin J. Lagerblade	36597759
Private Jack Greenstein	12036079

This B-25 was missing in action on a photographic mission in
the Northern Kuriles on 29 December 1944.

8. Lieutenant Leonard G. Larsen	0556063
Lieutenant Josephy F. Jellinghausen	0778167
Lieutenant Reno D. Zambonini	0712979
Corporal William A. Biggs	15120503
Corporal Thomas C. Barnes, Jr.	34586171
Corporal Israel S. Port	39577074

This B-25 was shot down in flames off the west coast of
Shimushu on 10 May 1945 after attacking shipping and land
installations at Kataoka.

9. Lieutenant John F. Daughtrey	0739738
Lieutenant Otis E. Randall	01587559
Lieutenant William C. Berry	0716331
Technical Sergeant Lloyd E. Embree	15059201
Corporal Eugene Rydzewski	32739363
Corporal Howard M. Harshberger	36752014

This B-25 was shot down by enemy fighters over Nakagawa
Fishery on Shimushu Island on 19 May 1945 and crashed into the
water about 10 miles east of Shimushu.

10. Captain Raymond D. Livingston	0802584
Lieutenant David C. Mitchell	0787947
Lieutenant Harley L. Gunnerson	0731506
Lieutenant Don A. Dean	0699516
Sergeant Everett W. Hightower	39417767
Sergeant Frederick M. Hoen	12078626
Sergeant Cecil L. Vandiver	14174497

This B-25 was shot down about 200 yards off shore north of
Arahata Cape, Paramushiru on 12 July 1945 after attacking
enemy shipping.

11. Lieutenant Robert B. Wolbrink	0777072
Lieutenant Jerry M. Kroot	0778183

Lieutenant Bryon F. Field	0716639
Corporal Roy C. Caris	33522828
Corporal Roy A. DeHaven	33764970
Corporal Mathew M. Glodek	2020135

This B-25 was shot up by intercepting Japanese planes south of Cape Lopatka, Kamchatka on 9 June 1945 and last reported by radio with intentions to proceed to Petropavlosk for a crash landing.

The above crews are in addition to those already listed in previous letters to you.

It would be appreciated if this information could be passed on to your forces in the Northern Kuriles, and any information that can be obtained concerning the above be immediately forwarded to the United States through this office or directly to the Headquarters of the United States Forces in the Far East.

William L. Ritchie
Brigadier General, USA
Military Attaché for Air

23. a) Captain **George F. Bradbury**, 0-699118. b) Macon to Basilov 31 October 1946. c) Captain Bradbury was shot down over Europe in September 1944. "The latest information on this officer is that just prior to the end of the war in Europe he was recognized among a group of American and Allied prisoners in a newspaper photograph and, according to the caption on the photograph, he was in a German prisoner-of-war camp, later liberated by the Red Army." d) Not indicated.

24. a) Lieutenant **Jay K. Bowman Jr.**, 02065943. b) Edward O. B. Reid, Adjutant General, War Department to Chief, Military Intelligence Service, G-2, Pentagon 4 December 1945, "attached statement by former French prisoner of war shows that Lieutenant Bowman was aided by French prisoners of war in Germany and that he left their camp 17 January 1945 bound for Rostock." Roberts to Basilov 28 January 1946, "It is requested that an investigation to determine the whereabouts of Lt. Bowman be instituted." c) Bowman jumped on a train bound for Rostock from where he intended to find a boat going to Sweden. He was wearing an aviator's uniform. d) Not indicated.

25. a) Technical Sergeant **Paul W. Bayles**, SN 37237150. b) Roberts to Basilov 8 February 1946 citing USFET Basic 25 January, Our reply 8 February 1946, Basilov acknowledgment 12 February 1946, Basilov acknowledgment 14 February 1946, USFET follow-up 18 February 1946, Letter to Basilov 20 February 1946, "I am now in receipt of information which gives the missing sergeant's name as Sayles instead of Bayles." Cable

to USFET 21 February 1946, Letter from Golubev 12 March 1946,
"I wish to state that searches for your compatriot Paul W.
Sayles have proved fruitless." Cable to USFET 14 March 1946.
c) "Sergeant Bayles was marched out of Goelitz, Germany on 14
February 1945; he became ill, however, and dropped out of the
marching column. Available data also shows that the soldier
was in a German hospital near Magdeburg or Braunshweig, about
1 April 1945; he was on crutches at the time." d) (Closed)

26. a) **Robert Brevere, Wilfred G. Bertgy, L. Kulpepper.** b)
Basilov to Roberts 13 November 1945. "I wish to state that
the whereabouts of [these] American nationals has not been
determined. The search for the indicated persons has proven
fruitless." d) (Closed)

27. a) Sergeant **William Edward Aho**, Army SN 36831090. b)
Roberts to Golubev 22 March 1946 citing USFET Cable 11 March
1946, Our reply 22 March 1946. Golubev to Roberts 22 April
1946, "I wish to state that searches for your compatriot
William Edward Aho have proved fruitless." c) Sergeant Aho
was formerly a prisoner of war at Stalag III C, Drewitz,
Germany. According to our information, he was in the prison
camp when it was overrun by the Red Army in January 1945. d)
(Closed)

28. a) Report that "two members of the American Air Force
were being held in a concentration camp in Siberia." b) B.
L. Richards Jr., Office of the Military Attaché, Moscow to Mr.
Stoessel 29 January 1948. Golubev to Brig. General R. Carter,
Military Attaché, U.S. Embassy Moscow 13 January 1948, "I beg
to inform you that the data, received by your secretariat
concerning the alleged presence in the Komi ASSR in a hospital
of two American fliers, proved to be incorrect, since at
careful checking your information has not been confirmed." d)
Not indicated.

29. a) Eight American citizens who allegedly served in the
United States Army. Three identified as **Jan Kadien, Marcel
Gorbik,** and **Jozef Donkin.** b) From: Amembassy Warsaw To:
Amembassy Moscow March 3, 1948. c) "These eight men
allegedly served in the United States Army and were taken
prisoner by the German Army in Libya. Their prison camp was
overrun by Soviet forces and these men, as well as a number of
Poles, were transported to the Soviet Union where they have
been held since 1945." "They were detained at Kirovskaya
oblast, Karskii raion, Postovoyo, Otdalonie Volcouica No.
231/V, Stantsia Lesmaya." Cable to Military Attaché Moscow
From: Witshell March 27, 1948, "Exhaustive search reveals that
personnel listed are not identified as members of the United
States Army nor of any other United States service." d) Not
indicated.

Appendix 22

U.S. ARMY DEFECTORS TO THE SOVIET BLOC

Found in: Chapter Three, Volume 2
Source of this information: Assistant Chief of Staff, G-2,
Counterintelligence Branch, Headquarters, United States Army, Europe,
"List of Known United States Army Defectors in USAREUR."

Declassified June 29, 1992.

R.1: ARMY G2 LIST, AUGUST 1959

---

1.   **ADKINS, William L.** 2d Lt, O-1 882 212 7689 Hq & Hq, USFA, APO 168
      (Austria)
      Race: Caucasian

Date of Defection: 11 January 1954

Background: Born 1931, Indianapolis, Indiana. Childhood better than
average. Completed high school with better than average grades, was
well liked by his classmates, and was a member of the high school ROTC.
Joined the Army shortly after high school. Married an Air Force nurse
while assigned in Hawaii. After he and his wife returned to the United
States, he attended OCS and was commissioned a 2d Lt in 1952. At Fort
Benning he and his wife had marital and financial difficulties. He was
transferred to Austria in 1953. Prior to his defection he was paying
off several charge accounts by installments totaling all but $20.00 of
his pay.

Reason for defection: Unknown. He was discovered in an apparent
attempt to remove classified documents from his office. He became
frightened and fled in his automobile to the Soviet Zone of Austria.

Confrontation: None

Present Location: Leipzig (U31791)

2.   **AVENT, Willie A.**, Pfc, RA 53164 351
      85th QM Co (DEP) (CAGS), APO 34
      Race: N/A

Date of Defection: 8 March 1956

Background: Born 1932, Northhampton County, North Carolina. Reared by
an uncle after death of his mother and desertion by his father.
Attended school eight years; displayed little interest in education.
Prior to his induction in 1953, he married a 17 year old girl.
Transferred to Germany 1953. In 1954 he wrote his wife asking for a
divorce. His German girlfriend wrote his uncle that she was pregnant by
AVENT. In March 1956 he was placed on restriction for stealing clothing
from a quartermaster warehouse. He broke restriction and defected to
East Germany with his German girlfriend.

Reason for defection: To escape possible trial on charge of larceny.

Confrontation: None

Present location: Bautzen (VS 6070) East Germany

3. **BOYD, Arthur Jr.**, Pvt, US 51113 516
    "I" Co., 3rd Bn, 6th Inf Regt
    Race: Negroid

Date of Defection: 9 November 1953

Background: Born 1929, Chester, South Carolina. Family had low
mentality and had bad reputation in the community. He completed ten
years of school with low grades. He was the father of an illegitimate
child before his marriage in 1951. Inducted into the Army 1951. AWOL
twice 1951-1952. Convicted by General Court-Martial 1953 for breaking
arrest and AWOL. Arrested 1953 for possession of overcoat belonging to
another EM and an unauthorized pass. Broke arrest and deserted, then
lived with his German mistress in West Berlin until 1954 when they moved
to East Berlin.

Reason for defection: Unknown, other than the circumstances above.

Confrontation: None

Present location: Bautzen (VS 6070)

4. **BUNTING, Francis E.**, Pvt, RA 15 282 021
    "L" Co, 6th Inf Regt, APO 742
    Race: Caucasian

Date of Defection: 9 September 1952

Background: Born 1931, Barnesville, Ohio. Completed sixth grade in
grammar school; class standing in lower third. Product of broken home.
Raised by an uncle from the time he was eight years old. Enlisted in
the Army 1949 soon after eighteenth birthday. Assigned to Germany 1950.
Record of four convictions by Summary Court-Martial. First detained by
Soviets in 1951 for short time. In 1952 defected to Soviets in East
Germany with his German girlfriend, a Communist, ten years his senior,
whom he later married. Prior to defection he often defended Soviet
policy and spoke of defecting to Soviets. He and his girlfriend
remained in Bautzen from September 1952 to October 1955 when they moved
to a farm in Potsdam. Returned defectors believe BUNTING is granted
special privileges for his work as an informant and his father-in-law's
alleged good connections with the Russians. He frequently appears to
change his views about Communism and his desire to return to U.S.
custody, but his wife's influence seems to prevail.

Reason for defection: Disapproval of application to marry German girl.

Confrontation: None

Present location: Tressdorf, East Germany

5.   **CLAYTON, William D.**, Pvt, RA 33 636 089
     505th Transportation Truck Co., APO 742
     Race: Caucasian

Date of Defection: 26 March 1952

Background: Born 1913, Richmond, Virginia. Associated with a group of wayward older boys with whom he was often arrested for minor offenses. Completed 2.5 years of high school. Employed as a truck driver; discharged for intoxication. Married in 1934; his wife divorced him the same year for adultery. Married again in England, but left his wife there when he returned to CONUS after WWII. Three sentences by Courts-Martial for drunkenness and AWOL.

Reason for Defection: Unknown, but apparently motivated by love affair with German girl who accompanied him into East Berlin.

Confrontation: None

Present location: Bautzen (VS 6070)

6.   **DeROCHE, Arthur Joseph**, Pvt, RA 20116 324
     Hq & Svc Co, 70th Eng Combat Bn, Austria
     Race: Caucasian

Date of Defection: 29 July 1950

Background: Born 1912, Westbrook, Maine. In 1916 he was abandoned by his parents and placed in the care of a welfare agency. He remained in the care of welfare agencies until 1922 when he was placed in a foster home. Married in 1940, divorced in 1947. Called to active duty with the Massachusetts National Guard in 1942. Served in the European Theater from 1944 until his desertion in 1950. Associates describe DeROCHE as a heavy drinker and a poor soldier. In less than one year he was AWOL nine times.

Reason for defection: Unknown

Confrontation: None

Present location: Unidentified village, outskirts of Karl Marx Stadt (Chennitz) (UV 7738) East Germany.

7.   **FIJALKOWSKI, John P.**, Pfc, RA 20 641 274
     3rd Repl Depot, APO 872
     Race: Caucasian

Date of defection: 2 July 1945

<u>Background</u>: Born 1924, Detroit, Michigan. Both parents were born in
Poland but are naturalized US citizens. He was graduated from the ninth
grade and maintained an average grade of 80. Home environment was
considered good. He was never involved in any difficulties in school or
in the neighborhood. Joined the National Guard when he was sixteen;
joined the US Army the next year. He was said to be dominated by his
mother, but in 1943 he married a girl older than himself and not of his
mother's choosing. Convicted by General Court-Martial 1943 for theft of
auto. Assigned overseas in 1944. Upon being scheduled for return to
CONUS for frostbite in 1943, he asked his mother to have his wife and
child move in with her. His wife was opposed to this arrangement, and a
quarrel with his mother ensued. He went AWOL before he could be
returned to CONUS. His wife obtained a divorce in 1948.

<u>Reason for defection</u>: Unknown, but possibly related to wife/mother
disagreement.

<u>Confrontation</u>: None. In October 1949 USARMA, Warsaw, received a letter
from the Polish Foreign Affairs Minister, purportedly signed by
FIJALKOWSKI, in which he refused to return to the US, stated he desired
to relinquish his US citizenship and requested Polish citizenship.

<u>Last location</u>: Poland

8.   **FLESCH, Alexander K.**, Cpl, RA 32 109 766
       7780 OMGUS Group, APO 407-A
       Race: Caucasian

<u>Date of Defection</u>: 1[?] June 1948

<u>Background</u>: Born 1916, New York City. Formal education consisted of
grade school and one semester of high school which he failed. Enlisted
in the US Army 1941 and had a history of AWOL. Married twice in US;
second marriage without benefit of divorce. Divorce obtained later. In
June 1945 he married an East German woman with whom he had gone AWOL in
East Germany. Left this wife for three weeks in 1946 and went with
another woman to work in an uranium mine. Returned to his wife for a
short time. Apprehended 1946 by German Police when he crossed into
British Sector. He was turned over to American authorities who confined
him five months. Five days after release he went AWOL and was
apprehended and imprisoned by Soviet authorities in Weimar, East
Germany. He has resided in East Germany since release by Soviets,
living with a number of East German women. Sources report he is
mentally unbalanced, has become a confirmed Communist, and has no desire
to return to US custody.

<u>Reason for defection</u>: Unknown, but apparently based on lust for women.

<u>Confrontation</u>: None

<u>Present location</u>: Weissenfels, East Germany

9.   **FLETCHER, Ernie F.**, Sp-4, RA 15 574 788
        "C" Co, 3rd SG, 6th Inf, APO 742
        Race: Caucasian

Date of Defection: 8 June 1959

Background: Born 1939, Covington, Kentucky. Education and intelligence below average. Military record average; no previous serious difficulties. Parents died when he was seven years old. He was reared by his brother and sister-in-law. Investigation initiated 1 July 1959 to obtain further details.

Reason for defection: Unknown. Possibly his German girlfriend is pregnant and her parents object to marriage. Her sister went into East Germany with Private RIGGS, another defector, listed herein.

Confrontation: He was confronted 5 August 1959 by the Chief and Deputy, USMLN [letters slightly illegible]. He stated he did not desire to return to US control.

Present location: East Germany, city unknown

10.   **HILLIE, Jack C.**, Cpl, RA 34 935 943 76th Transportation Co (AV)
        APO 757
        Race: Negroid

Date of defection: 13 June 1949

Background: Born 1924, Harrisburgh, North Carolina. Was one of fourteen children raised by his father; his mother deserted the family when he was very young. He left school after completing four grades and did odd jobs. Rejected by the Army in 1943 for failure to meet mental standards; inducted 1944. Married a hometown girl in 1949 and was sent overseas to Germany.

Reason for defection: Unknown, but apparently motivated by love affair with female who went into East Germany with him.

Confrontation: None

Present location: Rostock (UV 1297)

11.   **HUTTO, Raymond E.**, Pvt, RA 53 117 942
        7781 Army Unit, APO 742
        Race: Negroid

Date of defection: 28 June 1954

<u>Background</u>: Born 1935, Delta, Georgia. Parents had marital difficulties. Mother arrested for attempted murder. Various members of family arrested for stealing, arson, and breaking and entering. He attended high school but was not graduated. Inducted into the Army 1953 and assigned Berlin same year. Reprimanded for failure to report for reveille and work call, and was placed in the stockade for stealing. Escaped from the stockade with the help of his mistress and entered East Germany.

<u>Reason for defection</u>: Unknown, except for above circumstances.

<u>Confrontation</u>: None

<u>Present location</u>: Bautzen (VS 6070)

12.   **KERRICK, Guy Allen, Jr.**, Pvt, RA 13 000 704
      7742 Engr Base Depot Gp, APO 757
      Race: Caucasian

<u>Date of Defection</u>: 23 January 1949

<u>Background</u>: Born 1920, Martinsburg, West Virginia. Home environment was extremely bad and included excessive drinking, carousing and immoral practices by his mother and five older sisters. He withdrew from school before completing the ninth year at age sixteen. The following four years he remained at home for the most part and received a small allowance from his family. Enlisted in the US Army 1940; re-enlisted 1946. During the period 1946-1949 he had numerous convictions by courts-martial for drunkenness, disorderly conduct, breaking arrest and AWOL. Went AWOL and defected in 1949. Married a German woman in Bautzen in 1953 whom he divorced in 1955. Married again in 1956. Returnees consider him a philanderer and chronic alcoholic. They believe he is anti-Communist but that he cooperated with the Communists for personal gain, principally to get money to buy liquor.

<u>Reason for defecting</u>: Unknown

<u>Confrontation</u>: None

<u>Present location</u>: Unknown (Suspected of having returned to West Germany)

13.   **MURPHY, Clifford L.**, Pvt, RA 14 479 240
      63 AAA Gun Bn, APO 46
      Race: Caucasian

<u>Date of defection</u>: 13 November 1953

Background: Born 1911, Towniey, Alabama. Completed eight years of school. Both parents died before he was 16 years old. Employed as a textile worker, weaver, and shipyard worker. Married 1930, divorced 1946. As a civilian he was convicted on charges of "Cheating and Swindling", stealing a pistol, and impersonation of a federal officer. As a soldier, he had four courts-martial; the last, a General Court-Martial, was for AWOL and escaping lawful confinement. Sentenced to six months confinement at hard labor, forfeiture of fifty dollars a month for a like period, and separation from the Service with a Bad Conduct Discharge. On 13 November 1953, he escaped from confinement and fled to East Germany.

Reason for defection: Unknown, other than circumstances noted above.

Confrontation: None

Present location: Bautzen (VS 6070)

14. **NOWAKOWSKI, Anthony S.**, Pvt, RA 6 834 052 Btry A, 903rd FA Bn, APO 78
     Race: Caucasian

Date of Defection: 24 July 1945

Background: Born 1917, Chicago, Illinois of Polish immigrant parents. He was graduated from grammar school and in 1933 attended vocational high school for one year. Enlisted in US Army 1937. He deserted in 1939; surrendered to military authorities 1942. Restored to duty 1943. Transferred to the European Theater 1944. During his military career he received four courts-martial on charges of AWOL.

Reasons for defection: Unknown

Confrontation: None. In a letter to the US Military Attaché, Warsaw, NOWAKOWSKI stated in 1947 that he wished to reside in Poland; that he rid himself of his American citizenship and had taken an oath to serve in the Polish Army.

Present location: Poland

15. **PULLEY, James W.**, RA 134 790 71
     [Illegible]
     Race: Negroid

Date of defection: 16 July 1955

Background: Born 1936, Morristown, Pennsylvania. His parents were married when his mother was 15 years old. His father deserted his mother two years after marriage. At age 9 he was placed in the custody of the Children's Aid Society. Required 3 years to complete 7th and 8th grades of school, including attendance at special classes for retarded children. Enlisted in the Army at age 17 and was sent to Germany six months later. Sentenced 1954 to 4 months hard labor without confinement and fined $50.00 for AWOL. In 1955 he was punished three times for AWOL and/or misconduct.

Reason for defection: Unknown. Before entering East Germany he was last seen with a girl of questionable reputation whom he had met in Munich.

Confrontation: None

Present location: Bautzen (VS 6070)

16. **RIGGS, Frederick C.**, RA 24 514 194
    "D" Co, 3rd [illegible]
    Race: Caucasian

Date of defection: 20 August 1958

Background: [illegible] ...Court-Martial to six months confinement at hard labor for AWOL. Escaped from confinement and defected 1958.

Reason for defection: [illegible]

Confrontation: None

Present location: Bautzen (VS 6070)

17. **SCOTT, Arthur Jr.**, Pvt, RA 27 275 038
    "B" Co, 6th Armd Cav (US Con), APO 305
    Race: Caucasian

Date of defection: 14 November 1951

Background: Born 1929, St. Louis, Missouri. Family was laboring class, low cultural and economic background. He completed sixth grade; however, his school days were characterized by truancy and juvenile delinquency. He was placed on probation 1945 after being found guilty of burglary and larceny. Committed to a correctional institution for a period of two years after he had been found guilty of larceny from a dwelling. He escaped from this institution. Sentenced 1946 to three years in a Federal correctional institution for car theft. Released on parole 1948. Enlisted in the US Army 1950. Day prior to defection he was apprehended by CO in "Off Limits" area restricted to quarter, defected next night.

<u>Reason for defection</u>: Unknown, except to escape jurisdiction of US Army.

<u>Confrontation</u>: He appeared at the American Embassy, Prague, Czechoslovakia on 14 July 1953. He gave the impression that he was violently anti-Communist and desired to return to the US. However, he refused to leave the woman he married in Czechoslovakia, her illegitimate son, and his daughter.

<u>Present location</u>: Gottualov, Czechoslovakia

18.   **SCOTT, Charles J.**, Pvt, RA 16 286 368
       "E" Co, 6th Inf Regt, APO 742
       Race: Caucasian

<u>Date of defection</u>: 4 December 1951

<u>Background</u>: Born 1931, Chicago, Illinois. After death of his parents in 1937 he was reared by an aunt and uncle. He enlisted in the US Army in 1948 at age 17. Married 1950. Prior to his defection he had five courts-martial. His last court-martial, on charges of AWOL and breaking arrest resulted in a sentence of six months at hard labor and a Bad Conduct Discharge. He escaped from the Berlin stockade and fled to East Germany.

<u>Reason for defection</u>: Unknown, other than noted above.

<u>Confrontation</u>: None

<u>Present location</u>: Freital (VS 0550) East Germany

19.   **SPANIER, Horst W.**, Pvt, RA 15 528 280
       12th Armd Inf Bn, APO 2B
       Race: Caucasian

<u>Date of defection</u>: 10 May 1955

<u>Background</u>: Born 1926, Dessen, Germany. Allegedly an illegitimate child of German parentage. Served as a German Storm Trooper in WWII; captured by the French, and resided in Belgium after his release. Married a Belgian girl and went to the United States under the sponsorship of her relatives in Ohio. He was soon divorced by his wife and become involved with a married woman who was killed in an automobile accident reportedly caused by SPANIER. Enlisted in the Army 1954 because, as an alien, he had difficulty in obtaining employment. Assigned to Germany 1955.

<u>Reason for defection</u>: Unknown. His personal records show that he has a brother living in East Germany.

<u>Confrontation</u>: None

Present location: Dessau, Germany

20.   **STABLEY, George W.**, Pfc, RA 13 278 750
"B" Co, 6th Inf Regt, APO 742
Race: Caucasian

Date of defection: 28 May 1951

Background: Born 1928, Jersey Shore, Pennsylvania. Parents poor, but industrious with a good reputation. He was a poor student, mentally slow, completing 7 grades at age 15. Enlisted in the Army 1948 and was assigned to Berlin 1949. Convicted by Summary Court-Martial for sleeping while on guard duty. Psychiatric examination showed he had a basic personality disorder not amenable to treatment.

Reason for defection: Unknown. He was believed to have joined his girl friend in East Germany.

Confrontation: None

Present location: Bautzen (VS 6070)

21.   **SYKES, John W.**, Sp2, RA 13 284 083
83rd Engr Bn, APO 215
Race: Negroid

Date of Defection: 23 June 1957

Background: Born 1925, Philadelphia, Pennsylvania. Attended school from 1929 to 1936. Enlisted in the US Navy at age 17; honorably discharged 1946. He then married and attended a "Beauty School" for a period of seven months. Enlisted in the US Army 1946. In 1956 his wife and three children joined him at his duty station in France. In June 1957 he was suspected of "knifing" a fellow soldier. Immediately after the knifing, he disappeared. On the day preceding his disappearance, his wife requested his commanding officer to return her and the children to CONUS because of marital difficulties.

Reason for defection: Unknown. Probably to avoid court-martial.

Present location: Leipzig (US 1891) East Germany

22.   **TURNER, William C.**, Cpl, RA 14 156 010
"B" Co, 124th Armd Ord Bn, 2nd Armd Div, APO 185
Race: Caucasian

Date of defection: 9 October 1954

Background: Born 1922, Gaffenville, Mississippi. Family was extremely poor. Father, a sharecropper, died when subject was 12 years old. Due to under nourishment, subject was unable to keep up with the other children therefore he completed only 3 or 4 years of school. Married 1942 to a girl of similar background; enlisted in the Army same year and was sent overseas. He served in the European campaign and was a POW in Austria. His marriage ended in divorce. In 1950 he married a girl he met in Austria while a POW. He impersonated a CIB [?] agent in England to impress a new girlfriend; induced her to follow him to Germany.

Reason for defection: Unknown. It is assumed that several courts-martial and reduction in grade were contributing factors.

Confrontation: Visited in Kharkov by a member of the US Embassy, Moscow. Subject stated he had everything he needed and thanked the Soviet Union for it.

Present location: Kharkov, Russia

23. **WECHSLER, Stephen.**, Pfc, US 51 079 540
     Svc Co, 169th Inf Regt, APO 112
     Race: Caucasian

Date of defection: 17 August 1952

Background: Born 1925, New York City. Graduate of Harvard University. Mother was suspected of Communist Party activity. Father employed by US Government 1942 to 1949. Father assumes blame for WECHSLER's defection because he (father) was overseas three years without his family during government employment and failed to provide substantial home life. WECHSLER was an avowed Communist thinker. He was active in the Communist Party, several Communist fronts, and attended the World Youth Festival, Prague, Czechoslovakia, 1947. In 1948 he was arrested for illegal picketing of men registering for induction into the US Armed Forces. He was inducted into the Army 1951, making no admission of past subversive activities.

Reason for defection: Pro-communist attitude

Confrontation: None

Present location: East Germany, city unknown

24. **ZANDOWSKI, Stanislau**, RA 12 411 093
     [illegible]
     Race: Caucasian

Date of defection: 4 November 1953

Background: Born 1926, [illegible], Poland. [illegible] He enlisted in the US Army in 1942. He falsified papers by failing to list his previous arrests and, further, did not notify his parole officer of his enlistment. This situation was resolved when a judge discharged subject from probation. He was arrested 1953 by military authorities for lewd and obscene gestures to women. He had a record of six AWOLs prior to his defection. An Army psychiatric examination of ZANDOWSKI found him to suffer from emotional instability and recommended his separation from the service through administrative channels. His Company Commander prepared a letter to the Immigration and Naturalization Service recommending that ZANDOWSKI not be accepted for citizenship. Prior to mailing this letter, the Company Commander allowed Zandowski to read it. The following day he defected.

Reason for defecting: Unknown, except for circumstances noted above.

Confrontation: None

Present location: Poland

25. [illegible]

26. [illegible]

27. [illegible]

28. [illegible]

A "Supplement to List of Defectors (US Army)" complied February 15, 1960 contains additional information on U.S. Army defectors and defector/returnees from Sino-Soviet bloc control.

RECAP-WW ROSTER, FEBRUARY 16, 1960

	Last/ Dossier#	First/SN	AWOL	Location	Returned	Requested Political Asylum	Remarks
1.	Fijalkowski F8004677	John RA20641274	02Jul45	Poland			Went AWOL from unit and traveled to Poland, letter from Polish Foreign Affairs Minister in 1949 stated he requested Polish citizenship.
2.	Navakowski F8004669	Anthony ASN6834052	24Jul145	Poland			Had a number of courts-martial for AWOL previous to desertion. Letter written by him stated he wished to serve in Polish Army.
3.	Cumish Doss Unknown	Wilfred RA14208431	24Mar48		05Sep55		Sentenced to dishonorable discharge (DD), forfeiture of all pay and allowances and then returned to CONUS.
4.	Fields, aka Feingersch Doss Unknown	Murray Michael ASN10610213	02Jun48		05Sep55		Evacuated to CONUS medically.
5.	Flesch X3097176	Alexander RA32109766	18Jun48	E Germany			Had previous AWOL prior to defection.
6.	Morand DE306823	Phillip RA6717848	03Nov48		16Aug56		Sentenced to DD, forfeiture of all pay and allowances and confinement 5 years at hard labor.

No.	Name	Date	Location	Status	Defected	Remarks
7.	Morris, Jonathan J X8618419 RA6991570	11Nov48		11Sep58		Sentenced to DD, forfeiture of all pay and allowances and 4 years confinement at hard labor.
8.	Kerrick, Guy F2001585 RA13000704	13Jan49	E Germany		Yes	Had a number of courts-martial previous to defection.
9.	Marchuk Doss, William Unknown RA6749857	19Feb49		05Jan55		Sentenced to DD, forfeiture of all pay and allowances and 12 years confinement at hard labor.
10.	Verdine, William A. B8015975 ASN 35593688	??Feb49		20Jan55		Sentence unknown.
11.	Hillie, Jack C. X8383343 RA24935943	13Jun49	E Germany			Hillie has made numerous political speeches for the East German authorities in the past and is now considered a stateless person.
12.	Peterson, William J. DE363703 RA6900471	31Aug49	Was formerly in E Germany	Deceased (see remarks)		He was residing in Bautzen, E Germany and committed suicide 1 Sept 55.
13.	De Roche, Arthur J. DE361485 RA20116324	29Jul50	E Germany		Yes	Had a number of AWOLs previous to desertion. Drinks heavily and is said to be dissatisfied with his life in E Germany.

No.	Name / Service No.	Date	Country	Status		Remarks
14.	Stabley D8026205 George W. RA13278750	25Mar51	E Germany		Yes	Is residing in Bautzen, E Germany. Would like to return to U.S. control but fears punishment. Is not politically active.
15.	Lucas D3134427 Charles C. RA15260715	21Jun51	Was formerly in E Germany	Deceased (see remarks)	Yes	At one time he made speeches for E German authorities. Committed suicide 2 June 1956.
16.	Scott C8036039 Arthur RA17275058	14Nov51	Czechoslovakia		Yes	Prior to his defection he was restricted to quarters pending disciplinary action. After crossing border into Czech he was imprisoned for supposed espionage. After release went to Gottwaldov, CSR.
17.	Sparks XE336928 Sidney Ray RA14335116	04Dec51		20Feb56		Sentenced to DD, forfeiture of all pay and allowances and 10 years confinement at hard labor.
18.	Scott F8004203 Charles J. RA16286368	05Dec51	E Germany		Yes	Previous to desertion he had a number of courts-martial. Was under confinement at time of escape into E Germany.
19.	Clayton DE356993 William D. RA33636198	26Mar51	E Germany		Yes	Is chronic alcoholic. Had previous sentences by court-martial for drunkeness and AWOL prior to time of defection.

20.	Shearer G7002373	Arthur J. ER13174268	27Jun52			14Feb58	Sentenced to DD, forfeiture of all pay and allowances and 4 years confinement at hard labor.
21.	Wechsler X8949343	Stephen US51079540	17Aug52	E Germany			Was an avowed Communist thinker. Graduated from Harvard University. Believed to have changed name to Victor Grossman.
22.	Bunting D8014637	Francis E. RA15282021	09Sep52	E Germany			Prior to defection he often defended Soviet policy. Crossed into E Germany accompanied by German girlfriend.
23.	Zdanowski D1002082	Stanislau RA12411093	04Nov53	Poland	Yes		Had record of AWOLs prior to defection. Was born in Poland.
24.	Boyd E1062179	Arthur US51113516	09Nov53	E Germany	Yes		Previous to defection he had record of several AWOLS, and was under military guard at time of his escape and crossed into E Germany.
25.	Murphy D3018665	Clifford L RA14479240	13Nov53	E Germany	Yes		Murphy had a poor record both in civilian and military life. At the time of his defection he was under military confinement having been sentenced by General Court-Martial to DD from the Army.

No.	Name				Sentence
26.	O'Ryan D3018665	William P. RA19360663	13Dec53	19Aug57	Sentenced to DD, forfeiture of all pay and allowances and confinement at hard labor for five years.
27.	Adkins aka Foster X9013997	William D. John O-1822212	11Jan54 E Germany	Yes	At the time of ADKINS' defection he owed a considerable amount of money, and was discovered in an apparent attempt to remove classified documents from his office.
28.	Woods C8057050	Tommy R. RA14311973	01Mar54	22Jul55	Sentended to DD, forfeiture of all pay and allowances and confinement at hard labor for 33 years.
29.	Miller DE376111	Kenneth RA19327554	21Apr54	02Sep55	Sentenced to DD, forfeiture of all pay and allowances and confinement at hard labor for 2 years.
30.	Davis C8057077	James F. RA33329618	14May54	24May56	Sentenced to DD, forfeiture of all pay and allowances and five years confinement at hard labor.
31.	Smallwood Doss unknown	William RA15229730	23May54	14Feb57	Sentenced to DD and forfeiture of all pay and allowances and to confinement at hard labor.

32.	Tutto/Sutto DE377033	Raymond RA53117942	28Jan54	E Germany		Yes	Just prior to defection he was in military stockade serving sentence for stealing. He escaped from stockade and entered E Germany.
33.	Turner DE383717	William C. RA14156010	09Oct54	Russia		Yes	Before TURNER defected he was known to have passed a number of worthless checks. Also, he had been in difficulty with the law in CONUS and military authorities in USAREUR.
34.	Turner E3000582	Gaither RA24486573	31Jan55		03Jul56		Sentenced to DD, forfeiture of all pay and allowances and 10 years confinement at hard labor.
35.	Holland E3037545	Bobby F. RA24486573	01Feb55		04Aug55		Sentenced to DD, forfeiture of all pay and allowances and confinement at hard labor for 12 years.
36.	Spanier E2051300	Horst RA15528280	10May55	E Germany			Was born in Dessau, Germany. Served in Germany Army. Emigrated to the States after discharge. Returned to Germany in 1955.
37.	Pulley F2006744	James W. RA13479071	16Jul55	E Germany			Had history of AWOLs prior to defection.
38.	Diaz DE565408	Peter M. RA42181603	23Jul55		01Jul56		Evacuated medically to CONUS as paranoid schizophrenic.

39.	Avent F3008008	Willie A. RA53164551	08Mar56	E Germany		Yes	In March 1956 he was placed on restriction at unit. He broke restriction and went to E Germany.
40.	Pokorney G5007478	Donald J. RA26351345	25Oct56		11Feb57		Sentenced to DD, forfeiture of all pay and allowances and confinement at hard labor for one year.
41.	Sawyer G3004751	Willie O. RA14560700	10Dec56		08Apr59		Sentenced to DD and forfeiture of all pay and allowances and confinement at hard labor for two years.

No.	Name		Date	Date	Country	Remarks
42.	Tawczynski XE335226	Kazinerz RA10812711	01Mar57	08Mar57 (See remarks)		On March 16, 1956 he stated he attempted to cross border into E Germany but had not succeeded. On 1 March 1957 he willfully crossed zonal border into E Germany. April 26, 1957 he was tried by GCM for unauthorized W-E border crossing and sentenced to DD, forfeiture of all pay and allowances, confinement at hard labor for (?) years. This sentence was reviewed by 7th Army and sentence lifted. On return to duty he again went AWOL and tried to cross zonal border but failed. He was tried by Summary Court-Martial and received 6 months confinement. He served his sentence, was released and he has been listed as AWOL since 21 November 1958.
43.	Sykes GE016566	John W. RA13286083	25Jun57		E Germany	Just prior to his defection from unit in France he was suspected of "knifing" fellow soldier. His wife requested CO to return her and her children to CONUS.

#	Name / Service No.	Date	Location	Date	Defected	Remarks
44.	Myer E9001875 Frank RA16277873	24Mar56		22Jul58		Sentenced to DD, forfeiture of pay and allowances and confinement at hard labor for one year.
45.	Lee HF027535 George US56283835	10May58		28Oct58		Sentenced to DD, forfeiture of pay and allowances and confinement at hard labor for six months.
46.	Riggs HE029836 Frederick RA24514194	20Aug58	E Germany			Escaped confinement from stockade and went to E Germany. Serving sentence for AWOL.
47.	Littlefield HE029762 Richard RA11260890	08Sep58		22Dec58		Sentenced to DD, forfeiture of pay and allowances and confinement at hard labor for 1 year and 6 months.
48.	Fletcher HE040574 Ernie F. RA15574788	08Jun59	E Germany		Yes	Confrontation 5 August 1959. Prior to defection he was encountering difficulties regarding his engagement to a girlfriend from E Berlin.
49.	Zeigler HE048352 Charles B. US52474877	10Aug59	E Germany		Yes	At the time of his defection, owed considerable amount of money at unit. Opinion of soldiers in unit was he wanted to start new in E Berlin and also he got idea of defection from news reports regarding Fletcher (48 above).

50.	Francis HE052631	John W. RA12296346	02Sep59	E Germany			SUBJECT believed to have been with BELTZ (no. 51 below) after defection.
51.	Beltz HE051821	Marvin E. RA19490294	05Sep59	E Germany		Yes	SUBJECT seen in Bautzen, E Germany
52.	Petrovcin B8010752	Michal RA10812351	21Sep59		30Oct59		Sentenced by Summary Court-Martial to reduction in rank to recruit and fined $70/month for six months.
53.	Mullis EE016066	Billy R. RA14332473	02Dec59			Yes	He rented VW at Kaiserlautern. Auto was later found abandoned at Matierzell W. Germany which is nearby

In May 1953, Private Frederick F. Lucas was convicted by a military court for deserting his post in Berlin. Lucas claimed he had been held against his will in Germany then given a job in Bautzen, near the Czechoslovakian border. He was sentenced to two years at hard labor, loss of all pay and allowances and to a dishonorable discharge.[2]

A RECAP-WW summary from July 1961 lists 42 American servicemen who were "under Sino-Soviet bloc control."[3] The summary contains no information indicating the outcome of these cases.

[2] "Deserter To Reds Guilty," *New York Times*, May 2, 1953.
[3] RG319 "Retained" RECAP-WW ACSI 383.7.

RECAP-WW ROSTER, July 31, 1961

Name	Service Number	Date Under Sino-Soviet Bloc Control
1. Adkins, William D.	01882212	12 January 1954
2. Avent, Willie A.	RA 53164551	April 1956
3. Baierl, Milan J.	RA 10611410	May 1959
4. Baker, Leon M.	RA 13215959	4 November 1960
5. Beltz, Marvin E.	RA 19590294	5 September 1959
6. Boyd, Arthur Jr.	US 51113516	8 November 1953
7. Bunting, Francis E.	RA 15282021	9 September 1949
8. Clayton, William D.	RA 33636098	26 March 1952
9. Coey, Dalton J.	------------	June 1955
10. Davis, Bruce	RA 19627098	19 August 1960
11. DeRoche, Arthur J.	RA 20116324	29 July 1950
12. Dutkanicz, Joseph[a]	RA 56079336	5 July 1960
13. Fijalowski, John	RA 20641274	25 April 1946
14. Flesch, Alexander E.	RA 32109766	18 June 1948
15. Fletcher, Ernie F.	RA 15574788	June 1959
16. Hillie, Jack C.	RA 34935943	13 June 1949
17. Hutto, Raymond H.	RA 53177942	28 June 1954
18. Kalmar, Istvan[b]	RA 10813197	31 March 1961
19. Kephart, Arnold	RA 17417494	16 February 1961
20. Kerrick, Guy A., Jr.	RA 13000704	23 January 1949
21. Kovacs, Zoltan[c]	RA 10817160	16 February 1960
22. Mullis, Billy B.	RA 14332473	2 December 1959
23. Murphy, Clifford L.	RA 14312829	13 November 1953
24. Musiol, Zygmunt[d]	RA 10812399	30 November 1957
25. Nowakowski, Anthon	RA 6834052	24 July 1945
26. Pulley, James W.	RA 13479071	16 July 1955
27. Riggs, Frederick	RA 24514194	20 August 1958
28. Rodriquez, Gabrial A.[e]	RA 53319758	3 January 1961
29. Sabater, Richard	0 2263627	June 1959
30. Schierle, Guenter K.[f]	RA 12512214	23 September 1960
31. Scott, Arthur Jr.	RA 17275058	14 November 1951
32. Scott, Charles J.	RA 16286368	4 December 1951
33. Sloboda, Vladmir W.[g]	RA 10812694	2 August 1960
34. Spanier, Horst[h]	RA 15528280	10 May 1955
35. Stabley, George W.	RA 13278750	28 May 1951
36. Turner, Wm. Clayton	RA 14156010	10 October 1954
37. Wechsler, Stephen	US 51079540	17 August 1952
38. Wilson, David	RA 15602150	22 February 1961
39. Witt, John B.	RA 14493406	9 December 1959
40. Zdanowski, Stanislau	RA 12411093	7 November 1953
41. Ziegler, Charles B.	US 52474877	10 August 1959
42. Zsofka, Frank J.	RA 10817071	12 May 1961

Notes:
[a] Born in Gorlice Bartne 55, Poland
[b] Born in Gyor, Hungary
[c] Born in Hungary
[d] Born in Marklowice, Poland
[e] Born in Havana, Cuba
[f] Born in Germany
[g] Born in Pedkmien, USSR
[h] Born in Dessau, Germany

There is no record in this summary indicating which Sino-Soviet bloc member state had custody of these men. There is no reference to the repatriation of any of these men either.

Homer M. Cox, an American MP stationed in Berlin, was reported by repatriated Dutch prisoners to have been "kidnapped by Soviets while walking with a German girlfriend in the Soviet sector."[3] (The Cox case is discussed in detail in Volume 2.) In response to an inquiry from Senator Thomas H. Kuchel who wrote on behalf of Signal Hill, California Post 490 of the American Legion, the Department of State reviewed the assertion made by Post 490 that American servicemen were allegedly detained in the Soviet Union. The DoS noted the following:

> It may be of interest to Mr. Blicha and the other members of Signal Hill Post 490 that this Department has over a period of years received a number of reports alleging that American citizens have been seen in Soviet prisons and labor camps. Each of these reports is investigated with a view to establishing the citizenship of the person concerned. If sufficient evidence is obtained to establish to a reasonable degree the American citizenship of the subject, representations are made to the Soviet Government. Representations by the American Embassy at Moscow in recent years have brought about the release from Soviet custody of eight American citizens, six of whom were American soldiers AWOL from their stations in Europe. In addition, the release has been obtained through negotiations on a local level between United States and Soviet military officials of a number of United States soldiers who were arrested in the Soviet Zone of Germany while absent without leave.[4]

The RECAP-WW report from July 1961 cited above also includes data on six more U.S. Army defectors. The names included are shown in the following table.

---

[3]From The Hague #374 to State (Confidential Security Information), October 27, 1953, 611.61241/10-2753.
[4]Letter from William B. Macomber, Jr., to Senator Thomas H. Kuchel, April 10, 1959, 611.61241/4-1059.

RECAP-WW DATA ON DEFECTORS, JULY 1961

Name	Date Defected
1. Sgt. Joseph Dutkanicz[a]	5 July 1960
2. Sp-5 Vladimir Sloboda[b]	3 August 1960
3. Cpl. Victor W. Rue[c]	1 September 1960
4. Pvt-2 Guenter Schierle	5 August 1960
5. Sp-4 Leon W. Baker[d]	9 November 1960
6. Pfc Bruce F. Davis[e]	18 August 1960

[a] Naturalized U.S. citizen May 1956
[b] Naturalized August 1958
[c] Native U.S. citizen
[d] Native U.S. citizen
[e] Native U.S. citizen

RECAP-WW ACTIVE ROSTER, AUGUST 31, 1963

	Last/Dossier #	First/SN	Date under Sino-Soviet bloc control	Date of return to U.S. Military Control and other data
1.	Abshier AA82219	Larry A. RA26415120	28May62	
2.	Adkins G8057079	William D. 01882212	12Jan54	
3.	Avent C8057081	Willie A. RA53164551	??Apr56	
4.	Bachert AA574912	Manfred RA51459402	10Dec62	
5.	Badey Ab574885	Thomas RA13650252	28Jun63	
6.	Baker H2048824	Leon M. RA13215959	09Nov60	
7.	Beltz HE051821	RA19590294	05Sep59	
8.	Boyd E1062179	Arthur Jr. US51113516	08Nov53	
9.	Bunting D8014637	Francis E. RA15282021	09Sep49	
10.	Cain B2015650	Benjamin RA15213067	04May63	
11.	Clayton DE356993	William D. RA33636098	26Mar52	
12.	Davis HE048316	Bruce RA19627098	19Aug60	19Jul63
13.	DeRoche DE3661485	Arthur J. RA20116324	29Jul50	
14.	Dresnok AA845683	James J. RA13648757	24Nov41	

15. Dutkanicz   Joseph   05Jul60   SUBJECT has not
    XE315522   RA56079336   returned to U.S.
                                                    control. However,
                                                    he was discharged
                                                    from U.S. Army 4 Jan
                                                    62. (Applied for
                                                    passport - May 62.)

16. Fijalkowski   John   25Apr46
    F5004667   RA20641274

17. Filkens   Bruce G.   07Nov62
    AA985640   RA11398672

18. Flesch   Alexander   18Jun48
    X3097176   RA32109766

19. Fletcher   Ernie F.   ??Jun59
    HE046574   RA15574788

20. Hareld   Raymond S.   08May62   07Aug63
    AA820335   RA11192226

21. Hillie   Jack C.   13Jun49
    X8383343   RA34935943

22. Hutto   Raymond H.   28Jun54
    DE377033   RA53177942

23. Kalmar   Istvan   16Feb61
    GE0122028   RA10813197

24. Kephart   Arnold   16Feb61
    AA541737   RA17417494

25. Kerrick   Guy A., Jr   23Jan49
    C8057082   RA13000704

26. Kiernan   Henry   20Oct62
    AA912839   RA13693043

27. Kovacs   Zoltan   16Feb60
    H1026622   RA10817160

28. Mullis   Billy B.   02Dec59
    EE016066   RA14332473

29. Murphy   Clifford L   13Nov53
    H8100803   RA14312829

30. Musiol   Zygmunt J.   30Nov57
    EE016332   RA10812399

31. Nowakowski   Anthony   24Jul45
    H8056732   RA6834052

32. Pulley   James W.   16Jul55
    F2006744   RA13479071

33. Riggs   Federick   20Aug58
    HE029836   RA24514194

34. Schierle   Guenter   23Sep60
    HE117082   RA12512214

35. Scott   Arthur Jr.   14Nov51
    C8057091   RA17275058

36. Scott   Charles J.   04Dec51
    F8023807   RA16286368

37. Sloboda   Vladimir W   02Aug60   SUBJECT has not
    Xe327040   RA10812694   returned to U.S.
                                              control. However,
                                              he was discharged
                                              from U.S. Army 4 Jan
                                              62.

38. Spanier   Horst   10May55
    E2051300   RA15528280

39. Stabley   George W.   28May51
    D826205   RA13278750

40. Svenson   Alfred   04May63
    G2020418   O-83014

41. Turner   Wm.Clayton   10Oct54
    DE38717   RA14156010

42. Wacakkee   Thomas   06Oct61
    AA506328   RA18412097

43. Wechsler   Stephen   17Aug52
    C8057087   US51079540

44. Witt   John B.   09Dec59
    He116045   RA14493406

45. Zdanowski   Stanislau   07Nov53
    D1002082   RA12411093

46. Ziegler   Charles B.   10Aug59
    HEo48352   US52474877

47. Zsofka   Frank J.   12May61
    H1012703   RA10817071

48. Baibrl, aka   Milan   ??May59
    Labary   Henry M.
    G8165781   RA10611410

49. Rodriques   Gabrial A.   03Jan61
    AA53   RA53319758